WOMEN OF THE WASHINGTON PRESS

Medill School of Journalism
VISIONS *of the* AMERICAN PRESS

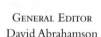

GENERAL EDITOR
David Abrahamson

Selected titles in this series

WOMEN OF THE
WASHINGTON PRESS
POLITICS, PREJUDICE, AND PERSISTENCE

Maurine H. Beasley

Foreword by Sandy Johnson

MEDILL SCHOOL OF JOURNALISM

Northwestern University Press
Evanston, Illinois

Northwestern University Press
www.nupress.northwestern.edu

Printed in the United States of America

10 9 8 7 6 5 4 3 2 1

ISBN 978-0-8101-2571-1

Library of Congress Cataloging-in-Publication Data

Beasley, Maurine Hoffman.
Women of the Washington press : politics, prejudice, and persistence / Maurine H.
Beasley ; foreword by Sandy Johnson.
p. cm.—(Visions of the American press)
"Medill School of Journalism."
Includes bibliographical references and index.
ISBN 978-0-8101-2571-1 (pbk. : alk. paper)
1. Women journalists—Washington (D.C.)—History. 2. Journalism--Washington
(D.C.) I. Title. II. Series: Visions of the American press.
PN4888.W65B46 2012
070.4834709753—dc23

2012005926

♾ The paper used in this publication meets the minimum requirements of the
American National Standard for Information Sciences—Permanence of Paper for
Printed Library Materials, ANSI Z39.48-1992.

To my husband, Henry R. Beasley, who has never failed to support my scholarly endeavors with love and understanding

CONTENTS

FOREWORD

Sandy Johnson

I was socializing with friends at the National Press Club in the summer of 2011, telling stories, as journalists do, over drinks at the bar. I walked down the hallway and chuckled as I passed the wall of fame, filled with stern portraits of the NPC presidents through the years. All men, of course, until 1982, when Vivian Vahlberg of the *Daily Oklahoman* broke the barrier. A few months later, I was attending the memorial service for my friend, Allan Cromley, who worked alongside Vahlberg at the *Oklahoman* bureau in Washington. Friends and colleagues told story after story about Cromley, an extraordinary journalist who had a sage suggestion and a kind word for everyone. Yet I cringed at one story. Cromley, so friendly to me in person, had fought tooth and nail to keep women out of the Gridiron Club. As one colleague recounted, even his wife finally had enough and asked, "Allan, when are you and the other dinosaurs going to climb out of the tar pits?" Everyone laughed. But there was a painful truth behind our smiles.

Only five years after my graduation from South Dakota State University, I was transferred to Washington. It was 1983, and the city was still very much a good ol' boys town. On the day of my interview, my boss took me out to lunch at one of the stuffy, expensive K Street restaurants and proceeded to drink three Manhattan cocktails. As I nursed a glass of chardonnay, I wondered how I could compete journalistically if I couldn't throw back liquor like the men did. But there were signs of change in the air. Helen Thomas covered the White House for United Press International (UPI). Sara Fritz of the *Los Angeles Times* was elected the first woman president of the White House Correspondents' Association. Helen Dewar of the *Washington Post* was the dean of the Senate Press Gallery. And the first women had finally cracked the all-male Gridiron Club, dinosaurs be damned.

As I read Maurine Beasley's wonderful book, I laughed, shed a tear, nodded in agreement, and shook my head in amazement at her ability to capture the trials and tribulations of generations of women journalists in Washington. Every woman's story is unique, yet together they form a collective sisterhood of journalism in the nation's capital. We have not only survived, we now thrive. For that, we stand on the shoulders of all the women who came before us, and we are humbled.

Every one of us has stories similar to those so well and insightfully chronicled by Professor Beasley. I had a boss who insisted on driving me home from a farewell party and then tried to kiss me at the doorstep. I had a boss who asked me, as part of an interview for a promotion, how I would balance my young family with the demands of being a senior manager. Would he have asked a male candidate that question? Of course not. I had a boss who unfailingly called me dear. I was never sure whether he couldn't remember my name or was being condescending. I had a boss who asked me why I didn't wear more skirts because I had nice legs and should show them off. I had a boss who, under pressure from a pending Equal Employment Opportunity Commission lawsuit against the company, said he was told to hire a woman—so he was going to hire a woman with the biggest tits he could find.

On the other hand, I also had bosses who mentored me and generously shared their knowledge and wisdom so that I could rise in my chosen profession. I recall with gratitude my very first boss, the news director of the public radio station at my college.

He sent me out on assignments that no rookie could nail—city council meetings, zoning boards, even a murder trial—and then patiently taught me what I didn't know. I am forever grateful. Another boss took me under his wing and taught me everything I needed to know about Washington, and then gave me the freedom to soar on my own. For several years, I secretly kept a note taped to my computer, "WWJD" (as in, "What would Jon do?"), as a reminder of his unflappable ability to see the forest for the trees in every story.

When I became assistant Associated Press bureau chief in charge of politics and national security, only one thing intimidated me: the leonine reporter who was the dean of the diplomatic press corps. I actually took a college course in nuclear proliferation so I could talk throw weights with him. (If the throw weights reference seems obscure, please Google "Donald Regan" and "throw weights" for another major sexist moment in the history of Washington.)

After one of my greatest tests as a journalist—refusing to call the 2000 election for George W. Bush even though all the TV networks had done so, a decision that was a Pulitzer finalist for public service—my boss wrote a letter of admiration that ended with the phrase, "You had brass ones when we needed them." It amused me to picture his struggle to use the *über*-male phrase, "brass balls," in the context of his very female bureau chief.

Washington was and still is a city whose power circles are dominated by middle-aged white males. But women are breaking those glass ceilings in every profession, including the news media. There was a golden moment when every network bureau chief in Washington was a woman—at ABC, NBC, CBS, Fox, and CNN—plus a goodly number of those directing the print media, too, including the Associated Press, Newhouse, and the *New York Times*. While a number of us were cooling our heels waiting for a meeting at the White House, I recall marveling at the collection of so many powerful skirts. Not suits.

When I was promoted to Washington bureau chief for the Associated Press in 1998, I chafed when the PR shop wanted to bill me as "the first woman." Like so many others, I had been "the first woman" this and "the first woman" that many times. By the end of the twentieth century, weren't we beyond that? Yet ten years later I secretly delighted in the team of top political reporters I trained to cover the 2008 presidential campaign. For the first time in the AP's history, the political team was led by women—four strong, determined, hard-nosed, well-sourced reporters who beat the pants off "the boys on the bus" with regularity. For good measure, they reported to a political editor who was a woman and a bureau chief who was female, too. Six more cracks in the glass ceiling.

As Maurine Beasley so ably recounts, it has been a slow evolution. But as the newsrooms and clubs and back rooms of Washington have finally given up their all-male facade, perhaps it is a comfort to note that the sun still rises in the east and sets in the west—even with women in the room.

Today women journalists constitute a growing number of Washington women journalists, holding high-profile as well as more mundane jobs. The last forty years have brought them success undreamed of by their predecessors and allowed women to lay the groundwork for playing ever more significant roles in the rapidly changing field of journalism. Barbara Cochran, president emeritus of the Radio-Television News Directors Association (RTNDA), voiced aspirations for young women now entering the ranks after she received the Giants of Broadcasting Award from the Library of American Broadcasting of the University of Maryland, College Park, in October 2009.

Cochran looked back over her own twenty-eight-year career in Washington, which included her working as managing editor of the *Washington Star* newspaper, vice president for news at National Public Radio (NPR), executive producer of NBC's *Meet the Press,* and vice president and Washington bureau chief at CBS News. Before retiring in 2009, she had directed RTNDA for twelve years.

"With so much change roiling the news business today, a lot of journalism students wonder whether they're making a good career choice," Cochran said in an alumni publication of the Columbia University Graduate School of Journalism, where she received her master's degree in 1968.[1] "I envy them because they have the opportunity to participate in a revolution—a revolution as exciting as the one I experienced when I started my career just as newsrooms were opening up to women and people of color. They will get to design the new journalism, to figure out how to use new technologies to have more impact. They will need to master and defend the traditional standards—journalism that is accurate, ethical and meaningful. But they can be the pioneers who will invent the way to tell news in the future."[2]

Her comments implied that women have both professional capability and responsibility. Few today would argue otherwise. As the first decade of the twenty-first century unrolled, staff members at the U.S. Senate estimated that half of the five thousand correspondents accredited to the Capitol press galleries are women.[3] But for years that was not the case. Women journalists in Washington, like their counterparts in general, faced gender discrimination and stereotyping that made it difficult for them to be (1) employed and (2) taken seriously, particularly as political reporters, for most of the twentieth century.

Even today gender matters, leaving women to deal with the fact that they are not simply journalists but women journalists. Maureen Dowd, the caustic *New York Times* Washington columnist who won the 1999 Pulitzer Prize for column writing that dissected the Clinton White House, referred to the social costs paid by women who challenge prevailing authority. Promoting her book, *Are Men Necessary? When Sexes Collide,* she commented, "Any woman who criticizes men for a living—which I do because politics is still male-dominated—may have a harder time getting dates," although she quickly added that she "gets plenty."[4] Bringing to journalism experiences different from those of their male colleagues, women have offered an array of voices to both circumvent and uphold the dominant power structure of both politics and mass media. This book tells the story of what they did and how they did it in the midst of technological change and shifting ideas about gender relationships. It questions to what extent women have been able to combine their professional and gender identifications. It also asks, based on historical experience, to what degree Washington women journalists will be in a position to do what Cochran suggests—defend the ideals of traditional journalism based on perceptions of accuracy, fairness, and balance.

As is well known, the whole idea of a professional journalism dedicated to finding that elusive substance called truth has come under increasing attack in recent years, with opinion and the celebration of celebrities themselves substituting for what once was considered political news and discourse. Numerous pundits have mourned the loss of what has been called mainstream journalism with its emphasis on public service and what one sociologist has termed *altruistic democracy,* which leads it to identify winners, losers, and bureaucratic mismanagement in the political process.[5] In past decades women journalists in Washington fought for a chance to participate in this news process. Now that they have proved themselves and arrived in force, the old idea of news itself is under attack. New forms of media have produced new forms of communication, among them social networking, and a consuming thirst for insider looks at sports, entertainment, and the lifestyles of superstars. Even in Washington, the political capital of the nation, if not the world, as some believers in American hegemony contend, political news seems stale and bombastic, riveted to polarized positions.

Yet, historically, Washington women journalists have viewed news differently and more broadly than their masculine competitors. Due to their own roles, engendered by societal expectations, they had to move beyond the limitations of a journalism that focused on reporting and commenting about conflicts and controversies chiefly of interest to a male-run world. If journalism today has to move outside the box of customary topics and practices, it might start by examining the careers of Washington women journalists, who saw events through a different prism than their male colleagues.

WOMEN OF THE WASHINGTON PRESS

ONE

PRELUDE

CONGRESS: We trust in heaven for three things. First—that members may give us the means to pay for this paper, perhaps three or four cents a member. . . . Second—that Washington may escape that dreadful scourge, the Cholera. Our third prayer is that the Union of these States may be eternal.

— *"Farewell," The Huntress, July 24, 1854*

With these words Anne Royall, the first woman to report, edit, and publish a Washington newspaper, ended her career as the capital's first and most notorious woman journalist. She died three months later at the age of eighty-five. In her "farewell" she identified issues that have continued to concern her successors up to the present: economic survival, general conditions in Washington, and personal interest in politics emanating from the U.S. Capitol.

A slight, disputatious individual in a trademark plaid coat who carried a green umbrella, Royall pursued congressmen into the Capitol seeking both news items and subscriptions for her newspapers. Those who subscribed received her flattering comments, those who did not fell prey to her pen. Yet Royall was more than a gossipmonger, and her newspapers more than scandal sheets.

A penniless widow seeking a pension based on her husband's service as a major in the Revolutionary War, she launched her first Washington newspaper, *Paul Pry,* to support herself at the age of sixty-one. The name came from a popular drama, but Royall used her weekly newspaper mainly to investigate wrongdoing and give her views in sharp-tongued comment. Five years later she converted it into the *Huntress.*

Her second newspaper featured more literary works, which could be copied readily from other publications in an era of lax copyright laws, but Royall's main interest lay in being a public watchdog. Intent on making democracy function, she terrified politicians by exposing abuses of power, such as improper use of government horses and carriages by public officials. She stood up for states' rights, opposed the Bank of the United States, and campaigned for internal improvements, sound money, free schools, free thought, free speech, and tolerance for Catholics.

Curiously, by today's standards, she supported neither an end to slavery nor woman suffrage. A penniless servant girl, she had been educated by her husband, William Royall, a Virginia aristocrat who was twenty years older than she and an ardent Freemason. He encouraged her to use his well-stocked library, and she soaked up many of his ideas, which were based on the thinking of Voltaire, Thomas Paine, and other Enlightenment figures. Her husband left his estate to her, but jealous relatives managed to break the will, claiming that she and the major had cohabited before marriage. Destitute at the age of fifty-four, she accepted charity from members of Masonic orders but wanted to earn her own living.

Before Royall turned to newspapers, she wrote and peddled ten volumes of travel books, full of facts, figures, and descriptions of the places she visited throughout the new United States. Eager to see all parts of the nation, she traveled by stagecoach, collecting material for each book while selling the previous one and writing shorthand notes by candlelight in uncomfortable inns. Readable and detailed, her books remain a useful source of nineteenth-century social history.

To push her pension claim, Royall made the capital her base of operation. A vitriolic exchange with Washington youth who mocked her verbal assaults on evangelicals led to her being the first and only American ever tried and convicted under an old law of being "a common scold."[1] Her scorn for evangelicals stemmed from her support of Masons during a period of anti-Masonic feeling in the United States spurred by some church members.

At her 1829 trial, John Eaton, Andrew Jackson's secretary of war, testified to her good character and proper conduct, although others testified to her venomous speech. She was fined ten dollars, but due to her age was spared the indignity of being placed on a stool and publicly dunked into cold water. Two newspapermen paid her fine, saying they did so to "stand up for the honor of the press."[2]

The following year Royall settled permanently in Washington. She acquired an old printing press, hired boys to run it, and with the help of a loyal companion, Sally Stack, published pamphlets before starting her first newspaper. Her pension case dragged on for years. Finally, in 1848 an act of Congress gave her $2,400, of which Royall's legal heirs took half. After paying her debts she was left with only ten dollars. In the last issue of the *Huntress* she said she had nothing but thirty-one cents.

For years Royall endured ridicule as a Washington character, chastised for her vitriolic pen. Male newspaper editors of the day also engaged in personal polemics, but Royall was treated like a town freak. One biographer stated that if a man with her mental abilities had been inculcated with the same political passion, he would have been elected to Congress.[3] Long after her death, Royall remained a comic figure in the lore of Washington journalism.

The best-known legend claimed that she followed President John Quincy Adams to the banks of the Potomac River, where he took his morning swim in the nude and sat on his clothes until he agreed to an interview. Historians doubt that this occurred, since Adams was a friend who willingly spoke to Royall and supported her pension claim, but the story still persists, testifying to the kind of journalistic zeal considered shocking in a woman of Royall's era. Royall herself gave lip service to conventional femininity, writing in a travel book, "No woman has any business with politics; there is something so masculine and opposed to female delicacy in meddling with the affairs of state that I view it with sovereign abhorrence."[4] Her actions belied her words, but they illustrated the difficulty of integrating personal identification as a woman with the masculine world of Washington reporting.

Even at the end of the twentieth century Royall remained a contested symbol among women journalists in the capital. In 1990 the Society of Professional Journalists, a national organization, placed a plaque in the Senate Press Gallery as part of its program to mark historic sites in journalism. The plaque honored Royall as a "fearless champion of freedom of the press" and "the first woman to cover the U.S. Congress."[5] Helen Dewar, a distinguished *Washington Post* reporter assigned to the Senate, objected strongly to the plaque, apparently unwilling to honor Royall as a legitimate journalist, and refused to be present for its unveiling, although she originally had been one of two women journalists chosen for special recognition at the ceremony.[6]

By contrast the second honoree, Helen Thomas, a veteran White House reporter for UPI, spoke of Royall as a pathbreaker for women. Thomas said she was sorry to see the debunking of the "wonderful legend" of Royall sitting on the president's clothes but was glad there was "no regulation against irritating presidents with impudent questions—[otherwise] Sarah and I would be behind bars." This was a reference to Sarah McClendon, an outspoken journalist who, like Thomas, appeared regularly at presidential press conferences and strongly backed women's equality. "Women in journalism of our vintage have risen above outrageous prejudice," Thomas said, "from the blatant—'we don't hire women' pronouncements of editors in an earlier day—to the more subtle forms of discrimination today."[7] It had taken more than a century and a half for women to move to that point.

Aside from Royall, the most remarkable nineteenth-century Washington woman journalist was Jane G. Swisshelm, a well-known abolitionist editor from Pittsburgh credited with being the first Washington woman correspondent. In 1850 Swisshelm, a small, slender woman said to have an enchanting smile, marched into the Senate Press Gallery, located in back of the presiding officer's rostrum. She was determined to claim a right to sit there, even though Vice President Millard Fillmore had tried to dissuade her. He told her the "place would be very unpleasant for a lady, and would attract attention."[8] Since nineteenth-century ladies were supposed to be retiring in public, Fillmore in effect told Swisshelm not to make herself disreputable. Swisshelm, on the other hand, contended she was a journalist and that she simply could not hear what was going on in Congress from the noisy public gallery, where fashionable belles gossiped during history-making proceedings.

Having been hired by Horace Greeley, publisher of one of the most famous newspapers of the day, the *New York Tribune,* to write Washington columns, Swisshelm was determined to witness for herself how Congress would act on the issue of allowing slavery to spread to newly annexed territories. Covering Senate debate, which she apparently had difficulty hearing, she wrote in pungent prose in her second column, "They [the Senators] keep such a dingdong about 'supporting the Constitution.' One might suppose it was some miserable, decrepit old creature that was no longer able to totter on crutches but must be held on every side, and dragged along like a drunken loafer, on his road to the lock-up."[9]

For her third column Swisshelm claimed her press gallery seat, where she got a ringside look at Sen. Henry S. Foote of Mississippi drawing his pistol as Sen. Thomas Hart Benton of Missouri advanced toward him. She told her readers, "I sat in the reporters gallery, directly opposite the gentlemen, and saw it all."[10] In her next column, which was her last, she explained that she had invaded the press gallery because of disgust with crowded conditions in the public galleries, adding, "So much for a fit of ill-temper! It has established woman's right to sit as a reporter in our legislative halls."[11]

Yet she did not remain in the capital but returned home to Pittsburgh. Why? Because she had broken an unwritten law—that certain topics involving sex and power could be talked about, but not written about, in Washington. Swisshelm had published allegations, not in the *Tribune,* but in her weekly newspaper, the *Saturday Visiter* (a British spelling that she insisted on using), against the character of a famous statesman, Daniel Webster. She reported that he drank to excess and had African American mistresses. She knew the accusations would be too shocking to allow her to continue as a correspondent, so she left Washington, according to her autobiography, so that "Mr. Greeley should not discharge me."[12]

Were the allegations true? In her autobiography, written thirty years later, Swisshelm wrote that she had been assured by credible sources, including Gamaliel Bailey, editor of the *National Era,* Washington's abolitionist newspaper, that Webster had fathered a mulatto family. At the time, abolitionists had targeted Webster for attack because he backed the Fugitive Slave Act, requiring the return of runaway slaves to their masters. Swisshelm contended it had been her moral duty to print the story, which had been widely circulated by word of mouth in Washington, even though Bailey and other abolitionists warned her against doing so, on grounds that Webster's powerful "friends would ruin her."[13]

At the time Swisshelm's charges made their way into print, male editors, including Greeley, castigated her for making the accusations, which they reprinted with no effort to determine their veracity. Early biographers of Webster ignored them, but recent biographers have pointed to unseemly details of Webster's personal life and attached some importance to the allegations. One concluded, "reliable or not, Swisshelm did permanent harm to Webster's reputation."[14]

Regardless of the accuracy of the allegations, it took an iconoclast to publish them. The personal conduct of political figures remained off the news agenda of almost all Washington journalists—then and for many years thereafter. As outsiders, women like Swisshelm and Royall were not bound by the same rules, but they paid a high price for being outspoken—they lost their own status by being ridiculed as unwomanly. A woman journalist did not fit the nineteenth-century ideal of the "lady," who personified what historians have identified as the "cult of true womanhood."[15] It equated virtue with "piety, purity, submissiveness and domesticity."[16]

Swisshelm refused to limit herself to this narrow role. After leaving the capital, she returned to Pittsburgh, where she gave birth to a daughter and subsequently left her husband. With her child she moved to St. Paul, Minnesota, the home of her sister, and revived a defunct frontier newspaper. Her antislavery stand so enraged an opposing editor that he led a gang of toughs in destroying her press and type. Not one to give in, she started another newspaper, the *St. Cloud Democrat,* and became a crusading lecturer, but not always as a liberal.

Swisshelm favored women's rights but was far from being a bleeding heart. She returned to Washington in 1863 after a national lecture tour calling for harsh treatment of Sioux Indians involved in the Dakota Rebellion the previous year. While in the capital, she nursed wounded soldiers in makeshift hospitals and was hired as one of the first woman clerks in the federal government, replacing men fighting in the Union army. She did not return to the Capitol press galleries, although she mailed reports criticizing conditions in military hospitals to her St. Cloud newspaper, which she sold to her nephew. As a well-known figure, she published a column in Greeley's *Tribune* begging readers to send her pickles and lemons, believed useful for fighting gangrene.[17] Consequently, pickles and lemons soon flooded her home.

Curiously, in her autobiography, Swisshelm glossed over her journalistic career and reaffirmed traditional gender roles, devoting about a third of the volume to her service as a Civil War nurse. Assuming that her foray into the Senate Press Gallery three decades earlier had paved the way for women journalists to claim the same privileges as men, she declared she had "felt the novelty would soon wear off, and that women would work there and win bread without annoyance."[18]

Unfortunately, for many years this did not materialize, although Swisshelm was not the only woman to act as a Washington correspondent during the Civil War. Journalism, particularly when

practiced on a part-time basis, presented itself as a relatively respectable occupation for a woman. For example, Mrs. John A.
Kasson, wife of a congressman from Iowa, used the name Miriam
to send letters back to the *Iowa State Register* in Des Moines.

More remarkable was Laura Catherine Redden, a deaf poet
and writer from Missouri who used the male pseudonym Howard
Glyndon. Redden traveled alone by train from St. Louis to Washington in 1861 and became a correspondent for the *St. Louis Republican.* She wrote several columns about troop movements and
battles near the capital and reported on the Lincoln White House.
Redden also gathered material for a book, which contained biog-
raphies of members of the House of Representatives, although her
chief interests remained writing poetry, some of which Abraham
Lincoln called "very pretty," and travel articles.[19] She made no
attempt to hide her gender or deafness in Washington and com-
municated with news sources by giving them a tablet and pencil
to write down answers to her written questions.[20]

Another correspondent, Lois Bryan Adams, a widowed Michigan poet and editor residing in Washington, contributed letters
to the *Detroit Advertiser and Tribune* from 1863 to 1865. Like Swiss-
shelm, she was among the first women government clerks. Adams
signed her columns L and was never identified by name in her
newspaper.[21] Her readers knew who she was, however, since she
had used that pseudonym for years in her literary career. It centered on publication of her work in the *Michigan Farmer,* a leading
regional agricultural journal. After that periodical moved to Chicago, Adams secured a job in the newly organized U.S. Department of Agriculture. Like the other women clerks she received
$600 a year, exactly half of what male clerks were paid.

In her letters to the Detroit newspaper, Adams described the
department in detail, along with other government agencies in

wartime Washington, which she called "shabby-looking" and "very dirty" with open sewers "channeled across the pavements."[22] In an easy, conversational style she expressed sympathy for the newly freed African American population, described the Civil War hospitals where she took relief supplies and volunteered as a nurse, and commented on women's activities, politics, and war news. In November 1865 she attacked Swisshelm, who had written a widely reprinted column disparaging women clerks, all of whom were appointed by members of Congress, as incompetent, overly dressed, and "perhaps a little piece of painted impertinence."[23]

Adams disagreed in her column of November 17. She charged that "Mrs. S. uses no discrimination, so far as her own sex is concerned, but rates them all alike, and all of very little account because they differ from herself."[24] Further excoriating Swisshelm, Adams wrote that Swisshelm had some good ideas, "which if enforced by attractive personal example, and without the accompanying termagant spirit seemingly inherent in her nature and inseparable from her name, might be of appreciable weight and influence."[25]

Swisshelm appeared again as a topic of Adams's last column on December 5, 1865. In it Adams changed her normally mild-mannered tone to one of contempt for Swisshelm's plan to start a new Washington newspaper called the *Reconstructionist,* with intent to protest President Johnson's lenient policies toward the defeated South. Adams wrote, "The belligerent lady requires some such safety value as a newspaper under her own control will afford. Brawling women have pretty much the same propensities in these days as they had in the times of Solomon, and delight to exhibit themselves on housetops."[26]

The journalistic voices of both women soon were stilled in the capital. Swisshelm published only a few issues of her newspaper before she lost her job, which she blamed on President Johnson, and an arsonist tried to burn her press.[27] She suspended publication in March 1866 and left the capital. Adams did not continue her correspondence after 1865 but stayed on at the Department of Agriculture.

Other women were eager to follow their example. Enterprising individuals saw new career opportunities in writing colorful columns for out-of-town newspapers. Their work appealed to a growing number of middle-class women who had some formal education and leisure time for reading and shopping. As department stores became prominent features of city life, newspapers instituted women's and society pages that carried advertising and some content geared to their interests.

In 1870 four women were accredited to the Capitol press galleries; by 1879 that number had risen to about twenty. These women took advantage of the fact that the Civil War had widened opportunities for them even though they could not vote. Having left their homes to act as nurses, participate in relief activities, and advocate on behalf of newly freed slaves, women had proven that they could play a part in the public sphere. The ideology of the lady itself stimulated women's reform interests because women were expected to be purer than men and more interested in moral issues.

As a group, the post–Civil War Washington women journalists came from abolitionist backgrounds and defended the civil rights of African Americans. Some saw their work as correspondents as an outgrowth of their support for the North in the war. Not all favored woman suffrage, even though suffrage leaders like Elizabeth Cady Stanton and Susan B. Anthony argued that women should oppose slavery on moral grounds. The more outspoken mocked the scandals of the post–Civil War period, even as they chronicled in detail the lavish lifestyle in the capital during the era known as the Gilded Age. Some signed columns with their real names; others did not, in keeping with the nineteenth-century idea that true women avoided the public eye. The group sought to give their readers vivid pictures of Washington life. As they surveyed the capital scene, some sparked a new genre of society reporting, describing extravagant entertaining based on the wealth of new post–Civil War industrialists, later known as robber barons.

Two of the most renowned, however, did not write specifically for women, although their columns traded heavily on their gender. Sara Clarke Lippincott used her pen name, "Grace Greenwood," to write weekly "Washington Notes" for the *New York Times* from 1873 until 1878. Mary Clemmer Ames, a strong proponent of civil rights for African Americans, was known for her "Woman's Letter from Washington," which appeared in the New York *Independent,* an influential weekly, from 1866 to 1884.

Like other women writers of her day, Lippincott, whose maiden name was Clarke, began her career as a poet, adopting a floral pseudonym to suit a sentimental age that praised her verses and essays on topics such as "Sly Peeps into the Heart Feminine."[28] Before the Civil War she had been an assistant editor on Bailey's *National Era,* where she had edited installments of Harriet Beecher Stowe's compelling novel against slavery, *Uncle Tom's Cabin.*

Bailey hired her in 1850 after she lost an assistant editor's job on *Godey's Lady's Book,* the most successful of the new pre–Civil War magazines aimed at middle-class women, because Louis Godey feared her antislavery stance would offend Southern readers. Reinforcing the "cult of true womanhood," *Godey's* and its imitators avoided political issues but, nevertheless, widened some horizons for women because they published the work of women authors like Lippincott, known as literary ladies.

Leaving Washington in 1852, Clarke visited Europe, sending back lighthearted travel columns and interviews to various publications. In 1853 she married Leander K. Lippincott, whose charm exceeded his character. He joined her in starting one of the nation's first children's magazines, the *Little Pilgrim,* published in Philadelphia until 1875. During the Civil War she gave numerous lectures in support of the Union army, prompting President Lincoln to call her "Grace Greenwood, the patriot."[29]

By the time Lippincott returned to Washington in the 1870s, she had established herself as a prolific author of children's books, contributor to magazines, and professional lecturer on literary and reform causes, including the abolition of capital punishment. Her husband, who obtained a clerk's job in the General Land Office due to her contacts, disappeared in 1876 after being indicted in connection with fraudulent Indian land claims, leaving her to support their only child, a daughter, through journalism.

In her columns for the *New York Times* and other newspapers, Lippincott satirized corruption in Congress, employing witty domestic metaphors to carefully claim her femininity. The first woman to write regularly for the *Times,* she never set foot in the newspaper's city room, although she was listed in the *Congressional Directory* of 1874 as a representative of that newspaper.[30] She sided with the Radical Republicans, who advocated for African American men to have voting rights in the South, and supported woman suffrage.

Castigating the Crédit Mobilier Scandal, a corrupt scheme of railroad promoters who gave stock to congressmen in return for political favors, she referred to those taking bribes as the "irresponsible lords of creation."[31] Ridiculing a proposed pay increase for members of Congress, she wrote, "To be able to meet their needs, let a deaf ear be once more turned to the demand of the poor clerks of the departments for an increase of salary, refuse yet again the humble petition of the women for equal pay for equal services."[32]

Like Lippincott, Ames, said to be the highest-paid newspaperwoman of her day, told her readers of misconduct in Congress. In one column she pictured a scene of drunkenness described as "a senator vomiting over the costly furniture of the Secretary's room, and . . . other senators who seemed to be mounting the air, or pawing the ground, or lying back in their seats telling ribald stories."[33] The column continued with a plea for woman suffrage amid disgust for the low tone of Congress. "Remember, brother, you abide on the plane of tobacco-juice, brandy-bottles, and doubtful stories. . . . You can't awe me, simply because you are a man."[34]

Ames arrived at a career in journalism after her experiences during the Civil War. Like Lippincott, she had published poems as a young woman and tried to continue writing essays and poems for newspapers during her unhappy marriage to a Methodist minister before the war. During the conflict the couple lived in Harpers Ferry, West Virginia, where she was taken prisoner briefly by Confederate forces. Subsequently she served as a nurse in Union hospitals, left her husband, and launched a literary career through contracts with influential friends. In addition to corresponding for the *Independent,* which had started as a radical antislavery newspaper, she wrote book reviews and other articles for the *Brooklyn Daily Union,* the *Independent*'s sister publication from 1869 to 1872, earning a total salary of $5,000 a year, considered a record for a woman.

Following her divorce in 1874 she used her maiden name, Clemmer, for her byline. She retained it after she married another Washington journalist, Edmund Hudson, a year before her death in 1884. Divorce was almost unthinkable for genteel women of her era, but Ames countered any perception of scandalous behavior with fulsome praise of prevailing ideas on women's roles.

Both Ames and Lippincott insisted that they were truly feminine in spite of their careers. In a collection of her writings in 1850, Lippincott had defined "true feminine genius as ever timid, doubtful and clingingly dependent; a perpetual childhood."[35] By the time she became a Washington correspondent for the *New York Times,* she had outgrown this description of ideal womanhood, having become a convert to woman suffrage and a fervent supporter of African Americans. She had asserted herself to the extent of sitting in the Capitol press galleries. Nevertheless, she assured her audience that "American home life is not declining," refusing to consider divorce or other remedies for unhappy marriages like her own.[36] When it was suggested that no woman had the right to speak out on political issues, she retorted, "I can 'rastle' with cooking and sewing as well as any of my gentler sisters, but just at present I confess I prefer serving up a spicy hash of Southern Democratic sentiment to concocting a pudding."[37]

In her columns Ames insisted that professional success did not appeal to the "womanly" woman. She contended, "That fame is a curse which soils the loveliness of the womanly name by thrusting it into the grimy highway, where it is wondered at, sneered at, lied about, by the vulgar, the worldly, and the wicked."[38] Unlike Lippincott, she declined to enter the Capitol press galleries, one in the Senate and one in the House of Representatives, which offered not only sweeping views of Congress but also provided working space for journalists, and even pens, ink, and stationery furnished at taxpayers' expense.[39]

Considered personally timid herself, Ames told her readers, "Because a woman is a public correspondent it does not make it at all necessary that she as an individual should be conspicuously public—that she should run about with pencils in her mouth and pens in her ears, that she should invade the Reporters' Galleries."[40] According to Ames, no woman "should go anywhere as a mere reporter where she would not be received as a lady."[41] To her, women journalists who made themselves conspicuous brought reproach to all women correspondents.

In her view women journalists had a moral obligation to expose questionable actions by politicians, although she urged women to remain behind the scenes politically, claiming "only in this higher realm of politics can woman reign without detriment to herself or without reflex injury to man."[42] She favored woman suffrage, but found it less important than the right of women to earn money if they lacked male providers, arguing, "Women can live nobly without voting; but they cannot live without bread."[43]

Attacking the low moral tone of President Grant's administration, she defended the press against criticism of it, calling on women journalists to uphold morality. A graceful and dignified woman with blue eyes and light brown hair, Ames wrote, "Because she is a woman, hers is a higher work. It is her work to help exalt the standards of journalism, and in the midst of an arduous profession to preserve intact the dignity and sweetness of individual womanhood."[44]

Neither Ames nor Lippincott was dependent on use of the press galleries to gain material for their columns. As leading literary ladies of their era, they enjoyed the acquaintance of political figures, particularly Radical Republicans, who willingly gave them news items. Although accredited to the galleries, Ames found her close friendship with Sen. Justin S. Morrill of Vermont and his wife far more productive of news.

Another woman correspondent had an even closer connection to power. Mary Abigail Dodge, who wrote under the pseudonym Gail Hamilton, lived in the home of Sen. James G. Blaine of Maine, whose wife was her cousin. Before the Civil War she had lived in Washington as a governess in the home of the editor of the *National Era,* Gamaliel Bailey, who had encouraged her to write for his newspaper as well as to send columns on antislavery issues and congressional proceedings to the *Congregationist,* a Boston religious newspaper that included general news. So concerned was she about concealing her identity as a woman that Dodge did not sign her column Gail Hamilton, but "Cunctare," a Latin epithet commending reserve.[45] She gained much of her material from conversations in the Bailey drawing room, where leading abolitionists gathered.

A shy woman who had suffered a disfiguring eye injury as a child, Dodge left Washington during the Civil War to care for her ailing mother in Massachusetts but continued to write as Gail Hamilton. Her sharp-witted essays, mainly on domestic themes, appeared in the *Atlantic* and other magazines. Collected in five books by Ticknor and Fields, the Boston firm that also published the work of John Greenleaf Whittier, Nathaniel Hawthorne, and Harriet Beecher Stowe, Dodge personified the successful literary lady. On her return to Washington, her reputation as an author, as well as her attachment to Blaine, a presidential aspirant, made her a personage of importance.

Standing aloof from other women correspondents, she echoed the opinions of the powerful Blaine, a conservative Republican and former Speaker of the House who unsuccessfully ran against Grover Cleveland for president in 1884. She wrote a long series of articles for the *New York Tribune* in 1877 attacking civil service reform, which Blaine opposed. Unlike her contemporaries, she rationalized the Crédit Mobilier Scandal, presumably because it came close to Blaine, himself a journalist who had gained a fortune by questionable means.[46] In a magazine article she defended the extravagance of the social circles in which she and the Blaines moved.[47]

The journalistic fraternity in general dismayed her. She sniffed, "I do hate that whole style of writing—newspaper correspondents. It is meddlesome and mischievous. It does small harms and great harms. It does its little all to make people petty, and it is arrogant and pretentious."[48] Clearly, she saw herself far above the press galleries and the women who used them.

For most women correspondents, factual material mattered less than their ability to convey interesting impressions of the Washington scene, which included the White House and government agencies. Photography had not advanced to the point where newspapers could reproduce pictures. Women reporters filled in this lack by sketching pen portraits of leading figures, describing their appearances, clothing, and personalities.

They paid special attention to presidential wives, making their wardrobes and entertaining perennial news subjects and judging their performances in the White House. Ames described Julia Grant as lacking "the natural gifts or graces which could have made her a leader of other minds," but praised her "good nature."[49] A close friend of Lucy Hayes, Grant's successor, Ames pictured Hayes far differently—as having "that tender light in the eyes which we have come to associate with the Madonna."[50] She referred to Hayes as "the first lady of the land," marking one of the first times that the president's wife received the title of First Lady in print.[51]

Unlike Ames, Lippincott, and Dodge, a well-known correspondent, Emily P. Edson Briggs, who used the pseudonym Olivia, concentrated on society reporting during the twenty years that she covered the capital, although she also touched on political issues that affected women. She came to Washington in 1861 with her husband, John R. Briggs Jr., an Iowa newspaper publisher and friend of Abraham Lincoln. Briggs obtained a clerkship in the House of Representatives, where he worked under John W. Forney, who owned two newspapers, the *Washington Chronicle* and the *Philadelphia Press.* Forney hired Emily Briggs to write daily columns for his Philadelphia paper after she sent a letter to the *Chronicle* in favor of women government clerks.

As a reporter Briggs had little need of the Capitol press galleries, even though she was granted admission there, because her husband had a Capitol office and many contacts who could give her information. The first woman to go regularly to the White House to get news, she accompanied her husband when he reported to President Lincoln on political trends. Over the years her columns befriended Mary Todd Lincoln; included lists of matrimonial eligibles among capital bachelors; reported on inaugurations, receptions, and parties; and pictured the "delicate life-currents and details" of the impeachment trial of President Johnson, while the actual trial coverage was handled by a male reporter.[52]

Although she had little interest in woman suffrage, she covered the National Woman Suffrage Convention in Washington in 1870 and heard "Grace Greenwood" give the keynote speech. After watching Susan B. Anthony give news items to a rival, Nellie Hutchinson, of the *New York Tribune,* who favored the suffrage cause, Briggs decided not to be outdone again.[53] The next year Olivia presented a more enthusiastic account of the suffragists' meeting.[54]

Her husband died in 1872, but Olivia continued to write, using contacts originally made through him to interview leading male figures in Washington. Readers enjoyed her lively style and original descriptions. She called the railroad lobby a "huge, scaly serpent . . . winding in and out through the long, devious basement passage, crawling through the corridors, trailing its slimy lengths from gallery to committee room, at last it lies stretched at full length on the floor of Congress."[55] A good-looking Union Pacific lobbyist appeared in her column as an accomplice of Satan: "He might easily be mistaken for something more than human, yet neither horns nor tail are visible."[56]

Briggs's work became so popular that she was one of the few women correspondents whose editors paid for her to send some of her dispatches by telegraph, while her counterparts mailed their copy. A recognized hostess herself after she used an inheritance from her father to purchase a Capitol Hill mansion, Olivia was known for her arched eyebrows, gracious manner, and fashionable dress. Seeing herself as a judge of Washington society, she wrote, "The 'society women' at Washington are expanding the last show of vitality in the adorning of their bodies. Flitting from one 'palatial mansion' to another . . . these human butterflies make no more impression on the world at large than the moths which they so much resemble."[57]

Her comments, designed to show that she was a true woman who disliked displays of riches, probably pleased readers who lacked access to high society. They differentiated her from Gail Hamilton, the apologist for conspicuous consumption. Briggs's career dwindled after 1876, when she stopped corresponding for the *Philadelphia Press,* although she sent columns to other newspapers, and she devoted more energy to entertaining. She subsequently published her columns in a book, *The Olivia Letters.*

In 1879 Briggs was the best known of nineteen women listed in the *Congressional Directory* as entitled to Capitol press gallery privileges, representing about 11 percent of the total of accredited correspondents.[58] By contrast only four had been listed in 1870— Briggs, Lippincott, and two others, Austine Sneed of the *New York World* and Maria A. Stetson of the *State Record* (Topeka, Kans.). Lippincott's name was not there in 1879. She had left Washington the previous year to seek a musical education for her daughter in Europe. Ames and Dodge long had eschewed the press galleries, leaving them to lesser-known correspondents, who mainly wrote social notes. But by 1880 Briggs, along with the other women listed in 1879, was banished from the galleries.

New rules made by the Standing Committee of Correspondents, the group of male journalists who oversaw the galleries, had been put in place, effectively banning the women. In 1877 the Speaker of the House and the Senate Rules Committee, which had jurisdiction over the galleries in the House and Senate respectively, transferred authority for policing the gallery to a select group of correspondents, ostensibly eliminating pressure for admission from lobbyists, government clerks who worked part time as correspondents, and hangers-on.[59] Detailed records have been lost, but those few in existence show a five-member committee of leading correspondents that met in the *New York Times* Washington office in 1879. They drew up rules that limited gallery privileges to persons principally employed as reporters for daily newspapers.[60] These journalists dispatched their news stories by telegraph over special lines set up in the galleries.

The rules said nothing about women per se, but women correspondents were not their newspapers' prime representatives in Washington. With an occasional exception, as in the case of Briggs, editors did not think dispatches from the women—some of whom worked for weekly newspapers—important enough to be sent over costly telegraph lines.[61] As a result the women were forced out of the galleries just when it appeared they were making inroads in a male domain. Since editors did not think that women were capable of reporting political news as well as men, newspaper hiring policies ensured that the galleries would be closed to women for years to come.[62]

As the Civil War faded into history, the ideology of the abolitionist movement, which had led the foremost women correspondents to praise Radical Republican politics and call attention to
the plight of former slaves, wore thin. Journalists like Lippincott
could no longer gain an audience on the grounds of having a
higher moral sense than men and by pointing out unseemly behavior in Congress. Ames had suffered a skull fracture in a carriage accident in 1878 and curtailed her output thereafter. Dodge
increasingly devoted herself to writing about religion and helping
Blaine write his memoirs. Of the leading correspondents only
Briggs remained active in journalism.

Women correspondents increasingly were limited to writing social news, although this had a political dimension because
it came from Washington. Even in covering society they found
rough going. In letters to former President Rutherford B. Hayes
in 1887, Austine Sneed, who wrote for various New York newspapers, expressed her frustrations about making a living from Washington correspondence. She told Hayes bitterly, "Editors always
help the man who is trying to get a woman's work on their paper
away from her."[63]

Aside from motives of self-expression and desire to make an impression on the political scene, the rationale for nineteenth-century
women correspondents in Washington remained the same as it was
for their foremother, Anne Royall. Single, divorced, or widowed,
with few exceptions, most of the women journalists needed to
make a living through their pens, choosing Washington, like Royall, because they wanted to be close to their nation's government
and watch it in action. After the loss of press gallery privileges in
1880, women journalists did not return to the Capitol in sizeable
numbers until the campaign for suffrage reached a crescendo in
the World War I era.

———————————◇———————————

TWO

A NEW GENERATION

Remember too I shall return
From Athens, Naples, and Lucerne;
From castles I have found in Spain—
And then I'll see you all again,
Whenever I can get the chance.
For Persia, Palestine, and France
Can give me nothing much, I guess,
That I'll love better than the Press
Club, so for Monday lunch
I'll soon be back here with the bunch;
And don't let anybody cry
Because I now must say goodbye.

So wrote Frances Parkinson Keyes, the Washington correspondent for *Good Housekeeping* magazine and a novelist of note, when her colleagues at the Women's National Press Club (WNPC) feted her in 1925 before she left on a trip to circle the globe. The wife of Henry W. Keyes, a Republican senator from New Hampshire from 1919 to 1937, she became one of the early members of the WNPC. As a Washington writer who herself laid claim to celebrity, Keyes had managed a successful transformation from literary lady in the style of the nineteenth century to professional journalist. Membership in the WNPC proved she was not a dilettante but a respected member of the working press.

Writing her columns in the form of chatty letters to friends from 1921 to 1924, Keyes told *Good Housekeeping* readers about the rigorous rules of the WNPC that restricted membership to those "at least partially self-supporting by contributions to magazines or newspapers of recognized standing or by publicity work of national scope."[1] Keyes explained that "this requirement naturally means that the members of the club are a very alert, up-and-coming group of women, with whom it is a great pleasure as well as a great stimulation to be."[2] With a voluminous outpouring of fiction and nonfiction that contributed greatly to her family's finances, Keyes took pride in being eligible to join this small but impressive group founded just after World War I ended.

By this time women journalists in the capital had acquired some experience in banding together for professional advancement and personal enrichment. Even before the advent of the twentieth century, Washington women journalists had organized as part of the women's club movement of the day. Clubs appealed generally to white, middle-class Protestant women, most of whom were housewives, who met to pursue cultural and educational goals. Committed to what was called municipal housekeeping, women's clubs also pressed for social improvements.[3] Club women argued on behalf of causes like the abolition of child labor and the sanitary production of milk on grounds they were needed to improve life for women and children.[4]

Club activities, prominently featured on the women's pages that were staples in newspapers of the 1920s, offered women journalists fruitful opportunities for the sale of news. At a time when cities had numerous competing daily newspapers—twenty-nine in New York City alone in 1899—editors frequently bought copy from stringers (so-called because they strung together all the news items they had supplied to submit them for payment).[5] By organizing themselves, the women could write about their own events as well as those of other groups. Club activities played a major role in women's pursuit of news in the face of widespread gender discrimination.

Surprisingly, Washington women journalists predated their male competitors in setting up a viable club. On July 10, 1882, Briggs, better known as Olivia, took office as the first president of the Woman's National Press Association (WNPA), itself an outgrowth of a short-lived Ladies' Press Club. It took until the next year for male reporters, after a couple of false starts, to start a Washington Press Club. It met in the back rooms of the *Baltimore American*'s office adjoining Newspaper Row, an area near the White House just off Pennsylvania Avenue between Thirteenth and Fourteenth streets, where dozens of newspapers had dingy offices.[6] One history said the club, which mainly offered a place to drink, soon died, a casualty of "unpaid bar bills" and "rent long in arrears."[7] Women decidedly were not welcome.

Two years later a group of newspapermen formed the elite Gridiron Club, still in existence, known for its annual "roast" of the president of the United States and other leading political figures. Then, as now, only a select few were allowed to belong. Although the Gridiron had a rule that "ladies are always present," this did not refer to actual attendance, but meant only that members were not allowed to use indecent language or tell smutty stories.[8] It held only three actual "ladies' dinners," to which female family members and correspondents were invited, between 1885 and 1898.

Briggs's organization sought to bring together women engaged in literary and journalistic work for personal growth, social betterment, and mutual assistance. Meetings revolved around teas, not alcohol. In 1893 the WNPA joined the General Federation of Women's Clubs, founded in New York by a journalist, Jane Cunningham Croly, after the male-only New York Press Club refused to invite women journalists to a reception to meet Charles Dickens.[9] By 1895 the Washington group listed 130 members and welcomed press women visiting the capital at its headquarters in the well-known Willard Hotel, which anchored one corner of Newspaper Row.[10] The previous year the group itself had started the Federation of Women's Clubs in D.C.

Two years later women journalists helped establish a second organization—the League of American Pen Women, later the National League of American Pen Women, that remains headquartered in Washington today. Founders included Margaret Sullivan Burke, who gained admission to the congressional press galleries in 1890 after telegraphing dispatches to the daily *Philadelphia Item*. Assured by an Associated Press correspondent, Perry Heath, that he would assist her in case she became ill, she started her own Washington bureau, using her initials, M. S. Burke. Unfortunately she soon lost her affiliation with a daily newspaper and was not reaccredited.[11]

She was followed by Isabel Worrell Ball. Not a suffragist, unlike many of the nineteenth-century Washington women reporters, Ball reveled in her Western roots, having survived attacks by marauding Indians and ravenous wolves.[12] Starting her newspaper career in Kansas, she worked for the *Kansas City* (Mo.) *Star* before moving to Washington in 1891. Arriving as a correspondent for the *Lawrence* (Kans.) *Journal* and *Arkansas City Traveler,* she wrote that male journalists admitted her to the galleries "with the enthusiasm of a case of smallpox."[13]

Nevertheless, men and women sometimes joined reportorial forces, since overworked correspondents frequently bought tidbits from both male and female stringers, who reported on mundane matters, including routine social events and fashion.[14] Writing in the *Journalist,* an early trade publication, Burke told the story of her short-lived press gallery triumph: "The world did not know that I many times did work for the gentlemen of the press that they could not do for themselves; but at last, when the session was half over, I received the magical endorsement that opened the 'sacred precincts' to a woman."[15]

For most women writers, however, the press gallery remained a foreign field. Another founder of the pen women's league, Marion Longfellow O'Donoghue, niece of the beloved poet, Henry Wadsworth Longfellow, herself frequently contributed prose and poetry to Boston and Washington newspapers but did not deal in political news. The third founder was Anna Sanborn Hamilton, social editor of the *Washington Post.* The league did not limit itself to journalists and writers, although many of the members fell into the category of literary ladies, who sold work occasionally to periodicals. The organization also included women artists, dramatists, lecturers, and composers and planned programs that appealed to genteel middle-class women.[16]

In 1921 Keyes, who spanned women's social and professional worlds in Washington, held the office of vice president of the league, which saw itself as an uplifting force in women's lives. She reported in *Good Housekeeping* that it was the largest organization of women writers and illustrators in the United States.[17] Calling the league "very democratic," she explained that "though nearly all the big women writers—the ones whose names are 'top-liners'—belong to it, any woman who has written or is writing professionally is eligible."[18] The league symbolized womanly achievement, so much so that it was prominently mentioned when Keyes became one of four women awarded honorary doctoral degrees from George Washington University in 1921. Her citation began, "Doctor of Letters, Frances Parkinson Keyes; Vice President of the League of American Penwomen; frequent contributor to many reviews and periodicals of the highest literary standards."[19]

In her *Good Housekeeping* columns, Keyes invited readers to join her personal world in official Washington. As a senator's wife, she had no need of accreditation to the Capitol press galleries, since she had automatic access to a reserved seat for senatorial wives. In the same column in which she announced her honorary doctorate, Keyes told of being part of a committee of the National Woman's Party to unveil a statue of three suffrage leaders, Susan B. Anthony, Lucretia Mott, and Elizabeth Cady Stanton, in the Capitol Rotunda. Arguing against criticism of the work, Keyes wrote, "I can think of no way in which the heads of three women . . . could be treated with more dignity and effectiveness than rising from the massive block which forms their base . . . didn't those three women have to fight through, and rise above, something as hard as marble in their lifetime?"[20]

In contrast to the self-improvement atmosphere of women's organizations, male journalists wanted a club where they could swap gossip, drink after the Washington bars closed at midnight, and play poker all night long. In 1908, some thirty newsmen organized the National Press Club (NPC) on Newspaper Row. Graham Bright Nichol, a police reporter for the *Washington Times,* laid down the basic concept of a club that "shall forever be emphatically a newspaperman's club, with the management exclusively in the hands of newspapermen, and with all the officers elected, and all the policies formed by men actively engaged in earning their livings by the pen, the pencil or the artist's brush [a reference to cartoonists and illustrators]."[21]

Obviously, women journalists were excluded. This fact reinforced the idea of separate journalistic spheres for males and females, just as the women's groups did, although separate did not mean equal. Located two floors above a jewelry store, a new NPC opened its doors on May 2, 1908, to a crowd of newspapermen and several members of Congress, as well as to British and Japanese ambassadors who packed the card room and bar.[22] Members were not allowed to charge food or drink, a rule that enabled the club to survive, unlike its predecessor. The club immediately established itself as the place for politicians and the press to congregate in a distinctive outpouring of male bonding. Needing more space, it moved to the corner of Fifteenth and F streets across from the Treasury Department, on the inaugural day parade route.

Members gained $5,000 by renting out club rooms to a wealthy financier who wanted to watch the inauguration of President William Howard Taft, soon to be a club visitor.[23] Both his presidential predecessor, Theodore Roosevelt, and successor, Woodrow Wilson, followed suit. When the club moved again to still larger quarters, Wilson came to its housewarming in 1914. As the club yearbook put it, he bared "his soul," describing his inner struggle to "restrain the emotions inside me."[24] Reporters pressed him to allow them to quote his remarks, which he agreed to, including a comment about the demands of the presidency, which ended with a comment, "If I were free I would come not infrequently to these rooms."[25]

Meanwhile, the WNPA faded from the scene as the woman suffrage campaign heated up in the capital. The longtime president, Mary S. Lockwood, a founder of the Daughters of the American Revolution (DAR), was in her eighties and unsuccessful in recruiting new members at a time when women were becoming far more active politically in Washington following decades of struggle over suffrage.

After its beginning in Seneca Falls, New York, in 1848, the suffrage campaign had been marked by a split between two rival organizations, the American Woman Suffrage Association, which pushed for women's voting on the state and local levels, and the more radical National Woman Suffrage Association. This organization initially opposed the Fifteenth Amendment to the U.S. Constitution on grounds that it gave citizenship rights to African American men but excluded women. The two groups finally merged in 1890, forming the National American Woman Suffrage Association. This umbrella group lumbered on toward suffrage, which women gained successfully in some states partly through the influence of suffrage newspapers.

It was not until Wilson's administration from 1912 to 1920 that the campaign moved to the federal level. A dynamic new group, the Congressional Union, held a massive parade in Washington in 1913 led by a famous suffragist, Inez Milholland, who rode her white horse straight into mobs of hoodlums who tried to disrupt the orderly protest.[26] The Congressional Union sought to mobilize those women who had the ballot to vote against Democratic candidates unless Wilson and the Democratic Party came out for suffrage. Led by Alice Paul and Lucy Burns, the Congressional Union, which changed its name to the National Woman's Party in 1916, modernized by using the new tools of publicity and propaganda.

Paul's small band of followers, mainly young, white, and upper class, was influenced by suffragists in England who engaged in acts of civil disobedience, undertook hunger strikes, and endured the indignity of being force-fed by police. The National Woman's Party employed similar tactics of confrontation, including picketing the White House.[27] Outside the fence, the party stationed "silent sentinels," well-dressed women carrying banners with slogans like HOW LONG WILL WOMEN HAVE TO WAIT FOR LIBERTY?[28]

Women with backgrounds in journalism came to the capital as both publicists for suffrage and reporters to cover the movement. A handful returned to the press galleries, where women constituted about 10 out of 213 accredited correspondents in 1920.[29] One veteran newspaperman asserted that "if women had not been discriminated against from the beginning in this as in many other fields where men were the pioneers, they probably would make up a much larger fraction of the correspondents than is the case."[30] The suffrage campaign proved a godsend to the women since it gave them a wedge for writing political news. With the campaign increasingly dependent on publicists to promote its activities and lobby members of Congress, camaraderie developed between publicists and women journalists, almost all of whom now favored the cause.

When the United States entered World War I in 1917, suffragists were divided over support of the war, although most backed Wilson's decision to fight. The National Woman's Party did not. Paul led demonstrations at the White House protesting the hypocrisy of the nation fighting for democracy in Europe while denying the vote to half the population of the United States. Accusations of being unpatriotic led to demonstrators being arrested and imprisoned in a workhouse in Virginia where Paul was forcibly fed. Newspapers carried stories about the harsh treatment of the suffragists and swung public opinion in their favor.

Supporters of Paul contended that the arrests helped convince Wilson and members of Congress to come out in favor of the Nineteenth Amendment to the U.S. Constitution granting women voting rights. The National American Woman Suffrage Association disagreed, citing victories in state referendums and women's general support for the war effort as the rationale for the amendment's passage. In 1920 it became law after ratification by thirty-eight states.

The year before this finally occurred, three publicists and three journalists who had become friends during the years of suffrage struggle decided to form a new organization to advance their professional standing. The publicists, Florence Brewer Boeckel, Eleanor Marsh Nelson, and Alice Gram Robinson, all had worked for the National Woman's Party. Robinson had spent nine days in jail as part of the mass arrest of suffragists picketing the White House.[31] The journalists represented news organizations outside Washington, in line with the growing number of bureaus set up in the capital to cover its lively political and social scene. They were Cora Rigby, who as bureau chief of the *Christian Science Monitor* was the first woman to head the Washington office of a major newspaper; Carolyn Vance Bell, a syndicated feature writer for the Newspaper Enterprise Association; and Elizabeth King (later Stokes), a reporter for the *New York Evening Post*.[32]

In September 1919 the founders sent letters inviting women journalists working on local newspapers and in news bureaus and government publicity jobs to attend an exploratory meeting. The session was held in the office of the public relations firm run by Boeckel, Nelson, and Robinson, but the letter did not mention the inclusion of publicists in the proposed organization. It simply stated that "it might be both pleasant and profitable for the newspaper and magazine women of Washington to have some means of getting together in informal and irregular fashion."[33] The letter promised that a club would give members "an opportunity to hear more intimately than we otherwise could, prominent men and women who come to Washington."[34] This constituted a slap at the NPC, which barred women from its lunches with newsmaking figures. The letter went out just after the NPC announced that it would entertain the Prince of Wales but made it clear that women journalists would be barred from activities and interviews with him.[35]

Bell recalled years later that she had suggested the idea of the women's press club to the publicists who represented women's groups like the Visiting Nurses Association. After passage of the suffrage amendment seemed assured, Boeckel, Nelson, and Robinson were "looking around for new worlds to conquer, establishing a partnership for what we call today 'public relations,'" Bell continued; "The idea of starting a woman's press club where they could peddle their wares enthused them."[36]

Some forty women attended the organizational meeting and twenty-eight of them decided to join the group, which named itself the Women's National Press Club (WNPC). It held its first luncheon business meeting on November 6, 1919, electing Rigby honorary president for that year and a *New York Times* correspondent, Lily Lykes Rowe (later Shepard), active president. Bell herself did not attend the event because she was pregnant. "It was considered shameful for a woman to show herself in public when there was the slightest evidence of the blessed state," she remembered.[37]

Of the women who did not join, some seemed reluctant to associate themselves with publicists. As Vylia Poe Wilson, a newspaperwoman who later became a member, expressed it, "We were suffragists ourselves and had nothing against the causes represented. Just wanted it [the club] to be more professional."[38]

Wilson was one of the indefatigable Poe sisters, a journalistic pair descended from Edgar Allan Poe who were well known to the *cave dwellers* of Washington, a term used to refer to members of its old-line society. She and Elizabeth Ellicott Poe worked for years for the *Washington Post,* chronicling the history of the capital along with its social events, reviewing books, and "doing a little of everything," according to Ishbel Ross, who wrote the first history of the women journalists.[39] In common with other journalists, both male and female, the sisters saw themselves as having professional autonomy and being superior to publicists, who were hired by special interests to influence news copy.

The WNPC dealt with the tensions between journalists and publicists by setting up two types of membership: a mainstream category for journalists and a subordinate one for publicists. Only journalists were allowed to be presidents and take charge of the club's operations. Although Keyes claimed that members had to be only "partially self-supporting," club rules stated that the journalist category was limited to "reputable publishers, editors, writers, correspondents and reporters, actively engaged in Washington on well established newspapers, press associations or periodicals including government publications, and deriving therefrom all or the greater part of their income."[40] Women doing publicity work could join only "if engaged in such work professionally and deriving the greater part of their incomes from it, and maintaining direct and regular contact with the press."[41]

A testimony to the relationship of the WNCP with its predecessor organization lay in the fact that one of the club's charter members was Grace Porter Hopkins, identified as a special writer, who as vice president of the old Woman's National Press Association, ended that organization. Following the death of Lockwood, its president, in 1922 at the age of ninety-three, Hopkins decided not to hold any more meetings. She placed the association's records in a bank with the notation, "most of the members having passed away."[42]

During the club's formative period, Rigby, considered the most distinguished woman journalist in Washington, took over as sole president, serving from 1920 to 1926. She saw the club as a necessary means for combating "the discrimination of men to keep women off the newspapers—or at least to reduce their number, wages, and importance to a minimum."[43] Posing for her photograph wearing a white blouse and dark skirt and seated behind her rolltop desk, Rigby personified the capable, childless woman correspondent who devoted herself to her profession. She lived with her closest friend, Margaret Williamson, another *Monitor* staff member.

Rigby, the daughter of an Ohio judge, started her career in Columbus, Ohio, writing unsigned columns of local political news that proved so trenchant, rumor had it the governor's male secretary was the actual author.[44] Moving on to New York, she worked for fifteen years for the *Herald* owned by James Gordon Bennett Jr., rising to the editorship of its Sunday magazine, even though Bennett generally disapproved of women in responsible positions. When Rigby proved exceptionally capable, Bennett gave her a Pekingese puppy in appreciation.[45] After his newspaper was sold, she joined the staff of the *Christian Science Monitor,* where she stayed until her death in 1930. Described as unobtrusive in manner, Rigby wrote copy so gender neutral that colleagues praised it for not showing "it was written by a woman."[46]

Working for a daily newspaper started by a woman, Mary Baker Eddy—founder of the Christian Science religion—Rigby, herself a Christian Scientist, extended a helping hand to other women. In her will she left money to the WNPC to aid newspaperwomen who needed financial assistance. According to Keyes, Rigby "was a little wisp of a woman with faded hair and a faded face" and an infinite capacity for work, easily "getting off five thousand words a day."[47] When Keyes became ill while covering a political convention in New York, Rigby put her to bed in a hotel room and told her she was working too hard. She even saw an editor to line up an easier job for Keyes and did not realize that she herself had gotten no sleep at all in her eagerness to help "until I reminded her of it," Keyes recalled.[48] Although Keyes did not take the other job, she appreciated Rigby's actions. "There was a feeling of having touched rock bottom, of being allied to something fine and enduring, and still stimulating, in associating with Cora Rigby," Keyes wrote, crediting Rigby with establishing the WNPC as a prestigious organization.[49]

Rigby's willingness to mentor other women led her to hire Mary Hornaday, a Swarthmore College graduate, for the *Monitor* bureau in 1927. Hornaday's father was a well-known Washington correspondent for the *Indianapolis News.* Under Rigby, Hornaday became one of the few women journalists regularly assigned to Congress. When she telegraphed her first story to the *Monitor* from Washington, the bureau's telegraph operator paid her the optimum compliment for a woman journalist of her day: "You write like a man."[50] Hornaday eventually followed Rigby as president of the WNPC, serving in 1936.

Determined to be a professional organization, not a traditional women's club composed of stay-at-home matrons, the WNPC prided itself on admission standards that excluded those who sold occasional offerings to the press. "Our qualifications are so high that from the beginning our membership committee has had an exceedingly difficult job—one requiring members who are smart, sharp, and with backbone and tact," Shepard, the first president, wrote in the 1960s for a proposed book on the club's history that was never completed.[51] She said the committee had the task of saying "gently but firmly to a member why it cannot recommend for membership her friend Susy Doaks on the basis of Susy Doaks' nice letters from her Congressman to the committee telling how she sends back such interesting social items about the Congressman's wife, which appear in the Bingville Bugle."[52]

Following the example of the men's NPC, the WNPC decided to hold luncheon programs featuring speeches by newsworthy individuals, both male and female. Not only did the members obtain news stories from the speakers, but the speakers helped elevate the status of the women by meeting with them. Margaret Bondfield, a British labor expert, gave the first speech on November 13, 1919. Lowell Thomas, a world traveler, spoke shortly thereafter, telling for the first time in Washington of his adventures with Lawrence of Arabia.[53]

Although the members had been committed to suffrage, they did not join forces to push protective legislation for women. The WNPC did not see itself as an arm of the Women's Joint Congressional Committee, which was established in 1920 to lobby for maternal and infant health projects, the elimination of child labor, and efforts to develop women's economic independence. This organization, which lasted for a decade, drew in groups such as the Women's Trade Union League, the National Consumers League, the Women's Christian Temperance Union, and the League of Women Voters.

In particular, the committee pushed for the Sheppard-Towner Maternity and Infancy Act of 1921 and the Child Labor Amendment, both of which were fought by conservative forces. Although individual members of the WNPC wrote stories from time to time about legislative debates over these and other measures, both the club and its members made no overt commitment to publicize legislation sought by mainstream women's organizations. Like women in general, journalists split on the actions that should be taken by newly enfranchised women voters.

Some members of the WNPC belonged to the National Woman's Party, which favored an equal rights amendment to the U.S. Constitution and opposed the concept of protective legislation for women workers. Other journalists looked favorably on the League of Women Voters, the largest of the organizations that had joined in the campaign, but as a group did not press for what became known as the politics of maternalism.[54] One strong supporter of maternal legislation was Keyes, whose husband backed the Sheppard-Towner Act, which was supported by the Republican administration of President Harding.[55] Keyes herself testified on behalf of the bill before Congress.

"I believe I'd be willing to camp on the Capitol steps all summer to see it passed," she wrote in one of her magazine letters. "A woman who feels that the job of a senator's wife should be purely social said to me the other day that if I wasn't careful my name would go on that bill as a rider!"[56] Far from being dismayed, Keyes applauded the idea, replying "that I was very proud of my name, and that there was no place where I would rather see it."[57]

Unlike Keyes, most members of the WNCP did not want to be associated simply with women's issues or, more pointedly, with news destined to appear on the women's pages of the day. They did not want to be restricted in news assignments. "There is no more reason for this feature [the women's page] than there is for a men's page," exclaimed a woman writer for the *Philadelphia North American*.[58] "News belongs to the people, not to a sex."[59]

Unlike their male counterparts, members of the WNPC had no permanent meeting place, refusing to accept the help of well-connected associate members in financing club quarters, as the NPC did.[60] While President Warren G. Harding, publisher of an Ohio newspaper, frequented the NPC, where members circumvented Prohibition by hiding liquor in a small room called the Turf Club, his wife, Florence, endeavored to make friends with women journalists. She invited WNPC members to cruise on the presidential yacht, where she astounded the group by slapping the dignified Rigby on the back and exclaiming, "Well, here we are, all girls together."[61]

One club member proposed that the First Lady be taken into the club on grounds she had managed her husband's newspaper in Ohio before his election as president, but the officers ruled she was ineligible because her work had been in the business office, not the editorial rooms of the *Marion Star.*[62] While Keyes praised her effusively, other women journalists gave her mixed reviews. She had refused, for example, to tell social writers what dress she planned to wear for her husband's inauguration in 1921.[63]

After the First Lady invited WNPC members to the White House, according to Bell, her patronage helped put the club "on the map," by giving it social standing in the capital.[64] Not all the women were favorably impressed by the president's wife. Recovering from a near-death experience in 1923, Harding held an informal tea in her bedroom, "pasty white [and] heavily made up as she could be," according to Vylla Wilson.[65] She received the group in a red velvet negligee and went into such detail about her health that it "revolted" one reporter.[66] Harding used the occasion to reveal that she supported a federal prison for women, giving the reporters an actual news story.[67]

While club members showed up for the social opportunities that fell their way, they sought to be taken seriously as journalists who could cover important assignments as well as men. When male officials appeared to belittle the group, the women became angry. William G. McAdoo, secretary of the treasury under Wilson, talked down to his audience at a club luncheon, one member remembered later. "He treated us as if we were debutantes to be flattered by pretty compliments instead of giving us at least some shreds of information about current affairs."[68] He left the women "angry and deflated."[69]

The women met over the years in an assortment of restaurants, tea rooms, hotels, and headquarters of women's groups like the American Association of University Women.[70] By contrast, having outgrown its rented quarters, the NPC broke ground for an impressive new fourteen-story building in 1926 at the corner of Fourteenth and F streets, on old Newspaper Row, about two blocks from the White House. President Coolidge, who laid the cornerstone, returned two years later to speak for the official dedication, broadcasting his remarks across the nation. As a special concession, the club was opened during the fete to "ladies of the members' household," but not to women journalists unless by chance they were married to members.[71] Subsequently, the club maintained a separate ladies' dining room, until Prohibition ended in 1933 and it wanted to use that space for its bar.

Determined to prove their competence as journalists, WNPC members persevered in seeking their own luncheon speakers so they would have access to fresh news. In 1927 they held the club's first "stunt party," a takeoff on the Gridiron Club's annual all-male roast of the president and other government leaders. As the years went by, the parties became more elaborate and drew scores of honored female guests: the wives of cabinet members, top political figures and Supreme Court justices, women members of Congress, and celebrities like Amelia Earhart.

The WNPC published its own mock newspapers to celebrate

these occasions, carrying out the theme of the evening. In 1931, when the club had eighty-five members, the theme was "Station WNPC broadcasting its annual Cabaret Toasting Party from the roof garden of the Willard Hotel," presented in a four-page oversize broadsheet, the *Toaster*.[72] The satirical sheet featured take-offs on the kind of news that members wrote for women's pages. Under the heading ERRORS OF OTHERS LOST ON SCRIBES, the *Toaster* reported that "these ladies of the Fourth Estate, who so readily and anxiously tell the world of the disorder found at elections of prominent women's organizations, are sadly in need of seeing themselves as others see them."[73] An account of a "colorful fray" in last year's election of WNPC officers followed.[74]

Other "news flashes" appeared such as this: "[The] president general of the D.A.R. has just sent a messenger to Continental Hall for her missing forty-ninth medal of service. Says she cannot eat without it."[75] The item mocked members of the conservative patriotic organization, who frequently were photographed wearing large badges and similar paraphernalia. In a fashion column spoof, the DAR came in for another swipe: "The D.A.R.'s are wearing search lights on their hats this year. Their bonnets are attractively trimmed with the scalps of Pinks and Reds won in their last Communist hunt through the halls of Congress."[76]

Prohibition, then in its heyday, came in for potshots. "Club Notes" referred to "the committee of the thirsty" and a revelation of "what the decanter said to the goblet in the days when they bravely faced their doom and the determination of those who bore from within the hogshead to crack them all up."[77] The "Order of the Grand Exchange of New Coats for Old" announced a forthcoming "Battle of the Cloak room," a drama that would include passage of resolutions "in favor of civil service reform and padlocks on all sable coats."[78] Rivalry with male journalists along with hints of jealousy underlaid the "stunt parties." As Keyes expressed it: "The Gridironers who decided that they would never ask us to their dinners would repent their rash action in sackcloth and ashes if they realized what our retaliation in not asking them to ours has cost them. But, then, that is just like men ... we have a perfectly good time without them."[79]

In 1927 the club held its first luncheon for a First Lady, honoring the vivacious Grace Coolidge, a personal friend of Rigby. Coolidge graciously accepted, but did not break with her husband's admonitions. President Coolidge refused to let his wife give interviews or make speeches, just as he forbade her to ride horses, drive a car, fly in an airplane, bob her hair, or express her views on politics.[80] In keeping with her well-known charm and diplomacy, she displayed a unique way of communicating at the luncheon even though at the time "there was an unwritten law that no First Lady should ever be called upon to speak in public," according to an official history of the WNPC.[81] When "a brash member arose and asked if she wouldn't say a few words," Grace Coolidge "smiled her famous smile" and quickly began to talk in sign language that she had learned before her marriage as a teacher in a school for the blind and deaf.[82] The astonished club members made no attempt to translate it.

Although some WNPC members were accredited to Capitol press galleries, few of the women had the option of covering politics. Since many club members wrote for women's and society sections of newspapers, disagreements took place over whether the club should be oriented to general news of the type covered by men or to women's and society events. Two members who were society editors, Sallie V. H. Pickett of the *Washington Star* and Ruth Jones of the *Washington Herald,* were presidents in 1928 and 1930, respectively.

Both women had long newspaper careers and represented the apex of society writing, considered a special art in the capital. As Ross put it, "The capital ... is paradise for the society reporter. There is a constant influx of interesting figures from all over the world. The political aspects of the social scene add a measure of color and excitement to a job that, too often, is one of mere routine."[83] In Ross's view, publicity in the social columns counted as part of the capital's political game: "A woman who could never hope to crash the social column in the town from which she springs, may rate the most conservative grouping in Washington because of her husband's political standing."[84]

After coming to the capital in 1892, Pickett became a society editor and feature writer for several Washington newspapers as well as out-of-town publications during a career that spanned forty-four years. Keyes pronounced Pickett, known as Aunt Sally, as "extremely discreet in all her writing," but less so in conversation.[85] She recalled an occasion when "well-worn gossip about the paternity" of a child was revived, and Aunt Sally placidly commented, "I have always felt that every lady is entitled to have at least one child about whose father not too many questions are asked!"[86] A similar affectionate nickname was bestowed on one of Pickett's contemporaries, Maude McDougall, who covered Washington society for the *Philadelphia Public Ledger,* and was known as Maudie by her colleagues.[87]

At the time of her death in 1939, Pickett was referred to as society editor emeritus of the *Evening Star* and dean of Washington newspaperwomen. A total of twenty-one *Star* executives served as honorary pallbearers.[88] Her contemporaries said Pickett saw presidents "come and go, administrations rise and fall, but never missed a move in the social picture."[89]

Jones, who wrote as Jean Eliot, attained even greater recognition. Starting as a society reporter for the *Washington Times* in 1914, Jones, whose father was a prominent lawyer and mother a famed Baltimore beauty, capitalized on her family connections. These included a senator and a mayor of Washington, who helped her gain access to presidents, cabinet officers and their wives, diplomats, and members of Congress. Leaving the *Times* in 1928, she worked as society editor of the *Washington Post* before Eleanor M. "Cissy" Patterson took over the *Washington Herald* and lured Jones to her newspaper.

Jones's obituary in 1940 said that "reticent cave dwellers confided in her and their confidence was never misplaced" and lauded her for gaining the "esteem and affection" of social leaders like Evalyn Walsh McLean, owner of the Hope Diamond.[90] It called attention to her early journalistic feats—scooping the country on news of the engagement of President Woodrow Wilson's daughter Eleanor, who married Secretary of the Treasury McAdoo in 1914, and the "brilliant parties" during the Harding administration, "when the city swarmed with glittering missions and dignitaries from all parts of the globe."[91]

Described as "handsome, sophisticated and smart," Jones was known for getting on "equally well with the debutantes and their mothers."[92] Keyes rated Jones as "incontestably the outstanding society editor in Washington in the 1930s," calling her "aristocratic of background, pleasing of person, trustworthy of character, wise of policy . . . [putting] wit, punch, and class" into her society page.[93] She said Jones had "a flair for finding fresh material in a field already apparently gleaned bare."[94]

Jones's employer, Patterson, led a life far removed from those of other Washington women journalists, although she too was a member of the WNPC. Not a working journalist but an exceptional editor and publisher, Patterson's flamboyant style, immense fortune, and extraordinary family connections placed her in a class by herself. A granddaughter of Joseph Medill, founder of the *Chicago Tribune,* Patterson, whose brother, Joseph Medill Patterson, founded the *New York Daily News,* had newspaper ink in her veins.

After a failed marriage to a Polish nobleman, which gave her the title of Countess Gizycki, and a foray into writing novels—one of which featured a poorly disguised Alice Roosevelt Longworth and Countess Gizycki herself as society rivals in Washington—she took charge of the morning *Washington Herald.* Owned by William Randolph Hearst, the most powerful media mogul of the day, the *Herald* ranked fourth in circulation among the city's five dailies in the 1930s.[95] Patterson set out to brighten its women's and society coverage and increase its circulation. She recognized public interest in society news at a time when women journalists themselves were split over whether they ought to make efforts to enhance their personal contacts with social leaders.

Under both Pickett and Jones, the WNPC's main orientation continued to be luncheons with speakers on political topics instead of social events. Society reporters, however, frequently invited socially prominent women to attend these events to foster relationships with them. The society journalists pressed to have these women admitted to membership, but the majority of the club members disagreed.[96]

As a result, most of the society reporters withdrew from the group in 1932 and formed a rival organization, the American Newspaper Women's Club (ANWC), which offered associate memberships to prominent women featured in women's and society pages. In addition, it established an honorary membership category for women either known in their own right or through their husbands. Grace Coolidge was promptly made an honorary member, as were all the First Ladies who followed her. Six months

after the club's formation, it held a party in honor of First Lady
Lou Henry Hoover and conferred membership on her.

Cofounded by Katharine H. Brooks and Margaret Hart Canby,
two society journalists from the *Evening Star,* then considered
Washington's leading newspaper, the new group also listed Pickett and ten other women from Washington newspapers, the *Post,
Times,* and *Herald,* as organizing members.[97] Charter members included women who represented newspapers outside the capital:
Leila W. Bathon of the *Baltimore Sun,* Mary MacCracken Jones
of the *Springfield* (Mass.) *Republican,* Ann Parks Marshall of the
El Dorado (Ark.) *Times-News,* and Mrs. George F. Richards of
the *Worcester* (Mass.) *Telegram,* who signed her columns only as
Richards.[98]

Brooks became the first president, serving from 1932 to 1935,
followed by Hart Canby from 1935 to 1937. The group met at
teatime in the ladies' dining room of the NPC until evicted in
1933, when the dining room changed into the bar. The ANWC
then moved into rented space until it finally acquired a clubhouse
nearly thirty years after its formation.[99] Initially hostile, eventually
the women's clubs had considerable overlapping membership, although Jones did not join the Newspaper Women's Club.

Unlike the WNPC, the ANWC showed less interest in speakers than in staging social events and its own benefits for worthy
causes, supported by its associate members, and publicized on the
women's and society pages for which members wrote. The two
clubs represented different viewpoints toward the role of women
journalists in Washington. Members of the WNPC wanted to
cover the news like men; ANWC members saw women's news as
separate from men's news. With their orientation to women's and
society pages, ANWC members pictured news in terms of fashions
as well as socially elite women, particularly well-known hostesses.

ANWC members also specialized in the activities of traditional women's clubs and charitable organizations, attempting, perhaps unconsciously, to identify a separate women's culture in the capital linked to the male power structure. Illustrating the journalistic adage that names make news, women's and society pages carried items with long lists of names of family members of influential men. Weddings rated descriptions of minute detail, ranging from the social standing of the families involved down to embroidery on wedding gowns and the refreshments served at receptions.

Women in both clubs attuned themselves to politics, since the capital's social scene revolved around those in political power. The White House stood at the apex of the socio-political structure, and society reporters clamored for full details of the entertaining that went on there. Rather than the Capitol, the White House became their special province, with the First Lady's social secretary routinely providing guest lists and seating arrangements for state dinners and other events. Women reporters wrote about Christmas decorations, garden parties, diplomatic receptions, musicales, and family members.

Women reporters who were accredited to the Capitol press galleries did not spend much time covering legislative actions or political maneuvering, but generally were confined to the fringes of politics. This group included stalwart members of the WNPC like Winifred Mallon, who had been hired in 1929 as a political writer in the *New York Times* Washington bureau, but also covered social events as the bureau's token woman. Mallon, originally a cable clerk at the State Department, had begun writing news dispatches from Washington for the *Chicago Tribune* in 1902.[100]

Her first contribution to the *Tribune* was an item for a column that revealed First Lady Edith Roosevelt's choice of children's books for the White House library.[101] Mallon corresponded for the *Chicago Tribune* and other newspapers for two decades. She wrote as "Raymond" for stories on immigration and armed forces recruiting. Her own name appeared only on stories related to women's issues, such as this one for the *Pittsburgh Dispatch* in 1903, headlined, MRS. SECRETARY OF COMMERCE CORTELYOU CHATS EN-TERTAININGLY OF HER NEW SOCIAL DUTIES, LIVES FOR HUSBAND AND CHILDREN.[102]

In 1913 Mallon started a column on the suffrage campaign, but it was not until 1918 during World War I that she was admitted to the Capitol press galleries and made a regular bureau staff member, assigned to do a column on pending legislation.[103] Considered an expert on immigration, having worked on Ellis Island as a government employee, she was called before a congressional committee to testify on the subject.[104] After a disagreement with the *Tribune* in 1925, she left that newspaper to handle publicity for the National Woman's Party. Developing a relationship with the *Times* bureau, she reported on women's views of the presidential election of 1928 during a campaign swing through five states, prior to being offered a full-time job on the *Times* staff. Ross called this "a distinct innovation for the Washington bureau."[105]

The first woman who regularly covered political stories for the *Times,* Mallon tackled hearings held by the Senate Interstate Commerce Committee in 1929 and 1930 on the legislation that created the Federal Communications Commission. She received compliments from the committee's consul for her accurate and clear coverage.[106] More typical assignments revolved around women's organizations, social life at the White House, and similar women-oriented fare. One task was to report on a longstanding feud between Dolly Gann, the sister of Vice President Charles Curtis, and Alice Roosevelt Longworth, wife of Nicholas Longworth, Speaker of the House of Representatives, over whether the brother or husband should have precedence in seating at official dinners during the Hoover administration.

As a veteran observer of the Washington scene, Mallon had a well-stocked memory of newsworthy events and a habit of peering at other reporters over spectacles that repeatedly slipped down her nose.[107] Small in stature, she presented a somewhat eccentric appearance, clutching an oversized handbag that trailed behind her. Her contemporaries conceded that she had a "lively mind and the ability to think clearly and to write clearly."[108]

Another committed WNCP member, Bess Furman, a red-haired former schoolteacher from Nebraska, arrived in Washington in 1929 to work for the Associated Press. She won a prize for a story written in Omaha on a campaign appearance of Alfred E. Smith, the unsuccessful Democratic candidate for president in 1928. Her colorful, chatty style suited the AP, which was just beginning to use women's bylines on feature stories mainly aimed at women's pages. It hired her for the top woman's job in the Washington bureau, where her gender both defined and minimized her opportunities.

In the *Congressional Directory,* Furman's name was last on the list of thirty-six persons from the AP accredited to the Capitol press galleries. On the AP's weekly assignment sheet, "my beat trailed all the rest," Furman wrote in her autobiography.[109] She described herself as limited to the "outer edges of government town, plus news of interest to women."[110]

Furman's rounds included government agencies that lacked much appeal to her male colleagues. She sought stories at the Department of Labor's Women's Bureau and Children's Bureau, the Department of Agriculture's Bureau of Home Economics, the Public Health Service, the Veterans Bureau, the post office, and the

Census Bureau, as well as the Red Cross. She also covered national women's organizations, particularly the DAR, whose annual conventions filled columns of women's and society news.

When Furman finally got a chance to go to Capitol Hill to write about the opening of Congress from "the women's angle" in December 1929, she found the experience "tense and strenuous."[111] Having arrived in Washington the previous April, she easily could have sought out the eight women members of Congress before the regular session began, "but the AP men on Capitol Hill kept it as holy ground, on which I was not supposed to set foot without explicit orders," she recalled.[112] "I had to meet and interview all eight Congresswomen in one day, in addition to picking out the women notables in the galleries."[113] Fortunately, Furman again proved her competence and became the first woman reporter regularly assigned to the House of Representatives by a press association.[114]

By no means did Congress represent Furman's main reportorial responsibility. She later recalled as the "most peculiar chore" of her first year in Washington her reporting on a conference to negotiate the division of water and electric power from Boulder Dam, which was still in the planning stages, among the competing Western states of California, Arizona, and Nevada.[115] She learned that another woman, Ruth Finney, a reporter for the Scripps Howard newspaper chain, stood out as the most knowledgeable journalist on water resources, but the two did not work together. To help her understand the complicated issues involved, Furman turned to a man, George W. Malone, the state engineer for Nevada.

Finney, in the words of Ross, ranked "with the best men in the press gallery."[116] Ross named her the top Washington example of the "front page girl," the name bestowed on newspaperwomen of the period who covered the same news as men—politics, courts, and public affairs, even though they generally received less pay.[117] As a star for Scripps Howard, Finney wrote political stories making use of her gallery contacts and was recognized as an authority on issues of power, oil, labor, and federal budgeting. She arrived in Washington in 1924 as a correspondent for Scripps Howard newspapers in California and New Mexico. Recognizing that her male colleagues had preempted most of the important assignments, she decided to concentrate on a neglected area—power—specializing in legislation pertaining to public utilities. In addition, she developed expertise in government oil reserve leases and reported on leasing scandals that stemmed from actions of the Harding administration.

According to Ross, Finney pounded "out her stories in the press gallery with the assurance that comes from having complete grasp of her subject."[118] Married to another journalist, Robert S. Allen, who wrote a Washington investigative column called "Daily Washington Merry-Go-Round" with Drew Pearson, Finney was said to mask intellectual vigor "behind a quiet feminine manner."[119] Undoubtedly, Furman knew Finney and must have seen her as a quasi-role model at least, although Furman prided herself on writing lively features and showed limited interest in complex subjects like power legislation.

Determined to cultivate sources in Congress in spite of discouragement from her male counterparts at the AP, Furman paid frequent social visits to the office of Rep. Ruth Bryan Owen, a Democrat from Florida, whose famed orator father, William Jennings Bryan, had been a Democratic presidential candidate. The two women became so close that Furman was married in Owen's apartment overlooking the Capitol plaza on March 18, 1932, to Robert J. Armstrong Jr., a reporter for the *Los Angeles Times*.[120] Furman continued to use her given name professionally.

She was not the only woman in the AP Washington bureau. Close friend Sue McNamara, who had worked with her in Omaha and helped her get the Washington job, wrote for the new AP feature service. Among her tasks was covering parties. When a society matron sent her giant dahlias with four-foot-long stems mingled with huge gladioli, according to Furman, McNamara stuffed them down an incinerator, pronouncing them "the symbol of social Washington, blatant and without fragrance, and blown up beyond natural size."[121] Society news was far from a preferred assignment at the AP.

Furman's closest competitor inside the AP was Marguerite Young, whom Furman referred to as "remarkably beautiful [and] anything but my idea of a collaborator," although the bureau management paired them occasionally.[122] Furman accused Young of using sex appeal to cut her out of stories. "Every time I worked a joint story up to the cream-skimming stage, or so it seemed to me, she would have been out dancing with the man 'on desk' the night before completing all arrangements to skim all the cream," Furman claimed.[123] She described the competition as "deep and elemental."[124]

A lively redhead who took to radical ideas, Young was the daughter of a Louisiana planter who encountered financial reverses. After working on a New Orleans newspaper, she arrived in New York in 1928 with forty dollars and persuaded the head of the AP to hire her for the Washington bureau. Not content with her assignment to women's features, she pinch-hit for men temporarily absent from their regular beats and learned the Washington scene.[125]

Shocked by the machinations of politicians, Young studied communism but left the anonymity of the AP to work for the *New York World-Telegram,* a conservative publication out of keeping with her own philosophy.[126] In 1934 she resigned from that newspaper, denounced it for publishing "uncounted reams of woman-story piffle" and moved to the *Daily Worker,* the newspaper of the Communist Party, as its Washington correspondent.[127] Paying little attention to the party line, she was fired two years later but managed to land on her feet with a job at the Republican *New York Herald Tribune.*

Other women who gained admission to the press galleries in the 1920s and 1930s included two outspoken feminists, Ruby Black and May Craig. Black, a slight woman with fashionable bobbed hair, had graduated with a Phi Beta Kappa key from the University of Texas, pursued graduate work at the University of Wisconsin, where she taught journalism, and served as president of a national journalism sorority, Theta Sigma Phi, for which she edited its magazine, the *Matrix.* Married in 1922 to Herbert Little, a reporter for the United Press, she refused to take his surname. After Little was transferred to Washington from St. Louis, where she had been labor editor of a newspaper, Black was unable to find a job in the capital because of her gender, so she started her own news bureau in 1928, providing political and governmental news to some twenty newspapers.

Craig, a diminutive correspondent for the Gannett newspaper chain in Maine, had learned the journalistic craft from her husband, Donald A. Craig, a newspaperman. After he was injured in an automobile accident in 1923, she helped him write political columns and eventually became his successor as a Washington correspondent. Like Black, Craig was a member of the National Woman's Party and committed to equal rights.

Along with Furman, Black and Craig, as well as other women reporters, benefited professionally from news stories generated by Eleanor Roosevelt, who became First Lady in 1933. Roosevelt provided a focal point for them and other Washington women journalists for the next twelve years. Without the professional camaraderie and organizational experience gained during the 1920s and early 1930s, Washington women journalists would not have been able to take advantage of the opportunities offered by Roosevelt to gain more bylines and headlines. She used the Washington women's press corps to publicize her activities, while the women used the conferences to help keep themselves employed.

◈

THREE

ELEANOR ROOSEVELT AND THE "NEWSPAPER GIRLS"

It will save my time enormously if I see you all together once a week and do not have to see three now and three later and so on. I feel that your position as I look upon it is to try to tell the women throughout the country what you think they should know. That, after all, is a newspaper woman's job, to make her impressions go to leading the women in the country to form a general attitude of thought and mind. Your job is an important one and if you want to see me once a week I feel I should be willing to see you, and anything that I can do through you toward this end I am willing to do. The idea largely is to make an understanding between the White House and the general public. You are the interpreters to the women of the country as to what goes on politically in the legislative national life and also what the social and personal life is at the White House.

With these words a nervous Eleanor Roosevelt explained to a group of about thirty-five women journalists on March 6, 1933, that she appreciated their importance and planned to hold weekly White House press conferences for women only during her tenure as First Lady. These events, which totaled nearly 350, continued during the three full terms that her husband, Franklin D. Roosevelt, spent in the presidency, ending on the day of his unexpected death on April 12, 1945, after the start of his fourth term. In many ways they defined the role of Washington women journalists during the 1930s and World War II. These journalists covered other women and their activities, no matter how much some aspired to the same assignments as men. Covering a president's wife who was believed to wield power herself appeared to enhance their own importance.

Looked down on by male journalists, Roosevelt's press conferences pictured a president's wife for the first time as a key political player who created her own news. By banning men, she compelled some male editors to hire women journalists to report on these gatherings. Vague in their intent and execution, the conferences illustrated the dimensions of news assignments considered appropriate for most women reporters. By male standards their news value may have been minimal, but they acquired significance in the context of increasing opportunities for Washington women journalists.

Unlike her predecessors who had limited contacts with reporters, Eleanor Roosevelt started planning for press contacts after a Depression-stricken nation elected her husband president in a landslide in 1932. An immediate rationale was to keep women journalists employed in Washington. Since they were considered less capable than their male counterparts, they were in danger of losing out as some newspapers cut payrolls in the midst of declining revenues.

In her autobiography Roosevelt expressed fears of layoffs: "Unless the women reporters could find something new to write about, the chances were that some of them would hold their jobs a very short time."[1] She wrote that Lorena Hickok, an AP reporter who had covered her during the presidential campaign and became an intimate friend, "pointed out many of these things to me, because she felt a sense of responsibility for the other women writers."[2] Mary Hornaday of the *Christian Scientist Monitor* recalled later, "I think Lorena Hickok persuaded Mrs. Roosevelt that everything she did was news."[3] Her press conferences helped make her into a media celebrity and influenced the careers of women who covered her, but not always positively.

By 1933 Hickok herself, pictured by a contemporary as "hard-boiled and soft-hearted at the same time—a big girl in a casual raincoat with a wide tailored hat," had worked her way up to being one of the top women reporters in the United States.[4] She specialized in political coverage and other prize assignments given to only a few women who won the coveted title of "front-page girl" in the early twentieth century.[5] A servant girl during her poverty-stricken youth in South Dakota, Hickok mastered the journalistic craft at the *Minneapolis Tribune,* where she was assigned to both football and politics, before arriving in New York City in 1927 and landing a job with the AP. Although the U.S. Census counted some fourteen thousand women reporters and editors in the United States in 1930, most, including those in Washington, were confined to women's and society pages, women's magazines, or sentimental "sob sister" feature stories.[6] A versatile and hard-working exception who outdid her competitors, Hickok became the first woman trusted by the AP to write "hard news" leads on major stories.[7]

Overweight and somewhat erratic, Hickok appeared to India Edwards, a journalist and Democratic Party official in Washington, to be "the most mannish woman I've ever known; she walked like a man; she dressed like a man (in tailored suits; in those days women didn't wear pants); she styled her hair like a man."[8] Edwards said she was told by "old friends of Hick she had admitted having a lesbian affair."[9] According to Edwards, "Mrs. Roosevelt was an angel to Hickok."[10]

The dissimilar pair, drawn together during long rides on campaign trains, undoubtedly exercised extraordinary influence on each other at a pivotal time in the lives of both women. Through her favorable news stories on Roosevelt during the campaign, Hickok introduced her to the nation as a different kind of First Lady, eager to identify with ordinary Americans and help them in a time of turmoil. Roosevelt admired Hickok's successful career in journalism and skill in dealing with news. Hickok found herself mesmerized by Roosevelt's aristocratic background and interest in the unfortunate.

Almost consumed by her relationship with the First Lady, Hickok stopped thinking like an AP reporter; for example, not phoning in the gist of Franklin Roosevelt's inaugural address, which Eleanor showed her in advance.[11] On inauguration day Hickok interviewed Roosevelt in a White House bathroom after the two women could not find another place to meet where they would not be interrupted. The AP copyrighted the interview, which announced that the First Lady would serve as her disabled husband's "eyes and ears," seeing as many Americans as possible and reporting back to him.[12]

To Hickok's great disappointment, it got relatively little news play, ending up on page seven of the *New York Times,* while a lively AP story by Furman landed on page one, beginning, "The century-old White House wore a startled air today, as though listening to the sound of shattering precedents."[13] Editors obviously preferred bated-breath features to more substantive fare that pictured a First Lady as a political partner.

Within months, Hickok's closeness to the Roosevelts forced her to give up her AP job, since she could not maintain the objectivity required of a wire service reporter. She went to work as an undercover investigator of relief programs for the Roosevelt administration, visiting hard-pressed areas throughout the nation and writing confidential reports on what she found. Between assignments she lived in the White House and occupied a bedroom near Eleanor's. Historians do not agree on the exact nature of their relationship, but letters of endearment exchanged between the two testify to their emotional closeness and suggest physical intimacy.[14]

Although Hickok never worked as a news reporter in Washington, she encouraged Eleanor to befriend women reporters, who in turn capitalized on their access to the White House. During Hickok's coverage of the 1932 campaign, she detected that Eleanor had mixed feelings about acting as First Lady—unwilling to give up her own career interests, which included writing, teaching, and commenting on women's issues on the radio—to serve as her husband's hostess. The niece of President Theodore Roosevelt, Eleanor did not relish the traditional role of a First Lady, like Theodore's wife, Edith Carow Roosevelt, who had hired a social secretary to pass out posed pictures and release innocuous details of dinner parties.

Holding press conferences seemed one way in which Eleanor could continue to promote a social feminist agenda, while maintaining her own personal identity. Spurred by Hickok, she saw them as a way of using reporters to communicate with women across the United States. "I began to wonder if there was anything besides the purely social doings [at the White House] that might be of special interest and value to the women of the country and that the women reporters would write up better than the men," she explained in her autobiography.[15]

The idea of women-only conferences appealed to most of the Washington women journalists. Six weeks before Franklin Roosevelt's inauguration as president on March 4, 1933, Furman drove all night from Washington to New York to meet Eleanor for lunch as Hickok suggested. Roosevelt broached the subject of press conferences, saying she believed "that news of interest to women the country over was being bypassed," Furman noted in her diary.[16] Roosevelt also talked about dispensing with Secret Service agents, which she subsequently did. An enthusiastic Furman endorsed that possibility along with the idea of press conferences: "Immediately I saw vast news possibilities opening before me—what you could do with a President's wife if she didn't have the Secret Service tagging along to fend you off—what you could do if you could ask questions and get answers," she wrote.[17]

The prospect of the press conferences in itself made news, perhaps because Eleanor's single conference between the November election and March inauguration had led to an uproar. Roosevelt had questioned the propriety of holding inaugural balls due to the Depression. After hearing protests from the fashion industry as well as florists and musicians, she quickly reversed herself and came out in favor of the dances.[18] Hornaday announced the conferences with enthusiasm in the *Christian Science Monitor:* "The feminine contingent of the Washington press corps is anticipating more 'copy' than they have had for a long time."[19] She added that "a number of newspaper women have already obtained additional contracts on the strength of announcements from Mrs. Roosevelt that she will hold meetings with women writers."[20]

This category included Ruby Black, to whom Roosevelt's plan for regular press conferences came as a godsend. Black had found it so hard to get information about Lou Henry Hoover for an article in a women's magazine that she resorted to bribing a male journalist to reveal details of the First Lady's daily activities by, as she put it, "snooping around among the Secret Service men."[21] During the 1932 presidential campaign, the United Press had hired her on a part-time basis, in spite of its rule against employing women, to compete with Hickok's AP coverage of Eleanor Roosevelt. The press conferences meant that Black, whose news bureau was struggling, could stay on the UP payroll at twenty-five dollars a week.

After discussing the proposed conferences with other women reporters, Black proposed that Roosevelt's secretary, Malvina Thompson, meet with an informal committee "to work out such eligibility rules as may be necessary."[22] In a letter to Roosevelt, Black recommended that committee members represent the three different groups of women reporters who covered Capitol Hill and the White House. These included the Green Room Group, the informal name given society reporters, the few women like Craig, Finney, and Hornaday, who had credentials to cover the president's press conferences and consequently belonged to the White House Correspondents' Association, and the "more than twenty women" admitted to the congressional press galleries.[23] The prospect of frequent meetings with the new First Lady seemed an unexpected antidote to frequent reminders of their second-class status. Women members of the White House Correspondents' Association, for example, paid dues to that organization but were not allowed to attend its male-only dinners.

Recognizing she was venturing into a new arena, Roosevelt replied to Black that she was unsure of what she would say at press conferences since political news "must come from my husband."[24] Black quickly wrote back that she should not worry since "your wide interests will give us much news."[25] Two weeks later Black assured Roosevelt that she was working with Louis Howe, a former newspaperman who acted both as Franklin's chief political strategist and Eleanor's trusted adviser, to set up the organizing committee for the conferences. She listed committee members from the three categories of women journalists referred to previously—they were Furman and Finney, who also covered the president; Katharine Dayton of the Consolidated Press Association; and Black herself—all of whom were accredited to the Capitol press galleries, as well as Ruth Jones, society editor of the *Washington Herald,* who under the pseudonym Jean Eliot ranked at the forefront of the Green Room Group.[26] Assuming that at least one woman from each of Washington's five newspapers should be eligible to attend along with representatives of press associations, news bureaus, and out-of-town newspapers, Jones made up a tentative list of women to be admitted.

She gave it to Stephen T. Early, Franklin Roosevelt's press secretary. In response, Early certified forty reporters.[27] The group constituted a cross-section of Washington women journalists: two from the AP; seven from other news services; seven, including Cissy Patterson, from Washington newspapers; seven from Washington bureaus of major metropolitan newspapers; and the remainder correspondents from other daily newspapers.[28] While there is no record of the swashbuckling Patterson actually attending the conferences, she declared in her newspaper, "Mrs. Roosevelt has solved the problem of living better than any woman I have ever known. . . . Eleanor Roosevelt is the master of her soul."[29]

After visiting the Roosevelts at Hyde Park, New York, following Franklin's nomination for the presidency, Patterson wrote an article for the *Washington Herald* refuting criticism of Eleanor. She said, "This picture of Eleanor Roosevelt with her school books under her arm, self-righteous and somewhat bossy, is simply all wrong. . . . As one close to her said to me, 'There are about ten sides to her, and it's pretty hard to catch up on all of them.'"[30]

The First Lady occasionally attended Patterson's parties, which led to sprightly items for Patterson's society pages.[31] At one summer buffet held at Patterson's estate outside Washington for Roosevelt and her female press corps, Eleanor held her nose and jumped into the pool, confessing she wished she could learn to dive.[32] On another occasion, Cissy herself dived into the pool wearing real pearls, exclaiming, "Oh, I forgot to take them off, but water is good for them."[33]

Patterson gave instructions to the photography department at the *Herald* to make the First Lady's pictures as attractive as possible.[34] Still the *Herald* was owned by Hearst, who split with the New Deal after supporting Franklin's campaign in 1932. Mildred Gilman, who reported on Eleanor for the *Herald* in 1934, said that "too friendly stories were often cut, and I envied the reporters who could go all out in their administration of her."[35] Patterson purchased both the *Herald* and the *Times* from Hearst in 1939 and merged the two into a twenty-four-hour newspaper, giving the *Times-Herald* the largest circulation in Washington. Her criticism of Franklin Roosevelt's policies increased, particularly when he appeared to favor intervention in World War II prior to Pearl Harbor. Still, she championed Eleanor and their friendship never cooled.

Times-Herald circulation figures may have been related to the newspaper's relatively large number of both women reporters, many of them attractive and talented, and women readers. When *Time* magazine referred to the growing number of women on Patterson's staff in an article headlined CISSY'S HENHOUSE, it enraged Patterson, who thought it implied, as rumor had it, that she engaged in romantic relationships with some women on her staff, particularly Jackie Martin, her picture editor.[36] Irrespective of her personal life, Patterson used women journalists to draw a female audience. The *Times-Herald* proudly reported in 1939 that a company producing a diet bread had surveyed women in Washington and been assured that it was the most popular newspaper in the capital among women readers, many of whom worked for the federal government.[37] Patterson's interest in attracting women readers may have been among the reasons she displayed less hostility toward Eleanor Roosevelt than to her husband.

Early's role in controlling admittance to Eleanor Roosevelt's press conferences showed that the administration saw them as part of its overall political communication program. At their inception Eleanor knew that "many people around my husband were doubtful whether I could handle press conferences without getting myself and him into trouble," even though both Howe and her husband were unworried.[38] She met the women reporters with trepidation on March 6, 1933, just two days after the inauguration and before Franklin held the first of some nine hundred press conferences of his own during his years in office.

Hornaday recalled that Roosevelt tried to conceal her nervousness by grabbing a box of candied grapefruit peel and passing it around as if she were a hostess.[39] Roosevelt detected disapproval from the White House staff, which thought a First Lady should not be so undignified as to hold press meetings, and she herself feared the newspaperwomen, most of whom she did not know. "I only hope they did not know how terrified I was in entering this untried field," she wrote.[40]

Her worries proved unfounded. Grateful to her for giving them news, the press women shielded her from adverse publicity that might cut off their access to the White House. Roosevelt reported to Hickok, "Well, the girls were so friendly and nice, I really think I'll have another conference."[41] And so she did, forming close ties with a small group of the reporters.

In fact, women journalists had shown feelings of empathy for her before the inauguration. Years later Dorothy Roe Lewis, in 1933 a reporter for Universal Service, Hearst's night wire service, wrote in the *New York Times* that on the eve of Franklin's first inauguration Roosevelt told her and three other reporters of her husband's refusal to join with President Hoover in closing the nation's banks to prevent widespread bank failures.[42] Writing in 1981, Lewis said that she and the other three, Hickok, Black, and Dorothy Ducas (who worked for International News Service, Hearst's day wire service), refused to print the story, telling Roosevelt that the story could cause a "worldwide panic."[43]

Ducas, the only other member of the group alive in 1981, admitted that it was common for women journalists to cover up for Roosevelt. "All kinds of things were said [by her] that shouldn't be said in print," she commented.[44] She also said Hickok, who returned to New York after the inauguration and never attended the press conferences, tried to guide Roosevelt on how to handle herself. "I think Hickok helped her not to dissimulate—made her say the wise things, not the impulsive. Mrs. Roosevelt had a tendency to ramble on."[45]

Roosevelt took pains to limit direct quotations. She required reporters to get her permission and to check their notes with her secretary, Malvina Thompson, who kept a shorthand record. At her first conference Roosevelt consented to be quoted on only one comment, "The time is one that requires courage and common sense on everybody's part," a reference to anxiety gripping the nation as it faced the Depression.[46] Hardly a sensational statement, it resulted in a modest one-column headline, ALL ALIKE IN CRISES, on a brief, unbylined story buried inside the *New York Times* written by Winifred Mallon.[47] The story explained that Roosevelt had no message addressed specifically to American women because she considered them part of the larger public to whom her husband had directed his inaugural address.

Antagonism from male reporters came to the fore with publication of a photograph taken at the second conference on March 13, 1933. It depicted Roosevelt seated in a chair with women reporters clustered about her, some standing and other sitting at her feet. Furman thought it ridiculous, sending a copy to her family in Nebraska with the following note: "The girls ... all crowded around to get in the picture—just like they were a bunch of tourists who never saw a President's wife before. . . . It is not my original idea of the way the picture should look and I was the one who asked for it."[48]

Male reporters promptly scoffed at the photograph, targeting the women as Roosevelt's "incense burners."[49] They had not thought much of the gatherings to begin with: Byron Price, Furman's bureau chief at the AP, expected them to fold within six months— the "only poor prediction I ever heard him make," Furman said.[50] Hornaday thought the editors' scorn reflected prejudice against women in general: "Mostly the men preferred to ignore Mrs. Roosevelt and her views."[51] Franklin himself made a jest about the newspaperwomen sitting at his wife's feet.[52] Black published a comment that "Mrs. Roosevelt, without ever mentioning it, put an end to this 'girls at Mrs. Roosevelt's feet' crack of the columnists, by giving orders that chairs be provided for all attending."[53]

Not all women reporters found the conferences satisfying. Mrs. George F. Richards, who insisted on identifying herself as a wife, although she wrote a column signed "Richards" for New England newspapers, declared herself appalled by the sight of the women gazing up at Roosevelt.[54] A veteran correspondent who sported a tippet (a long fur stole), jet beads, and a bonnet, Richards, a Republican, vowed she would not attend another of the gatherings.

Most of the women wished the conferences produced more news that met the generally accepted news values of conflict and controversy. Even Furman and Black expressed discontent. Furman confided to her diary that Roosevelt readily answered mundane personal questions such as "when she gets up in the morning and what she eats for breakfast ... [but] she rules out all controversial subjects, and won't be queried on anything in the province of the President."[55] In an article for the *Matrix,* a magazine for her journalism sorority, Black noted that the First Lady would speak only in generalities about social concerns, including housing, education, and legislation that aimed to bar married women from working, avoiding direct comment on pending bills in Congress.[56]

Furman and Black provided the nucleus of a small group of admiring women who constituted Roosevelt's inner circle at the press conferences. These included Craig; Martha Strayer of the *Washington Daily News,* who, like Thompson, took shorthand notes of the proceedings; and Genevieve Forbes Herrick, nicknamed Geno, of the *Chicago Tribune.* Emma Bugbee, the chief woman reporter for the *New York Herald Tribune,* stayed in Washington for four months after the 1933 inauguration and returned frequently to cover the First Lady. Although she worked for a leading Republican newspaper, she too was counted an inner-circle member, turning out stories about the homey furnishing preferred by the Roosevelts in the White House living quarters, and similar subjects.

Regardless of their newspapers' editorial policies, most of the women reporters basically agreed with the political views of both Franklin and Eleanor Roosevelt and liked them personally. A society editor definitely not among the First Lady's intimates, Hope Ridings Miller of the *Washington Post,* said the reporters applauded Eleanor Roosevelt for acting as her disabled husband's "eyes and ears." She added, "We all felt that she was absolutely marvelous to look after him so well."[57]

According to Rosamond Cole, who worked as Black's assistant, "She [Roosevelt] stood for everything they stood for [thinking] the New Deal would rescue us."[58] The reporters also benefited professionally and personally, at least in the beginning, from their close friendship with the president's wife. Cole observed, "They were smart, intelligent women who were well established in journalism before Mrs. Roosevelt came along, but their friendship with her didn't hurt their standing with their editors."[59]

At times women reporters received unexpected news benefits—but sometimes with a price attached. Shortly after Franklin Roosevelt's inauguration in 1933, Eleanor took Furman and a few other women journalists along on what the AP reporter called "a most glorious night of high adventure, flying with Mrs. R. and Amelia Earhart to Baltimore and back—in evening dresses."[60] The trip, a publicity stunt for Eastern Air Lines that constituted Roosevelt's first night flight, provided Furman with a bylined feature. The flight apparently came as a reward for Furman keeping quiet about Roosevelt being blacklisted for active membership in the DAR, then a potent political force. Roosevelt became an honorary member in 1933 as the president's wife.[61] The blacklisting, presumably on grounds of her liberal sentiments, could have made a front-page story, but Furman chose not to pursue it to strengthen her friendship with the First Lady.

Favored women reporters and their families were invited to visit the Roosevelt family at the White House, Hyde Park, and Campobello, the Roosevelt summer home in Canada. Black's baby daughter, Cornelia Jane Little, attended her first birthday party and her first movie at the White House as the guest of Roosevelt's grandchild, Eleanor "Sistie" Dall.[62] Any reporter covering the First Lady's press conferences "received flowers from the White House greenhouse if she stayed home even a day with the sniffles," recalled Dorothy Roe Lewis.[63]

Hickok, who kept a close eye on the conferences from afar, considered only one of the women who covered them her own journalistic peer. "God damn it, professional I ranked so far above the rest of that mob, except Geno," Hickok exploded in a letter to Malvina Thompson after Roosevelt had left the White House.[64] "I had ... the kind of assignments for the AP that even Geno never got."[65]

Her outburst came after reading a draft of Roosevelt's 1949 autobiography, *This I Remember,* in which she referred to Hickok's exclusive inauguration day interview with her but added that later she realized "in the White House one must not play favorites [with reporters]," an assertion that Roosevelt's ties with her inner circle tended to belie.[66] Hickok thought the statement belittled her own professional stature and made it appear she got the interview because she was a "nice, tame, pet reporter."[67] In the published version of the autobiography, presumably changed to please Hickok, Roosevelt referred to Hickok as "the outstanding woman reporter for the Associated Press" and "an excellent reporter whose sense of duty to the news was always paramount."[68]

Herrick, described by Keyes as "tall and slim and graceful, with short dark curls and a mobile sensitive face," had been a star reporter for the *Chicago Tribune* before joining the *Tribune*'s Washington bureau along with her husband, John, an editorial writer.[69] In Chicago she won accolades for exclusive interviews with Al Capone and other gangsters, as well as for such feats as posing as an Irish immigrant and crossing the Atlantic in the steerage to document the mistreatment of immigrants.[70]

The Herricks lived in Alexandria near Black and Keyes in a

house that featured violets, Geno Herrick's favorite flower, as a decorative motif, but Herrick did not see herself as a shrinking flower. In a speech to women journalists, she said, "An editor may give a woman her assignment but she gives herself her style. She should strive to write all the news she can better than as many men as she can."[71]

As admirers of Franklin and Eleanor Roosevelt, both Geno and John Herrick ran afoul of the editorial politics of the *Chicago Tribune,* a rock-ribbed Republican newspaper. According to Edwards, women's editor of the *Tribune* in the 1930s, staff members geared their copy to the watchful eye of Robert R. McCormick, always called Colonel, who ran the newspaper: "Reporters on the TRIB were always trying to write the way they thought he wanted them to write."[72] While McCormick backed Franklin Roosevelt for his handling of the banking crisis in 1933, he grew increasingly angry at the New Deal and labeled the president a dictator.[73]

A few months after the 1933 inauguration, both Herricks resigned from the *Tribune.* Geno switched to a newspaper syndicate, the North American Newspaper Alliance, where she continued praising the Roosevelt administration. She also served as president of the WNPC from 1933 to 1935. Her husband took a public relations job working for Harold Ickes, secretary of the Department of the Interior.

Geno Herrick, unfortunately, suffered major injuries in a car accident in August 1935 while touring pueblos in New Mexico with Harold Ickes's wife, Anna Wilmarth Ickes, who was killed. Herrick never fully recovered either physically or professionally. After her "brilliant years," she "had a tragic life," unable to find suitable employment, according to Edwards, who said false pride kept Herrick from seeking help from Roosevelt.[74]

As the First Lady's press conferences continued, members of the inner circle coached Roosevelt by planting questions and advising on statements. After the Roosevelts decided that Eleanor, not Franklin, should release the news on April 3, 1933, that beer would be served again at the White House as the first step in ending Prohibition, Eleanor discussed the subject with Strayer in advance. The prim Strayer, a teetotaler, advised her to hand out "a carefully thought-out statement . . . written in advance so everybody could have one," along with a "carefully worded expression of hope that the change would contribute to temperance."[75] Roosevelt accepted these suggestions, but she did not follow Strayer's recommendation to deal only with the beer announcement. Instead, she took questions on other subjects as varied as Easter hats and her views on sweatshops.

At least obliquely, in featuring herself Roosevelt broadened the scope of the institution of the First Lady and her position as part of the administration. On May 16, 1933, for example, she described her visit to a camp set up by the so-called bonus army, a large contingent of unemployed World War I veterans seeking a promised bonus for their past service. President Hoover had used the army to try to disperse the men; the New Deal administration dealt with them differently, sending Roosevelt, accompanied only by Howe, to visit the encampment. According to Strayer, Roosevelt acted to defuse the situation, telling the press women of a "remarkably clean and orderly camp."[76]

A week later the gatherings served as a trial balloon for a New Deal program for unemployed women. Roosevelt endorsed the idea of forest work camps for unemployed women, but backtracked after a public outcry against taking women away from their families.[77] Subsequently, the camps were limited to the unmarried with both the First Lady and Secretary of Labor Frances

Perkins issuing a joint statement in June that the first camp, at Bear Mountain, New York, relatively close to Hyde Park, would be for unattached women only.[78]

Roosevelt repeatedly violated her own rule—that she would not answer political questions—by putting some issues that concerned feminists on the public agenda. In December 1933, for example, she pointed out that women on relief doing skilled work in sewing, nursing, and teaching received less pay than unskilled male laborers on relief projects. When journalists subsequently asked Harry L. Hopkins, head of federal relief efforts, about the discrepancy in pay, he replied, "Yes, I know it's lower. We think that's right."[79] Women's pay was not raised, reflecting a period when male wage earners were expected to be primary breadwinners and women to work, if at all outside the home, only to supplement male incomes. The First Lady's opposition to the two-tiered wage structure received little news play. The discriminatory provisions were not repealed until four years later.

Male journalists displayed more respect for the conferences as legitimate news-making events after the news release on beer. Another announcement nine months later made front-page headlines—wine would be available again at the White House, marking the final repeal of Prohibition. Roosevelt offered to hold a special press conference on the subject, but her husband turned down the suggestion, unwilling to draw extra attention to the issue. Instead, a brief statement was passed out at Roosevelt's regular conference on January 29, 1934, saying that wine, preferably American, would be back, but not distilled liquor.

After a society reporter raced to a telephone to call in the story before Roosevelt wanted it to be released, the First Lady let Furman, Black, and Marie Manning, representatives of the three leading wire services, use the telephones in White House bedrooms so they would not be scooped.[80] Manning, a columnist offering advice to the lovelorn, reported on the conferences for Hearst's International News Service. She saw Roosevelt's gesture as recognition of her concern for women journalists.

At least one woman reporter thought it was unfair to exclude men. The irrepressible May Craig, a strong believer in equal rights, argued that if women wanted the same privileges as men, they should not discriminate themselves. Roosevelt disagreed, claiming that male reporters would force her to "encroach on my husband's side of the news," a tacit admission that she wanted news divided along gender lines.[81] She held fast to her women-only rule until World War II forced an exception, although she allowed men to cover her press conferences outside the White House.

Most of the women reporters concurred on the woman-only rule. They relished the opportunity to go to the White House, rushing up the stairs to the Monroe Room on the second floor, where the conferences usually were held, in a dash for front-row seats. The sorority-like atmosphere led to invitations to White House events, including Gridiron Widows' parties. These gala evenings featured skits, costumes, and other entertainment for journalists and top women in the Roosevelt administration excluded from the all-male dinners of the Gridiron Club, the capital's most prestigious organization of journalists.

Black, although one of the most fervent members of the National Woman's Party, did not want to jeopardize her own United Press connection by upholding the abstract principle of admitting men. Her gratitude to Roosevelt became almost embarrassing as she passed on political information to the administration that she gleaned from other clients, which included Maine's only liberal newspaper. When Franklin remarked at his press conference, "Ruby Black brought Mrs. Roosevelt some clipping about the

Gannett [businesses] in Maine," a reference to powerful Republican banking, waterpower, and publishing interests, Black wrote to Eleanor, "Can't you persuade your husband to be more discreet? Was my face red?"[82]

Influenced by Black, who spoke Spanish fluently and was a correspondent for *La Democracia,* a Puerto Rican newspaper, Roosevelt became the first president's wife to travel outside the continental United States while in the White House. Black persuaded her to visit Puerto Rico and the Virgin Islands in 1934, ostensibly to inspect social conditions there. Accompanied by Black, Furman, Bugbee, Ducas, and a male photographer, Sammy Schulman, Roosevelt kept up a frantic pace, visiting slums, shanties, and factories, greeting exploited needle workers, sightseeing, giving speeches, and talking to officials. The women eagerly wrote about Roosevelt's exhausting schedule, but barely mentioned the presence of Hickok, who went along in her capacity as the chief investigator of New Deal relief programs. *Time* magazine, however, pictured the trip, which coincided with Hickok's fortieth birthday, as a boondoggle for the former reporter, whom it called a "rotund lady with a husky voice, a preemptory manner, [and] baggy clothes" who has "gone around a lot with the first lady."[83]

Although the Puerto Rican trip enhanced Black's standing with *La Democracia,* her professional reputation suffered as a result of her closeness to Roosevelt. When Roosevelt resumed commercial radio broadcasting, Black, as a working wife herself, overlooked ethical questions that arose about the propriety of the First Lady making money as a result of her position and stressed that Roosevelt intended to donate her earnings to charity. Black asked her United Press readers rhetorically in 1935: "If the wife of the President of the United States cannot live on her husband's prestige and money, what other wife can? Mrs. Franklin D. Roosevelt, only working First Lady this country ever had, is earning for charity by radio talks and writing, at least as much as the government pays her husband for being President."[84]

Franklin Roosevelt received a salary of $75,000 a year as president, and Eleanor Roosevelt received substantial sums for magazine articles, books, and broadcasts while in the White House, but she never announced the total amounts. Her broadcast earnings went directly to charity, although detractors said this was a way of avoiding income taxes.[85] Black was less interested in specifics than in glorification of the principle of a woman's right to earn money, even though it stemmed from her relationship to her husband. Writing in the *American Mercury* in 1935, a male journalist sniped at Black, claiming, "Even the women reporters in Washington today are amazed at the extremes of Ruby's idolatrous attitude toward the First Lady."[86] Five years later Black was believed to be the main target of a magazine article written by Dorothy Dunbar Bromley, a New York newspaperwoman, who called Roosevelt's press conference reporters her "willing slaves."[87]

Even though Furman and the AP were not singled out, to her great dismay Furman's bosses decided to take her off the First Lady beat in 1935, perhaps fearing she also was too close to Roosevelt. Furman was dispatched over her protests to cover congressional hearings, while another woman staff member, Sigrid Arne, who specialized in New Deal legislation like social security, was sent "pouting and protesting" to Roosevelt's press conference.[88] Furman soon returned to coverage of the First Lady.

When Black's marriage faltered and her news bureau failed as the 1930s ended, Black tried to recoup her losses by writing *Eleanor Roosevelt: A Biography,* the first full-length account of Roosevelt's life. She sent the manuscript to Roosevelt and her secretary, Thompson, for approval in advance of publication, but the work was not officially authorized by Roosevelt. Published on Roosevelt's birthday, October 11, 1940, the book claimed that Roosevelt had been instrumental in setting up programs to give surplus farm products to the jobless and employment to white-collar workers, women, and youth.[89] Relatively few sources were given and it sold poorly, to Black's dismay.

Society writers remained on the outer fringes of Roosevelt's press conference group, even though society and women's news in general carried overtones of political importance, particularly in the nation's capital, because it measured family standing within the local power structure. Women helped their husbands' careers by gaining publicity as outstanding hostesses and patronesses of important organizations. Society pages also could be utilized to bring in advertisers. For instance, in 1936, when Patterson's *Herald* decided to enthrone Gwendolyn Cafritz, wife of a real estate tycoon, as the new leader of Washington society, her husband's advertising soon landed in its pages.

Similarly, Washington society pages could be viewed as billboards for political interests. Political insiders read them carefully, tracking White House guests and social events. Roosevelt fully understood the importance of social reporting and the strata of society at which it was directed. The same day she held her first press conference, March 6, 1933, she accepted honorary membership in the American Newspaper Women's Club, the organization set up by society writers to take in the wives of prominent men as associate members. Roosevelt attended a tea, the first party that honored her as First Lady, given by the club for her and her daughter, Anna Roosevelt Dall.

Possibly because they were not interested in women's news per se, the top women journalists did not attend the conferences. Anne O'Hare McCormick of the *New York Times,* the first woman to win a Pulitzer Prize in reporting, ignored them, although she went through Eleanor to make arrangements to interview the president.[90] Ruth Finney, busy with her coverage of power issues, objected to the length of the conferences, which sometimes produced an hour and a half of chitchat but little solid news.[91]

Busy at the *Daily Worker* bureau, Marguerite Young paid little attention to the First Lady's press conferences. Her reappearance in the Capitol press galleries in 1934 as a representative of the mouthpiece of the American Communist Party raised few eyebrows, both because some other reporters had leftist sympathies in the midst of the Depression and she was remembered from her AP days for her "good work," according to Ross.[92] Young also attended Franklin Roosevelt's press conferences. In Ross's view, if Young asked a "disturbing question," she received "a candid and ready response from the President."[93] Until she was fired in 1936 for not always following the party line, Young wrote serious fact-oriented stories about relief activities and efforts to organize labor from the communist angle.[94] The First Lady's press gatherings with their eclectic subject matter did not produce the kind of story Young considered worthwhile.

The press conferences lasted throughout Roosevelt's tenure in the White House because they offered some news that most women reporters otherwise would not have been able to get, although their friendship with the First Lady frequently overshadowed pointed questioning and they readily agreed to avoid writing on some topics. Prior to Franklin Roosevelt's reelection campaign of 1936, Furman recorded in her diary that the First Lady did not want comments reported on the issue of birth control. Similarly, she ruled out comments on a magazine article criticizing her role in the Arthurdale resettlement project, an effort to move destitute West Virginia coal miners to a new community that had experienced large cost overruns.[95] Earlier, Furman had glossed over the fact that reporters had been barred from Roosevelt's meeting with Arthurdale residents, who complained that they had not able to move into their new houses as soon as they had expected. Instead, Furman had emphasized their gratitude for Eleanor's help.[96]

Other subjects Roosevelt kept off the record included her frequent meetings with Hickok and their lengthy summer vacations together in 1933 and 1934. In a letter to Hickok, Roosevelt exclaimed that she had concealed their weekend rendezvous from the women reporters: "They smelled a rat but were kind and didn't press me!"[97] "For all her friendliness, Mrs. Roosevelt made it plain that there were certain subjects on which she did not wish to chat," wrote Kathleen McLaughlin in the *New York Times Magazine*.[98]

Even during her "off-the-record ramblings," as Furman put it, Roosevelt maintained informal, if unconventional contact, with some of the press women.[99] Furman wrote in her autobiography that there was "something bizarre about picking out of the home mailbox a picture postcard of Maple Grove Inn, St. Johnsbury, Vermont, carrying the signature 'E. R.' and knowing that it came from the wife of the President of the United States."[100] While such gestures may have struck some of the women as odd, they also engendered a feeling of loyalty toward the First Lady. Ducas saw her as a somewhat "prissy" woman who sought to "do good" and was "easily led by people she felt were her friends."[101] The women felt sorry for Mrs. Roosevelt, with "that nervous little laugh," Hornaday recalled.[102]

This feeling of compassion for the First Lady carried over even when Roosevelt did not welcome members of the press at a controversial White House event. Frances M. Lide, who in 1935 was hired by the *Washington Evening Star* as the first woman to report city as opposed to social news, recalled a half century later how she and other women reporters were forced to peer through the iron fence surrounding the White House to watch a lawn party for delinquent young women, most of whom were African American. Lide, nevertheless, muted her dismay by keeping in mind that her employment resulted from the *Star*'s desire to have a city-side reporter cover Roosevelt.[103]

Lide struggled to write a story on the party, given on May 16, 1936, that featured uniformed butlers offering refreshments to in-mates of the National Training School for Girls. The previous day the First Lady had surprised her press conference by announcing she had invited the "delinquents" to the White House after visit-ing their reformatory, a dilapidated District of Columbia facility for young women from fourteen to twenty-one years old. She said that "twenty-six of the girls had syphilis and almost every girl had gonorrhea," and that no vocational program existed ex-cept one to teach laundry work, even though there was "no hot running water."[104] Asked why she wanted to entertain the "girls," she answered, "These youngsters should have an occasional good time."[105]

Although the African American guests were served in segre-gated tents, Lide called the party "a great shocker for those days," which explained why Roosevelt wanted to keep the press at bay.[106] In her autobiography Roosevelt wrote that Early thought the party "very unwise, politically, and I did get some bad publicity in the southern papers."[107] The publicity from the press conference corps, however, led Congress to appropriate funds to renovate the reformatory.

Notwithstanding the garden party for "delinquents," most of Roosevelt's White House entertaining, like many of her press conferences, fell within traditional boundaries for president's wives and resulted in typical women's and society page stories of the 1930s. Women reporters wrote about accompanying Roosevelt to an Appalachian music festival and covering her descent into a coal mine in Ohio. Stories appeared on leading women in the New Deal invited to speak at her press conferences: Secretary of Labor Frances Perkins; Nellie Tayloe Ross, director of the mint; Ellen S. Woodward, director of women's relief work in the Federal Emergency Relief Administration; Louise Stanley, chief of the Bureau of Home Economics; and Mary Anderson, head of the Women's Bureau.

More exciting guests from outside the administration produced other stories. They included Amelia Earhart, the famous aviator, Ishbel MacDonald, daughter of the British prime minister, and, before and during World War II, royalty seeking aid from the United States. Roosevelt arranged special opportunities for the press women to meet Queen Elizabeth of England—accompanied by her husband, King George VI, who visited the White House in 1939—and Queen Wilhelmina of the Netherlands in 1942.

Roosevelt kept careful track of what she allowed to be quoted. When Madame Chiang Kai-shek, wife of the leader of China, stayed at the White House in 1943 and appeared at Roosevelt's press conference, she urged the United States to supply more munitions to China. But, Roosevelt gave reporters permission to quote only one sentence of Madame Chiang's comments directly: "I have never known brains to have any sex," a remark made when asked her view of the proposed Equal Rights Amendment in the United States.[108]

In her autobiography Furman likened her relationship to Roosevelt as "swinging on a star" as she wrote stories about the First Lady for the 1,400 newspapers that belonged to the AP.[109] Without Roosevelt, Furman would have been relegated mainly to news "about parties and women's clothing, and chasing women dignitaries."[110] The same could be said for many of the other women journalists, although Furman attached herself to Roosevelt more firmly than most, except perhaps Black. During Roosevelt's first year as First Lady, Furman filed more than sixty stories about her, dined at the White House six times, and took tea there four times.[111] Furman returned the invitations by entertaining the First Lady at her home, and the two exchanged Christmas presents. McLaughlin remembered Furman years later as a "petite, brown-eyed, auburn-haired girl," who was "indefatigable in gathering news," and concluded, "of us all, I tend to think that Mrs. Roosevelt cherished her most."[112]

Furman had to give up her AP job in 1936 due to pregnancy, a condition that required her to resign in the climate of the day, but she continued to benefit from her contact with Roosevelt, who kept her on the invitation list for scrambled-egg suppers at the White House. When Furman surprisingly gave birth to twins on April 4, 1937, Roosevelt, who already had knitted one baby blanket, made the twins, one boy and one girl, the subject of her news conference and sent word that she was knitting a second blanket.[113] Furman named the girl Ruth Eleanor, and Eleanor Roosevelt became the godmother, maintaining ties with the Furman family. Confronted by the need for more income than her husband could make, Furman started a freelance news service, Furman Features, with her sister, Lucille, and continued to attend the First Lady's press conferences in the 1930s. Roosevelt helped her obtain writing assignments for the *Democratic Digest* and other work for the Democratic Party.

Although many of the conferences had a mundane ring, even queries on social questions sometimes made news, such as when a reporter asked Roosevelt if artists who performed at the White House for the king and queen of England would be introduced to the monarchs. Roosevelt's affirmative answer outraged segregationists, since it was known that Marian Anderson, a world-famous African American contralto, would sing at the state dinner honoring the monarchs. Furman thought the inquiry was "asked with malice" by a reporter who did not like the Roosevelt administration.[114] It is likely the White House preferred to keep quiet on the subject due to the power of conservative Democrats in Congress who upheld segregation.

By this time Anderson and Roosevelt had become linked in the public mind. A few months before, Anderson had been refused the right to sing in Constitution Hall, Washington's chief concert hall in the 1930s, because of her race. In protest Roosevelt resigned from the DAR, which owned the hall. She played a backstage role in arranging for Anderson to give an open-air concert on Easter Sunday, April 9, 1939, at the Lincoln Memorial. It drew an integrated crowd of seventy-five thousand and set the stage for civil rights demonstrations to come.

Roosevelt's resignation from the DAR drew front-page headlines, but the First Lady made little mention of her action at her press conferences. Instead, she publicized her decision to withdraw from an organization because she disagreed with its policies (without naming the organization) in her own newspaper column, "My Day." Roosevelt started writing the daily syndicated column, billed as a diary of her activities, at the end of 1935.

Her press conference group at first laughed at "My Day," considering it amateurish and shallow, although they viewed it differently after she used it to break news stories that otherwise might have come out at the conferences. Disregarding her friendship with Roosevelt, Patterson engaged Evalyn Walsh McLean, the eccentric socialite and owner of the ill-starred Hope Diamond, to write a column, "My Say," which parodied "My Day."[115] Writing did not become McLean, who noted in her first column, "It seems fantastic that Cissy, who has done so much good and done such wonderful things with her newspaper, would be willing to allow such a waste of space."[116] "My Say" did not last long; neither did a rival column by Eleanor Roosevelt's acid-tongued cousin, Alice Roosevelt Longworth.

Yet "My Day" went on and on, continuing until 1962, the year of Roosevelt's death, to the surprise of professional journalists. Ducas called the column, somewhat akin to a blog today, "very naïve," while Hornaday saw it mainly as a reflection of Roosevelt's desire to earn money. "We resented that when she wrote her column competing with us," Hornaday said.[117] After Roosevelt also signed a contract for commercial radio broadcasts in 1937, some of which paralleled her paid lectures on topics aimed at women, such as "A Typical Day in the White House," the press women had an additional reason for seeing her as a competitor. Learning that she planned a broadcast immediately after the wedding of her son, Franklin Jr., to Ethel DuPont on June 30, 1937, the press women complained to Early that they feared the First Lady would "scoop" them on details of the lavish event.[118] He assured them she would not, but he urged her to avoid "a descriptive account of the wedding."[119]

On the basis of having written "My Day" for two years, in 1938 Roosevelt won election as an active member of the WNPC. Doris Fleeson, a political columnist for the *New York Daily News,* proposed her for membership, and Black and Furman eagerly seconded the nomination. The election posed a dilemma for club members, many of whom had displayed their fondness for the First Lady as part of their own social events. In 1935 Black, Bugbee, and Furman presented a skit at the annual WNPC stunt party in which they posed as residents of the Eleanor Roosevelt Home for Broken Down Newspaper Women, worn out from trying to keep up with the inexhaustible First Lady. Two years later, in the midst of labor unrest, reporters depicted her as demanding "Union Hours for First Ladies" and one day's rest in forty.[120]

Still, nine members cast votes against her election on grounds that club rules required members to earn most of their living from writing. Roosevelt obviously did not, contending she gave away most of what she made, although not offering detailed reports. The First Lady was admitted after Black, then serving as president, denied reports that she was Roosevelt's ghostwriter, and Frances Parkinson Keyes joined Fleeson, Furman, and Black in arguing on Roosevelt's behalf.[121]

Black also acted as Roosevelt's guide after she joined the American Newspaper Guild, a union of newspaper employees, in 1936 to demonstrate her belief in the labor union movement. When Roosevelt was nominated for national president in 1939, Black warned the First Lady that radical, communist-led forces were trying to use her name to conceal their own activities. Roosevelt declined the nomination.

The close relationship between Roosevelt and members of her press conference group attracted the attention of Drew Pearson, the ex-son-in-law of Cissy Patterson, and Robert S. Allen in their "Daily Washington Merry-Go-Round" column. Comparing Eleanor Roosevelt's press conferences with her husband's, Pearson and Allen declared that "the 'girls' are always on the alert to protect [the First Lady] from a slip of the tongue or an incautious comment."[122] According to Pearson and Allen, if Roosevelt made a comment such as "That is ridiculous," about some subject, her devotees would immediately say, "You mean 'regrettable,' don't you, Mrs. Roosevelt?" and she would respond, "Yes, thank you, I think that would be better," while "beaming gracefully."[123]

Not all the reporters saw themselves as giving Roosevelt special treatment. Beth Campbell Short, who succeeded Furman in covering the First Lady for the AP, denied that the press women showed favoritism. Short said she gave Roosevelt the coverage she deserved, adding, "I don't think those women wrote puff pieces just because she was nice to them."[124]

Press conference regulars did not always please the First Lady. Winifred Mallon of the *New York Times* ran afoul of the First Lady for a story claiming that she had been behind the selection of Mary Winslow, who was backed by the League of Women Voters, for the Inter-American Commission of Women and, in addition, had pushed through the appointments of two men to the Interstate Commerce Commission.[125] Roosevelt used her press conference on February 27, 1939 (when she also declined to discuss her resignation from the DAR), to deny that she had proposed "anybody for anything," and directly upbraided Mallon, accusing her of printing "mere rumors."[126]

Black rushed to Roosevelt's defense, asking, "Now that we are clearing away the gossip, did you send cables as to what you wished done at Lima [where the Inter-American Commission of Women was meeting]?"[127] Roosevelt denied sending cables, but then restated opposition to the proposed Equal Rights Amendment. It had been supported by Winslow's predecessor, Doris Stevens, a lawyer and member of the National Woman's Party. Unlike Stevens, both Roosevelt and Winslow favored protective legislation for working women rather than a commitment to equal rights. Roosevelt said Latin American women were "even less ready for [a] blanket equal rights treaty and loss of protective legislation than in [the] United States."[128] Instead of questioning Roosevelt further on her involvement in the commission, the women reporters moved on from politics to trivia frequently associated with women's pages, such as rumors of ghosts in the White House.

In spite of the uneven nature of the conferences, an increasing number of women sought permission to attend them as Franklin Roosevelt completed his first two terms and was reelected for an unprecedented third term in 1940.[129] Speculation over whether he would run drew journalists to the conferences, where they asked a variety of what Eleanor called trick questions, such as, "Will the social season next winter be the same as usual?" to gain hints of his intentions. She avoided direct answers. Before the United States entered World War II on December 7, 1941, the number eligible to participate in the conferences grew to a total of 115 newswomen plus some sixteen publicity writers from governmental agencies.

All of the women at the First Lady's press conferences were white, except Pilar N. Ravelo, who represented the *Philippine Herald*.[130] African American reporters were not admitted in spite of overtures to be taken in. In February 1941 Early told the First Lady he had rejected a request from Mrs. Bedford Lawson, who "represents colored weekly newspapers printed in Pittsburgh," because she worked for weekly, not daily newspapers.[131] He viewed her as the pawn of "certain colored leaders" attempting to "force their admission to the President's conferences with the press," which also excluded African American journalists on the grounds they were employed by weekly, not daily, newspapers.[132]

The following November, Early advised Malvina Thompson, to whom he often delegated the admission of reporters to the First Lady's press conference, against accepting a reporter from the *Washington Afro-American,* a weekly newspaper.[133] Since some women admitted to the First Lady's conferences were freelance writers who were not employed full-time, Early's reasoning seemed a subterfuge to uphold segregation. Many of the journalists accredited in 1941 wrote Washington columns for small newspapers. This category, for example, included Chrissie J. Anderson of the *Warrensburg* (Mo.) *Star-Journal,* Margaretta Campbell of the *Southwest Times* (Pulaski, Va.), and Eleanor Cox Tribby of the *Daily Herald* (Columbia, Tenn.). The wives of at least four congressmen were accredited on the basis of columns they wrote for their hometown newspapers. They were listed as Eva Buck, wife of Rep. Frank H. Buck, *Woodland Democrat* (Calif.); Maude Elizabeth Kee, wife of Rep. John Kee, *Williamson Daily News* (W.Va.); Mrs. John R. Murdock, wife of Rep. John R. Murdock, *Phoenix Republic & Gazette;* and Mrs. W. R. Poage, wife of Rep. W. R. Poage, *Temple Daily Telegram* (Tex.).[134]

By this time six radio reporters had joined the roster. Gertrude V. Chestnut and Eleanor Ragsdale represented Transradio Press Service and Madeline Ensign the Mutual Broadcasting Company, while NBC had two reporters eligible to attend, Mary Mason and Marian Phebe Gale (Mason's alternate). Ann Gillis was listed from CBS.[135]

Members of the original inner circle remained on the roll. Black and Strayer attended faithfully, along with Craig. Also included was Furman, who listed herself as representing the *San Francisco Chronicle,* one of the clients for her feature service, and Herrick, an occasional correspondent for the *Chicago Daily News.*[136] The press conferences obviously had become a Washington institution reflecting the gender, racial, and reporting practices of the day.

By the time of Franklin Roosevelt's third-term reelection in 1940, the gatherings had lost luster as career-building vehicles. The novelty of reporting on an activist First Lady had worn off, and Roosevelt herself was communicating directly with the nation via her "My Day" column, magazines articles, and lecture tours. The conferences, however, still drew journalists eager to gain access to the White House. Whether they helped or hurt women reporters in the long run remained an open question. Most of the news they produced remained strictly gender segregated, but they aided in establishing the position of the First Lady as an important part of the American presidency, turning her into a voice for administration policy. Consequently, the conferences allowed some women journalists to be drawn, if only marginally, into the political maneuverings that marked life in Washington.

FOUR

WORLD WAR II SHATTERS
PRECEDENTS—AT LEAST FOR A TIME

They yelled, "Boy!" and I jumped. I've always said that if I ever wrote
an autobiography, I'd call one chapter "When I Was a Boy."
—Reminiscence of Eileen Shanahan, who started in journalism as
a copyboy at the Washington Post during World War II

The impact of World War II on Washington women journalists
changed the dynamics between journalists and their male employers in line with major shifts generally in women's roles from
housewives to war workers. All over the nation women replaced
men in defense plants, took jobs as drivers and pilots of cargo
planes, and volunteered for women's units within the military.
Just as it produced Rosie the Riveter, the war produced Rosie the
Reporter. Yet Rosie was expected to go back to the kitchen, or
the women's pages, after the war ended.

Employers had no choice except to hire women as war clouds
came ever closer to the United States. Even before the Japanese
attacked Pearl Harbor on December 7, 1941, Betty Hinckle Dunn,
national secretary of the journalism sorority Theta Sigma Phi, ex-

claimed, "Odd isn't it, how the job picture has changed in war months."[1] She continued, "Flippantly I tell my friends, 'The war means more opportunities for women and Negroes.'"[2] Only a year earlier a group of editors had given women journalism students at Ohio State University such a gloomy picture of the discrimination facing them in newsrooms that the *Matrix,* the magazine of Theta Sigma Phi, had concluded, "There seemed to be a general agreement among the members of the employers' symposium that women don't have any more chance for jobs on newspapers than Jews have of surviving in Germany."[3]

In Washington, as elsewhere, the war gave women far more chances than existed previously to show what they could do in journalism. By 1944 about one hundred women had been accredited to the Capitol press galleries, compared with about thirty-six years earlier.[4] Their presence revealed the ambiguity in the way they saw themselves. The Capitol press galleries lacked facilities for women, yet the women themselves disagreed on the propriety of demanding them.

May Craig became known for her insistence on equal facilities for women as well as for the attention-getting hats that served as her trademark. Her newspaper column, "Inside Washington," which ran in several Maine newspapers, as well as radio broadcasts over two Maine stations, mixed political and social news, presenting Washington as a "regular sewing circle" of gossip and intrigue in government circles.[5] Craig finally won her long fight for women's restrooms adjoining the galleries in 1945, achieving her victory without the formal backing of the WNPC, even though she had been elected its president in 1943. The club refused to speak up on the subject because some members thought it appeared unladylike to campaign for the same facilities as men.[6]

In 1944 Mary Hornaday protested on her own when women members of the White House Correspondents' Association were banned from the annual male-only dinner with the president, although they paid the same dues as the men. A former president of the WNPC, she too lacked support from the organization for her effort. The entire membership declined to support her for fear of being thought unfeminine.[7]

Both Craig and Hornady remained active in Eleanor Roosevelt's press conference group, which was forced to reorganize because of wartime security. When Roosevelt accepted an official, but unpaid, appointment as assistant director of the Office of Civil Defense prior to U.S. involvement in World War II, she held press conferences in her office rather than the White House. Men attended as well as women, making the gatherings more formal and news-oriented than those in the White House.

Even before Roosevelt started her new duties on September 29, 1941, an effort was underway to tighten accreditation. It started after Florence Shreve, formerly a government publicity writer, had been "dramatically ejected from the White House by ushers," according to a newspaper account of the First Lady's press conference on May 31, 1941.[8] The White House press office claimed that Shreve, pictured in the column as a "red-haired and aggressive matron," had posed as a reporter for the *Hemet* (Calif.) *News,* but actually was a lobbyist for shipping and mining interests, claiming to have White House contacts.[9]

After the Shreve incident, women reporters debated whether to form an organization that would restrict admission to full-time professionals. On December 22, 1941, the women held a meeting at which Craig called attention to the need "to prevent exploitation of the conference" and "to avoid the danger of subversive activity."[10] The group decided to establish itself as Mrs. Roosevelt's Press Conference Association. Hornaday was elected the first chairman.

Roosevelt's press conferences at the Office of Civil Defense proved confrontational as she was asked tougher questions with men, as well as women, reporters present. By January 1942 Roosevelt had come under fire for both alleged administrative inefficiency and putting personal friends on the government payroll. In particular, she was attacked for employing Mayris Chaney, a professional dancer, to set up a program to teach dancing to children in bomb shelters. The revelation that Chaney had been hired at a salary of $4,600 per year, more than that paid to an army colonel, was reported in February 1942 by Christine Sadler of the *Washington Post*. The uproar over Chaney's appointment dominated a press conference on February 9, 1942, in which reporters asked, "What is Miss Chaney doing?" and Roosevelt declined to give a definite answer, saying, "That's not for me to discuss."[11]

This conference proved the last Roosevelt held at Civil Defense headquarters. She told women reporters that she was moving the conferences back to the White House, where there was not "the difficulty here that other people [men] want to come."[12] She resigned her post on February 20, 1942, amid waves of criticism. The resignation came just after Roosevelt informed Hornaday that the Secret Service wanted her to limit the size of the group.

Consequently, attendance was restricted to employees of daily newspapers, press associations, broadcasting companies, and weekly news magazines. This policy excluded part-time journalists and sharply cut the number of women eligible to attend from 115 accredited in June 1941 to thirty-three in 1942.[13] With four exceptions, those accredited to NBC, CBS, Transradio Press Service, and a local Washington radio station, WWDC, all the women were correspondents for newspapers or press associations.

Women seeking admission as journalists were required to submit letters from their employers, samples of their recently published work, and statements of plans for attendance, since only about half of those previously accredited showed up for conferences. A five-member committee took care of actual accreditation. Members included Hornaday, Strayer, Craig, Gertrude Chesnut of Transradio Press Service, and the stately Esther Van Wagoner Tufty, who represented a group of Michigan newspapers and was called Duchess after being mistaken for royalty in Europe.[14]

Two familiar names, Ruby Black and Bess Furman, did not appear on the list of accredited journalists. Black left the United Press after an argument over her pay in 1942 to be a publicist for the Office of the Coordinator of Inter-American Affairs headed by Nelson Rockefeller, a job obtained partly through Eleanor Roosevelt's influence. The UP then relied on Strayer to cover the conferences for it as well as her own newspaper. Furman gave up freelancing to become assistant chief of the magazine division of the Office of War Information, where she worked under another of the First Lady's journalist friends, Dorothy Ducas (by then Herzog). These women joined the ranks of scores of Washington journalists who left civilian employment to work in government publicity efforts during the war.

According to rules set up by the association, Roosevelt was allowed to select government employees she wanted to attend the conferences. Not surprisingly, she picked Black and Furman along with a handful of others. The new rules forbid questions from government employees. Black fought the ban vigorously, but Furman withdrew support for Black's position, saying the Office of War Information had decided to ban "more planted questions."[15] After Craig objected to any "hint of government propaganda" at the First Lady's conferences, the group refused to back Black.[16]

Returned to the White House, the First Lady's press conferences continued to attract some interest from male reporters. The conference association divided over the request of Gordon Cole, who reported for the liberal New York newspaper *PM,* and Frederick Othman, a Washington humor columnist, to attend the gatherings.[17] "Some members seemed to feel it is up to us to end the discrimination against men; others felt that women have so many strikes against them in this business that it is wise to keep this one advantage," Hornaday informed Roosevelt, who ended the discussion.[18] She warned that she might stop the conferences if men were admitted, causing the group to turn down Cole's application. Tufty told her colleagues that the women-only gatherings were "precious" to Roosevelt.[19]

The conferences continued to offer some nuggets of news for women reporters. In 1943 Ann Cottrell (later Free) became the first woman hired in the Washington bureau of the *New York Herald Tribune,* both to replace men gone to war and to cover the First Lady's gatherings. A graduate of Columbia University, where she had studied English, Cottrell began her Washington career in 1940 as the first woman in *Newsweek*'s bureau before moving on to the *Chicago Sun.*

Cottrell saw one aspect of her *Herald Tribune* job as providing fresh coverage of Roosevelt's press conferences. "I remember my boss, Bert Anderson, saying 'Nobody gets this right. Go in there 'n' picture it. Just put in everything.' I wrote long detailed stories. They wanted them, they really did," she said.[20] Cottrell's coverage produced few surprises, as she dutifully reported Roosevelt's focus on women's participation in the war effort. One of her biggest stories dealt with Roosevelt's denial of repeated rumors of widespread immorality among servicewomen.[21] Roosevelt branded these as originating in a Nazi-inspired whispering campaign.[22]

Younger than many of the women, Cottrell, who succeeded Hornaday as head of the press conference association, saw the group as a collection of extraordinary individuals who fought their way forward both literally and figuratively. Her older colleagues surprised her with their "surprising agility and ferocious front-row-seat grabbing."[23] Decades later, she remembered Marie Manning dressed in mannish suits and flat-heel shoes like Martha Strayer. She recalled how the aged Mallon failed to submit an application for accreditation under the new press conference rules. Initially denied access, she stood outside the White House, protesting, "You can't do this to the *New York Times!*"[24]

Roosevelt's worldwide travels, first to England and then to the Pacific, brought her extensive reportorial attention during the war. When she returned to the White House after a twenty-five-thousand-mile trip that included stops at seventeen islands as well as Australia and New Zealand, she allowed men to attend her press briefing, after male reporters insisted the trip was "of such unusual significance that it justifies an exception to your rule."[25] The presence of men became the story, rather than her account of the trip, with headlines such as this one in New York's *PM:* MALES SQUIRM AT FIRST LADY'S PARLEY.[26] A male reporter was quoted as saying, "I felt like I had blundered into the powder room of an art gallery."[27]

Women reporters avoided making fun of the conferences, even though as the war proceeded, the First Lady herself came under occasional attack. Helen Essary, writing for the *Washington Times-Herald,* snidely commented that Roosevelt "talked, not as a woman who had gone traipsing off on her own to see the sights, but as the other half of a working team ... maybe for five or six terms."[28] So Essary expressed oblique opposition to Franklin Roosevelt's fourth term.

Women still sought accreditation, with the number of women eligible to attend increasing from thirty-three in 1942 to fifty-six in 1945, nine of whom represented radio networks and stations. Preceding Franklin Roosevelt's reelection campaign in 1944, the conferences drew headlines when Eleanor discounted reports that her husband's health would not allow him to remain in office. After his victory she asked members how the sessions could be made more productive, expressing dismay that "the reporters could not make me a better conveyor of ideas and of information and of thoughts that they could make use of."[29] The women journalists responded on February 13, 1945, objecting to Roosevelt's desire to make the conferences "into sessions resembling a forum."[30]

At this point some women journalists showed little admiration for the First Lady. Ruth Montgomery, a reporter for the anti-Roosevelt *New York Daily News* and successor to Cottrell as conference head, described the First Lady as conducting her conferences "with the giddy informality of an Aunt Nellie."[31] She claimed Roosevelt's answers to some questions "evoked squirming discomfort" from the president's press staff, giving this example: "'Did Mrs. Roosevelt think it was right for her to accept an $11,000 mink coat during wartime, a gift from the Canadian mink ranchers?' Mrs. Roosevelt assured us that she did, since there were no legal restrictions against a President's wife receiving presents."[32]

Clearly, by this time Roosevelt's press conferences were far from the only game in Washington for women journalists. As the war progressed, women made up at least half of the staffs of newspapers in smaller cities across the United States.[33] The scene in Washington was no different, although a few experienced women journalists gained accreditation as war correspondents. Washington seemed a likely spot from which to seek credentials to go overseas, but the State Department, which issued passports, and the

War Department, which accredited correspondents, did not look favorably on women. In all a total of 127 women managed to get overseas, but once there, some encountered hostility from generals and male correspondents.[34]

Ruth Cowan, in spite of working for the AP in its Washington bureau, had difficulty getting credentials. No stranger to discrimination, Cowan, a high school teacher in Texas who longed for the more exciting world of journalism, covered the state legislature in Austin for the United Press in the 1920s using a male byline, R. Baldwin Cowan. She lost her job when top executives discovered her gender.[35] Hired by the AP in Chicago, she managed to cover crime during the Al Capone era, as well as women's stories, before being transferred to Washington in 1940 and assigned to Eleanor Roosevelt's press conferences.

When Cowan found it hard to gain accreditation as a war correspondent, she asked Eleanor Roosevelt to intervene and went to Europe in 1943 with the endorsement of both Roosevelt and Oveta Culp Hobby, the first director of the Women's Auxiliary Army Corps (WAAC).[36] Along with Inez Robb, a New York–based feature writer for International News Service, Cowan covered the first two companies of WAACs sent overseas. The two were the first uniformed women correspondents attached to a military unit headed directly for war. Once in Europe, Cowan encountered resentment from male correspondents and officials in charge of press arrangements until she sent a cable to Eleanor Roosevelt complaining about the situation. Military censors refused to deliver the cable, but it prompted authorities to give Cowan and Robb better treatment.[37]

Craig obtained accreditation as a war correspondent in 1944. She toured American bases in England and advanced to the front lines in France and Germany. In doing so, she circumvented rules that kept women off military planes and ships because of lack of "facilities" for women.[38]

Another Washington woman journalist, Doris Fleeson, resurrected her career by reporting from Europe for the *Woman's Home Companion*. Fleeson, an economics graduate of the University of Kansas, had married John O'Donnell, a fellow reporter for the *New York Daily News,* where she had emerged as a talented "girl reporter" in 1927. In 1933 the two arrived in Washington to write a political column, "Capitol Stuff," under a joint byline, but the marriage collapsed under the stress of personal and political differences.[39]

Fleeson admired Roosevelt and the New Deal; O'Donnell, in keeping with the increasingly anti-Roosevelt stance of the *Daily News,* did not. When the couple divorced in 1942, he remained the newspaper's Washington correspondent, while she was recalled to New York to write radio news.[40] The war gave her a chance to cover battlefields in Europe before eventually returning to Washington and launching her own political column.

The real breakthrough in reporting for women occurred on the home front, in Washington as well as elsewhere.[41] Rosie the Reporter endured the snubs of males who thought in general she lacked their physical and mental ability. The *Saturday Evening Post,* a widely circulated weekly magazine, ridiculed wartime women journalists in 1944 in an article titled PAPER DOLLS, which estimated the number of replacements at eight thousand nationally.[42] *Time* magazine reported that newspapers scraped the "bottom of the manpower barrel" as they recruited "more and more women."[43] Nevertheless, male journalists were forced to admit, even if reluctantly, that there were at least a few exceptional women who proved themselves to be as good as or better than their male colleagues.

Some of these women held on to their jobs after World War II ended. In Washington the United Press bureau, which became the United Press International bureau in the 1950s, served as the professional home of three women who went on to successful careers following the war—Eileen Shanahan, Helen Thomas, and Charlotte Moulton. Before the war the bureau had only one woman reporter, Ruby Black, and she worked part-time. During the war the number increased to eleven women assigned to beats while several others worked in the office itself.[44] Shanahan, later an economics reporter for the *New York Times,* explained that Moulton, who covered the U.S. Supreme Court, was kept on because she reported "rings around a whole series" of competitors.[45]

On the other hand, Shanahan continued, both she and Thomas stayed because they rewrote news from Washington papers at odd hours for the UP radio wire and "nobody else wanted those lousy jobs."[46] Thomas arrived in Washington in 1942 with a new journalism degree from Wayne State University in Detroit and worked as a restaurant hostess before moving to the *Washington Daily News* as a wartime copygirl and then on to United Press. She persevered to become the first woman assigned to the White House permanently by a wire service, covered ten presidents, and established herself as the dean of the White House press corps.[47] Her career continued until 2010, when a remark construed as antisemitic forced her retirement from full-time employment.

Like the UP, the AP bureau also hired women to take the place of men, but few, if any, were groomed to move up in the ranks. Patriotic motives prompted Jane Eads, who had left Patterson's *Times-Herald* for an advertising job in New York, to seek a return to the capital after Pearl Harbor. She hoped for a spot at the AP "if they'll take me."[48] Editors readily did.

Virginia Van Der Veer, a youthful graduate of Birmingham-Southern College who had been employed to type stories dictated to her by AP reporters, leaped at the opportunity to cover congressional delegates from the South. She found herself limited to routine items, such as the appointment of postmasters. Members of Congress greeted her in "extravagant, albeit patronizing, language," such as that used by a representative from Mobile, Alabama, who called out, "Hello there, honey! Everything's made for love!" and Sen. Lister Hill, who rhapsodized, "My you lookin' pretty today, Miss Virginia!"[49] If important news happened on her beat, the AP gave the story to a man.

Undaunted, Van Der Veer advanced to the AP's national staff and wrote an important story on the Interstate Commerce Commission. When the war ended, however, editors made it plain she need "no longer worry about complicated subjects like freight rates" and should stick to topics such as the First Lady's wardrobe.[50] Six months after reporting on a speech from Republican Rep. Clare Booth Luce urging women to marry in lieu of a career, Van Der Veer decided do just that. She gave up Washington reporting for marriage but later became a professor of history in Alabama.

At the *New York Times* bureau, the absence of men during the war finally gave bylined stories on the front page to the venerable Winifred Mallon, who was assigned to report on wartime coal strikes.[51] In 1943 Bess Furman left her Office of War Information job to cover education, science, and medicine as well as Eleanor Roosevelt for the *Times,* taking over most of Mallon's beat. Furman stayed in the bureau until 1961. A feminist writer saw her as the first woman in the office to make a lasting name for herself.[52] Yet James Reston, the influential Washington correspondent and bureau chief of the *Times* during Furman's tenure at the newspaper, referred to her in his autobiography only as a staff member who took important film to New York on the train.[53]

The war advanced the career of Elsie Carper, who fought against sex discrimination, at the *Washington Post,* where she started as an assistant librarian immediately after graduation from George Washington University. When the librarian went into the army, she got his job, but not for long because the picture editor soon left, too, and she replaced him before moving up to assistant city editor.[54] "I was twenty-three and I was assigning reporters to cover stories and sending out photographers, reading copy, and it was marvelous, the things I was allowed to do," Carper told an interviewer in the 1980s.[55]

In her autobiography, Katharine Graham, who turned the *Post* into one of the world's leading newspapers in the 1970s, noted that Carper was "able to move up quickly, many women were taking over the jobs of men who had gone off to war."[56] She added that "unfortunately, like all publications, the *Post* sank back into its old ways after the men returned," although "a nucleus remained . . . largely on the women's pages and in what were regarded as women's issues, welfare and education."[57]

Among the wartime journalists, Graham's mother, Agnes Meyer, who wrote two lengthy series of articles, occupied a special place. Following the purchase of the *Washington Post* in 1933 by her wealthy husband, Eugene Meyer, Agnes, an imposing individual who had been the first woman reporter in the city room of the *New York Sun* before her marriage, insisted on writing for the *Post* on social and literary subjects. Meyer, with whom she frequently disagreed, both personally and on policy, discouraged her contributions, leaving editors caught between demands from two awe-inspiring figures.[58]

The war gave Agnes Meyer opportunity to broaden her journalistic activities, as she traveled throughout the United States to report on home-front conditions. She campaigned against over-crowded schools, lack of community facilities for health and welfare, and racial discrimination, helping build the *Post* into a strong liberal voice. Reporting from the South on March 28, 1944, she observed that the military "uniform worn by a Negro affects the ignorant white population as a red flag does a bull. . . . Southerners said to me quite frankly: 'You've got to teach a nigger in uniform that he's still a nigger.' "[59] After the war she wrote a series of articles on migrant workers in the Southwest, scrambling along a dirt bank to inspect "burrows" occupied by "wetbacks."[60] The managing editor first refused to run the articles, but she insisted until he agreed to try them out, and they met an enthusiastic response from readers.[61]

During the last months of the war, Katharine worked on the paper in the circulation department, answering subscriber complaints. Prior to her marriage in 1940 to Philip Graham, she had been in charge of "Letters to the Editor." When one stalwart employee, Marie Sauer, a Columbia University Journalism School graduate who edited the Sunday review of national and international news, left to join the U.S. Navy Waves in 1942, Graham worried about her father. She knew that he was dependent on women to run his newspaper during the war.[62] When Sauer came back, she was "banished to head the women's department where she was topnotch," according to the centennial history of the *Post* by Chalmers M. Roberts.[63]

The manpower drain led to an "influx, first, of female 'copy boys' and then of women reporters; some from outside, others coming down a floor from the women's department to the city room," he wrote.[64] It also led to changes in content directed at women with greater emphasis on the war effort than social events.

On July 19, 1942, Hope Ridings Miller, society editor, declared in her column "for the duration—and probably longer—we are finished with society-as-such. We are interested only in contributing our bit toward preservation of the only kind of world in which any of us would care to live."[65]

Once in the city room, women journalists received an inhospitable welcome in what appeared to be a male fortress where one editor, "in the Hollywood casting couch tradition, demanded a sexual price for good assignments," according to Roberts.[66] Helene Champlain, who wore harlequin glasses and black fishnet stockings, attracted notice as the first woman to replace a male copyboy. She faced such resentment that male staff members refused to call out "girl" to pick up their copy. Instead they yelled "boy."[67]

At the *Times-Herald* most of Patterson's experienced journalists also went off to war, leaving the paper to be run by "amateurs," according to Patterson's biographer.[68] The paper continued, as before, relying on sprightly local coverage and national copy from Hearst stars. Adele Rogers St. Johns, Hearst's top woman feature writer who worked out of Washington in the 1930s, managed a reconciliation in 1942 between Patterson and her old enemy, Alice Roosevelt Longworth.[69] That same year the erratic Patterson broke with Drew Pearson, her ex-son-in-law, who also may have been one of her many romantic conquests, and eventually dropped his syndicated, coauthored "Daily Washington Merry-Go-Round" column. Increasingly disliked by the public because of her isolationist stance before the war and attacks on Franklin Roosevelt, Patterson could no long count on attention from her editor, Frank Waldrop, busy directing newspaper operations with a skeleton staff. It fell to the glamorous Evie Robert, who wrote a social column called "Eve's Rib," to put Patterson to bed when she drank too much.[70]

Even if Washingtonians disagreed with its editorial policy, Patterson's lively, around-the-clock *Times-Herald* appealed to readers. By 1943 it had the largest circulation in the city and finally was earning a profit.[71] Called a "women's newspaper," because of its many columns on cooking, society, fashions, movies, etc., there also were two columns aimed at men, one on fashions and one on advice-to-the-lovelorn-male."[72]

For example, in 1942 Inga Arvad, in her column on personalities billed as "Did You Happen to See," described Katherine Smith, the women's page editor, as looking "like a page from *Vogue.*"[73] After pointing out that the attractive Smith, pictured in a head shot, carried six different shades of lipstick, made her own hats, and enjoyed cooking, Arvad concluded that Smith was "a grand little gal."[74] Such women-oriented feature copy, favored by Patterson herself, appeared aimed at the "government girls," as they were called, an estimated nine hundred thousand young women who flocked to Washington to handle the flood of wartime paperwork.[75] St. Johns dramatized them in a 1944 magazine series on wartime Washington titled "Government Girl," which became a Hollywood movie.

Another staff member assigned to "Did You Happen to See" was Kathleen Kennedy, the sister of John F. Kennedy. She started at the newspaper in 1940 as a secretary, hired because her father, Joseph P. Kennedy, Roosevelt's ambassador to England, held isolationist views that mirrored Patterson's own.[76] Able, willing, and likeable, she left in 1943 to go to England, where she married the Marquis of Hartington. When news of their deaths in a plane crash hit the city room five years later, the staff wept openly.[77] Her brother Jack liked to visit the city room, partly because it "boasted the prettiest distaff staff in town," according to a Patterson biographer.[78]

The war years were hard on the fiery, redheaded Patterson, called "the most powerful woman in America" by *Collier's* magazine and "the most hated woman in America" by *Time*.[79] Increasingly dependent on drugs and alcohol, her interest in the *Times-Herald* slackened, although she remained the newspaper's queen bee, writing commentary that revealed her personal weaknesses as she lashed out against drunkenness and mental instability.[80] Outraged by Franklin Roosevelt's election to a fourth term, she printed horrifying pictures of the war dead to show that Roosevelt's promise not to send American boys "into any foreign wars" had not been kept.[81]

On July 24, 1948, Patterson's servants found her dead in bed, apparently of a heart attack, at her estate outside Washington at the age of sixty-six. She left the newspaper to seven executives, soon dubbed the Seven Dwarfs.[82] Her cousin, Robert R. McCormick, publisher of the *Chicago Tribune,* bought the *Times-Herald* from the heirs within a year of Patterson's death, but "killed Cissy's Page 3, 'the rape and murder page,'" as it was called.[83]

Content became duller, but the "Inquiring Photographer" column continued, carrying the byline of Jacqueline Bouvier, destined to achieve celebrity status as the wife of Senator Kennedy. Before her marriage in 1953, Bouvier handled the daily column for nearly two years.[84] It generally featured an innocuous question ("Have you done your Christmas shopping?") or occasionally one with an overtone of misogyny ("Do women marry because they are too lazy to go to work?").[85] Replies appeared alongside pictures of individuals answering the questions. The column illustrated the *Times-Herald*'s emphasis on local news as entertainment and use of attractive young women as staff members, but Patterson's old formula no longer worked.

Without Patterson's brassy presence at the helm, the newspaper slipped in circulation and losses mounted. McCormick sold it in 1954 to Eugene Meyer, who merged it with the *Washington Post,* a move that Cissy would not have approved. She viewed Meyer as her arch rival and once sent him an elegantly wrapped chuck of raw meat during a dispute over the right to publish popular comic strips. Meyer was puzzled, but his wife was not: "It must be a pound of flesh [for] a dirty Jewish shylock," Agnes told her husband.[86] The Meyers were appalled; Patterson said later, "I guess I made a mistake that time."[87]

Patterson viewed her newspaper as light and bright, while Meyer wanted his to appeal to government policy makers. Meyer won out, as Patterson's death brought an end to personal journalism in Washington. The purchase gave the *Post* domination of the morning newspaper scene in Washington and set the stage for its emergence as a leading national newspaper.

Among those writing columns about Patterson after her death was Evelyn Peyton Gordon of the *Washington Daily News,* who had once worked as Patterson's society editor. Gordon remembered standing outside the Russian Embassy to cover a reception one cold night, when Patterson came along and draped her own mink coat over the shivering journalist's shoulders. When Gordon dropped the coat off at Patterson's Dupont Circle mansion, Patterson berated her, saying, "Why did you bother to return the coat, my dear? I've dozens of them."[88]

A veteran society reporter, Gordon was one of the women who enabled the *Daily News,* a feisty Scripps Howard afternoon newspaper in Washington, to keep publishing during World War II. According to Dorothy Jurney, the *News* depended on women because it had no men left except "the physically handicapped and the drunks."[89] A 1930 journalism graduate of Northwestern University who had worked for the newspaper owned by her father in Michigan City, Indiana, Jurney was hired in 1943 as a "city-side deskman" on the *Daily News* by Charles Stevenson, the managing editor.[90]

Jurney soon advanced to assistant city editor and then to acting city editor. Stevenson praised her as "one of the greatest finds ever to enter our doors. She was an excellent copy editor, a good writer, an editor of rare judgment, an exceptional executive—and one of the hardest workers it ever has been my privilege to know."[91] It looked like she would be made the actual city editor, but that did not happen.

When the men came back, she received a telephone call from a top editor, who told her, "We have this young man who was a cub reporter in the sports department and I want to make him the city editor. And Dorothy, I would like you to teach him his job."[92] She said he added, "I just don't think it would work to make you the city editor, and you know the reason why. And I said, 'Yes, I'm a woman.' He agreed."[93] Jurney tried to teach the young man the job but "he wasn't smart, and I got tired of it and quit," she said.[94]

Jurney soon moved to Miami, where she became the women's page editor of the *Miami Herald*. Disillusioned by her *News* experience, she gave only a tepid response when asked in Miami about her professional goals. Later she learned that editors there had been considering her for city editor but decided against giving her the job because "she didn't show any ambition."[95]

The most profitable Washington newspaper before, during, and after the war, the *Star* depended on women for assignments of increasing importance during World War II. Miriam Ottenberg, a journalism graduate of the University of Wisconsin, joined the newspaper in 1937, assigned to human interest features and public service campaigns. Talented in disguising herself, she laid a claim to covering major murder stories.[96] The war allowed her to report on vital topics of the day—the draft, manpower, and civil defense issues. "If a good murder came along, I did that, too," she noted.[97]

Like Ottenberg, another women hired at the *Star* during the early 1940s went on to a fruitful career. Mary Lou Werner dropped out of the University of Maryland to take a job as a seventeen-year-old copygirl. Her widowed mother's lack of money forced Werner, who had been studying math, to quit college and seek employment. She sought work in the *Star*'s accounting depart-ment but was assigned to the newsroom instead because of the need to replace men. Werner rose to reporter and state editor and was metropolitan editor in charge of all coverage in Washington, Virginia, and Maryland before the *Star* folded in 1981. Decades later she said that she thrived at the newspaper as long as editors did not think she was interested in marriage or planning to have children.[98]

The excitement of the capital in wartime captivated a young woman who persuaded her parents to give her $250 to seek her future in Washington after she got her degree in journalism from the University of Texas at Austin. "The National Press Building [where many news organizations had offices] looked lively but frightening," Liz Sutherland Carpenter wrote in her memoir.[99] "I put on my best clothes, took my scrapbook of clippings, and timidly began knocking on its doors for a job."

Fortunately, she found opportunity, she explained, "in the form of a dynamic blond newswoman from Michigan who looked like Brunhild and was known as the 'Duchess.'"[100] She was Esther Van Wagoner Tufty, a leading member of Eleanor Roosevelt's press conference who presented a regal appearance with braids wrapped around her head like a coronet. Tufty's news bureau provided Washington columns for Michigan and other newspapers.[101] News bureaus like hers, which served some three hundred newspapers at the peak of her career, remained an important component of journalism in the mid-twentieth century when some 1,800 daily newspapers still dominated the news agenda in the United States. Tufty hired the novice from Texas "as assistant everything—reporter, secretary, bartender."[102]

In 1944 Sutherland married Les Carpenter, a journalist on duty with the navy, and moved to Philadelphia, where she worked in the United Press bureau until the war ended and the couple returned to Washington. After working for the Bascom Timmons News Bureau, a regional news-gathering operation run by a fellow Texan, Carpenter opened his own news service. His wife joined in the operation, while also having children, two in three years. "He got the by-line, and I did all the work," Liz Carpenter said.[103] "Raising children while working for a dozen newspapers is no way to grow old gracefully. Rapidly, but not gracefully."[104]

During the war Timmons had hired another journalist from Texas, Sarah McClendon, destined to become well known in the capital. McClendon, a young woman from Tyler, Texas, had graduated from the University of Missouri journalism school and enlisted in the WAACs after working on newspapers at Tyler and Beaumont, Texas. As a first lieutenant, she was stationed at the Pentagon to write publicity releases for the Army Surgeon General's office. When a disastrous wartime marriage left her pregnant, she was discharged from the military in line with the rules of the day, after concealing her pregnancy for eight months and insisting on her right as an army officer to give birth at Walter Reed Army Hospital.

Abandoned by her husband, in 1944 McClendon was hired by the short-staffed Timmons only nine days after the birth of her daughter, Sally.[105] She stopped in to see Timmons on her way home from an obstetrical checkup, and "when he realized I was an experienced reporter, he wouldn't let me out of the office,"

McClendon said.[106] After asking her babysitter to stay on until evening, McClendon sat down to work then and there. Timmons assigned her to be national correspondent for the *Philadelphia Daily News.* "I never told Timmons that I had a tiny daughter," she wrote in a memoir. "I had to work to support my child."[107]

Told to contact members of Congress, McClendon endeavored to track them for days before realizing that she could locate them easily through the congressional press galleries. When she asked Timmons's office manager why he had not sent her there, he answered, "Well, I figured you wouldn't be here but a few days."[108] It was a totally incorrect prophecy. Patching together child-care arrangements, McClendon doggedly pursued her career. Two and a half years later, Timmons let McClendon go, since he was obligated to give jobs back to returning servicemen, but he offered advice that she followed.

"You should be like May Craig; you should have your own news bureau," Timmons told her.[109] He gave her a few of his own clients so she could set up McClendon News Service. She ran it for decades, earning enough to take care of herself and her daughter, covering "Capitol Hill, the State Department, the Veterans Administration, the FBI and the White House or any place else where I thought there was a story," she noted.[110]

While working for Timmons, McClendon tipped off Les Carpenter about an upcoming vacancy in the office and helped him get the job. According to McClendon, Les and Liz Carpenter showed no gratitude as they competed with her to be Washington correspondents for the same newspapers. She blamed them for labeling her "a conservative for years, which hurt me and limited my effectiveness as a newspaper reporter."[111] Both McClendon and Liz Carpenter eventually emerged as Washington institutions, but that lay years ahead.

The Roosevelt years ended dramatically on the afternoon of April 12, 1945, when Franklin Roosevelt died of a massive stroke at his winter retreat in Warm Springs, Georgia, belying the assurances of his wife that he remained in good health. That same morning Eleanor held a press conference at which she was questioned concerning a "Daily Washington Merry-Go-Round" column that referred to a "cooling in relationship between Mrs. Roosevelt and the ladies of the press."[112]

The column, now running in the *Washington Post,* claimed that Jonathan Daniels, a White House press aide, accused a reporter of misquoting the First Lady on the issue of whether the United States would be able to send food to Europe after the war ended. It alleged that Roosevelt's secretary, Malvina Thompson, had doctored a transcript of the conference to prove that Eleanor did not make a controversial statement that the United States would not be able to feed Europe, when, in fact, she had done so.[113]

Claiming that her editor wanted to know, a reporter from the *Star,* probably Ottenberg, asked at the April 12 conference if the long "honeymoon" between the First Lady and her press corps had finally ended.[114] When Roosevelt started to answer, Furman moved to refer the issue to the conference association, and the reporters debated among themselves on taking this action. During the discussion Roosevelt said off the record that she did not think Pearson's assertions merited an answer.[115] News stories stemming from the conference focused on Roosevelt's request that the public withhold judgment on postwar treatment of Germany until more information on conditions there was available from the U.S. government.[116]

The president's death put an end to the controversy over the "Merry-Go-Round" column as well as to the First Lady's press conferences, since Eleanor's successor, Bess Truman, refused to continue them after realizing she was not required to imitate her predecessor. On April 19, 1945, Roosevelt gave a farewell tea at the White House for her press corps. She told the reporters that she planned to join their ranks as a newspaperwoman herself, continuing her "My Day" column and writing for magazines on her return home to New York.

Used to obtaining news from the First Lady's press conferences, even though it did not always result in significant headlines, Washington women journalists pressed President Harry S Truman's staff for items related to his wife and his daughter, Margaret. Advised to maintain cordial relations with press women, the matronly Bess invited them to tea and attended social events sponsored by women's press groups but said almost nothing. When journalists asked how they would "get to know you," she retorted, "You don't need to know me. I'm only the President's wife and the mother of his daughter."[117]

Reporters directed questions about her schedule to two aides, Edith Helm, social secretary, and Reathel Odum, a personal assistant, both of whom disliked dealing with the press. A woman's page reporter desperate for any tidbit resorted to innocuous inquiries such as "What will Mrs. Truman wear to the tea for the United Council of Church Women today?"[118] Relayed to the First Lady, a question of this type would result in Truman snapping, "It's none of her damn business," leaving the aide to politely inform the reporter that "Mrs. Truman hasn't quite made up her mind."[119]

The fact that women reporters pursued information on the First Lady showed that they continued to look at the distaff side of the White House as one of the relatively few avenues open to them for news. According to Malvina Stephenson, who corresponded for the *Cincinnati Times-Star* and other newspapers served by her one-person bureau, women reporters were "really caught short when we didn't have regular access to the first lady."[120] The women grasped at any morsel of news they could glean about Bess Truman, posing personal questions generally through Helm, who responded with the First Lady's monosyllabic replies.

At semimonthly briefings, reporters inquired about such details as Truman's favorite color ("blue"), favorite style of clothing ("tailored"), whether she liked costume jewelry ("very little of it"), whether she counted calories ("yes"), her dress size ("18"), her shoe size ("6"), and what type of centerpiece she used at her Independence home ("floral").[121] No record exists of any male reporters who wanted to attend the briefings, but the White House press secretary's office stood ready to offer accreditation for "each lady correspondent who wishes to attend."[122] Few did; by 1953, when the Truman administration ended, attendance varied from seven to fifteen out of a total of forty-six accredited journalists.[123]

The scarcity of information for women reporters from the Truman White House symbolized the uncomfortable terrain that women journalists encountered in Washington after the end of World War II. Women journalists found the pickings slim when Dwight D. Eisenhower was elected president in 1952, following Truman. Mamie Eisenhower cooperated with the desire of women reporters to impersonate her husband at a WNPC stunt party by lending them his golf apparel. But, the new First Lady's secretary, Mary Jane McCaffree Monroe, was the one giving out news, according to Isabelle Shelton of the *Evening Star,* "as sort of a catch-as-catch-can thing in which you had to ask the right questions or lose the game."[124]

Women who sought to cover the same news assignments as men faced intense discrimination. Some returned to the women's pages because they had no other option. Judy Mann, who worked first for the *Washington Daily News* and later wrote a feminist column for the *Washington Post,* wrote that the news media until the 1980s were "very much in the grip of white men whose wives had stayed home."[125] In 1949 *Mademoiselle* magazine discouraged its readers from newspaper work, relying on a survey of editors of twenty-seven daily newspapers who claimed women were too emotional to handle news except on women's and society pages.[126] Editors were quoted as saying women "get married and quit just about the time they're any good to you."[127]

On the surface many women journalists themselves either bought or were forced into the prevailing emphasis on marriage, families, and suburban lifestyle that marked the postwar years, as illustrated by the fact that the WNPC published a cookbook, *Who Says We Can't Cook,* in 1955. After her service as a war correspondent, Ruth Cowan (later Nash) returned to the AP Washington bureau, where she was booted off the Pentagon beat in 1950. Her new assignment: to cover wives of officials, appointments of women, White House social functions, and similar fare in a stereotypical feminine style. One scholar speculated that she "intentionally fluffed up her stories to mask the radical potential of the inroads women were making in society."[128]

Some women's page writers began to speak up with more authority on the rights of women. In 1946 Malvina Lindsay, a 1913 journalism graduate of the University of Missouri and women's page editor of the *Washington Post,* contended in her "The Gentler Sex" column that males clung to sex-segregated institutions out of anxiety. She claimed men feared the "energy, ambition and organizing talents" of women and were in a "last ditch retreat from 'mother knows best.'"[129]

A few women managed to make use of their wartime experience to further their careers in general news. At the *Star,* Ottenberg developed a career in law enforcement reporting after the war ended, covering congressional investigations and crime within the District of Columbia. In the 1940s and 50s she investigated phony marriage counselors, a multistate abortion ring, rising food prices, juvenile crime, sex offenders, and drug addiction.[130] Although she considered most of her work not particularly dangerous, she said when she got into "somewhat sticky situations" the city editor "very sensibly arranged for a man to go with me as both protector and witness."[131]

In 1958 Ottenberg won unprecedented tribute from Washington's law enforcement officers for more than a decade of what her newspaper called "zealous reporting of crime and its correction."[132] At a testimonial dinner attended by 150 policemen, jurists, and officials, including members of Congress, she received credit for spurring legislation to tighten prosecution of multiple offenders, fight juvenile crime, stiffen penalties for sex offenses involving children, and hospitalize drug addicts. In a foreword to a book by Ottenberg on federal investigative agencies in 1962, Robert F. Kennedy, then attorney general, wrote that she "has won the respect of the investigators about whom she writes—and whom she often assists with the results of her own digging for the facts."[133]

In 1960 Ottenberg received a Pulitzer Prize for local reporting for a series, reprinted in 120,000 pamphlets, on unscrupulous practices of used car dealers.[134] It spurred Congress to pass corrective legislation outlawing unethical practices. In announcing the award, the *Star* published a picture of Ottenberg demurely wearing a dark dress accented by a matching pearl necklace and earrings, her dark hair carefully arranged in a fashionable style.

This picture of conventional femininity obscured the determination that Ottenberg, a short, well-turned-out woman, showed in the newsroom. According to Washington newspaper legend, on one occasion Ottenberg took the belt off her dress and flayed an astonished male editor in a disagreement over the way her copy had been handled.[135] As a star reporter, she suffered no reprisals in the free-flowing newsroom atmosphere of the day.

Ottenberg was the second Washington woman journalist to win a Pulitzer Prize. The honor of being the first went to another *Star* reporter, Mary Lou Werner, who had won the previous year, also for local reporting. She covered the state of Virginia's attempt to use "massive resistance" to fight the U.S. Supreme Court ruling against school segregation in 1954, reporting on the tactics of the political machine of Sen. Harry F. Byrd Sr. that shut down public schools rather than integrate them.[136]

As an afternoon newspaper, the *Star* had multiple deadlines for different editions, requiring reporters to dictate stories to the main office under extreme time pressure. Werner succeeded in mastering the art of calling in both facts and historical context. Her Pulitzer citation praised "her comprehensive year-long coverage of the integration crisis in Virginia which demonstrated admirable qualities of accuracy, speed and the ability to interpret the news under deadline pressure in the course of a difficult and taxing assignment."[137]

The year Werner won the Pulitzer, Newbold Noyes Jr., whose family ran the *Star,* named her the paper's first full-time woman editor of news, after asking, "Do you think that men will take orders from you?"[138] "Of course, they will," she answered.[139] "They know I've been a very good reporter and will have done everything I ask them to do."[140] And so they did; Ludy, as her colleagues called her, known for her unflappable good humor, personal warmth, and uncommon competence, became a beloved figure at the newspaper. Her byline changed in 1965, when she married James D. Forbes and had a child.

Neither Forbes nor Ottenberg saw themselves as crusaders for women but as professional journalists. "I'm not a feminist, I'm a reporter," Ottenberg said.[141] Stricken with multiple sclerosis, which was diagnosed the same week she won the Pulitzer Prize, when she was hospitalized for tests, she said, "I would call my bad-guy targets for my stories and impersonate a beleaguered house-wife—to the wide-eyed amazement of the three other patients in the room."[142] After she was forced into medical retirement in the 1970s, she researched and wrote a book about victims of multiple sclerosis. Both Forbes and Ottenberg served as pathbreakers for others who needed role models in the aftermath of World War II, when the ideology of domesticity offered an excuse for outright discrimination.

Minority women journalists faced a different set of obstacles in an era when Washington's mainstream newspapers did not employ African Americans. In 1947 Alice A. Dunnigan, a school-teacher who had arrived in the capital during the war to work as a clerk-typist for the federal government, became the first African American woman to be accredited to the Capitol press galleries, White House, Supreme Court, and State Department. In 1955 she was invited to join the WNPC, making her the first African American member of that organization, but her pathbreaking career had not come easily.

A Kentucky sharecropper's daughter who had always dreamed of being a journalist, Dunnigan obtained accreditation as Washington correspondent for the Associated Negro Press (ANP), a news agency that served some hundred African American newspapers across the nation. She applied for press credentials one day after being barred because of her race from using the Senate Press Gallery to cover the ousting of the racist senator from Mississippi, Theodore Bilbo, for conduct unbecoming to his office.[143] Her gallery application coincided with an effort by Louis Lautier of the *Atlanta Daily World* to gain admission that led to a rules change forbidding segregation.[144]

Dunnigan had worked part time for Claude A. Barnett, the founder of the ANP, before he hired her as Washington bureau chief for one hundred dollars a month after male reporters to whom he had offered twice that amount turned him down. He later told Dunnigan, "I was not confident that a girl could do the type of job we needed in Washington."[145] In her autobiography she noted, "My salary was hardly sufficient to eke out a livelihood, and no expense account was offered. . . . I made personal sacrifices and paid my own expense."[146]

As a correspondent, she covered District of Columbia stories ignored by the mainstream press, such as the burning of a cross by the Ku Klux Klan in a Washington neighborhood and a suit brought by white families to evict an African American family that had purchased a house in a white neighborhood.[147] In 1948 she became the first woman journalist of color to travel with the press corps covering Truman's campaign trail, even though she had to pay her own way to do it. Barely able to support herself on her meager salary, she picked up extra money writing speeches for a woman government official, but a black male colleague tried to get her accreditation lifted on grounds of conflict of interest. The National Association for the Advancement of Colored People defended her, pointing out that white reporters also supplemented their income with speech writing.[148]

A woman destined to become one of Washington's top political writers appeared on the newspaper scene in 1947 in a marginal role. Mary McGrory started on the *Star* as a book reviewer, spending her days off on Capitol Hill to gain material for profiles and features on political figures. Her chance to write a witty and observant news column came after Noyes, the national editor, said, "Say, Mary, aren't you ever going to get married?"[149]

McGrory attracted favorable notice for columns on the Army-McCarthy hearings in 1954 that resulted in the downfall of Republican Sen. Joseph McCarthy, who engaged in communist witch-hunting in the State Department and other government agencies. Her coverage prompted James "Scotty" Reston to offer her a job at the *New York Times* Washington bureau. But she remained at the *Star,* telling her journalist friend Eileen Shanahan, "Scotty made me feel as though he wanted me to work the telephone switchboard part-time."[150]

McGrory took comfort in the fact that at least one woman made a significant dent in the atmosphere of male supremacy that dominated Washington journalism for some two decades after World War II. Doris Fleeson proved herself an exception to masculine rule. Buying a small house in Georgetown, where bricked sidewalks and Federal-style townhouses appealed to well-connected liberals, Fleeson established herself as a political columnist shortly after Truman moved into the White House.

McGrory called Fleeson an "able, tough reporter, an ardent feminist who was very kind to me."[151] She said when Fleeson was told she thought like a man, she would shoot back, "What man?"[152] McGrory pointed to Fleeson roaming through the Capitol, "a tiger in white gloves and a Sally Victor hat, stalking explanations for the stupidity, cruelty, fraud, or cant that was her chosen prey."[153] In 1952, McGrory noted, Fleeson was awarded "the abominable accolade, 'Capitol's top newshen' by *Newsweek* magazine."[154] The previous year *Time* magazine profiled her as "the capital's top woman reporter," listing her as the only woman among the thirteen leading members of the Washington press corps, and claiming that she "frequently knows what the Administration is up to before many of its brasshats."[155]

Before beginning her political column, Fleeson asked her close friend, Henry L. Mencken, the writer known as the "Sage of Baltimore," for advice. She told him that she had received an offer from the North American Newspaper Alliance, its affiliated Bell Syndicate, and the *Star* to write a five-day-a-week political column on a trial basis for three months for which she would receive $150 a week. "Do you think it is a risky enterprise?" she asked, noting that she had no private income and had to support her daughter as well as herself.[156] Mencken counseled her to go ahead, predicting the success that made her the first national syndicated woman political columnist, producing some 5,500 columns in the following twenty-two years.[157] Her column ran in some one hundred newspapers.

Using the colorful style that she had perfected in her previous reportorial experience, Fleeson, considered a voice of liberalism, drew on her contacts with notable figures and sources, following Mencken's advice to "avoid mere opinion as you would the pestilence."[158] Recognizing the hostility that many male editors had against women, she told a radio audience, "Thinking has no sex. We need a great flowering of mind and spirit on the part of men in the newspaper management."[159]

While joining with her good friend, May Craig, and other women journalists to protest discrimination, Fleeson gave readers an "insider's" view of secret meetings between political figures by maintaining contacts with Eleanor Roosevelt and others high in the councils of both the Democratic and Republican parties. Fleeson was one of the few women to attend President Truman's press conferences as well as those of presidents Eisenhower, Kennedy, and Johnson.

A slender woman with big hazel eyes and a wide smile, Fleeson engaged in a flirtatious relationship with Mencken. At least one of his biographers, Fred Hobson, declared that Fleeson was "too much one of the boys" for Mencken to woo as a serious romantic interest.[160] Hobson described her as "a lusty, good-humored, tough-talking woman with a 'healthy Kansas appetite.' "[161]

In 1958 Fleeson married Dan Kimball, an industrialist who had made a fortune in rocket engines and served as secretary of the navy from 1951 to 1953 under Truman. Those attending the fashionable Manhattan wedding ceremony at the home of another well-known woman journalist, Inez Robb, included Eleanor Roosevelt; Margaret Truman and her husband, Clifton Daniel; and the famed financier, Bernard Baruch, with whom Fleeson also had an affectionate friendship. Fleeson and Kimball lived in an elegant house on Washington's S Street and participated in elite social events.

Fleeson continued her column, having changed from the Bell Syndicate to United Features in 1954, the same year she attacked McCarthyism, which she called the "flower of evil."[162] After winning several awards, she was chosen as a celebrity guest on Edward R. Murrow's television show *Person to Person* in 1958. Fleeson collapsed while covering Lyndon B. Johnson's presidential campaign in 1964, suffering various circulatory ailments, and discontinued her column in 1967. She died in 1970 of a stroke thirty-six hours after the death of her husband.

Only one other Washington woman journalist during this period could claim a national reputation that came near Fleeson's. The flamboyant Marguerite Higgins of the New York *Herald Tribune,* who became the first woman to receive a Pulitzer Prize for war reporting, arrived in the capital in 1955 with her husband, Lt. Gen. William E. Hall, former director of U.S. intelligence in Berlin. The Halls had married three years earlier while Higgins, who shared a 1950 Pulitzer Prize with male reporters for coverage of the Korean conflict, was receiving great fanfare for her Korean reporting exploits. Her numerous awards included being named Associated Press Woman of the Year in 1951. In Washington she covered the State Department and wrote a weekly editorial page column for her newspaper.

Higgins, a Columbia University journalism graduate known for her competitive instincts, successfully pleaded with Helen Rogers Reid, the wife of the publisher of the *Herald Tribune,* for the right to become a World War II war correspondent in Europe. Her accounts of German concentration camps led to her being named the best foreign correspondent of 1945 by the New York Newspaper Women's Club.[163] Sent by the *Herald Tribune* to Tokyo as its Far East bureau chief in 1950, Higgins found herself almost immediately covering the outbreak of hostilities between North and South Korea.

When military brass ordered her to leave Korea because "there are no facilities for ladies at the front," Higgins and her newspaper appealed to Gen. Douglas MacArthur.[164] He lifted the ban, which helped make Higgins into a feminist heroine. She recounted her experiences in a best-selling 1951 book, *War in Korea: The Report of a Woman Combat Correspondent,* followed by three other popular books drawing on her journalistic accomplishments, including one on reporting from Russia.[165]

An attractive blond frequently photographed in the press, Higgins had the misfortune of being victimized by unfair gossip, according to Keyes Beech, a *Chicago Daily News* correspondent who covered Korea with her. "Maggie didn't need to use her sex to do a good job as a war correspondent. She had brains, ability, courage and stamina."[166] Rumors persisted that she took advantage of her good looks to advance her career, but a close friend, Judy Barden, told a Higgins biographer that "her relationships, sexual or otherwise, were mutually pleasurable associations."[167] Higgins's defenders contended that she simply refused to go along with the double standard that permitted men sexual freedom while punishing women for similar conduct.[168]

In Washington Higgins exercised her claim to being the *Herald Tribune*'s White House correspondent, invoking a clause in a contract she had signed with the newspaper's top brass that gave her rights to this prize assignment.[169] The terms of the contract were not known in the bureau, where her insistence on the White House beat caused internal friction. She relinquished that post in 1956, but controversy arose over her accreditation to the congressional press galleries.

As one of the best-known women of the era, Higgins accepted contracts to appear in ads for Crest toothpaste and Camel cigarettes, shocking her journalistic colleagues. The contracts violated a rule that correspondents entitled to gallery admission not engage in paid promotion or publicity work.[170] Higgins resigned her gallery memberships in protest and raised the question of what difference there was between being paid to do an ad and appearing in a sponsored television news show.[171] Commenting that she rarely used the press galleries or attended press conferences, she declared, "I depend upon personal contact for news."[172]

Higgins then covered the State Department, a beat where her bureau chief, Bob Donovan, thought she could be reined in and "could not go on free-wheeling the way she had been, without blow-ups all over the place."[173] In this job she continued to travel abroad, covering international conferences and presidential trips.

After suffering the loss of a premature infant in 1953, Higgins had two more children, a son born in 1958 and a daughter the following year, but she did not give up her career. She traveled to Vietnam in 1963 and supported U.S. military action there in the face of vigorous protestors against the Vietnam War. After leaving the *Herald Tribune* in 1963, she moved to Long Island's *Newsday* for which she wrote a thrice weekly column syndicated in ninety-two other newspapers.[174] She died two years later in Washington at the age of forty-five of a tropical disease contracted on a reporting tour to Vietnam, India, and Pakistan.

Apart from stars like Fleeson and Higgins, most Washington women journalists struggled to gather news through conventional channels sometimes closed because of their sex. Particularly galling to the women, the NPC—which prided itself on a men's club atmosphere symbolized by the display of a large oil painting of a nude titled *Phyrne the Courtesan*—refused to admit them as either members or guests.[175] Since many bureaus were located in the National Press Club building, women reporters found it grossly unfair that they were not allowed to enter the bar even to contact their bosses, or to have a quick meal there. Even more upsetting, the club's refusal to admit women reporters to its newsmaker luncheons restricted their ability to cover the news, especially since the State Department arranged for world leaders visiting Washington to deliver speeches there during the Cold War period.[176]

In 1955 the question of admitting women arose during a dispute over the admission of the club's first African American member, Louis Lautier, who represented the National Negro Press Association. While a minority of members opposed Lautier's application, a majority voted for him, contending the club was a professional, not a social, organization.[177] Fifty-four members of the NPC then signed a petition to admit women. Sarah McClendon, whose office was in the National Press Building, submitted an application duly signed by male sponsors. "When it was raining or cold and no restaurant nearby, I often wished I could go upstairs to the Club and get coffee or a sandwich," McClendon said.[178]

Somewhat surprisingly, the effort to admit women died when Liz Carpenter, then president of the WNPC, told James J. Butler, sponsor of the petition, that few WNPC members wanted to join the NPC. Carpenter questioned Butler's motives, since he had voted against the admission of Lautier.[179] Carpenter was quoted as saying, "We don't like being used by the Dixicrats [Southern Democrats against integration]. . . . Why, our organization is much purer than the Press Club. We don't have morticians, patent attorneys and lobbyists on our rolls [a reference to the NPC inclusion of associate members who were nonjournalists]."[180] Meanwhile, the NPC told McClendon that it had never received her application.

In November 1955 the NPC agreed to allow "any member of the working press" to cover luncheon addresses by noteworthy speakers. But women had to stay in the balcony overlooking the dining area and had no access to the food and drink being served below. Hot, crowded, and uncomfortable, the balcony became a symbol to women journalists of their second-class status. Decades later Bonnie Angelo, then with the *Newsday* Washington bureau and subsequently a writer and bureau chief for *Time* magazine, remembered being confined to the balcony "crowded up against Pulitzer Prize winners like Miriam Ottenberg and Marguerite Higgins [who came to the NPC on occasion]. . . . It was hard to hear. It was hard to see. . . . You entered and left through a back door, and you'd be glowered at as you went through the club quarters. It was discrimination at its rawest."[181]

When James Reston, the *New York Times* bureau chief, sent Maggie Hunter, a token woman staff member, to the NPC to cover a speech by Madame Nhu—viewed as the sinister wife of South Vietnam's leader, Ngo Dinh Nhu—Hunter found the balcony experience humiliating. "I stood on a rolled-up carpet in the back of the balcony and I couldn't hear a goddamned word going on down there—I couldn't hear a word," she told Nan Robertson, who wrote a history of sex discrimination at the *Times*.[182] Marching into Reston's office, Hunter "blurted out, 'Scotty, don't you ever send me to that damned National Press Club again.'"[183]

Reston was not sympathetic. He turned to an editor who had known Hunter when they both worked at the *Winston-Salem* (N.C.) *Journal* and asked with an "air of innocent wonderment, 'What's wrong with Maggie?'"[184] In 1969, two years before the NPC finally admitted women, Hunter served as president of the WNPC, which prided itself on inviting male as well as female journalists to its programs.

Newswomen retaliated against the NPC by petitioning speakers not to appear there unless women received dining room privileges. They pressed the issue with the State Department, foreign embassies, and members of Congress. Angelo was among those leading the campaign, which included Gladys Montgomery of McGraw-Hill publishing, Helen Thomas, Frances Lewine of the AP, Patty Cavin of NBC, and Elsie Carper of the *Washington Post*.[185]

Unlike other speakers, Soviet Premier Nikita S. Khrushchev sided with the women. After having been invited to speak at the NPC in 1959, Khrushchev took advantage of the opportunity to publicize American injustice to women as part of Cold War rhetoric.[186] Declaring that he would not speak unless women reporters were treated equally with men, he forced the NPC to allow thirty-three women reporters to have lunch with male members during his address. It highlighted the start of Khrushchev's tour of the United States and represented one of the biggest events in the club's history, although officially billed as a joint effort of the NPC, the WNPC, and the Overseas Press Club of New York.[187] Protesting against the scheduling of Khrushchev at the NPC, Doris Fleeson asked Vice President Richard Nixon to intercede with State Department officials who had "so cavalierly handed us over to the mercy of the NPC with the patronizing remark that we could expect them to be chivalrous."[188]

William H. Lawrence of the *New York Times,* NPC president, reluctantly agreed to abolish sex segregation at the Khrushchev luncheon, claiming "that's the way the Russians wanted it."[189] The club did not. When Molly Thayer, a *Washington Post* reporter, wandered into the NPC bar by mistake on that eventful day, she immediately was escorted out with Lawrence admonishing her to "try to act like a lady if you can while we must have you in here."[190] The furor reached the White House level with James C. Hagerty, press secretary to President Eisenhower, facetiously suggesting a "summit meeting" between Helen Thomas, then the WNPC president, and Lawrence "to blueprint a plan for an auditorium that has no balcony."[191] After the Khrushchev event, the women were relegated again to the balcony, giving rise to additional years of struggle to cover news events at the NPC.

Nevertheless, women were laying siege to the old idea of gender discrimination. One journalist, Vera Glaser of the North American Newspaper Alliance, wrote a poignant news article, commending Khrushchev: "Female writers in Washington had a communist dictator to thank for temporarily lifting them from their second-class status."[192] Spurred by their World War II experience, women journalists were gathering the strength to fight back against injustice, but victory did not come easily.

It was not until 1971 that the NPC finally voted, 227 to 56, to admit women after a contentious club fight. The previous month the WNPC had changed its name to the Washington Press Club (WPC) and decided to take in men. Both clubs operated until 1985 when the WPC merged with the larger NPC, although some WPC members refused to join the NPC on grounds that they had not been wanted there for many years.

FIVE

PARTIES, POWER, AND PROTEST IN THE SIXTIES AND EARLY SEVENTIES

I quickly learned that it was easier to talk my way into some place I didn't belong, grab the President of the United States, and ask him some awful question no one else would dare to, than it was to go back and have to admit to Miss Sauer (we never called her anything else) that I hadn't done it.

—Judith Martin (as quoted in Roberts, In the Shadow of Power, 400)

For many Washington newspaperwomen, the women's and society pages of the capital's three major newspapers, the *Washington Post, Star,* and *Daily News,* represented their professional homes in the mid-twentieth century, whether or not they wanted to be there. For example, at the start of the 1960s some 18 percent of editorial employees at the *Washington Post* were women, most of whom toiled under the dominating gaze of Marie Sauer, the formidable editor of the For and About Women section.[1] Nationally, *Time* reported in 1971 that women accounted for 35 percent of all editorial personnel, with most found working on women's sections or women's magazines.[2] By this time the *Post* had turned its women's pages into a lifestyle section, but other newspapers followed more slowly.

Flush with advertising aimed at women, the standard women's section catered to businesses who cultivated "the domestic consciousness of women in order to boost the consumer sector of a postwar economy," according to one researcher.[3] Regardless of their commercial aspects, the women's pages took seriously the efforts of their reporters, as Martin's recollection of her encounters with Sauer illustrated. Hot-tempered and shorthanded, Sauer dominated her department, cutting off one young woman who tried to say "good morning" with a curt, "We don't have time for that around here."[4] Her reporters, like their counterparts on other newspapers, covered what had been nicknamed the four *F*'s—family, food, fashion, and furnishing. Their beat included the four *F*'s at the White House itself, occasionally giving them an opportunity to question the president himself on a fine point related to entertainment of notable guests.

Ahead of her times, Sauer disagreed with the assumption that men and women had separate news interests divided between "hard" subjects and "soft" subjects. This ideology corresponded roughly to the Victorian idea of the public sphere for men, equated with power and politics, and the private sphere for women, equated with family responsibilities, personal relationships, and social life.[5] In a letter to a journalism student, she wrote that she had objected to the segregation of news at midcentury: "Even though at that time, they [women] weren't ready to be president, the most important issues to them were peace, budget balancing, honesty and efficiency in government, equal pay for equal work. . . . Hard news or soft news? I felt that women wanted both."[6]

Post editors dismissed Sauer's ideas of presenting general news in women's sections because they delivered a targeted audience of consumers to advertisers. Directed to separate, but clearly unequal, audiences, the sections brought in a growing stream of revenue. As sizeable segments of the population forsook the core city of Washington after World War II, advertisers sought to reach women consumers in the new suburbs. *Post* management, like that of other daily newspapers, eagerly provided content geared to advertisers' needs.

When Philip Graham took over the *Post* in 1946 from Eugene Meyer, one of his first acts was to pursue food advertisers by instituting a Friday food page in the women's section.[7] Editors at the *Star* and *Daily News* also favored news centered on traditional feminine pursuits, perceiving women readers as housewives and club members with limited horizons. This content supplied social signifiers of appropriate feminine behaviors.[8] An analysis of the *Post*'s women's section, for example, showed homemaking features jumped from 0.8 percent to 15.6 percent of the total content from 1945 to 1952, while child-care material increased 3.6 percent.[9]

As a result of advertising and editorial strategy, women's sections were restricted in what they wrote about and generally looked down on by male reporters. Men were not wanted as readers. Reporters for the *Post* women's section could cover Coretta King but not Martin Luther King Jr., the Women's Strike for Peace but not student protests.[10] But, because of close ties between Washington's party and political circles, the women's staff sometimes stumbled onto juicy news items as reporters chronicled the capital's dominant social and cultural activities, almost all of which were lily white. Sauer insisted that stories reported by her staff be printed in the women's section, giving rise to an inside joke that if the president resigned while speaking to a women's club, the news would lead the women's pages, not the front page.[11]

Luminaries of society reporting were led by Betty Beale of the *Star,* who promoted her column as "politics after six" and claimed the distinction of being the only syndicated society columnist in Washington.[12] She began her autobiography by noting "for over forty years I spent more time in the White House than in any house but my own."[13] A graduate of Smith College, Beale, a member of a prominent Washington family and the granddaughter of a Tennessee congressman, attended an estimated fifteen thousand parties from the Truman to the Reagan administration, chronicling in her words "the manners, customs and personalities of our times."[14] At the height of her career in the mid-1960s, about ninety newspapers bought her column that specialized in the human-interest aspects of society gatherings, including political comments overheard at parties.[15]

She began her lengthy career at the *Star* in 1945, continuing there until the paper's demise in 1981. At first she wrote who "poured," giving the names of guests honored by being asked to serve coffee or tea at receptions. When she started reporting what people actually said, editors told her "to cool it for a while," convinced that "real news—that is comments by politicos on topics of national or international interest—should not fall into the delicate hands of genteel ladies who wrote for the 'Women's Section,'" Beale recalled.[16] Gradually she won out, becoming a recognized writer of social chit-chat that included political tidbits. She entertained presidents in her home and mingled with monarchs, enjoying a "special bond" with Ethiopian Emperor Haile Selassie because of "the love we shared for Chihuahuas."[17]

At the 1952 Democratic convention Beale met Adlai E. Stevenson, the Illinois governor running for president. The two later engaged in a love affair that lasted until his death in 1965, according to her 1993 memoir, *Power at Play.* She announced her engagement to George Graeber, whom she married in 1969, in her column, calling herself "Washington's biggest party trotter"; the couple soon was feted at a White House luncheon.[18] While Beale's column rarely criticized those she wrote about, during the Eisenhower years Beale raised White House ire by reporting as a "pleasant surprise" that "Ike" served hard liquor at an afternoon diplomatic reception in contrast to the traditional bourbon-laced fruit punch.[19] This disclosure created storms of protest from non-drinkers, and hard liquor never appeared again at functions where reporters were present, Beale, herself a nondrinker, noted.[20]

Beale's greatest rival, Maxine Cheshire, an investigative reporter from Kentucky, became a society reporter for the *Post* in 1954 because it was the only job she could get.[21] Like Sauer's other reporters, she looked for links between parties and politics, eventually writing a VIP (Very Important People) column loaded with political gossip. Cheshire faulted the Washington press for failing to raise questions about Mamie Eisenhower's acceptance of gifts from foreign governments, criticizing what she called the "Emily Post approach to reporting about the occupants of the White House."[22] Cheshire lamented she was limited to writing "scoops" about a discount factory where the First Lady bought evening slippers to dye to match her gowns.[23]

At the same time, Cheshire appreciated the professionalism that Sauer brought to the *Post*'s women's section and relished the insights into Washington power provided by careful study of its social scene. She said, "If a reader was sufficiently sophisticated, knew enough about the way this city operated, then the women's pages of the *Washington Post* held more inside information than any other section . . . a close reading of who went where and with whom generally proved quite instructive."[24]

While Beale enjoyed the prestige of high-level social contacts and Cheshire chafed at constrains, another woman reporter encountered outright hostility. Ethel Payne, the granddaughter of slaves, arrived in the capital in 1954 to take over the one-person bureau of the *Chicago Defender,* an African American newspaper. A native of Chicago, Payne had stumbled into journalism during the Korean War when she worked as a hostess in an Army Special Services club in Japan, organizing recreation for African American troops. After she showed her diary to a visiting *Defender* reporter, he arranged for his newspaper to print excerpts about discrimination faced by black soldiers. Readers wanted more, although the U.S. government complained that Payne disrupted troop morale.[25] The *Defender* editor called Payne in Japan and offered her a job, which she accepted.

In Washington Payne recognized that the battle for civil rights constituted the biggest story of the era for African Americans. As an accredited correspondent, she attended President Eisenhower's press conferences and raised pointed questions. When the Interstate Commerce Commission ruled against segregation in interstate travel, Payne asked the president, "When can we expect that you will issue an executive order ending segregation in interstate travel?"[26] Eisenhower barked back, "What makes you think I'm going to do anything for any special-interest group?"[27]

Instead of dealing with the issue involved, the press pictured the exchange as a slap at Payne. The *Star* headlined it in a front-page box, captioned, "Negro Woman Reporter Angers Ike."[28] The *Defender* applauded her efforts, but other newspapers did not. "I was pilloried by the black press as being over-assertive," Payne said later.[29] "They wrote columns about it, that I was an embarrassment, that I had gone down and I was showboating, just disturbing the President."[30]

Eisenhower retaliated by refusing to call on her at press conferences. His press secretary, James Hagerty, threatened to withdraw her credentials on grounds she worked part time for the Congress of Industrial Organizations (CIO), violating a rule against accredited correspondents engaging in political activities.[31] Payne countered that she was a full-time correspondent and no longer worked for the CIO.[32] Hagerty stopped his attack only after Drew Pearson reported in his syndicated column that the press secretary had harassed Payne by attempting to investigate her income tax returns.[33]

Although it was not until 1961 that segregation was outlawed on buses and trains, Payne felt that her controversial question aided integration. "Suddenly, civil rights began to be the big issue," she said.[34] From her Washington base she subsequently traveled throughout the South, covering the Montgomery bus boycott and desegregation efforts at public schools and universities, profiling Rev. Martin Luther King Jr., and writing a notable *Defender* series on "The South at the Crossroads." She also traveled to Africa to report on liberation movements there, gaining the title, "First lady of the black press."[35]

Following John F. Kennedy's election as president in 1960, most Washington women reporters, unlike Payne, had little to do with civil rights issues, although they increasingly dominated the national agenda. One who did, both personally and professionally, was Dorothy Gilliam, the first African American woman journalist hired by the *Post*. Gilliam, one of two African Americans in the class of 1961 at the Columbia University School of Journalism, impressed Ben Gilbert, the *Post* city editor, who routinely interviewed Columbia graduates for jobs.[36] After she wrote reports for the *Post* from Africa, where she went on a fellowship following Columbia, Gilbert offered her a job.

Gilliam, whose maiden name was Butler, was the eighth of ten children (only five of whom survived), the daughter of an African Methodist Episcopal Church minister. When he became ill, the family struggled economically, moving from Louisville to rural Kentucky and existing as sharecroppers. After graduation from a segregated rural high school, she won a scholarship to help integrate Ursuline College, a women's school in Louisville, which she attended for two years. Gaining initial journalistic experience on the *Louisville Defender,* an African American newspaper, she obtained a bachelor's degree in journalism in 1957 from Lincoln University in Jefferson City, Missouri, a historically black institution. She worked two years for an African American company, Johnson Publications in Chicago, becoming an editor of *Jet* magazine before enrolling at Columbia.[37]

No stranger to inequality, she nevertheless found it taxing to keep a calm demeanor at the *Post.* Washington itself, still a segregated city, raised barriers against her. As one of three African American reporters working for the *Post,* she experienced countless indignities. "There were lots of restaurants around here [the *Post* building] that I couldn't eat at," she said. "Remember, the Civil Rights Act didn't pass until 1964."[38] To make her feel more at home, Gilbert asked Elsie Carper to go to lunch with her. The two ate at a YWCA cafeteria, one of the few integrated restaurants nearby.[39] When Gilliam was assigned to stories in all-white neighborhoods, doormen tried to steer her from front doors to servants' entrances. Taxicabs passed her by, unwilling to stop for a black woman who drivers assumed wanted to go to black neighborhoods where they had little chance of getting return fares to downtown.

In addition, after she married an artist—Sam Gilliam, who later won acclaim for his work—in 1962 and had a daughter the next year, she found her working environment uncongenial: "It was a place that was very kind of overwhelmingly white male and relatively few women," she said a half century later. "Not the kinds of women you have in newsrooms today ... women who are in active numbers, pursuing their career, having children and families. I don't know of any woman in the newsroom—I don't know about the women's section (that's what it was called in those days)—who really had any children."[40] After her daughter's birth, Gilliam received permission to work less than full time, but it was withdrawn after other reporters complained that she was getting special treatment, an objection she considered "very typical of attitudes toward women and children."[41]

Gilliam gained recognition for her articles on Junior Village, an appalling facility for homeless children controlled by District of Columbia committees in Congress. In a late stage of pregnancy she covered a visit to the institution by Virginia Sen. William F. Byrd, one of its congressional overseers and a well-known segregationist. "He reached back and helped me across—I don't know if it was a ditch or a divide or something," she said. "I remember remarking to somebody, 'I bet I was the first black woman he had ever held his hand out to help or escort,'" she told an oral history interviewer.[42]

When the *Post* sent Gilliam to Oxford, Mississippi, to cover the riots stemming from James Meredith's integration of the University of Mississippi in 1962, she stayed at a black funeral home because there were no accommodations for African Americans, while the white *Post* reporter also sent to Oxford checked into a motel.[43] At the funeral home, she learned that two African Americans had been killed "during the night, and we figured out that these [murders] were the warning to the local black community ... this is to let you know who's still boss, who still runs things."[44] Expecting her second child, she left the newspaper in 1965, although she returned to the *Post* in the years ahead.

White women reporters had relatively little opportunity to cover civil rights stories. One who did, Susanna McBee, was among the few women on the *Post*'s city staff in the late 1950s and early 1960s. McBee, who had been the first nonwartime woman editor of the University of Southern California's *Daily Trojan,* was hired as a *Post* news aide in 1956. She advanced to the rank of reporter the following year after writing book reviews and volunteering to take night assignments. She covered school desegregation cases in Northern Virginia and a lunch counter sit-in demonstration there in June 1960. Taken off the sit-in story when the *Post* city editor told her it was "too dangerous" for a woman to handle, she used her reportorial contacts to find out by telephone when the lunch counter event would happen and was the only reporter to cover it, scooping the rest of the press corps with a page one story.

After taking a leave in 1961–62 to earn a master's degree in political science at the University of Chicago, McBee went back to the *Post* planning to cover the massive civil rights march on Washington in August 1963 but was suddenly taken off that story. "I had spent months as the only reporter going to New York nearly every weekend with a D.C. local delegation making plans for the demonstration with national civil rights leaders including Rev. Martin Luther King Jr.," she said.[45] This time the city editor told her he did not want her to endure the hassles she would face attending a press conference by A. Philip Randolph, one of the march organizers, at the National Press Club, since she would be confined to the balcony and forbidden from asking questions.

McBee was outraged that the *Post* would not fight the NPC discrimination. "My career was suffering," she said.[46] The incident angered Elsie Carper, who had just been installed as president of the WNPC, propelling her to intensify the club's campaign to persuade political figures not to speak at the NPC. After persisting in following civil rights cases and covering Senate passage of the 1964 Civil Rights Act, McBee left the *Post* in 1965 for *Life* magazine's Washington bureau, where she won awards for disclosing dangerous practices of the diet pill industry.

In contrast to Gilliam, many women reporters received traditional assignments in the 1960s. Those assigned to the White House followed the photogenic activities of Jackie Kennedy and her children, who were prominently featured in women's sections nationally. Helen Thomas of UPI and her rival, Frances Lewine of the AP, matched wits with the First Lady, who wanted press coverage on her own terms, while they sought to feed public appetite for endless detail about the First Family. "She's such a good reporter everyone forgets she's a woman," a male broadcaster said of Lewine.[47]

A virtual godsend to the women's press corps, Jackie furnished copious amounts of copy. Her elaborate parties, White House redecorating, trend-setting fashions, youthful glamour, jet-set lifestyle, appealing small children, and even their pets—all made news—some of which the First Lady resented. Dorothy McCardle, a *Post* social writer, incurred Jackie's enmity for reporting that the White House curator had slapped the hands of little Caroline Kennedy when she touched antiques on display.[48] A grandmotherly looking woman, married to Carl McCardle, a journalist who served as an assistant secretary of state during the Eisenhower administration, McCardle, who joined the *Post* in 1960, saw herself as a reporter, not a guest, at the White House. She had a background in journalism that dated back to her first job at the *Philadelphia Inquirer* in 1924, where she covered crime.

As Thomas noted, "The irony is that Jackie Kennedy unwittingly gave a tremendous lift to me and many other women reporters in Washington by escalating our beat . . . to instantaneous front-age news."[49] Eleanor Roosevelt's liberal good works had drawn headlines, but Jackie's celebrity looks and status offered even more. "One biting quip from Jackie or a spill from a horse could launch a thousand headlines," Thomas said.[50]

Jackie offered little cooperation, informing her inexperienced press secretary, Pamela Turnure, rumored to have been one of Jack Kennedy's numerous romantic interests, "My press relations will be minimum information given with maximum politeness."[51] Yet, Jackie was the first president's wife to name a press secretary. In spite of her hostility to the press except when she wanted to publicize specific activities, she made the White House such a magnet for reporters that "a lot of women started going there every day learning on the job what to do," according to Winzola McLendon, a social reporter for the *Post*.[52]

Privately, Jackie referred to female reporters as "harpies," whose obtrusive presence marred her elegant entertaining.[53] In a memo seen by Esther Van Wagoner Tufty, Jackie, who preferred that reporters stay out of sight behind pillars and potted palms, caustically suggested "keeping the harpies at bay by stationing a couple of guards with bayonets near them."[54] President Kennedy on the other hand recognized the importance of the women on the political scene. Tufty claimed that on one occasion he took hold of his wife "very hard" and told her to "say hello to the girls, darling," referring to the social reporters, leaving "the imprint of his hand in her flesh."[55]

Jackie particularly disliked Thomas and Lewine, whose wire service jobs required them to keep close tabs on her movements. One Sunday she took revenge on the women as they stood watch outside while she attended a church service in Florida, reporting to the Secret Service that she was being followed by "two strange

Spanish-looking women."[56] As a result the two were briefly arrested. Thomas noted this as "a brilliant carom shot since Fran is Jewish and I'm of Arab descent."[57] Both women gained professionally from their assiduous coverage of the First Lady. Each moved up in her news organizations and won the opportunity to cover the president as well as his wife.

President Kennedy befriended women reporters when Bonnie Angelo, president of the WNPC in 1961–62, fought to open the annual all-male White House Correspondents' Association Dinner to women members of the organization. Angelo's career in the capital dated back to the 1950s when she worked in the Washington bureau of *Newsday* alongside her husband, Hal Levy, the bureau chief. Impressed with Angelo's feature-writing skills, Alicia Patterson, the founder of *Newsday*, had assigned the couple to the capital after employing both in *Newsday*'s home office on Long Island. The two had married after a newsroom romance while working on the *Winston-Salem Journal* (N.C.).

In her WNPC role, Angelo campaigned against the scheduling of speakers at the NPC in spite of its discriminatory policy against women reporters as well as battling for their right to attend the White House Correspondents' Association Dinner. She was one of a small group of reporters who took up the dinner issue with Pierre Salinger, President Kennedy's press secretary. "He got President Kennedy to say, to let it be known, not to announce but to let it be known that he was not going to the dinner if women members were not allowed," she said.[58]

The club changed its policy, and Angelo found herself sitting at the head table with Kennedy for the "jolliest of all nights."[59] But, she added, "I was assailed by men reporters; some of them who I thought were friends."[60] Clark Mollenhoff, an investigative reporter, told her that his secretary did not think women should go to the dinner. "I said, Clark, we're not concerned with your secretary; we're concerned with women who are journalists and who have the qualifications to be White House correspondents. . . . This was a rough time," Angelo said.[61]

After the assassination of President Kennedy in November 1963, women journalists found themselves covering a far different kind of White House presided over by a First Lady who herself had a degree in journalism. Lady Bird Johnson, a graduate of the University of Texas, and her husband, Lyndon Johnson, recognized the value of the women's press corps in publicizing administration activities. Far from talking about "harpies," Lady Bird patterned herself after Eleanor Roosevelt and became an advocate for causes, particularly those related to increased environmental awareness.

Under the direction of Liz Carpenter, who served as her capable press secretary, Lady Bird staged event after event and trip after trip that engaged her press corps. As Thomas recalled, "Climbing mountains pursued by gnats, riding Snake River Rapids in Wyoming, watching from the beaches as she—not I—snorkeled in the barracuda-filled Caribbean, bobbing in a flotilla of rubber rafts down the Rio Grande . . . no newswoman wanted to be left behind when Lady Bird set out on her adventures."[62] Some seventy reporters joined the First Lady for a raft trip down the Rio Grande in Texas as part of her campaign to promote environment issues.

Her efforts received the trivializing name of *beautification*. According to Lewis Gould, a historian of first ladies, use of the term showed the constraints on women in public life in the 1960s, since Lady Bird Johnson had no real choice except to accept the "attribution of inferiority toward women that the word beautification implied."[63] Newspapers shortened the term to *beauty* to fit into headlines, further diluting her advocacy of conservation.

The *Star,* for example, headlined a typical beautification story by Betty Beale, A PLEA FOR U.S. BEAUTY, and ran it on the front page of its society/home section, with the headline FIRST LADY DISCUSSES BEAUTY marking the continuation of the story on an inside page.[64] Lady Bird's campaign, which resulted in flower- and tree-planting projects in the city of Washington, paid for by private funds, also involved backing federal legislation, the Highway Beautification Act of 1965, to regulate billboards along highways.

By the time Lyndon Johnson left office in 1969, women's sections, where most of the beautification coverage was centered, were coming under increasing attack for failing to do serious reporting on women's lives. Whether focused on the White House or on the parties of famous hostesses, Washington's women's and society pages pictured aspects of life removed from the experiences of most women. In 1961, for example, the ANWC with its large contingent of society and women's page reporters as well as socially prominent hostesses, held a "Gala Garden Party" on July 11 at Hillwood, the grand Washington estate owned by Marjorie Merriweather Post, one of the world's richest women.

Other club events that year included a reception for opera stars and a festive Christmas party in the eighth-floor lounge of the State Department, an impressive area usually reserved for important foreign dignitaries.[65] In addition, the club held parties for authors and a reception for Letitia Baldridge, Jackie Kennedy's social secretary, at its stately headquarters, a turn-of-the-century townhouse near fashionable Dupont Circle.[66] It entertained the women members of Congress at a reception at the U.S. Capitol and put on a "Fashion Spectacular" at the historic Willard Hotel.[67]

Some members oriented to general news complained that the club was unprofessional in its pursuits, but it continued to plan events featuring celebrities and political figures, which it publicized in women's and society sections. In 1964–65 it counted 420 members, with one associate member for every two working professionals.[68] Associate members included wives of current and former diplomats and current and former members of Congress, as well as congresswomen themselves and the highest-ranking women in the military.[69] Sarah McClendon, who as president in 1960 had overseen purchase of the club's handsome clubhouse, expressed concern in 1969 over the club's image as a social organization and called for more attention to professional achievement.[70] The heyday of Washington social coverage was about to end, in response to women's changing roles.

Newspapers were slow to recognize that an increasing number of women, mothers as well as wives, were working outside the home. Nationally women workers increased from 24 percent of the total employed in 1940 to 32 percent in 1960, with both husband and wife working in more than 10 million homes by 1960, although women often worked part time.[71] Widespread use of the birth control pill and other forms of contraception altered women's lives at the same time life expectancy was increasing. Betty Friedan's best-selling book, *The Feminine Mystique,* published in 1963, tapped into anxieties of middle-class life, charging that mainstream media, particularly magazines, brainwashed women into accepting a narrow world of housewifery, subordination, and stifled ambitions.[72] The two major Washington newspapers, the *Post* and the *Star,* as well as the *New York Times,* did not even review the book.

The social movement that culminated with passage of the Civil Rights Act of 1964 directly fueled protest activities known as women's liberation, which included criticism of women's and society sections. Ironically, a Virginia congressman, eighty-one-year-old Howard W. Smith, tried to block the act's passage by adding the word "sex" to Title VII, which outlawed employment discrimination on the basis of "race, color, religion, or national origin." Smith hoped to ridicule and defeat the legislation by including women. His attempt, which insiders tagged the "May Craig Amendment," in honor of Craig's well-known views on equal rights, backfired. Sen. Hubert Humphrey of Minnesota assured Craig, a regular panelist on *Meet the Press,* by then a televised press conference program, that the Democratic leadership in Congress backed the legislation.[73]

Even though initial coverage of women's liberation activities took place in women's sections, the National Organization of Women (NOW), founded in 1966 by Friedan and others as the nation's largest feminist organization, complained that these sections ghettoized news of women. NOW's campaign against employment discrimination struck at the wage differential common between men and women reporters, particularly pronounced on women's section staffs. As part of women's liberation, feminists attacked the assumption that men and women should occupy separate, and unequal, spheres within journalism.

In 1962 Katharine Graham, described as a shy housewife, took over as head of the *Post* following her husband's suicide, becoming the most prominent woman in journalism, not only in Washington but in the United States. As a publisher, Graham, like Patterson before her, made crucial decisions but left implementation to key male editors. As she felt her way forward, she aimed to enhance the renown of the *Post* as a watchdog of the political scene, including its social side. "In most places in America nobody cares what the upper crust does anymore," she said. "Here, because the upper crust is basically political, everyone cares."[74]

Nevertheless, the *Post*'s women's section was transformed into a trend-setting feature section, Style, in 1969, after Graham hired a brash, innovative editor, Ben Bradlee. He joined the newspaper in 1965, pushing Sauer into retirement. Bradlee was convinced that "traditional women's news bored the ass off all of us."[75] He envisioned Style as featuring profiles, cultural trends, the arts, and reviews.

The shift to Style represented only one of the major decisions taken at the *Post* under Graham's leadership. In 1971 she boldly decided to publish the Pentagon Papers, a secret account of how the United States became involved in the Vietnam War. It had been appearing in the *New York Times* in spite of legal efforts by the Nixon administration to restrict publication on grounds of national security. The *Post*'s lawyers argued against publication, especially since the company was getting ready to sell its stock publicly, while its editors wanted to proceed. Graham recalled herself being frightened and tense as she "took a big gulp" and said, "Go ahead."[76] Fortunately, the U.S. Supreme Court ruled in favor of the newspapers.

The next year Graham committed the newspaper to controversial coverage of the Watergate scandal, a saga of political corruption that ended with the resignation of President Richard M. Nixon in 1974. The scandal unraveled after burglars were arrested for breaking into the Democratic National Committee headquarters at Washington's posh Watergate complex in 1972. Due partly to the exhaustive work of two *Post* reporters, Bob Woodward and Carl Bernstein, the burglars were tied to the White House. Investigation of the break-in, part of a widespread scheme to reelect Nixon, led to Attorney General John Mitchell making threats against Graham herself. He screamed at Bernstein that if he printed a story on a secret campaign fund, "Katie Graham's gonna get her tit caught in a big fat wringer."[77]

The Nixon administration put intense pressure, economic and psychological, on the *Post* to cease its coverage, resulting in a decline in its stock value. Even social news was affected. The White House cut off Dorothy McCardle's access to evening entertainment for twenty-eight days in 1972 in retaliation for *Post* reporting about Watergate. The ban was lifted only after Isabelle Shelton, McCardle's counterpart at the *Star,* decided to boycott any event that McCardle could not attend in a show of solidarity.[78] While it was in effect, McCardle, in the words of Graham, was left "cooling her heels in her evening dress all alone in the White House press room while parties went on without her."[79]

As Graham described it, "Of all the threats to the company during Watergate—the attempts to undermine our credibility, the petty slights, and the favoring of the competition—the most effective were the challenges to the licenses of our two Florida television stations."[80] Eventually, the challenges failed. Although Nixon easily won reelection, he resigned rather than be impeached after the disclosure of White House tapes that revealed his complicity in illegal activities, including a cover-up of the Watergate burglary. The *Post* won a Pulitzer Prize in 1973 for public service in exposing Watergate-linked corruption. A Hollywood movie, *All the President's Men,* based on Woodward and Bernstein's book about Watergate, further publicized the *Post*'s role in Watergate and dramatized investigative reporting.

Except for Graham, all the leading characters were men, showing the male domination of reporting and editing in Washington during the Watergate period. In her autobiography Graham said her relationship with Bradlee "was solidified forever by Watergate," in spite of "numerous sexist comments."[81] She wrote that she had complained to the editor of the *Boston Globe* about a news article on Bradlee, asking, "Why is it if a female publisher and a male editor get along, he is accused of stroking and she of being susceptible to manipulation?"[82]

Graham's ascension to power initially made little difference to most women journalists in the capital. A count of women at the *Post* in 1970 revealed 33 women among 272 reporters, columnists, and editors, while of the 14 editors and 22 reporters on the national desk, only 2 were women.[83] The *Daily News* had a little better percentage—10 women out of a staff of 54, while the *Star* counted 63 women out of an editorial staff of 256, but the numbers included secretaries, aides, and others not actually employed as reporters or editors.[84]

In 1969, when the *Post* became the first newspaper to actually eliminate its women's section, it struck some readers as odd that its new Style section, which at first almost ignored women's news, appeared in a newspaper controlled by a woman.[85] Bradlee, former Washington bureau chief of *Newsweek,* thought differently. "I don't think in this day and age that women's interests are different from men's," he said. "I think it's insulting to infer that they are interested only in recipes, lovelorn problems, and where Mrs. Merriweather Post danced last night."[86] The counterculture of the 1960s as well as the women's movement influenced the change. It was illustrated by the lead story on the front page of the first issue of Style, an account of a twenty-six-year-old woman kidnapper written by a youthful woman staff writer who used unisex initials, B. J. Phillips.[87]

The first renditions of Style featured male editors except for Elsie Carper, who had a short unsuccessful tenure, and a colorful male columnist, Nicholas von Hoffman. Described as "an aging flower child," he favored the "groovy, sexy, beautiful, swinging, mellow, hip and hep."[88] His voice did not appeal to the multitude. Graham said she was willing to stand by him because he interested the "young and black whom we need to attract," but she did not want Style to appeal only to minority readers.[89] As a woman herself, she missed some of the content of the old women's pages, writing to Bradlee, "Clothes, fashions, interiors and the frothy side . . . are all taking a hosing . . . I am quite fed up with the really heedless eggheadedness of Style."[90] Bradlee retorted, "I can't edit this section unless you get your finger out of my eye."[91]

Eventually Style settled down, in part by covering social activities from a sharp-edged perspective offered by Sally Quinn. Bradlee hired Quinn, the young, unemployed daughter of a general, on the strength of her family connections. Her only previous journalistic venture was the article HOW TO WOO WASHINGTON MEN in the *Washington Post* magazine, written with the help of *New York Post* reporter Warren Hoge, to whom she was engaged at one point.[92] Far from flattering her hosts with what she called the "sycophantic, fawning" social reporting of the past, Quinn saw society and celebrities through a critical lens.[93]

"I covered parties the way they were, not the way the hostess wanted them to be covered. I covered them the way someone on the 'Metro' section covers a crime," Quinn commented.[94] Soon she was no longer welcome at embassy and socialite affairs, but her stories, allowed to run longer than those of many other Style staffers, attracted an audience. Quinn became Bradlee's third wife in 1978.

Style continued to have some women columnists and reporters, including those who had worked under Sauer, but typical social fare almost disappeared to the glee of the *Star.* Gwen Dobson, the *Star*'s women's editor who headed a staff of nineteen, claimed the *Star*'s circulation jumped markedly.[95] Under the direction of a male editor, Tom Kendrick, and an assistant editor, Mary Wiegers, described as a bright, pretty young reporter, Style resumed some society news in the early 1970s to compete with the *Star,* which, as two social reporters expressed it, "informed the reader right along every afternoon which parties would have been the right ones to be at the previous evening."[96] Jacqueline Trescott, one observer said, in an effort to gain African American readers for Style, "ground out frequent dull stories on such subjects as black society parties and sorority balls."[97] Most journalists working for Style, however, showed little interest in being typecast as traditional social reporters.

Less willing to be in awe of president's wives than in the past, some women reporters detected false notes in the performance of Richard Nixon's wife, Pat. Helen Thomas saw the First Lady reach out for a glass of sherry, then pull her hand back when she realized that newswomen were watching her. Thomas wanted to tell her to take the drink, but realized that Pat Nixon "had been brought up in the old school that first ladies have NO 'bad habits.' "[98] When Beale interviewed Pat Nixon on "the real Richard Nixon," the First Lady pictured her husband as "considerate, kind and gentle," dismaying Beale, who had hoped that "she would find some fault with him" for the sake of both credibility and, one assumes, an interesting column.[99]

In addition to Beale, the *Star* featured columnist Ymelda Dixon, the widow of George Dixon, a political humorist. She reported on embassy parties, refusing to drop in for cocktails before any dinner to which she was not invited. "I'd feel like a servant if I did," she said.[100] Another prominent staff member, Eleni, the fashion editor, was the wife of the *Star*'s managing editor, Sidney Epstein. Because the newspaper had a policy against staff members marrying, the two had to get special permission from management to proceed with the wedding. As a fashion arbiter, Eleni protested the cliché that Washington women looked dowdy, insisting that political transplants usually sharpened their appearances and wardrobes "once their figures and faces start appearing in the newspapers."[101] She said she gave them six months "to get the message."[102]

And that they usually did, rising to their new status with new wardrobes that made copy for the women's pages.

Another well-known *Star* stalwart on Dobson's staff, Isabelle Shelton, gained an exclusive interview with President Lyndon Johnson on the same day as her daughter celebrated her fourteenth birthday. Unfortunately for Shelton, the president insisted that she accompany him to a wedding in Maryland and complete the interview in his limousine while en route back to the White House.[103] Frantic to get home to oversee preparations for her daughter's birthday party, Shelton begged Johnson to let her out as his motorcade neared her neighborhood, making her, according to the rest of the press corps, "the only reporter in history who voluntarily broke off an interview with the President."[104] The incident underscored the difficulties in combining reporting with motherhood, an issue that was to get more attention in the decades ahead.

By the time Style was well established, the *Star*'s glory days were numbered. In 1970 it failed to make a profit for the first time, impelling it to buy out its afternoon competitor, the *Daily News,* in 1972. The combined *Star-News* continued to lose millions, prompting its family owners, principally the Noyes and Kauffmann families, to sell the property to Joe L. Allbritton, a Texas millionaire in 1974. Afternoon newspapers in general were declining due to competition from television and suburban development that complicated delivery problems.

For all of its quirks, Style attracted the attention of other newspaper editors who transformed their women's pages into lifestyle sections, hoping to attract male as well as female readers while responding to the women's movement. For example, The *Los Angeles Times* replaced its women's pages with View, while the *New York Times* renamed its Food, Fashion, Family and Furnishings section into Family/Style. The *Star* itself followed the trend, introducing its Portfolio section to counter Style.

The change from women's pages to lifestyle sections did not necessarily mean a gain for women in terms of coverage. News of the women's movement tended to be squeezed out of lifestyle sections, yet not printed in general news columns. At the *Post* Bradlee showed little interest in the women's movement, although Sauer's For and About Women carefully followed federal policy on the status of women.[105]

Reflecting on the change in 1979, Peggy Simpson, a longtime AP staffer, commented, "Many veterans of the women's movement credit Elizabeth Shelton of *The Washington Post* [no kin to Isabelle Shelton] with having written the most comprehensive and thoroughly researched articles on the mid-1960s's emergence of the Status of Women commissions . . . in every state of the country."[106] With Style on the scene, the *Post* "literally abandoned any systematic coverage of the women's movement."

Quinn, the controversial Style star, blamed women for their own problems. "There are so many jealous bitches," she told an interviewer for *Editor and Publisher,* a trade magazine.[107] "Just let one woman rise from the crowd and other women delight in tearing her down. Those Libbers who make the most noise get nowhere. And those of us who rise above them are the quietest."[108]

By no means did the creation of lifestyle sections mean more jobs for women journalists and editors, some of whom were forced into retirement, like Sauer, or pushed aside. Style cost women four jobs in two years, according to a group of women who organized to protest sex discrimination at the *Post* in 1972.[109] They noted that there had not been a compensating increase in women hired for other sections of the newspaper.[110] Feminist critics complained also that the focus on entertainment in lifestyle sections resulted in bland content that shied away from serious discussion of sexual and reproductive controversies, lesbian issues, alternatives to conventional marriage, and feminism as it affected women of color. While the front pages depended mainly on official sources for news, usually white males, lifestyle sections, like their predecessors, were not above using press releases from corporations seeking women consumers.[111]

As professionals who subscribed to the ideology of keeping themselves out of the stories and simply reporting what others were saying and doing, Washington women journalists themselves had a difficult time with the women's movement. Women's liberation, with its emphasis on careers outside the home, equal employment opportunities, and an end to a subordinate status to men, puzzled the news media in general, according to David Broder, the *Post*'s Pulitzer Prize–winning political columnist. While it was a political movement, it did not fit within the confines of routine newspaper beats: politics, education, police, courts, labor, etc. "We remain trapped in the assumptions and parochial limitations of our regular beats and the conventional thinking of the institutions and people we regularly cover," Broder wrote.[112]

Coverage of the movement eventually centered on the fight for ratification of the Equal Rights Amendment (ERA) and political stories that showed women flexing political muscle. These included attention to new political organizations that pushed female candidates such as NOW and the National Women's Political Caucus. Kay Mills, at the time a reporter in the Newhouse Washington bureau, wrote later that reporting on these groups and the women candidates they backed allowed her to get into political coverage, since "male reporters wrote all the key campaign stories on male candidates," and "politics was the only language my bureau chief understood."[113]

While concerned about maintaining their objectivity as professional journalists, a handful of Washington women reporters were pivotal in publicizing the women's movement. Mills said they "were at the seat of political power and they worked for news organizations with power."[114] She recalled that the group included Eileen Shanahan at the *New York Times* bureau, Shelton at the *Star,* Frances Lewine and Peggy Simpson at the AP, Marlene Cimons at the *Los Angeles Times* bureau, Sara Fritz at UPI, and Barbara Katz at the *National Journal.*[115]

It was not easy to push Washington news aimed at women, as press secretaries for First Ladies discovered after the conversion of women's pages into lifestyle sections. Instead of having a reserved spot on women's pages, stories vied for space based on the standard elements of political intrigue—conflict, controversy, criticism, gossip, use of unnamed sources, human nature oddities. During President Jimmy Carter's administration, Rosalynn Carter described herself as "crushed" when the *Washington Post* did not cover the formation of the President's Commission on Mental Health, which she headed.[116] Instead, it featured her decision as First Lady to omit hard liquor at state dinners and compared her to "Lemonade Lucy," the nickname given to the pious Lucy Hayes, wife of President Rutherford B. Hayes, who refused to serve alcoholic beverages in 1877.

None of the women identified by Mills were political columnists per se like Fleeson and Higgins, but all very likely had personal experiences that attuned them to the subject of discrimination. Cimons, for instance, came to Washington in 1969 to cover Southern Californians for the *Los Angeles Times.* As the first woman in the *Times'* bureau, Cimons, a graduate of Syracuse University, was assigned generally to social reporting. "I really found it a rather tedious and shallow field mostly because I wanted to be doing more substantive reporting," she said.[117]

Although she produced an award-winning series on the post-traumatic stress disorder afflicting Vietnam veterans, her editors in Los Angeles "still were gripped by traditional values of partying and socializing," she said.[118] "I had to prove that I could cover what the guys were covering."[119] On one occasion she answered the telephone in the bureau and told a caller that the reporter he wanted to speak to was not there. The caller then asked for another journalist, who also was absent, and ended up with, "Well, is anybody there?" to which she replied, "Sure, can I help you? I'm here," and he said, "No, I mean a reporter."[120] Had she been a male, the caller would have assumed she was a reporter. Cimons was not promoted to covering national news until the 1980s.[121]

Only a few Washington women journalists, primarily Marianne Means and Mary McGrory, occupied the political columnist category in the 1960s and 1970s, paying varying amounts of attention to the feminist movement as they pursued national stories on male political figures. Marianne Means worked for Hearst's King Features syndicate, while Mary McGrory's column for the *Star* also was sold to other newspapers. Means viewed the small number of women columnists as evidence of discrimination, but McGrory displayed a different attitude, contending that it was up to each individual to prove herself a capable journalist.[122]

Means, said by some peers to look "like the actress a casting agency would pick to play a glamorous girl columnist in Washington," decided to come to the capital after giving Sen. John F. Kennedy a ride to the airport when he campaigned for the presidency in Lincoln, Nebraska.[123] A journalism graduate of the University of Nebraska, Means landed a job as women's editor of the *Northern*

Virginia Sun, a suburban newspaper owned by prominent individuals with good political connections. Eventually she moved to the Hearst Washington bureau, explaining to readers five decades later in her final column for Hearst, "Luckily, I was assigned to cover the 1960 campaign of Sen. John F. Kennedy—the bureau was very short-staffed at the time, and my salary was peanuts.... The betting in the press corps was that the more experienced Vice President Richard Nixon would win."[124]

Contemporaries said Means incurred the envy of other journalists when Kennedy got off his boat while vacationing at Cape Cod and addressed only her by name out of a crowd of a hundred waiting reporters and photographers.[125] As she looked back over her career, she said that when Kennedy actually won the presidency, "the startled Hearst bureau looked around and decided to take a chance on a young woman who could write and who knew some of Kennedy's aides and the president himself."[126]

Remaining a White House correspondent during the Johnson years before becoming a political columnist, Means, accompanied by her husband, visited the Johnsons at their Texas ranch, and she joined them at Camp David for several weekends without her presence being announced. One of a group of journalists whom the president took for a car ride on his ranch, Means said accounts of her drinking beer while "batting my blue eyes" at Johnson were fabrications because she hated beer and was "sitting in the back seat."[127] According to Means, she did not use her proximity to presidents to gain information for news stories aside from anecdotes and background material.[128]

In the early 1960s, Means said, "I was usually the only woman in press gatherings and news events [involving the president]."[129] "The upside was that they all knew who I was."[130] But, she continued, "The downside was all the unwelcome late night telephone calls from married Big Deal males seeking companionship on the cheap for an hour."[131]

Lamenting the fact that the Hearst organization had no Washington outlet, which meant that her work did not necessarily reach government officials, Means, whose column appeared in some 129 newspapers by 1970, hoped that the *Post* would pick up it up, but that did not happen. At the time Means said that editors had "a hard time taking a young woman seriously."[132] She told an interviewer, "All I want is to have access to the same sources the men do."[133] She specifically referred to a series of breakfast meetings with cabinet members and other dignitaries organized by a reporter for the *Christian Science Monitor* who said "to my face he simply doesn't want a woman there, and that's unfair."[134] She added, "I wish I could remember who first said, 'You have to act like a lady, look like a girl, think like a man, and work like a dog.'"[135] She continued her column until her retirement in 2008.

Mary McGrory occupied a special place in Washington journalism for two decades before gaining national recognition with a Pulitzer Prize for Commentary in 1975. Her column appeared in some forty newspapers and many considered her Washington's top woman reporter.[136] Following the direction of her *Star* editor to write her column "like a letter to your favorite aunt," McGrory captivated readers with her "lovely flow of prose," as John Hohenberg, the administrator of the Pulitzer Prizes, commented, while praising McGrory for her "gift of language."[137] Contending that "the admiration that has come to her professionally has nothing to do with her womanhood," Hohenberg noted that her colleagues "seldom admit privately, whatever they may say in public, that a woman journalist can be as good as a man."[138]

According to McGrory, it was only during the unsuccessful Democratic presidential campaign of 1968 by Sen. Eugene Mc-

Carthy that she felt accepted as a political columnist. She said McCarthy's young aides took her work seriously, although they considered her a substitute mother figure and began any complaints with, "My mother didn't like what you said about ..."[139] In 1970 she was quoted as saying that men politicians "of the old school still regard the woman political reporter as a contradiction in terms," bowing politely, then rushing off "to tell the story to the men."[140] Political figures tended to tell her their troubles rather than to leak stories. "I've heard more than I care to know about unhappy wives and wayward children," she groaned.[141]

By 1970 there were an estimated three hundred full-time women journalists in Washington, assigned to various beats, according to two veteran social journalists, Winzola McLendon, a former social reporter for the *Post,* and Scottie Smith, the daughter of F. Scott Fitzgerald. Less than one-half of the women's press group was accredited to Congress. McLendon and Smith divided the group into three categories: (1) those covering chiefly women's news, including charity events, food, fashion, the First Family, and what Beale referred to as "politics after six"; (2) those holding traditionally male reporting jobs, such as Eileen Shanahan of the *New York Times,* who won *a Times'* Publisher Award for reporting on the 1969 tax bill, and Helen Dewar, who covered Northern Virginia politics for the *Post* and predicted the election of the first Republican governor since Reconstruction; (3) those who gathered news for both women's and general news sections, including White House wire service reporters, Lewine of the AP and Thomas of UPI, as well as Barbara Fulow of *U.S. News & World Report,* since all three covered both the president and the First Lady.[142] They also pointed to Lillian Wiggins of the *Afro-American,* a black newspaper, as a reporter assigned to both women's "soft" news and men's "hard news."

Wiggins, while called the society editor, covered a war between Nigeria and Biafra in Africa for three months in 1969 and did a series on conditions in Barbados. She was attending a seated dinner at the Ivory Coast Embassy when riots broke out in Washington in 1968 following the assassination of Dr. Martin Luther King Jr. She rushed home and changed from an evening dress to slacks and leather jacket, not daring to show a reporter's notebook as she moved to the center of the riots on Fourteenth Street.[143]

McLendon and Smith concluded that many of the women reporters made relatively little for their labors. They gave the women an average salary of about $250 a week—but wrote that their reward was "a ringside seat at the best show on earth."[144] Seeing reporting as a way of getting close to power, they noted enthusiastically that women journalists might lunch with the wives of ambassadors, have cocktails with senators, and dine at the White House all in the same day. A growing number of women journalists, however, did not view such assignments as producing meaningful careers, but sought to have more latitude to compete directly with men in the wake of the women's liberation movement. While Beale saw power in being associated with those who held it, the newer crop of women journalists wanted more than the opportunity to observe those who made decisions; they wanted to report on the decision making themselves.

In 1972 *Cosmopolitan* magazine looked at the women's press corps from another angle. It spotlighted ten white Washington women journalists complete with a picture of the group smiling and striding down the street in business attire. Far from flattering the women, however, the article was titled THE WITCHES OF WASHINGTON, with the subhead, GET TO KNOW A COVEN OF NEWS-WOMEN WHO CAST SPELLS, EXHUME STORIES, AND, BRRR! MEET THEIR DEADLINES.[145]

The ten featured: Cheshire and Judith Martin, both of the *Post;* Sarah McClendon; Hearst's Marianne Means; Vera Glaser of Knight Newspapers Inc. and at the time president of the Washington Press Club, an outgrowth of the old WNPC; Wauhillau La Hay, a columnist for Scripps Howard newspapers; Kandy Stroud of *Women's Wear Daily;* television commentator Nancy Dickerson; and the two wire service rivals, Lewine and Thomas. Curiously, no representative from the *Star* was pictured, but Beale was quoted as saying, "We all protect the President."[146]

Quinn was absent from the group, too, although she was named as the author of a Style story on Lady Esme Cromer, wife of the British ambassador, that led to the title of the *Cosmopolitan* article. It stated that Lord Cromer had been so displeased by the "ill-mannered publication" of his wife's comments on the Vietnam War that he had exploded on the subject of women journalists, telling another man, "Witches of Washington? My dear fellow, I think you've misspelled it."[147] Lady Cromer was quoted in Quinn's story hoping that the United States won in Vietnam because to Asians "life means nothing."[148]

According to *Cosmopolitan,* any one of the three hundred women journalists in Washington would be pleased to be "considered a 'witch,'" since this term put a journalist in an elite "coven" with a national audience.[149] As evidence it pointed to a Glaser column on a clash between the White House and State Department over a State Department employees' petition protesting Vietnam policy. First relegated to the *Star*'s women's section, the story was picked up by AP and UPI for national distribution, which made it front-page news.[150]

Stoud, described as a "pert and girlish" mother of two, was pictured as "neither sweet nor harmless."[151] It was she who had asked Lady Cromer her views on the Vietnam War, precipitating Quinn's offending news story. Stroud could not break the story herself because her newspaper was not published the day of Cromer's comments.

Stressing the competitiveness among the women, the article told of McClendon's fury when President Nixon invited nine favored women reporters into his office for an informal chat. She led other uninvited women reporters "in a noisy demonstration outside the President's Oval Office, ending with an off-key rendition of 'We Shall Overcome.' "[152] McClendon also appeared as a mistreated member of the press in *The Boys on the Bus,* Timothy Crouse's attention-getting book on the political reporters who covered Nixon's second presidential campaign in 1972.

While generally sympathetic to her, Crouse described McClendon as "a frumpish woman in a purple pants suit and star-in-circle earrings, with tousled platinum hair, and a sweet, toothy smile."[153] He called her the "comic relief at presidential news conferences," and contended: "Whenever they were in a tight spot, Kennedy, Johnson and now Nixon would point to her with an indulgent smile and wait for her to ask some stupid, irrelevant question, which, it was true, she sometimes did. But no matter what she asked, all the male reporters laughed."[154]

Presidents, however, did not always welcome her questions. Recalling his first press presidential press conference in 1962, Sam Donaldson, veteran White House correspondent for ABC, remembered years later, "A woman got up—yes, a WOMAN—and said, 'Mr. President, two well known security risks have recently been put on a task force in the State Department . . .' and Kennedy began sputtering, got red in the face and started looking for cover. I knew at that moment I had found a role model."[155]

In Crouse's view McClendon did not receive fair treatment in the 1960s and 70s, first, because she was a woman, and second, because she represented relatively inconsequential newspapers. While Crouse saw McClendon as a victim of gender bias, the *Cosmopolitan* article saw her and other women as competitive vixens. As an example of their "witchiness," it quoted La Hay as remembering, "At the first Congressional party I covered I didn't know who some of the people were, so I asked Maxine Cheshire to help me. She said, 'You must be out of your mind,' and walked away."[156]

As a put-down to women's liberation, the article concluded that "sisterhood, it seems, will never have the egoistic appeal of the front-page exclusive."[157] *Cosmopolitan* only begrudgingly admitted that the news women had banded together sufficiently to press for admission to the NPC, which had finally allowed them to join the previous year with Thomas and McClendon among the first twenty-four women inducted. It did not say that sometimes "sisterhood" did make headlines.

Simpson noted in her recollections that Glaser, then Washington chief of the North American Newspaper Alliance bureau, asked President Nixon at a 1969 press conference "whether we can expect a more equitable recognition of women's abilities or are we going to remain a lost sex?"[158] This referred to the fact that he had named only three women while filling some two hundred top-level jobs, as Glaser well knew since she was the former head of publicity for the women's division of the Republican Party. Her political connections forced Nixon to take her question seriously and prompted creation of a White House task force on women.[159] Her question led to a five-part NANA series on the status of women that ran in some fifty newspapers. It covered women's lack of economic and political power, court rulings that held women were not equal under the Constitution, and lobbying efforts by national women's organizations seeking change.[160]

From the mid-century pages of both Crouse's book and *Cos-*

mopolitan, one obvious point emerged, although perhaps unwittingly in the magazine article—newswomen remained apart from the cozy world of male-oriented political journalism in Washington during the Cold War and civil rights eras. In Crouse's opinion some of the "toughest pieces on the 1972 Nixon campaign came from McClendon, Thomas, Cassie Mackin of NBC, Marilyn Berger of the *Washington Post,* and Mary McGrory," whom he called "outsiders."[161] He argued that discrimination against them had toughened the women, giving them an uncompromising detachment and "bold independence of thought that often put the men to shame."[162]

With the exception of Thomas, these women were not among the small group of Washington national news reporters credited by Simpson and Mills with developing the expertise needed to cover feminist issues. Like Mills, Simpson pointed to Shanahan, Lewine, Isabelle Shelton, Katz of the *National Journal,* Cimons, and UPI's Fritz, along with Mills herself.[163] Simpson referred to Shanahan's surprise when she received a telephone call in 1971 from an unknown woman attorney who told her that the ERA was scheduled to be voted on in the House of Representatives within a week but that the *New York Times* had run only one story on it.[164]

Moving outside her normal beat, Shanahan, according to Simpson, subsequently covered the ERA debate herself, compiled the first national statistics on women lawyers (only 9,103 out of 324,818 law school graduates), and did a pathbreaking survey of the suits women were winning under new federal laws prohibiting sex discrimination in employment.[165] Shanahan launched her coverage of the ERA debate in Congress when Marjorie Hunter, who was assigned to the House of Representatives and the only other woman in the *Times* bureau, declined to do so, telling Shanahan that she preferred to concentrate on an education bill.[166]

Shanahan, who covered economics for the *New York Times* from 1966 to 1977, was no stranger to sex discrimination and harassment. In an oral history interview in 1994, Shanahan gave concrete examples of the harassment that she faced as a woman reporter on Capitol Hill. She said she did not report it to her superiors because it was such a common occurrence that women "just sort of pretended it hadn't happened in those days."[167] She said Sen. John Sparkman, chairman of the Senate Banking Committee, whom she considered one of the "worst ones [members of Congress] in terms of making 'crude lunges,'" once directed her to his "hideaway office" to get a copy of an important committee report.[168]

"He actually tore a button off my blouse, trying to get at me," Shanahan continued, "and I remember saying to him, 'You do one thing more and I will file charges of attempted rape, and I'm not kidding.' And he said, 'Oh, don't be like that,' and so forth."[169] She managed to get herself together "as best I could—and remembered to pick up the report—and walked out," she said, seeking future news from Sparkman "only when I was desperate to get some information . . . I never went to that hideaway office again . . . [sexual harassment] was just a hazard of life."[170]

So was lack of opportunities to advance, which Shanahan fought by becoming a plaintiff in a class action sex discrimination suit brought by women at the *New York Times.* She was the only plaintiff from the Washington bureau of the *Times* and the best known of the group of women who accused the newspaper of gender unfairness in hiring, promotion, and pay. A contemporary on the *Times,* Nan Robertson, described Shanahan as a "superstar" who had "endless energy, enthusiasm, and an intellect of singular clarity."[171]

Before being hired by the *Times* in 1962, Shanahan had experienced numerous instances of discrimination. She gave up her job with the United Press in 1947 to have her first child, but after eighteen months at home with her baby daughter she became so depressed that her husband insisted she go back to work. After numerous rejections, she was hired by Walter Cronkite, then a Washington correspondent for radio stations, in 1949, but he moved on in less than two years, leaving her jobless again. A stint on a newsletter led her to specialize in business news, but she was turned down for the staff of a premier business publication, the *Kiplinger Letter.* Its founder, William Kiplinger, told her that "a respectable woman, the only kind we would want here," would be unable to get "inside information."[172]

Shanahan also was turned away from the *Post* by an editor who said an economics story with a woman's byline would lack credibility, but she finally found employment with the *Journal of Commerce* in 1956.[173] After she wrote an acclaimed ten-part series on the economic policy of the Kennedy administration in 1961, she became the spokesperson for Secretary of the Treasury Douglas Dillon. One year later she joined the *Times* as its star economics reporter.

Her colleague, Hunter, was hired in 1961 to cover First Ladies and Congress, replacing Bess Furman, who had left for the public affairs section of the Department of Health, Education, and Welfare. Bill Kovach, a former *Times* bureau chief, said Hunter and Shanahan were "pigeonholed" at the *Times* because of their gender.[174] "Maggie Hunter was on Congress her entire career in Washington," he said.[175] "She was interested in the Pentagon ... interested in other assignments, but the *New York Times* did not see fit to allow Maggie to develop in broader ways the way any man in the bureau [would have been allowed]. It just was not done."[176]

Kovach continued, "Either one of them could have competed head to head, toe to toe, with any man in Washington. [Editors thought] it was just too much risk to make a major assignment to a woman. They figured that the natural prejudice of the old boy network would freeze the women out."[177] Gender operated against women reporters, he added. "If a woman succeeded on a story that no one else had gotten, someone was always certain to say that she probably went to bed with [the source]. The idea that a woman could beat a man on a story fairly was inconceivable to a lot of journalists in Washington."[178]

Events leading to the *Times* suit started in 1972, when women employees in New York formed a caucus and met with Arthur Ochs Sulzberger Jr., known as Punch, the newspaper's publisher, to point out major inequities, including a fifty-nine-dollar weekly gap in the pay of male and female reporters.[179] After the women received little satisfaction from management in addressing their concerns, they went to federal court in 1974. The seven named plaintiffs, including Shanahan, the last to add her name and the only Washington staff member, gained the right from a federal judge to represent other women at the newspaper in 1977. Shanahan added her name shortly before she resigned, after having been passed over for a promotion at the *Times,* to become press secretary for Joseph Califano, secretary of health, education, and welfare under President Carter. Hunter, who continued at the *Times* until her retirement in 1986, was not involved in the suit. To Robertson, "Maggie, a Southern lady and a thorough professional, was no feminist firebrand."[180]

In 1978 the *Times* settled the sex discrimination case out of court for $385,000, specifying timetables for hiring and promoting women. Women in the news and business departments received $223,500 in back pay. According to Linda Greenhouse, who later covered the U.S. Supreme Court for the *Times,* the suit forced editors "to scan the horizon and promote women."[181]

The *Times* suit represented one of a score of legal actions brought by women and minorities against major news organizations under the Civil Rights Act of 1964. Class-action discrimination complaints named some of the most respected names in the news business, including the AP, *Newsday, Detroit News*, the *Baltimore Evening Sun,* and the *Post,* as well as NBC and other broadcasters. After years of negotiating contracts that called for women's page staff members to be paid less than general news or sports reporters, the Newspaper Guild, the chief union of news and business employees, reversed its stand in 1970 and set goals for equality.[182] As Kay Mills put it, "the women were clearly successful, not so much for themselves as for the women who came after them."[183]

After dragging on for a decade, for example, the AP suit, backed by the Wire Service Guild, ended in 1983 with a $2 million out-of-court settlement. It set up affirmative action plans for women and minorities and gave $850,000 in back pay to more than eight hundred women who had worked for the wire service since 1972. Among plaintiffs in the suit were Simpson and Fran Lewine, who keenly perceived lack of equality at the wire service.

Long before the settlement was reached, both women had left the AP. The wire service took Lewine off the White House beat after twelve years in 1977. She spent the next four years at the U.S. Department of Transportation, leaving as deputy director of public affairs, a job that paid her much more than the AP. In 1981 she moved on to CNN as an assignment editor, holding that job until her death in 2008. Simpson, who transferred to the AP Washington bureau in 1968 after covering the Texas legislature, left the AP ten years later to work for the Hearst bureau in the capital, to help develop more coverage of women.[184]

Recalling her years at the AP, Lewine complained of a double standard in which women were praised for filling in for men but not seen as capable as their masculine colleagues.[185] She once asked President Gerald Ford at a televised news conference if he agreed with his own administration guidelines against federal officials patronizing segregated facilities. When he said he did, she inquired why he played golf weekly at the Burning Tree Country Club, which refused to admit women. Some AP editors were upset that she raised the issue, and Ford's press secretary, Ronald Nessen, declared that her question "was the worse misuse of a question at a presidential news conference to advocate a personal point of view."[186]

In an oral history interview, Lewine pointed to a general pattern of discrimination, noting there were only ten women out of a hundred AP employees in Washington in 1968.[187] "We never got paid as much as the men. We had discrimination of women who were mandatorily retired at age fifty-five versus sixty-five for the men; and the whole idea that the reason you were covering the White House was basically to cover first ladies and the put-down of that role," she said.[188] "There was basic discrimination in the entire profession. . . . The AP was an organization that was looked up to by other newspapers and they set the pace, more or less, for the profession and news gathering."[189]

As other groups of women journalists became increasingly restive, Katharine Graham found herself dismayed in her role as head of the Washington Post Company. The *Post* had long treated women differently than men. For example, when Susan Jacoby applied to the *Post* for an entry-level reporting job in 1962, she was required to submit an essay on how she planned to combine motherhood with journalism. She insisted that the combination "would pose absolutely no problem."[190] She added, "If the personnel head had told me to produce an essay on my method of birth control, I probably would have done that too."[191]

Graham became an ally of women's liberation due in part to her friendship with Gloria Steinem, a leading feminist figure, but it took years for her personal interest to filter down to the level of the individual employer. To her discomfort in 1970, forty-six women at *Newsweek,* owned by the Post Company but published in New York, filed a discrimination complaint with the federal Equal Employment Opportunities Commission (EEOC) set up by the Civil Rights Act. The complaint came after the women were passed over by male editors who hired a freelance journalist to write a cover story on women's liberation. Graham's reaction, when informed of the complaint: "Which side am I supposed to be on?"[192] The company offered *Newsweek* women—who previously had been confined to the role of researchers, not writers, at the magazine—more opportunity, but two years later women complained male editors had not lived up to their promises.[193]

Interested in the women's movement as the result of the "many rooms into which I walked, boards on which I sat, meetings I attended, as the only woman," Graham gave Steinem $20,000 for her feminist publication, *Ms.* magazine.[194] Yet Graham wrote in her autobiography that she continued to back male management "as the way the world worked."[195] Her closest female confidant at the *Post,* Meg Greenfield, deputy editorial page editor and eventual Pulitzer Prize winner, had succeeded in her career before the women's movement. Greenfield posted a sign on her office door, "If liberated, I will not serve," although she later warmed to feminist ideas.[196]

In 1970 Graham and Bradlee called for nonsexist language in the *Post,* with Bradlee responding to the concerns of a committee of women reporters by issuing a memo cautioning against use of "words like 'divorcee,' 'grandmother,' or 'housewife'" if corresponding words were not used for men.[197] Graham became one of the first five women initiated into the Washington chapter of the formerly all-male Sigma Delta Chi, a professional journalism fraternity, in 1970, along with Mary Lou Forbes. In her remarks Graham joked that the *Post* might run the story under the heading NEWSMEN'S FRAT TAPS WORKING GRANDMA.[198] She and Bradlee chose the dependable Elsie Carper to become head of personnel "to hire more women and minorities," and Graham credited her with making "a big impact with her hires."[199]

Efforts to widen hiring practices did not stop accusations of discrimination brought against the *Post* by both women and African American journalists. Women at both the *Post* and the *Star* held consciousness-raising sessions to talk about their inferior status, while male colleagues scoffed. One prime example occurred in 1970, when a group of eleven women reporters from both newspapers met at the Capitol Hill apartment of Nancy Beckham, who worked for the *Star*.

For two years as an entry-level newsroom employee, Beckham, a graduate of Hollins College, had diligently typed stories in triplicate called in by reporters, while covering civic meetings and other assignments at night on a freelance basis. Unlike men who also had started on the dictation bank, she was not promoted to being a reporter because Epstein, the city editor, contended he was uncomfortable sending women out on Washington streets at night. Finally Forbes "volunteered to put me on the state staff," Beckham (later Ferris) said.[200] She reported on the suburb of Arlington and won promotion to the position of assistant metro editor, staffing the night shift, but at that point, no issues were raised "about my being a woman," she said.[201]

Although she advanced in her career, a consciousness-raising session at Beckham's apartment in 1970 turned into a terrifying event. As women on both newspapers were sharing accounts of lack of deserved assignments, to their horror three armed men from the neighborhood entered the premises. They forced the women to lie on the floor and robbed them of their valuables, and two of the men threatened to rape one of the women. The incident received only semiserious treatment from the city desks at both newspapers, according to Ferris, who recalled that male colleagues sniggered and made snide comments about it.[202] She said that the group did not meet again, although both newspapers eventually took steps to deal more equitably with women and minorities.

Newsrooms remained inhospitable places for women in the 1960s and 70s, when they began to hire women in larger numbers. At the *Star*, Epstein, a former marine, barked orders amid the clank of typewriters, clouds of cigarette smoke, and wads of torn copy paper thrown on desks dirty from stacks of carbon paper. Grizzled veterans still occasionally drank on the job.

"It was really tough on us broads back then," Myra McPherson, a feature writer from Detroit who started at the *Star* in 1960 and later moved to the *Post,* recalled a half century later, paying homage to Betty Miles James.[203] One of the first women on the news staff at the *Star*, James had been hired during World War II and kept on after the war, writing features on subjects like the newspaper's "Send a Kid to Camp Fund."[204] In the face of male coolness to new women employees, James welcomed them warmly.

Nevertheless, women at the *Star* considered working conditions there generally more accommodating than at the rival *Post,* according to Ferris, a *Star* employee from 1967 to 1980 noted.[205] This stemmed partly from the presence of women stars like Ottenberg,

Forbes, and McGrory, as well as another woman, Shirley Elder, who covered the House of Representatives. *Star* staffers also attributed it to the fact that the *Post* had more competitive young journalists seen as "grim careerists" intent on getting ahead in an atmosphere of "creative tension" promoted by Bradlee.[206] Ferris said that the *Star* had a paternalistic style of management; she believed the city editor's refusal to make her a reporter was motivated by concern for her safety.[207]

As the *Star* lost money in the 1970s, concern for saving jobs dominated the agenda for employees, said Ferris, who served as chair of the Guild unit.[208] Beset by declines in advertising and circulation, the paper only made money when the *Post* experienced a crippling pressmen's strike in 1975 that ended four and a half months later after Graham had broken the pressmen's union and weakened the Guild. The *Star*'s gains did not last. In 1978, Allbritton sold the *Star* to Time Inc., which failed to reverse the losses.

By contrast the *Post* enhanced its profits and reputation, but some women and minority journalists increasingly protested unequal opportunities at the newspaper. In early 1972 a group of African American reporters handed Bradlee a list of questions, such as, "Why are there no black originating editors on the foreign, national, sports, financial and Style desks, and only one . . . on the metropolitan desk?"[209] Bradlee responded by saying the *Post* "now employs more black editors, reporters and photographers than any newspaper in America," a total of twenty-one in all.[210] Not satisfied, the protestors, known as the Metro Seven, filed discrimination charges with the EEOC. Similar protests from women soon followed. Acting through the Guild, women filed their own sex discrimination complaint against the *Post*. Both groups found support for their charges. The EEOC issued a finding of discrimination against the *Post* on the basis of race, but *Post* attorneys fought the finding and the commission finally voted, three to two, not to prosecute the newspaper.[211]

In 1974 the commission concluded that the newspaper "restricts the opportunities of female employees to occupy its higher paying positions."[212] The findings referred to evidence that married women employees "experience greater difficulty in getting hired or promoted into higher paying positions than single females and that such considerations do not affect the opportunities of male employees."[213] Two examples were given, one of a women turned down for a correspondent's job because she had a child, and another of a woman who said she was harassed and denied assignments because of her plans to marry another staff member.[214]

The *Post* moved to address these issues. In 1976, the newspaper reported, 46 percent of those hired during the preceding year were minorities, while nearly 20 percent of all news employees were women.[215] But tension remained. Katharine Graham took a philosophical approach: "My own reactions to these suits were mixed; I felt that some [charges] were unfair and some were not. But you always get pushed when things become confrontational, and that is often to the good," she wrote in her autobiography.[216]

Graham also got caught up in the furor over ending gender discrimination by the prestigious Gridiron Club. Composed of fifty high-level Washington newsmen, the Gridiron existed to lampoon the current president at an annual black-tie dinner attended by him and the cream of the political establishment. In 1971 about thirty women reporters picketed the dinner led by Rachel Scott, a freelance environmental writer, who carried a sign saying, "Gridiron Studs are Sexist Bigots" and was arrested for disorderly conduct.[217]

When the club tried to counter protests against its male-only policy by inviting a few women to its 1972 dinner, Graham first accepted, then declined the invitation. She backed out after women at the *Post,* some of whom were among journalists who picketed the event wearing evening dresses, urged her to stay away. The women were part of an ad hoc group called Journalists for Professional Equality organized by Ann Wood, a *New York Daily News* correspondent, and others who pressed leading political figures not to attend.[218] In addition to Graham, most of the invited women, including Coretta Scott King, Sen. Margaret Chase Smith, and anthropologist Mary Mead, declined with Rep. Shirley Chisholm, the first African American woman to serve in Congress, stating, "Guess who's not coming to dinner."[219]

"I couldn't bring myself to picket, however," Graham told an audience at the NPC.[220] With Greenfield playing chauffeur, the wealthy publisher hunched down to avoid being recognized, as the two drove around the hotel where the dinner took place, watching the picketers. They included Judith Martin, later the *Post*'s "Miss Manners" columnist, who pushed her baby in a carriage on the picket line. Observers were afforded "a hilarious perspective on this scene of limousines, white tie and tails, the baby buggy, and the picketers," Graham said.[221] She ended the evening by joining the picketers at the home of Eileen Shanahan for a buffet supper.[222]

While the Gridiron admitted its first African American member, columnist Carl T. Rowan, in 1972, it voted against taking in women members in 1973. This prompted the 1974 staging of a successful counter-Gridiron party in a college gymnasium. Billed as a carnival with celebrity auctioneers, it attracted a bigger crowd of more prominent people than the Gridiron itself.

Marlene Cimons of the *Los Angeles Times* was one of the organizers of the annual protests. She saw the effort change from symbolic picketing gestures, "where my publisher Otis Chandler . . . came over to me on the line and said, 'Hi, Marlene, are you having fun?'" to counter parties, which nailed the Gridiron members where it hurt—in their dinner guest list," she recalled.[223] "As professional discrimination against women became less 'fashionable' and officials began to take it more seriously, they recognized—finally—that attending the Gridiron was not in their best interests."[224]

In 1975 the Gridiron capitulated, voting to admit Helen Thomas as its first woman member. She was followed the next year by Fran Lewine. The counter-Gridiron event for 1975 turned into a celebration, with Sen. Ed Muskie of Maine calling bingo games and Steinem signing pardons for "past male chauvinist sins."[225] Protests continued at the club's slow pace of integration. Finally, in 1993, Thomas was elected its first woman president. Similarly she won election as president of the White House Correspondents' Association.

No suits charging discrimination were filed at the *Star.* "I think the *Star* had a large enough core of women, saw the lawsuits going on elsewhere, and dropped most restrictions and tried to advance women's careers," Jody Beck, now director of the Scripps Howard Foundation Semester in Washington program, said.[226] Beck started working at the *Star* in 1973 before women were allowed to take the night police beat, one of the first assignments given reporter trainees, although that soon changed, she recalled.[227] Beck remained on the staff until the newspaper folded in 1981, covering almost all beats given to local reporters—police, courts, schools, legislature, local, and statewide politics.

Beck considered Forbes and other women in the office to have been her mentors. When former *Star* employees held annual reunions, Ferris said they retrospectively concluded, "We never worked in a better place."[228] No doubt, the newspaper served as a training ground for a group of accomplished women who went on to distinguished careers at other newspapers and in broadcasting. Whether at the *Star*, the *Post*, or other news organizations, however, it took dedicated, determined individuals to counter the sexist prejudices that infused Washington journalism in the middle of the twentieth century. Their success depended not only on themselves but, in many cases, on the impact of federal legislation to require equal employment opportunity. Along with the women's movement, it effectively ended formal segregation of women in news operations, based on ideas of separate spheres for men and women, but numerous challenges remained for women journalists in a male-dominated capital.

© UNDERWOOD & UNDERWOOD
WASHINGTON

Figure 1. First Lady Eleanor Roosevelt (*center*), with Eleanor "Cissy" Patterson, editor and publisher of the *Washington Herald* (*left*), and popular author Mary Roberts Rinehart, opening a relief drive for victims of the Depression in 1933 in Washington

Figure 2. Eleanor Roosevelt holds one of the first of her 348 White House press conferences for women reporters only in the Monroe Room on March 13, 1933, with some of the press girls, as they were called, sitting at her feet FRANKLIN D. ROOSEVELT LIBRARY

Figure 3. "You're Telling Me," a cartoon drawn by Clifford K. Berryman and printed March 19, 1934, in the *Washington Star,* presents a male view of Eleanor Roosevelt's press conferences

Figure 4. Members of the Women's National Press Club present a skit about a nominating convention to choose the next First Lady at the club's annual stunt party in March 1940. They hold signs for wives of possible candidates: James (Jim) Farley, Robert A. Taft, Cordell Hull, and Thomas E. Dewey. The performers (*left to right*) are Mary Johnson, *Time* magazine; Bab Lincoln, *Washington Times-Herald;* Corrinne Frazier, publicist for the federal Works Progress Administration; May Craig, *Portland* (Maine) *Press-Herald;* Bess Furman, Furman Features; Malvina Lindsay, *Washington Post* women's page editor; and Hope Ridings Miller, *Washington Post* society editor.

Figure 5. Martha Rountree (*far left*), one of the founders of *Meet the Press,* returns to the radio program along with cofounder Lawrence Spivak (*second from left*) on April 8, 1949, to interview Eleanor Roosevelt (*third from left*) FRANKLIN D. ROOSEVELT LIBRARY

Figure 6. Helen Thomas of United Press International stands outside the White House taking notes, ca. 1970s

Figure 7. Katharine Graham addresses the staff in the *Washington Post* newsroom during the 1975 strike by union pressmen, which she is credited with breaking WASHINGTON POST / GETTY IMAGES

Figure 8. Judy Woodruff in November 1977 as an NBC news correspondent in Washington LIBRARY OF AMERICAN BROADCASTING/ UNIVERSITY OF MARYLAND

Figure 9. Sarah McClendon asks questions on how to cover diplomats and embassies at a National Press Club forum featuring embassy press attachés on September 11, 1979 NATIONAL PRESS CLUB ARCHIVES

Figure 10. Linda Wertheimer provides political commentary along with Pulitzer Prize–winning reporter David Halberstam (*standing*), John Sears (*left*), and Sanford Ungar for NPR in December 1980

Figure 11. Katharine Graham sits at her desk as chairman of the board of the Washington Post Company, ca. 1980s NATIONAL PRESS CLUB

Figure 12. One of the first successful Asian American women in television broadcasting, Connie Chung started her network broadcasting career in 1971 as a CBS reporter in Washington. She is shown here in 1985, when she anchored NBC's early morning news program. LIBRARY OF AMERICAN BROADCASTING / UNIVERSITY OF MARYLAND

Figure 13. Three of the first women members of the National Press Club—(*left to right*) Helen Thomas, United Press International, and Judith Ellen Randal and Mary Lou Werner Forbes, both of the old *Washington Star*—celebrate the twentieth anniversary of women being admitted to the club with the club president, Kay Kahler, Newhouse News Service, in 1991 NATIONAL PRESS CLUB ARCHIVES

Figure 14. Helen Thomas (*left*) receives a Breakthrough Award on May 15, 1996, from feminist author Betty Friedan (*center*) and Nancy Woodhull, formerly of *USA Today,* who cochairs the Women, Men and Media project to investigate the representation of women in mainstream media. The event commemorated the twenty-fifth anniversary of the admission of women into the National Press Club. NATIONAL PRESS CLUB ARCHIVES

Figure 15. One of the most durable television newscasters in Washington, Maureen Bunyan started her career in the capital in 1973 and worked there for more than twenty years, mainly as a news anchor. She left in 1995 but returned to an anchor slot in 1999 at WJLA, where she is today. LIBRARY OF AMERICAN BROADCASTING / UNIVERSITY OF MARYLAND

Figure 16. Dorothy Gilliam, the first African American woman reporter and columnist for the *Washington Post,* is portrayed by a *Post* photographer, ca. 2000 WASHINGTON POST / GETTY IMAGES

Figure 17. Gwen Ifill, current moderator and managing editor of PBS's *Washington Week in Review* LIBRARY OF AMERICAN BROADCASTING / UNIVERSITY OF MARYLAND

SIX

◆

CLOTHES, CAMERAS, AND DETERMINATION TO MOVE INTO BROADCASTING

Few Washingtonian newswomen could be called fashion plates, but by and large they are trimmer, slimmer, and better dressed today than thirty years ago when members of the corps sloshed around in raincoats and Aunt-Jennie-type shoes. Credit for changing the appearance of women in the press, making it better looking and younger looking goes to the newcomers in the media, the television girls.

—Winzola McLendon and Scottie Smith in Don't Quote Me!

In their 1970 account of Washington women journalists, McLendon and Smith called attention to the importance of good looks for women who moved into television as barriers fell following passage of the Civil Rights Act. For years women had faced limited opportunities in broadcasting. With the advent of commercial broadcasting in the 1920s, men took charge of almost all newscasting, contending that women's voices did not convey authority and believability. Women who claimed a place behind the microphone faced restrictions on subject matter—generally they presided over homemaking shows, sandwiching household hints in between interviews with persons deemed interesting for a feminine audience.

Women's programming paid less than sports programming and other shows aimed at male listeners. It received less respect from male broadcasters. "I think a phenomenon of the early days of both radio and TV ... was that the women's director who had her own shows was inescapably considered a character by her station associates," commented Ruth Crane Schaefer, who spent twenty-seven years in broadcasting, from 1929 to 1956, in Detroit and Washington, D.C.[1]

"And the jokes directed at her were not always innocent," she continued. "Later on in TV it became almost the practice ... for the floorman, the cameraman and others to make away ahead of time with the food she had prepared ... she opens the oven door or the refrigerator door and ha-ha nothing is inside."[2] She added, "We tried putting locks on the refrigerator and all, but they'd [the male staff would] break it open. And the management didn't do anything about it."[3]

Few women were taken seriously as news broadcasters for decades, although some managed to have successful careers. Among them: Eleanor Roosevelt, who gave paid commentaries over network radio while First Lady from 1933 to 1945. Women like Schaefer took part in daytime radio, but as her experiences illustrated, they sometimes encountered covert hostility. As announcers, women were thought to be less appealing to listeners than men, based in part on a poll taken by WJZ in New York in 1926 that claimed to show listeners preferred men's voices over women's voices by a ratio of one hundred to one.[4] Prime-time, or nighttime radio, circumscribed women's roles and offered them little opportunity to move into news in most areas, including Washington.

Schaefer worked for WMAL, a station owned by the *Star*. Its rival, WTOP, was owned by the *Washington Post*. Newspapers originally acquired radio stations, which later turned into television stations, for prestige and experimentation. Publishers initially viewed radio as entertainment, although its reports on World War II showed its strength in news transmission. Not surprisingly, women, as well as men, were drawn to the new medium, seeking opportunities in an expanding field that depended on women's voices for daytime programming.

According to one radio historian, the "real-life world of radio itself—the world of writing, producing, and performing—provided a host of new careers for women," allowing some to succeed behind, if not in front of, the microphone.[5] One producer was Martha Rountree, creator and moderator for six years of the durable public affairs program, *Meet the Press*. It started on radio in 1945, moved to NBC television two years later, and is still being broadcast, making it the longest-running network show in the world.[6] Rountree sold out to cofounder Lawrence Spivak in 1954. The two first staged the program, which featured reporters asking questions of noteworthy guests, for the Mutual Broadcasting Company. Previously Mutual carried Rountree's successful show *Leave It to the Girls*, billed as a "battle of wits between the sexes" and "a roundtable of romance featuring glamorous career girls."[7]

One noteworthy broadcast of *Meet the Press* moderated by Rountree took place on December 10, 1949, when male journalists were attending the Gridiron dinner. Rountree presented an all-woman program, featuring journalists Doris Fleeson, May Craig, Judy Spivak (Lawrence Spivak's daughter), and Ruth Montgomery, who interviewed India Edwards, a Democratic political leader.[8] Generally, few women reporters with the exception of Craig appeared on the show, since most women journalists were not considered knowledgeable about the political issues discussed.

A native of South Carolina, Rountree maintained homes in both New York and Washington, where she stood out as an influential hostess. She relinquished her interest in *Meet the Press* a year after her marriage to an advertising executive, Oliver Presbrey. She and Presbrey then coproduced the program *Press Conference,* first on NBC and then on ABC, that soon faded from the scene.[9] In 1959, with another woman, Lucy Jarvis, Rountree launched *Capital Close-Ups,* a daily news show for Mutual radio, broadcast from her home on R Street in Washington's embassy section.[10] The program attracted notable guests like President Eisenhower, but by 1965 Rountree had left broadcasting. She started an organization called the Leadership Foundation to educate the public on current issues, which she ran until 1988.[11]

Beginning with the Eisenhower era, televised presidential press conferences afforded a chance for a few Washington newswomen to make fledging appearances on camera. Clearly recognizable with her trademark hats, diminutive May Craig drew on her radio and television experience on *Meet the Press.* Her short, peppery questions and "down East" accent gave her a distinctive air. "I would rather be grim than giggly," she said.[12] Sarah McClendon may have encountered ridicule, but she got attention. "I jumped up quicker, spoke louder, and was more determined than other reporters, so I was recognized regularly," she wrote in her autobiography.[13] Wearing bright red dresses, Helen Thomas stood out among the male reporters at the press conferences.

Broadcasting initially was seen as a perilous field for young women. When Patty Cavin, a journalism graduate of Stanford University who wrote women's political features for the *Washington Post,* chose to leave the newspaper in 1956 to work full time for the NBC affiliate in Washington, she received discouraging advice.

Cavin had moved to the *Post* after it purchased the *Times-Herald*, where she had been fashion and beauty editor. Asked to substitute on a noontime women's program on WRC, the NBC affiliate in Washington, she interviewed interesting people on the show while continuing to work for the *Post* until she was offered a full-time job at the radio station for twice her newspaper pay.

When she told Philip Graham, the *Post* publisher, she was leaving, he said something "rather nasty," implying she was not a professional journalist.[14] "He said, 'You know those radio types do nothing but pick pretty girls' brains and then throw them to the fishes,' " she recalled. "And with that I put on my white gloves and I looked him straight in the eye and I said, 'Mr. Graham, you may own WTOP but you'll always have an ambassadress in me at NBC. Good-bye.' And I walked out."[15]

Avoiding being "thrown to the fishes," Cavin specialized in live interviews, portions of which often were used on a weekend network program, *Monitor.* Among her subjects: Gandhi, Eleanor Roosevelt, and Danny Kaye. "It was great fun," she continued in an oral history. "I used to feel that I should pay NBC for the joy of spending eight hours there."[16] Taking "three or four weeks off for each child," she had two children, adding, "if I were to do it over again, I probably would have had the children earlier, but God knows what would have happened to my career."[17] At WRC, Cavin and Ingrid Rundel, the only other woman at the station, "were like baby stars, except we were much too down to earth [to take ourselves seriously] and we were busy constantly doing our own research. They never gave us enough secretarial help," she said.[18]

Not comfortable with the network's move to television, Cavin left NBC in 1963, joining the corporate staff of RCA as manager of news and information at double her salary. Her original title was manager of public affairs. She insisted it be changed after she received a note from an old friend, New York Sen. Kenneth Keating, who joked that "from here on in may all your affairs be public."[19]

Gender considerations greatly influenced the career of Nancy Hanschman (later Dickerson), the first woman television correspondent for CBS News. She became a popular subject for magazine articles with titles like "A Correspondent Who Could Be a Fashion Model" and "TV's Prettiest Reporter."[20] She gained her correspondent's status after six years of producing current affairs talk shows for CBS, including *Face the Nation,* taking the off-air job because radio and television news were virtually closed to women in the 1950s.[21]

True, Pauline Frederick had managed to move into radio in Washington and then television in New York in the 1940s, covering the United Nations, first for ABC and then for NBC. After obtaining a master's degree in international law in 1931 from American University in Washington, she wrote for the *Star* and the *United States Daily* (which became *U.S. News & World Report).* When she could not get interviews with male politicians because she was a woman, she specialized in interviewing diplomats' wives.[22] During World War II Frederick broadcast women's features for NBC, but worked mainly as a researcher for a male radio commentator, having tried unsuccessfully to get a network broadcasting job. Edward R. Murrow, the best-known newsman of his day, turned her down, writing in a CBS staff memo, "I would not call her material or manner particularly distinguished."[23]

While freelancing for ABC radio in 1948, Frederick was sent to cover the United Nations. She frantically dug up original stories after a desk editor told her secretly that, although some executives objected to her being on the air, if she turned in an exclusive story, he would have to use it.[24] ABC assigned her to the first televised national political conventions in 1948, expecting her not only to interview political women and wives of candidates in front of the camera, but to do their makeup as well.[25] Finally offered an ABC contract, she became the first full-time staff newswoman for a U.S. network. In 1953 she moved to NBC, where she distinguished herself by covering the United Nations until compulsory retirement due to her age in 1975.

Her dignified, serious demeanor personified the career woman of the day. Frederick's hard-driving approach to her work masked feelings of feminine inadequacy stemming from a hysterectomy performed without her consent at the age of seventeen when she suffered stomach cramps. "For a long time I felt like a freak," she told a graduate student years later.[26] Explaining her pursuit of news, she said, "When I have been busy at the United Nations during crises, it has meant working day and night. You can't very well take care of a home when you do something like that, or children."[27] She did not marry until the age of sixty-one. As a curious comment on her times, her first network assignment in television had been "How to Get a Husband."[28]

Hanschman followed a different type of career trajectory. A graduate of the University of Wisconsin, she sought more exciting work than teaching school in Milwaukee and moved to Washington in 1951. An attractive, green-eyed young woman working as an aide for the Senate Foreign Relations Committee, she met and sometimes dated influential men on Capitol Hill. Acting on a tip from a reporter friend that CBS was looking for a "man who knew Capitol Hill," she maneuvered herself into a job there in 1954, although her previous experience in journalism had been limited to her junior high school newspaper.[29]

She produced two radio public affairs programs before becoming associate producer of *Face the Nation,* which competed with *Meet the Press* on television. In 1957 she rose to being an assistant to Murrow, then at the apex of broadcast news.[30] At the same time she got so involved in a relationship with Kenneth Keating that she called herself his "secret campaign manager," although after his election to the Senate in 1958 their closeness ended.[31] Her association with him and friendship with other prominent politicians helped her obtain guests for her shows.

Hanschman was determined to follow Frederick and actually get on the air. After convincing network officials to let her broadcast from Europe, where she interviewed the pope in 1959, she became the first woman correspondent for CBS, covering political conventions and the presidential election in 1960. Murrow admonished her to dress conservatively because "frilly clothes might suggest frivolity."[32] Newspapers and magazines dwelled on her wardrobe, apparently more fascinated by what she wore than by what she did.[33] Publicity photos posed her in stylish garb with accessories ranging from kid gloves to feather boas.[34]

In 1962 Hanschman married a real estate magnate, C. Wyatt Dickerson, a widower with three children, and took his name. The couple had two sons, Michael in 1963 and John in 1968; she took only two weeks off work after each was born. Convinced that men at CBS were jealous of her success and sidetracked her reports to daytime television and radio, Dickerson left CBS for NBC in 1963. At the same time she achieved a reputation as a notable hostess at Merrywood, the Dickerson estate in Northern Virginia, which had been the girlhood home of Jackie Kennedy. Her son John recalled in a memoir of his mother that her dressing room contained "twenty feet of suits and gowns and silk shirts puffed with tissue paper to keep their shape," along with a wall of shoes, "at attention in their shoe trees."[35] In the back of the house she had "three more closets of colorful Dior, Cardin and St. Laurent outfits."[36]

Dickerson zealously covered the Kennedy administration. In her autobiography she described dating John F. Kennedy before either one was married, commenting, "Kennedy had great sex appeal."[37] Her son, also a network correspondent, said she "seemed to delight in having people think she might have had [an affair] with Kennedy."[38] Dickerson had a strong ally in Lyndon Johnson, who would spot her as the only woman in a crowd of newsmen, and drawl, "Hello, Nancy."[39] No doubt, she gained professionally from her friendship with both Kennedy and Johnson. She claimed in her autobiography that Johnson "only really propositioned me once."[40]

Dickerson's network career ended in 1970 when she in effect was fired from NBC. According to her son, "She was high maintenance, too close to her sources and she was expensive, the second highest-paid correspondent behind [David] Brinkley."[41] The network replaced her daily news show with Dinah Shore's entertainment program that brought in more advertising revenue. Reflecting on her ouster, Dickerson said, "I was raising five children, working a full day and often at night and on Sundays, and I simply did not have time to waste. As a result, I could be excessively abrupt, even arrogant, which naturally prompted retribution."[42]

Ironically, Dickerson left NBC shortly after she anchored a program on the fiftieth anniversary of woman suffrage, which she said her colleagues "giggled about."[43] After leaving NBC, she became an independent producer of documentaries. Her son discovered that her fan mail showed she was an inspiration for young women who "wanted to know how to train for a career like hers."[44]

By the time Dickerson left NBC, the rules of the broadcast

game were changing for women due to passage of the Civil Rights Act in 1964. Dickerson contended that the women's movement actually impeded her career by causing men to retaliate against her.[45] Other women saw the situation differently.

In 1964 Storer Broadcasting, which owned seven radio stations, employed Fay Gillis Wells as the first woman broadcaster to cover the White House exclusively, a job she held until retirement in 1977. Fifty-five years old in 1964, Wells, one of the first women pilots, had covered news around the world for decades with her journalist husband, Linton Wells. Fay Wells said male colleagues at the White House treated her well, perhaps because of her age and the fact that "I wasn't vying with anybody for time on the air."[46] Her most memorable assignment: accompanying President Richard M. Nixon on his historic trip to China in 1972.[47]

Some women sought redress under the Civil Rights Act to advance in broadcasting. Catherine Mackin was one of twenty-seven women who brought a discrimination complaint with the federal EEOC against WRC-TV, the NBC-owned station in Washington in 1971.[48] The complaint was based on a petition filed with the Federal Communications Commission by NOW seeking to require that station operators include women, as well as minorities, in counts of employees submitted as part of license renewal applications.[49] The rule, soon adopted, raised the specter of license challenges if stations did not hire women and minorities. The EEOC upheld the class action complaint and ruled that WRC had discriminated.

Even though Mackin, a journalism graduate of the University of Maryland, was a leader in the discrimination complaint, her career blossomed. Still, Mackin had doubts about being promoted due to gender. "I'm being used," she said at the time.[50] Made a network correspondent for NBC in 1971, she remained there until she joined ABC in 1977, where she stayed as a congressional correspondent until her death in 1982.[51] Apparently NBC had nothing to gain by retaliation against Mackin, since CBS was making overtures to her.[52] Her promising career, which included anchoring the NBC Sunday news, was cut short by death from cancer.[53]

While Mackin was covering Capitol Hill for NBC in 1974, Ann Compton of ABC became the first television newswoman to be named a full-time White House correspondent.[54] The wife of a physician and mother of four children, Compton decided the White House beat demanded too much travel and gave it up to work on Capitol Hill so she could be home more regularly.[55] Assigned as a floor reporter at national political party conventions in 1976, Compton went on to have one of the longest-standing network careers, covering eight presidential campaigns. In 2011 she was the national correspondent for ABC News Radio and president of the White House Correspondents' Association.[56]

The federal government's stand on equal employment advanced the careers of other notable broadcasters during the 1970s: watching the legal actions against NBC, its biggest rival, CBS reached out to hire more women in 1971 and 1972. Within six months it went from one woman reporter, Marya McLaughlin, to five newswomen on the air: Sylvia Chase; Lesley Stahl; Michele Clark, an Africa American; and Connie Chung, who is Asian.[57] Chase worked in New York, and Clark was killed in a plane crash in 1972 shortly after she had been made the anchor for the CBS morning newscast from Washington.[58] This left Stahl and Chung, along with Bernard Shaw, an African American, to stand out as what Stahl called the "affirmative action babies" in Washington.[59]

At the time, CBS, with its highly rated evening news featuring Walter Cronkite, represented the apex of the "Golden Age of Television News," according to Roger Mudd, one of its primary broadcasters.[60] Mudd called the Washington bureau "the heart of the CBS news operation."[61] With twenty-one correspondents and reporters, more than other networks, it thrived on competition. Rita Braver, who started out in the early 1970s as a desk editor and eventually worked her way up to being a national correspondent specializing in legal issues, said she learned from the bureau personnel who gathered nightly around newsroom monitors to critique newscasts on other networks: "You got to know what people who were good thought was good."[62]

McLaughlin, hired as an associate producer in 1963, became the only CBS woman reporter in 1965 and was made a correspondent—CBS's title for superior reporters—in 1971. She scored an exclusive that made worldwide headlines when she interviewed Martha Mitchell, wife of Nixon's attorney general, who suggested that America's anti–Vietnam War protestors should be sent to Russia.[63] McLaughlin appeared on camera less and less frequently during the 1980s, when she was CBS's oldest woman correspondent.

Mudd described her as a journalist with a sharp wit and mind but a lack of sharp elbows, "never body-slamming her way past a competitor," and surviving through "her sense of the absurd."[64] Like other "second- and third-stringers" in the bureau, she lacked an office, he noted, but she "brought in some miniature doll furniture and arranged it in her mail tray so that it looked like a dwarfed office."[65] Other employees thought it was funny, but the chief, Bill Small, was not amused. In Mudd's view, McLaughlin, having been the only woman for years, "decided she would not be a threat to anyone."[66]

The advent of Chung and Stahl changed bureau dynamics with the women routinely assigned to the "predawn stakeouts, minor congressional hearings, press conferences of little consequence—

which threw them into the all-male rough-and-tumble world of camera crews and courier corps," Mudd said.[67] He added, "Most of the men got along with Chung because she had a robust sense of humor and was not afraid to play their game," once calmly reaching out of a telephone booth on deadline to unzip the flies of a couple of male journalists who were teasing her.[68]

By contrast Stahl, whose father was a wealthy businessman in Massachusetts, initially had a "rougher time," Mudd noted, encountering difficulties with both an assignment editor who she thought had "little use for women and minorities" and camera crews who ridiculed her until she convinced them of her competence.[69] She had been a television producer and reporter for NBC in New York and London and a reporter for the Boston CBS affiliate before being hired by the network when a memo was floating around mandating "the next reporter we hire will be a woman."[70] Assigned to the Watergate hearings on Capitol Hill in 1974, she sat next to the venerated Mary McGrory and said she "squirmed" when McGrory "told me she resented the young women who had gotten their jobs through affirmative action."[71]

By this time all three major networks had added about a dozen newswomen and were looking for more.[72] But CBS still considered it an event when any of the three women in the Washington bureau, McLaughlin, Chung, or Stahl, each nicknamed Brenda Starr for their career orientation, appeared on the evening news.[73] When Stahl took part in a CBS Watergate roundup with correspondents Dan Rather and Daniel Schorr, a question was asked about Washington gossip. An investigative reporter famed for his role in leaking the Pentagon Papers—which detailed the futility of the Vietnam War—Schorr, who gave Stahl what she considered a "terrible hazing" when she joined the network, piped up to say, "If it's gossip you want, that's why we have a woman here."[74]

This comment represented continued friction between the two. Schorr resigned in 1976 after acknowledging he had been the source of a classified intelligence report on illegal activities of the CIA that appeared in New York's liberal weekly, the *Village Voice*. It ran under the byline of Aaron Latham, Stahl's boyfriend and later husband. Stahl contended that Schorr tried to pin the CIA leak on her before admitting his own responsibility.[75] After Schorr's departure, Stahl moved into his old office in the front row of CBS Washington correspondents.

In 1977 Stahl replaced Sally Quinn after Quinn failed as a coanchor for the *CBS Morning News*. Quinn had been hired away from the *Washington Post* for the coanchor job in spite of having no television experience, partly because of pressure to put more women on the air and partly because CBS executives reportedly thought she could be promoted as a "blonde bombshell who used sex to get stories."[76] Quinn became furious after learning that a comment she had made as a joke actually was used on the air with the approval of CBS executives—"A senator will tell you more over a martini at midnight than he will over a microphone at noon."[77]

Within six months Quinn returned to newspapers, smarting from criticism of her inexperience. Stahl successfully stepped into the coanchor role, although women anchors faced a chilly reception during this period. In 1976 Barbara Walters made history when ABC, hoping to improve the ratings of its evening news program, paired her with Harry Reasoner as the first woman to coanchor a nightly newscast. Her $1 million annual salary, huge by the standard of that day, sparked speculation that news broadcasts would turn into "showbiz," since Walters had appeared for fifteen years on NBC's *Today* program that featured entertainment more than news.[78]

A hysterical outcry greeted her move to ABC with headlines

like this one from the *New York Daily News:* DOLL BARBIE TO LEARN HER ABC'S.[79] Accused of flaunting her femininity while interviewing men, Walters wrote, "I love to flirt and be flirted with."[80] Beset by negative press criticism and faced with an unwilling partner in Reasoner, she was eased out of the coanchor role within a year and a half.

In 1979 Stahl, who had taken three weeks of maternity leave in 1977 to give birth to a daughter, becoming the first on-air network woman reporter to show her pregnancy, gained a major promotion. She was named CBS's chief White House correspondent, reportedly chosen for "her blond appeal," although she encountered some hostility.[81] One CBS executive asked her if she could manage the job and motherhood, too. Stahl interpreted the question as a how-could-you-leave-your child guilt-trip, designed to make her bow out in response to presidential pressure, since the Carter administration was angry over a magazine article written by her husband about a key presidential aide.[82] She recognized that she was promoted over Bob Pierpoint, a veteran correspondent far "more qualified than I."[83] Pierpoint wanted to resign, but Cronkite asked him to remain to help Stahl, and CBS gave him a 40 percent raise. To Stahl "they damn near bribed him to stay."[84]

Almost forty-two in 1983, the "age past which newswomen weren't supposed to survive on television," Stahl came out in support of Christine Craft, a television news anchor in Kansas City who sued for sexual discrimination after being demoted for allegedly being "too old, unattractive, and not deferential enough to men."[85] At the same time, Stahl said, she "spent as much time as I could spare on my appearance," getting "my hair done twice a week" and "buying and using enough makeup to open my own boutique."[86] Both her mother and her boss monitored her appearance; her mother told her not to wear glasses on television and both of them objected to her being seen in her fur coat. She followed their advice.

Stahl was embarrassed when her bosses told her to counsel another CBS White House reporter, Deborah Potter, one of the few brunettes in television news, to look better if she wanted to remain in front of the camera.[87] Stahl suggested Potter get a new haircut and pluck her eyebrows. Considered an excellent journalist and writer, Potter initially refused and was transferred to radio, but eventually hired a coach and returned to television.

The White House assignment pitted Stahl against Judy Woodruff of NBC to the glee of male colleagues. They insisted the two women "stand back-to-back to see who was taller," Stahl recalled, calling the incident a "weigh-in for what the men saw as the inevitable catfight between the two network ladies."[88] The two became friends, even though Stahl admitted she once stole a story from Woodruff by overhearing her record a news segment on a key appointment.[89] Both blonds, Stahl and Woodruff, the latter a beauty contest winner from Georgia, were addressed as "young lady" by President Ronald Reagan, who could not tell them apart.[90] Covering three administrations, those of Carter, Reagan, and Bush, Stahl revitalized *Face the Nation,* a public affairs program similar to *Meet the Press.* She subsequently became cohost of *60 Minutes,* the network's premier news magazine, which is produced in Washington.

Woodruff was not a chief network White House correspondent by herself, but shared the title with a man, John Palmer. "I'm not sure that the men running [NBC] thought that a woman could do the job by herself," commented Andrea Mitchell, an NBC White House correspondent passed over for her network's top slot there in 1988.[91] "It was considered the most authoritative beat among the correspondent jobs, and there was still a reluctance to assume that women could handle it."[92] A University of Pennsylvania graduate who began her television career in Philadelphia, Mitchell surmised NBC executives in the late 1980s remained wary of "the image of a woman standing on the White House lawn, giving the nation the view from the Oval Office."[93]

During her own White House assignment, which began in 1981, Mitchell, a blond like Stahl and Woodruff, said, "Sometimes I think women get criticized in subtle and not so subtle ways for being aggressive or ambitious. We're called pushy, bitchy, if we pursue a line of questioning at the White House aggressively.... It's really a matter of male expectations that we behave in a certain way."[94]

In place of moving up at the White House, Mitchell was dispatched to Capitol Hill, which turned into the "best decision that anyone had ever made for me," she said later, calling her years there "some of the most interesting and fulfilling of my career."[95] Looking back to days when "reporters had the freedom to roam the corridors, with few if any security restrictions," she said she covered foreign policy debates, budget hearings, disputes over energy policy—"the kind of substantive reporting I loved."[96] Mitchell returned to the White House as chief correspondent for NBC in 1993. The following year she was named chief foreign affairs correspondent, a position she continued to hold after her marriage in 1997 to Alan Greenspan, chairman of the board of governors of the Federal Reserve system.

Woodruff, the wife of Al Hunt, longtime Washington bureau chief of the *Wall Street Journal,* left NBC after the birth of her first child, who has spina bifida. She moved to PBS in 1983 as the first Washington correspondent for the *MacNeil/Lehrer NewsHour,* returning to commercial television in 1993 as a news anchor for CNN after having two more children. During her PBS decade, a contemporary broadcaster commented, "She rarely travels. Many network women envy her lengthy interviews and long reports on issues, as well as her control of her hours, and time for a personal life."[97] Woodruff left CNN in 2005 and took a visiting fellowship at Harvard University's Joan Shorenstein Center on the Press, Politics and Public Policy before returning to the PBS nightly *NewsHour.*

In 1971 Chung, then a twenty-five-year-old journalism graduate of the University of Maryland, made news herself as the first Asian American network reporter when she went from Channel 5, WTTG-TV, in Washington, to the CBS bureau there. Assigned to George McGovern's presidential campaign in 1972, Chung reported mainly for CBS radio, establishing a reputation for hard work. In his study of the campaign Crouse referred to her as the "pretty Chinese CBS correspondent, always in her hotel room at midnight, reciting a final sixty-second radio spot into her Sony or absorbing one late press release before getting a good night's sleep."[98] After substituting frequently as an anchor for the *CBS Morning News,* Chung left the network for its Los Angeles affiliate in 1976, becoming television's highest-paid local newswoman by 1983 with an estimated salary between $600,000 and $700,000 annually.[99] In 1993 she was named coanchor of the *CBS Evening News* with Dan Rather, but the two did not click as a team and she was dismissed from that position and released from her contract in 1995.

After returning to CBS, Chung, who married television personality Maury Povich in 1984, curtailed her broadcasting commitments and announced she wanted to have a baby at the age of forty-four. Yet, the announcement upset her: "I never wanted to be seen differently from a man [employee]," she said.[100] She did not become pregnant and the couple adopted a baby boy.

In part CBS wanted Chung back because Diane Sawyer, another blond television star, had decided to leave that network for more money at ABC. Kentucky-born Sawyer, whose father had been a judge and mother a schoolteacher, reigned as America's Junior Miss in 1963. A graduate of Wellesley College, she worked for eight years for President Richard Nixon, first as a writer in his White House press office and, after he was forced to resign, in California, where she assisted in the preparation of his memoirs. When he finished the manuscript, she returned to Washington in 1978 as a general assignment reporter in the CBS bureau at the age of thirty-two.[101] In 1981 she became coanchor on the network's morning news program.

Three years later she became the first woman staff correspondent for the highly rated *60 Minutes* news magazine. Impressed with her abilities, Don Hewitt, the producer, said he would have hired her if her name had been Tom Sawyer. "She is one of the girls who is one of the boys," he commented.[102]

Sawyer, who married Mike Nichols, a film director, in 1988, has expressed mixed feelings about not having a child, although Nichols has three from a previous marriage. "I cannot imagine having this job and having to pick up and go to Russia and then go straight on to Zaire and then come back here, and having a child at home. You would have to be so unfeeling and selfish to do it happily," she told an interviewer.[103] Describing conflict between career and family, Sawyer said, "It will always be a woman's problem."[104] At ABC Sawyer coanchored news programs and *Good Morning America* before being named anchor of ABC's *World News Tonight* in 2009.

As such, Sawyer competed directly with Katie Couric of the *CBS Evening News,* who in 2006 became the first solo woman anchor of a nightly network newscast. Although nightly news programs originate in New York, both are broadcast intermittently from Washington. In testimony to the glamour attached to the news anchor post in the twenty-first century, Couric's annual salary was $15 million, with Sawyer believed to get as much or more. Neither Couric nor Sawyer, however, was able to stop a steady drain of viewers from network evening news. Couric's contract was not renewed in 2011.

After graduating from the University of Virginia in 1979, Couric, who had been a high school cheerleader, started her broadcast career as a low-level assistant in the ABC Washington bureau where she brewed coffee, answered phones, and fetched sandwiches.[105] She left for an assignment editor/field reporter's job at the fledging CNN, where she was let go because of a "squeaky voice."[106] Following stints in Miami and at WRC-TV, Channel Four, in Washington, she joined NBC News in 1989. When NBC replaced the popular but aging Jane Pauley with a younger and prettier coanchor, Deborah Norville, on the *Today* show in 1991, the audience reacted negatively.[107]

Couric, known for her friendly, peppy personality, proved a hit when she was brought in to substitute for Norville and got the job permanently, winning high ratings that led to her nickname as "America's Sweetheart."[108] After her husband, Jay Monahan, a lawyer, died of colon cancer in 1998, Couric, the mother of two children, broadcast her own colonoscopy on the air in 2000 in a successful effort to encourage others to have the test to combat cancer.[109]

When Couric broke gender barriers to become the first solo woman anchor on a nightly news program, observers wondered whether she would trade in her sexy wardrobe on the *Today* show for more serious-looking "power" suits.[110] To some extent she did, but network publicity pictured both her and Sawyer as glamorous celebrities. CBS admitted to doctoring a photo of Couric in its company magazine to make her appear thinner, blaming an overzealous employee in the photo department.[111] ABC happily publicized the fact that viewers emailed questions about the shade of Sawyer's lipstick.[112]

As the careers of Couric and Sawyer illustrate, opportunities emerged for women in broadcasting after a federally mandated push for equality in hiring in the early 1970s. In 1971, for example, Betsy Ashton, an art teacher from Fairfax County, Virginia, outside Washington, heard Nicholas Johnson, an FCC commissioner, encourage citizens unhappy with television programming to present alternative ideas to local stations. Ashton did just that—a chance comment from a journalist friend prompted her to prepare a series of interviews on the women's movement that led to an interview for a job as the first woman reporter for WWDC radio in Washington in 1972.

She never forgot her first sight of the station's "tiny, smoke-shrouded newsroom, filled with the clackety-clack of a dozen machines and the noise of two typewriters being pounded by reporters sitting at a U-shaped desk. . . . Loud cackling came from a corner where the sports reporter undressed me with his eyes while sharing a joke with someone on the phone."[113]

In the midst of this cacophony, heightened by a young man who "yelled into a two-way radio to Captain Dan, the traffic reporter in a helicopter," Ashton was instructed to write a sample five-minute newscast in an hour on a typewriter with a broken *E* key.[114] Telling herself this was "no worse than teaching high school with a crazy student," she ignored the noise and the leering sportscaster to concentrate on writing her first newscast.[115] She soon was hired, but the news director still wanted to see if she could do a "man's job."

For a story on business conditions during a mild recession, he sent her to a strip club in Washington's then-seamy Fourteenth Street area. Ashton discovered a "young woman was dancing naked on a table but most of the few men inside were watching a football game on a big screen."[116] Picking up "unmemorable quotes" from the owner, she felt sorry for the dancer who had "taken it all off, and was being totally ignored."[117] Next, she was told to go by herself down Washington's blighted Seventh Street corridor and check on stores there. "They [station personnel] thought I would refuse to go," she said.[118] "They laughed about how one new woman reporter for another station had refused to cover a tough story and gotten herself 'justly' fired."[119]

Ashton proved them wrong. Driving right down Seventh Street, she parked in front of one of the few remaining businesses, and interviewed the owner and men who were hanging around the place. "They were actually glad that someone in the news media was interested in hearing their opinions," she said.[120] She soon moved to WMAL, the Washington station with the strongest news operation, switching from radio to television before the station changed its name to WJLA-TV in 1974. In 1982 she left Washington for WCBS-TV in New York, and wound up working for both that station and the *CBS Morning News*.

During the early 1970s Connie Lawn, a vivacious young woman who had worked briefly for an all-news radio station in the Washington area before becoming a television reporter in Massachusetts, set up her own syndicated radio service from Washington. She ran ads in *Broadcasting* magazine offering to cover congressional delegations and other local news events for stations around the country. "Soon I had a string of stations stretching from Canada to New York, south to Florida, and west to St. Louis and California," she wrote in her autobiography.[121] "I was constantly on the go, working eighteen-hour days, six days a week, with a few hours on Sunday."[122]

Lawn picked up international clients, particularly the Canadian Broadcasting Company, which she said "paid me quite well, for which I am grateful, [but] often treated me like a hired hand rather than a colleague."[123] She recalled that the male bureau chief grudgingly introduced her as someone "who occasionally does stories for us," whereas a man who reported far fewer stories was introduced as "one of our top free-lancers in Washington."[124]

Today the most senior freelance correspondent accredited to the White House, Lawn refused to give up her career when she was married and had children. At her wedding to Steven Rappaport, an accountant, in 1974 in New York's Plaza Hotel, she said she set up her tape recorder on the "virginal white bridal table" in order to do some broadcasts "a few hours before and after the ceremony."[125] When David, her first child, was born four years later, she "even filed a report on the Sunday interview shows for Israeli Radio moments before my labor began."[126]

She made it to the hospital two hours before her son David was delivered. A few hours later she watched the evening newscasts so she could phone in stories on a train crash and explosion to "my newly acquired stations in New Zealand and Australia."[127] Only months later did she let the stations know she had a baby. "I'd worked for years to get New Zealand as a client, and had just landed the Australian station, and was afraid both would fire me if they learned they had to share my time with a brand-new infant," she explained.[128]

Ten days later when her babysitter failed to appear, she "loaded David into his little plastic bed and set off on my rounds," placing him on a table in front of the secretary of transportation during a news conference.[129] Fortunately, David did not even gurgle. Her second son was born during the Mideast peace negotiations of the Carter administration. Two hours later, "determined to maintain my record," she said she broadcast a story in spite of difficulty in "getting an outside line from the recovery room."[130]

Antidiscrimination suits that were filed against network-owned-and-operated stations had led to a requirement by the Federal Communications Commission in 1971 that stations file affirmative action plans as part of their license renewal applications.[131] By the start of 1974 all three major networks had committees in place to improve the status of women. Although set up in New York, they had an impact on network operations in Washington, but change did not happen immediately.

According to Stahl, "sexual harassment hadn't hit the radar screen" in the 1970s.[132] "Yet I can remember going to Capitol Hill and being warned by the other women reporters to stay away from certain senators. . . . We relied on our ability to run faster (we were generally younger); complaining about advances was seen as futile or, worse, self-destructive," she said.[133]

In 1986, seven women employees of *Nightwatch*, a CBS overnight news program from Washington, sued the network, charging the executive producer with "sexual assault" and "international infliction of emotional distress" involving unwanted sexual advances in violation of the District of Columbia Civil Rights Act.[134] The producer left the program. The women, who had asked for $14 million in damages, settled the case out of court in 1987, but neither side would discuss the amount involved.[135]

Government regulations made it obvious to station managers that it was advantageous to employ minority women because they could be counted in two Equal Employment Opportunity categories, a phenomenon referred to as "twofer" hiring. A 1977 study found that a quarter of the women in television news were minorities, as were 16 percent of the women in radio news.[136] Frequently, minority women did not receive the same kind of "hard news" assignments as their masculine colleagues, yet a determined group persevered and established themselves as well-known figures in Washington, sometimes covering national stories because of their proximity to the Capitol.

J. C. Hayward, an African American who graduated from Howard University, became the first female news anchor in Washington in 1972 when she joined WUSA, Channel 9, the CBS affiliate, where she anchors the noon newscast today. Over the years Hayward set a national record for a woman anchoring the same evening newscast at the same station.[137] "Women were excited, but there were some diehards who said, 'What is this woman doing anchoring? She needs to be at home in the kitchen,'" she recalled.[138] Hayward became the first consumer reporter on the air in Washington. She also produced documentaries about world issues, including one on Somalia, which was broadcast on PBS and in other countries.[139]

Maureen Bunyan, who was born in Aruba, arrived in Washington in 1973 and joined Channel 9 as a reporter. Two years later she helped found the National Association of Black Journalists. Becoming coanchor for the 6:00 P.M. Channel 9 news in 1978, Bunyan remained at the station for more than twenty years, winning numerous awards. Faced with demotion in 1995, she resigned and ran her own public relations firm before returning to broadcasting in 1999 as an anchor at WJLA, Channel 7, Washington's ABC affiliate.[140] Bunyan is a founder and board member of the International Women's Media Foundation, set up in Washington in 1990 to cultivate women's leadership in media globally. She holds a master's degree from the Harvard University Graduate School of Education.

In 1978 Renee Poussaint, a graduate of Sarah Lawrence College who held a master's degree in African studies from the University of California, Los Angeles, left the CBS Washington bureau to become a coanchor for evening newscasts at Channel 7. She told CBS she was frustrated and restless because the size of the Washington bureau made it difficult for her and other reporters to get on the air. "Washington is a one-industry town, government," she said. "Most of the reporting involves standing around talking to men in three-piece suits about the government."[141]

Asked if she would like to become a network anchor, she replied that the odds against her were tremendous. "Watch network news on the weekends," she told an interviewer.[142] "That's where you'll see all the blacks and the women. But each network has a weekday blonde."[143] She attributed this phenomenon to men who did the hiring, suggesting "blondes are what they fantasize about."[144]

Previously Poussaint had worked for the CBS bureau in Chicago after a successful stint at the CBS-owned station there, where she had faced the difficulties of being a black woman covering racist activities. Sent to a meeting of the Chicago Firefighters Association, where the agenda centered on how to keep women and blacks out of the union, Poussaint kept calm and poker-faced. As she tried to exit, one firefighter, who watched her on television, rushed up and said, "Renee, we don't want you to leave thinking we're racist and sexists. But, well, it's just that the broads and the niggers are taking over the world!"[145]

His bigoted remark left a mixed impression. "As a black woman, I'm insulted that he could have said such a thing to me," Poussaint said. "But as a reporter, I almost felt flattered. He saw me as a professional and thought he could level with me."[146] At the same time, she recognized that many women in her audience gravitated toward her on the basis of style, not substance. "I envy men reporters because they don't have to worry about looking nice all the time," she said. "Women viewers can get very fixated on the accouterments. When I wore glasses, people called me up all the time to ask why I'd changed the frames."[147]

Poussaint gave up anchoring and became a correspondent for ABC's *Primetime Live,* but she did not remain in network television. She left in 1997, tired of "trying to make commercial broadcasting care about the issues I care about—poor people, education, women's issues, black people—and I got tired of having story ideas turned down."[148] She subsequently cofounded the National Visionary Leadership Project to preserve and distribute the stories of older African Americans as a way of inspiring the younger generation.

At the network level, Lee Thornton joined the CBS Washington bureau in 1975 and stayed there until 1982, when she left for an anchor job in Detroit. Thornton was the first CBS African American woman correspondent to cover the White House, although she did not report major stories. "I was fourth in line" in the network's correspondent hierarchy, she recalled years later.[149] "I was definitely going to get weekends . . . but I was not going to be the evening news reporter."[150] Frequently assigned to the president's wife, she said, "I learned in covering the first lady how to make a lot out of it."[151]

During her years at CBS, Thornton saw women bringing a special touch to television—"good hard news judgment plus human interest. A terrific combination. Are we the gentler sex? Innately softer . . . more loving . . . thank God. But the job of the journalist takes aggressiveness and tenacity, although that does not mean hard-edged rudeness."[152] She said it also took "physical health and stamina to meet unbelievable demands, such as working six nights a week for six months with two overnights (midnight to 8:00 A.M.) each week."[153]

Reflecting on her experiences, Thornton, a native of Washington who holds a doctorate in communications from Northwestern University, commented, "It's difficult for me to speak of women and minorities in one breath."[154] In her view, "broadcasting has allowed a far greater inflow of women, especially white women, since the early 1970s," but minorities have not fared as well as whites.[155] "I always fit into two categories and the old, unattractive, name for me was 'twofer,' two for one," she said. "But black women haven't made the same kinds of gains as white women in the business. In general, ethnic minorities have not made the same gains or had the same kind of success."[156]

After leaving full-time television news, Thornton taught broadcasting at Howard University. She also became the first African American to host NPR's *All Things Considered* program, which she did on Fridays and weekends. Later she was a Washington reporter for the American Business Network, which aired on cable channels, and produced a public affairs program at CNN's Washington bureau.

To Thornton "there's a male dominated corporate culture in newsrooms that leaves women and minorities and minority women at a distinct disadvantage. I tried appeasing it, fighting with it, bargaining with it and in the end resigning myself to it. But newsrooms aren't alone in this—by a long shot. I've found the same thing to be true in academics and in government," she said.[157]

Thornton moved to the University of Maryland, College Park, in 1997 as the first holder of the Eaton Chair in Broadcasting at the Philip Merrill College of Journalism. She served as interim dean at Merrill in 2009–10 and subsequently as the interim associate provost for equity and diversity at Maryland. "I am absolutely convinced that there exists an 'old boys' network. Sometimes it's a middle aged boys network, or, sorry to have to put it this way, a white 'boys' network," Thornton stated. "It exists and I have no doubt about it. And it is at the root of many things that result in inequality in journalism and in American society."[158]

The mainstream news culture offended Ethel Payne, who in 1972 became the first black woman commentator on network television. She commented on public affairs for six years on the CBS radio and television series *Spectrum*. The chauvinism of white male reporters irritated her. "There was always that haughty air about males in the press corps," she said in an oral history interview. "They had names and reputations. It was almost like they were holier than thou."[159]

When Eric Sevareid, a well-known CBS commentator, rebuked Sarah McClendon in public for alleged aggressiveness, Payne criticized his attitude. "I took him to task about his treatment of Sarah. I said, 'Let him drown in his own pomposity.' I got volumes of letters about that," she recalled.[160] Not all of them supported her.

During her CBS years Payne continued with the *Chicago Defender,* remaining with it until 1978 when she established herself as a Washington-based syndicated columnist for several African American newspapers.[161] A leader in the campaign to free Nelson Mandela in South Africa, Payne was arrested at the South African Embassy in 1985 during an antiapartheid demonstration there.[162] Seeing herself as an agent of change, she advised young journalists to "agitate, agitate, agitate."[163]

No doubt, the journalistic scene changed as the presence of women and minorities became accepted and expected by members of the audience. According to Cokie Roberts, a broadcast journalist and author, "At some point, being a woman became an advantage, at last for some of us."[164] She continued, "We went into the workplace as a group, an entire generation of educated women that was determined to break down barriers for ourselves and the women who came after us, and we have the scratches and bruises to show for it. But it mattered."[165]

Broadcasting represented a field in which intelligent, attractive women could stand out when given a chance. As Thornton put it, "We know that television, like film and advertising, is a cosmetic business. Physical appearance counts.... A well-kept appearance probably helps quite a bit in broadcasting. On air, definitely. But I honestly ... believe that if you don't know the journalism, this won't carry you."[166] Women had to fight to show that they were competent journalists.

Despite her privileged background as the fourth child of Hale Boggs, a Democratic congressman from Louisiana, and his wife, Lindy Boggs, who succeeded him in Congress after his death in a plane crash, Roberts had difficulty launching her career. When she entered broadcasting in Washington in the 1960s, she received encouragement from Nancy Dickerson, who extended a hand to new colleagues.[167] Following marriage to Steve Roberts, a *New York Times* reporter, two years after her graduation from Wellesley College, Roberts left an anchor job at WRC-TV in Washington to go with her husband to New York, where she encountered gender-based prejudice. "For eight months I job-hunted at various New York magazines and television stations, and wherever I went I was asked how many words I could type," she told an interviewer.[168]

Eventually, Roberts and two other women, Nina Totenberg and Linda Wertheimer, became known as the three musketeers of National Public Radio (NPR), when they found opportunities at the Washington-based operation during the 1970s and 80s that they developed into notable careers.[169] Begun in connection with the 1967 Public Broadcasting Act, which was primarily designed to deal with public television, NPR proved more hospitable to women than many other news organizations. In an interview with the three women in 1994, the *New York Times* credited them with "revolutionizing political reporting."[170] According to the *Times,* they had shown themselves to be "gutsy, witty, informed reporters who break stories from inside the Washington political machine," which twenty years ago had been "pretty much a male game, like football and foreign policy."[171]

The trio had struggled to get to a foothold in their field. Accompanying her husband to Greece, Roberts worked as a reporter for CBS there before returning to the United States. Totenberg encouraged her to apply to NPR. "When I came in for an interview, Linda and Nina were there, greeting me and encouraging me. And it just made all the difference in the world. NPR was a place where I wanted to work because they were there," Roberts said.[172]

To Totenberg, for many years NPR's legal affairs correspondent, "It [NPR] was, and still is, a shop where a woman could get considerable visibility and responsibility. NPR's wages were at least a third lower than elsewhere in the industry, and for what they paid, they couldn't find men."[173] Today considered the dean of Supreme Court reporters, Totenberg has won numerous awards for her reporting.

In the 1980s Roberts made a name for herself as congressional correspondent for NPR. Asked by Judy Woodruff, who coanchored PBS's gavel-to-gavel coverage of the Iran-Contra joint congressional hearings in 1987, to secure interviews from members of the bipartisan committee conducting the hearings, Roberts won a prize for her reporting. The coverage, which also featured coanchor Elizabeth Drew, longtime political reporter for the *New*

Yorker, drew compliments from women viewers who wrote to PBS that "they were bursting with pride," as one television insider put it, to see outstanding performance by three female correspondents.[174] Marlene Sanders of ABC, who had been named the first woman vice president for a major network news division, said it was "unlikely network executives [outside of PBS] would have dared to give such responsibility and star billing to their staff newswomen."[175] Roberts also hosted a weekly public affairs program on Congress on PBS from 1981 to 1984.

Joining ABC News as a political commentator in 1988, Roberts coanchored ABC News' Sunday morning broadcast, *This Week with Sam Donaldson and Cokie Roberts,* from 1996 to 2002. She also became the first woman panelist to appear regularly on ABC's *This Week* news program. She drew criticism in 1994, however, when a news broadcast showed her standing in front of the U.S. Capitol on ABC's *World News Tonight.* In actuality, she had donned an overcoat and stood in front of an image of the Capitol in ABC's Washington studio on her way to give a speech.[176]

Another controversy occurred two years later when Roberts insisted in an interview that Sister Dianna Ortiz, a Catholic nun, was lying about being raped and tortured by a death squad in Guatemala until an American who observed the attack realized that the nun was from the United States and ordered that she be freed. Considerable evidence supported the nun's account, and critics noted that Roberts's brother, Tom Boggs, one of Washington's most prominent lawyer-lobbyists, had been hired by the Guatemalan military to improve the image of its actions during bloody conflict.[177]

A senior news analysis for NPR and bestselling author of books on women in American history, Roberts marketed herself as a celebrity along with her husband. The couple started a weekly syndicated newspaper column in 1994 intended to merge the personal and the political. During the same period, Jim Warren of the *Chicago Tribune* lambasted her as a "journalistic cash machine" for receiving $20,000 or more for speaking appearances before business groups and for-profit organizations.[178] He cited such examples as a Chicago bank reportedly paying the couple $45,000 for three joint appearances during one weekend.[179] Warren ran a "Cokie Watch" feature in his Sunday column, prompting Steve Roberts to charge Warren with a "crusade to make his own reputation by tearing down others."[180] Steve Roberts declared no evidence existed that the couple's journalistic output had been influenced by money received from speeches.[181]

Wertheimer has been less controversial. The director of NPR's first program, *All Things Considered,* a daily news program that made its debut in 1971 on a hundred public television stations, she became its host in 1989.[182] Her audience expanded from 6 million to nearly 10 million listeners by 2001, making it one of the top five shows in U.S. radio.[183] At the same time, Wertheimer also appeared on CBS's Sunday morning news program, *Face the Nation.*

According to Wertheimer, "In the very beginning we had Susan Stamberg clearing a path for the rest of us, inventing her own kind of radio and ensuring that women would play an unprecedented role on the new network."[184] Stamberg, the first woman to anchor a national daily news program, influenced the novel development of *All Things Considered,* Wertheimer said, noting it was "difficult to overstate Susan's personal impact on the way NPR sounds now. . . . The opportunities that NPR has offered to women, to people of color, to very young people, to people who refuse to retire, to all sorts of voices and commentators have been unique."[185]

A native of Newark, Stamberg became program director and

then station manager of WAMU-FM, a public radio station located at American University in Washington, D.C., in the mid-1960s.[186] As cohost of *All Things Considered* from 1971 to 1986, she gave the program a personal touch, as illustrated by the fact that each Thanksgiving since 1971 she has provided NPR listeners with her mother-in-law's recipe for an unusual cranberry relish sauce.[187] In 1972 she referred to the infamous Watergate burglary as the "Caper of the Bungled Bugging."[188]

Over the years Stamberg reported on subjects as varied as the Carter administration, the AIDS epidemic, and white South Africa with an eye for human interest elements. When she interviewed Gloria Steinem in 1982 on the tenth anniversary of her feminist magazine, *Ms.,* Stamberg spoke of the defeat of the Equal Rights Amendment. She said she was struck by the "stiff upper lipped-ness that was so publicly demonstrated by the official speakers, by you and so many others. . . . Women are always talking about making room for feelings. . . . Why wasn't that kind of space made?"[189] Steinem agreed that perhaps she was right.

Born in New Mexico, Wertheimer became NPR's first senior national correspondent in 2002. Like Roberts, she graduated from Wellesley College. She began her career at the BBC in England. Returning to the United States, she applied for a job at NBC in New York. As she recounted the experience, "this 'gentleman' informed me that 'women are not credible on the air.' He then offered to introduce me to a woman at NBC whose career he thought I should emulate—she'd been a researcher for ten years—and I just started yelling at him."[190] Wertheimer added, "It was in neon: 'This Is the Only Job a Woman Can Have!'"[191]

After joining NPR Wertheimer scored several firsts. In 1976 she became the first woman to anchor network coverage of both a presidential nomination convention and an election night. Two years later she also became the first person to broadcast live from the U.S. Senate chamber, providing thirty-seven days of live coverage of the debate over the Panama Canal Treaty. "Our audience was fascinated and horrified, in about equal parts, to hear for themselves how the self-styled 'world's greatest deliberative body' actually sounds," she recalled.[192] She remembered "with great affection the late Senator James Allen of Alabama ... who habitually addressed me as 'little lady,' remembering not to do it only when I called him 'big senator.' "[193]

In 1987 Wertheimer won an award from the Corporation for Public Broadcasting for anchoring a special report on the Iran-Contra Affair. This series of forty-one half-hour programs looked into the claim of White House officials that they had proceeded without permission from President Ronald Reagan to act outside the law. "Whatever the real story, the Iran-contra affair had the effect of making the president a less significant figure in his last years in office," Wertheimer commented.[194] On occasion Wertheimer offered personal observations on the news. She noted during coverage of a ban on federal funding for abortions in 1977 that male decision makers had "an imperfect understanding of female sexuality and physiology," quoting a male Senate staffer who asked a female colleague, "Is ovulation the same as orgasm?"[195]

In 1997 she was named one of the top fifty journalists in Washington by *Washingtonian* magazine. The next year *Vanity Fair* cited her as one of the nation's two hundred most influential women.[196] She is married to Fred Wertheimer, past president of Common Cause, a prime advocate of campaign finance reform; she does not report on the subject to avoid conflict of interest.

Totenberg joined NPR in 1973 after a decade in print journalism. The daughter of a professional violinist, Roman Totenberg, and Melanie Totenberg, executive vice president of the Massachusetts chapter of the liberal Americans for Democratic Action, Totenberg dropped out of Boston University to work for the *Boston Record American,* where she edited recipes and wedding announcements. When she tried to get a job on a newspaper in Quincy, Massachusetts, in 1965, she recalled that "this male editor said to me, 'Oh, we don't hire women.' . . . It was so much the way things were that I wasn't outraged."[197] In contrast a decade later she felt "rage well up through my gullet" when a bureau chief of a newspaper chain reacted to her inquiry about a job by saying, "But, Nina, we already have our woman."[198]

After working for the *Peabody Times* in Massachusetts, Totenberg moved to *Roll Call* in Washington, D.C., and then on to another newspaper in the capital, the *National Observer,* where she developed a legal beat because "no one else was doing it."[199] In 1971 she broke a story about a secret list of candidates President Nixon was considering for the Supreme Court, all of whom later were rejected as unqualified.[200] After she wrote a profile of FBI director J. Edgar Hoover, he demanded that she be fired. The *Observer* responded simply by printing Hoover's letter along with an answer to his accusations of unfairness.

In 1972 Totenberg was fired for plagiarism after writing an article on Rep. Tip O'Neill, soon to be named Speaker of the House, which included without attribution quotes from members of Congress that previously had appeared in the *Washington Post.*[201] Some journalists, however, defended her on the grounds that the practice of using unattributed quotes was common in the 1970s. In 1995 she told the *Columbia Journalism Review,* "I have a strong feeling that a young reporter is entitled to one mistake and to have the holy bejeezus scared out of her to never do it again."[202] Totenberg also alleged that sexual harassment at the *Observer* figured into her firing. After she left the *Observer,* she worked for a short-lived

Washington magazine, *New Times,* where she wrote an article called THE TEN DUMBEST MEMBERS OF CONGRESS. It prompted Sen. William L. Scott, whose name stood at the top of the list, to call a press conference to rebut allegations of his stupidity.[203]

At NPR Totenberg's work continued to generate controversy. In 1977 she reported on private Supreme Court deliberations for the first time when she aired a story that the high court had voted secretly five to three against reviewing the case of three former Nixon administration officials convicted in the Watergate scandal. The story led to speculation that Totenberg had gained the story from a sitting justice, which she denied.[204] Subsequently she broke a story that a Supreme Court nominee, Douglas H. Ginsburg, had used marijuana. As a result Ginsburg withdrew his name from consideration.

Totenberg attained national prominence in 1991 when she disclosed sexual harassment charges by Anita Hill, a law professor, against Supreme Court nominee Clarence Thomas.[205] Totenberg revealed on NPR's *Morning Edition* that Hill had told the committee Thomas had harassed her while she had worked for him in two federal agencies. The disclosure forced the Senate Judiciary Committee to reopen Thomas's confirmation hearings and sparked widespread public debate on the issue of sexual harassment in general, although Thomas eventually was confirmed.

Totenberg herself was investigated by Congress in an unsuccessful effort to find out how she obtained the information. The hearings also resulted in Totenberg's firing from the *National Observer* being rehashed by Al Hunt of the conservative *Wall Street Journal,* which supported Thomas.[206] As she covered the committee hearing and coanchored its public broadcasting coverage, Totenberg herself became the subject of news stories—particularly after participating in a verbal shoving match involving Sen.

Alan Simpson, a Republican from Wyoming. The two engaged in a heated exchange following a joint appearance on the ABC *Nightline* program during which Simpson accused her of failing to be objective.[207] Totenberg also did commentary and reporting for ABC.

"I think there clearly was an attempt by some to switch the focus from the Thomas hearings and the charges to the so-called leak," Totenberg said. "Sen. Simpson has since said that I was just doing my job, and that I'm a fine journalist. He has backed off entirely. You can't do good investigative work without making some people mad."[208]

She added, "I just keep my head down and do my job. Whether liberals or conservatives like or dislike it is of no importance to me whatsoever."[209] Conservatives have targeted her for disapproval, especially in the wake of her 1995 comment about Rep. Sen. Jesse Helms of North Carolina, an opponent of funding for AIDS research: "I think he ought to be worried about what's going on in the Good Lord's mind, because if there is retributive justice, he'll get AIDS from a transfusion, or one of his grandchildren will."[210] NPR did not discipline Totenberg for her remark, a fact brought up by Juan Williams as an example of the network's proliberal bias after NPR fired him in October 2010 for unfavorable comments made about Muslims on Fox News.[211] The NRA also has criticized Totenberg's reporting on Second Amendment issues as skewed against gun rights.

Totenberg is the widow of Sen. Floyd Haskell, a Colorado Democrat, whom she married in 1979. She is also a personal friend of some persons in high places, including Supreme Court Justice Ruth Bader Ginsburg, who officiated in 2000 at Totenberg's marriage to Dr. David Reiner, a surgeon. He treated her for severe injuries sustained when she was hit by a boat propeller while swimming on their honeymoon.[212]

Diane Rehm, another woman whose career has flourished in public broadcasting, hosts a two-hour morning talk show that draws more than 2 million listeners across the country. She got her start in 1973 as a volunteer at WAMU-FM. The daughter of immigrants from Turkey who owned a Washington grocery store, she grew up in a Christian Arab household, subjected to beatings by her unstable mother. When she was nine years old, a congressman attempted to sexually abuse her, telling her family he wanted to make her a child movie star.[213]

Lacking money to attend college, she worked as a secretary after graduation from high school. After an early marriage ended in divorce, she wed John Rehm, a lawyer, and had two children. Finding herself "restless and edgy" as a suburban housewife in the early 1970s, she tried modeling swimsuits but felt like she "was part of a strip show" and "wasn't really comfortable with this kind of work."[214] Enrolling in a noncredit class at George Washington University to assess possibilities for a career, she was steered toward broadcasting. "It was a time of growth and experimentation [in public radio], a time when an inexperienced person like me could venture onto the airwaves without training, as long as she had something to say," she recalled.[215] On her first day at WAMU-FM, which had only a few full-time staff members, she filled in for an absent host, interviewing a representative from the dairy industry.

"At the end of the ninety-minute program [which included call-ins from listeners], I was exhilarated," Rehm recalled. "At the age of thirty-seven, without even realizing what had happened, I had embarked on my career in radio."[216] After volunteering for ten months, she became a paid assistant producer and hosted health-oriented programs. Leaving WAMU in 1976 for a try at television, she worked for Physicians Radio Network, a closed-circuit broadcasting service for doctors, for two years before returning to the station in 1979. Taking over *Kaleidoscope,* aimed primarily at women at home, she broadened the content to interest men.

Renamed the *Diane Rehm Show,* the program featured a weekly news roundup and interviews with guests as varied as former presidents of the United States, Nobel laureate authors, leading politicians, scientists, and reformed criminals. By 1999 her audience had grown from a few thousand listeners in the Washington area to more than seven hundred thousand NPR listeners around the country.[217]

Although she made forays into television, which included acting as the last host of CBS's *Nightwatch* before it left the air, radio remained more satisfying, she concluded, because it required the audience to concentrate on words. As Rehm expressed it, "With television, the image becomes an intense focal point, one that can, to a degree, get in the way of what's being said and done."[218] One of the pioneers of talk radio, she abhorred the biased, opinionated spectacle offered by ideologically oriented radio hosts, seeking instead to provide listeners with rational conversation. Occasionally she found herself subjected to offensive language because she was a woman. When she questioned actor Tony Randall about possible interview topics, he smirked and suggested she ask "about the size of my cock," while her youthful staff "burst into loud guffaws."[219] Livid with anger, she proceeded with the interview but refused to air it.

In 1998, after her program had achieved national distribution, Rehm feared that her career was over. Her voice became extremely hoarse and she was diagnosed with a rare neurological disorder, spasmodic dysphonia, which gave her tremors and forced her off the air briefly in 1999. She managed to treat the ailment with some success and returned to public radio. "There will always be a need, indeed a desire, for good, straightforward, honest dialogue," she insisted.[220] She interviewed President Bill Clinton in the Oval Office in 2000, marking the first time a radio talk show host had broadcast from the White House.[221]

Rehm has received numerous honors and awards, along with honorary degrees from several universities—including American University, which continues to host her show on WAMU. As the university's commencement speaker in 2007, she emphasized that public broadcasting and the university had the same goals—"to expand horizons, and to promote a deeper understanding of the world around us."[222]

Yet for some women broadcasting represented a contested field involving personal and professional turmoil. Jessica Savitch, considered a hot prospect in network news in the 1970s, died in a car accident in 1983 at a time when her career seemed to have leveled off. As one of the few women majoring in communications at Ithaca College in New York in the 1960s, she received a curt rebuke from a faculty adviser to a campus radio station. She said he told her, "There is no place for broads in broadcasting."[223] Determined not to give up, she protested and won the right to do a solo newscast.[224] Aided by a boyfriend, she did commercials on radio and television and on weekends broadcast on a Rochester, New York, rock-and-roll radio station as its first woman deejay.

After graduation in 1968 she sought a job in New York City. Hired as an assistant at WCBS-AM, she sought professional mentoring from correspondent Ed Bradley, with whom she also had a romantic relationship, and produced an audition tape that resulted in a television broadcasting job in Houston. Moving on to Philadelphia in 1972, her blond good looks resulted in "incredible viewer response" and a "magical" relationship with the camera, according to broadcast historians.[225] Her frantic pursuit of success led coworkers to call her "Jessica Savage," but it impressed the networks, which launched a bidding war for her services, eager to promote her mesmerizing qualities.[226]

NBC won out in 1977, offering the thirty-year-old Savitch a salary greater than that of any of its other newswomen. From a base in Washington she covered the U.S. Senate and occupied a weekend anchor chair on the network's *Nightly News,* as well as doing sixty-second news updates.[227] Far from welcoming Savitch, NBC staffers saw her as a personification of their fears that performers were taking over for journalists, and they were taken aback by the personal hairdresser she paraded into the building.[228] Lacking a Washington background and strong writing skills, she was taken off the Senate beat in 1978 and assigned to NBC's prime-time weekend news magazine.

During this period her first marriage failed after only ten months. For years she had been using drugs; now their use intensified and she threw fits at the office. In 1981 she married a Washington gynecologist, who committed suicide less than six months later, shortly after Savitch had ended a pregnancy.[229] Devastated, she poured herself into her career along with writing her autobiography, *Anchorwoman.*[230] "People look at my business and see it as all gloss and glamour, but the glamour is the tip of the iceberg," she told an interviewer, adding that she feared it might be "impossible" to attain success in both her professional and personal life.[231]

Savitch took a leave from NBC to appear on PBS's new series *Frontline,* a move that she hoped would give her more credibility in news. Nevertheless, NBC announced that Connie Chung would replace her as the Saturday anchor of *Nightly News,* although it did renew her contract. Tragically both she and her new romantic interest, Martin Fischbein, a New York newspaper executive, drowned in 1983 when he made a wrong turn on a Pennsylvania road during a rainstorm and their car landed upside down in a canal. Her biographer called her story "a nightmare, hung in the fragile balance of truth and illusion that is television."[232]

For women journalists in Washington, broadcasting offered both huge rewards and crushing disappointment. Network stars turned into glamorous role models that were far removed from the lives of many women viewers. Women at the top became well entrenched in the nation's power structure, themselves greater celebrities than most of the figures they covered. When they spoke with a voice different from that of their male colleagues, which they did on occasion, they brought up subjects that attacked the face of American politics—such as Totenberg's reporting on the sexual harassment charges against Clarence Thomas.

SEVEN

A QUESTION OF EQUITY AT THE END
OF THE TWENTIETH CENTURY

Traffic gridlock is a good metaphor for political gridlock; we can't get anywhere because no one will give an inch. Combat is prized over conflict resolution, conflict over consensus. Masculinist dynamics prevail in the political dialogue and they are mirrored abundantly in the coverage of it.

—Judy Luce Mann, syndicated Washington Post columnist

As politics and journalism became increasingly inseparable in Washington in the last decades of the twentieth century, white men continued to dominate in both fields. While television cut into print and women made gains in both print and broadcasting, males held sway. In 1994 a study by Women, Men and Media, a monitoring project headed by Betty Friedan, found that at newspapers men continued to write the majority of front-page news stories and nearly three-quarters of the opinion pieces on the nation's op-ed pages.[1] While the number of women's bylines inched up from an average of 33 to 34 percent the following year, the annual survey showed that the average percentage of stories reported by women correspondents on nightly network news broadcasts dropped from 21 to 20 percent.[2]

With the outstanding exception of Katharine Graham, the most powerful figures were men. In 1978 Stephen Hess of the Brookings Institution presented a picture of a press corps that was overwhelmingly male (80 percent), white (96 percent), and middle aged (63 percent between thirty and fifty years old).[3] While the *Star* perished in 1981 and UPI fought to stay afloat, other news organizations thrived, with some making enormous profits.

Aside from Graham, most women in Washington journalism were not highly paid movers and shakers. An "insider's" book on Washington in 1982 listed only four women among the top fifteen Washington media people, none of whom were minorities.[4] Although Graham had been replaced by her son, Donald (she relinquished the title of publisher to him in 1979 but remained chair of the board), at the top of the list, columnist Mary McGrory took fifth place, praised for having stayed with the *Star* "to the bitter end" before heading for the *Post;* and Meg Greenfield, editorial page editor of the *Post,* appeared in the eighth slot.[5] Helen Thomas of UPI, described as "past sixty" but able to "run for press buses and pool cars with the youngest," was tenth, judged "probably the best-known Washington woman reporter" because she spoke frequently at colleges and professional meetings.[6] Diana McClellan, who wrote "The Ear," a popular gossip column for the *Star* that moved to the *Post* after the *Star* folded, got the fourteenth spot.[7]

When the *Star* died, its reporters had relatively little difficulty finding other jobs. Barbara Cohen Cochran, named national editor of the *Star* in 1974 and managing editor in 1978, pursued broadcast management. She credited the transformation at the *Star* spurred by the women's movement for preparing her to move forward. "The *Star* went from a newsroom where women were few in number to a newsroom where women started at every position and had no limit on what they could aspire to.... Gender didn't matter.... You were never told what you couldn't do, only what you could," she said.[8]

Going from the *Star* to radio, she launched the successful *Morning Edition* on NPR, but found her gender a handicap in budget-cutting sessions after being promoted to vice president of news in 1982. "I felt I was subjected to a much tougher standard because there was an assumption that I was just a feather-headed woman who really didn't understand the budget or do what had to be done to get the budget in line," she said.[9]

Switching to NBC as manager of its political unit in Washington, in 1985 Cochran took over as executive producer of *Meet the Press*. She criticized "traditional male-clubbiness" at the network, commenting, "For women to get into management positions, they generally have to be not only good, but better than the men with whom they compete for those positions."[10] As president of RTNDA, a post she took in 1997, she received awards for advocating First Amendment rights, including the use of cameras and microphones in courtrooms.

Other women staffers at the *Star* who made successful transitions to new jobs included Sheilah Kast, who covered financial news. She moved to ABC where she covered the White House during the Reagan administration. Kast was among a small group of *Star* journalists invited to try out for network positions because they appeared to be photogenic.

Ironically, the *Star* died at a time when the Washington media had become, in the words of columnist David Broder, a ubiquitous "presence at the very heart of national political power."[11] The *Post,* which eagerly picked up notable *Star* staffers, dominated the scene with some 3,000 employees. A total of nearly 1,500 worked at two other daily newspapers, the *Washington Times* and *USA TODAY,* while some 1,180 had jobs at the Washington bureaus of ABC, CBS, NBC, and CNN.[12] More than 100 were employed at the AP, UPI, and Reuters, an international wire service, and some 700 at major news magazines, *Time, Newsweek,* and *U.S. News,* while scores of other print and broadcast operations also hired journalists.[13]

Convinced that women journalists were willing to "try new things," Jim Bellows, editor of the *Star* from 1975 to 1978, assigned Lynn Rosellini, who previously had written about gay athletes, to do a multipart profile of Katharine Graham, the "most powerful woman in Washington," to boost his newspaper's faltering circulation.[14] The controversial series did not run until after Bellows had left the *Star* to become editor of the *Los Angeles Herald-Examiner.* It pictured Graham, who had a reputation for changing her male executives as often as some women change hairstyles, as likable and vulnerable but also callous and caustic.[15]

In her reporting Rosellini encountered numerous individuals afraid to discuss Graham for fear of damaging their own careers. "Most people wouldn't even call back. And if they did, it was usually to say, curtly, 'I can't talk,' Rosellini recalled.[16] "When I look back I am reminded of what a snake-pit that whole episode was. And what power does to people in this town and what fear does, too."[17] Apparently Rosellini's career did not suffer. She moved to the Washington bureau of the *New York Times* and subsequently wrote fiction.

Bellows's interest in Graham spurred a *Star* question-and-answer interview with Graham in 1975 by Mary Anne Dolan, the features' editor, who later followed Bellows to Los Angeles and became the editor of the *Herald-Examiner,* making history as the first woman editor of a major metropolitan newspaper. Dolan tried to draw out Graham on whether or not she acted as the center of a political-social set that made national policy "over chocolate mousse and cognac in Georgetown [the affluent section of Washington where Graham's mansion was located]."[18]

Graham denied this was the case but called Washington the "one remaining town where social life is of interest."[19] Asked if she felt a responsibility to help other women, Graham replied affirmatively, "As a manager in a company these days, any executive feels a responsibility toward women, and if you're a woman in that role, you obviously feel it even more."[20]

A gap remained between Graham's philosophical commitment and the actual situation of women in the *Post* newsroom, employees said. *Post* women coalesced from time to time to fight discrimination, stirred by perceptions of inequity in pay, assignments, and gender and racial bias in spite of the newspaper's expressed commitment to equality. Although women at other news organizations in Washington faced similar situations, *Post* women, backed by their union, gained attention by actively filing complaints and approaching management directly. Minority women in particular felt lonely as trailblazers seeking to enlarge opportunities for themselves and others.

In 1975 Nancy Hicks Maynard, who had been the youngest reporter and the first African American woman on the metropolitan staff of the *New York Times,* moved to the *Times'* Washington bureau. She resigned in 1977 to launch a nonprofit organization with her husband, Robert Maynard, a *Post* editorial writer, to encourage diversity in American newsrooms. The organization, now the Maynard Institute for Journalism Education, initially known as the Institute for Journalism Education, was established in Berkeley, California, where the Maynards ran a summer program to train minority reporters.[21]

Dorothy Gilliam, who had come back to the *Post* as an assistant editor in the Style section in the 1970s, considered Nancy Maynard "a brilliant strategist" for efforts to bring minorities into newsrooms in face of covert hostility.[22] Decades later Gilliam remembered how "long the walk" seemed in 1979 from Style to the office of editor Ben Bradlee to ask if she could write a column directed at residents of Washington, a predominantly African American city.[23] She had proposed the column in a memo a year before but never received a response.

As she walked through the newsroom, Gilliam passed the desks of reporters coping with the paper's highly charged competitive atmosphere, which Bradlee had characterized as "creative tension."[24] These were, she recalled, "a lot of smart people with high ambitions," who keenly felt "the stress of these jobs."[25] Wary of approaching Bradlee face-to-face, she was still determined to present him with two options: that she be named editor of the newspaper's Sunday magazine or given a column. Bradlee chose the second, telling her to write features for the Metro section "so we can see if you are ready to write a column."[26]

Gilliam quickly produced stories on Washington that convinced editors to give her the go-ahead. For eighteen years, from 1979 until 1997, her column appeared in the Metro section, initially twice and later once a week, featured on the front page. Gilliam said she "approached the column like a "black woman out of the South."[27] While her picture did not run beside it, she said most readers knew that she was African American.[28] Bradlee approved the column partly because Gilliam moved in Washington circles where other *Post* staffers did not.[29] "We had nobody talking for that segment of our audience," he said.[30]

By the time the column started, Gilliam no longer was the only black woman journalist at the newspaper. In 1972, Alice Bonner, a graduate of Howard University who had been a copy aide at the *Post,* became the first person selected for a two-year reporting internship to advance minorities and women. Set up after complaints of discrimination from *Post* minority journalists known as the Metro Seven, the affirmative action internship program offered Bonner and others a chance to attend a summer training program at Columbia University for minority journalists.[31]

Bonner was one of the signers of two diversity petitions to *Post* management, the first in support of the Metro Seven in 1972, and the second a year later in support of improved newsroom opportunities for women.[32] For the next ten years she worked as a *Post* reporter, first on the local, then on the national staff and covered a range of stories from West Africa as a special correspondent. She also spent two years as editor of a weekly section and one year as an assistant city editor.

Yet she did not find it easy to move forward at the *Post,* even though she had been a Nieman fellow at Harvard University in 1977. "I am grateful that in one instance when I was denied an opportunity on the basis of my race AND gender, the editor, for whatever reason, told me explicitly that those were the prohibitive factors," Bonner said later.[33] "Surely many of us have been unfairly treated in employment situations without benefit of such stupidly overt expressions of bias."[34]

In 1984 Bonner, at the time an assistant Maryland editor, left the *Post* to join the staff of *USA Today,* the flagship of the Gannett Company, as a cover story editor. Her departure prompted publisher Donald Graham and editor Ben Bradlee to commission

an in-house survey to determine why African American journalists were leaving the *Post* for other newspapers.[35] The final report
moved far beyond racial issues, airing perceptions of sexism, favoritism, and lack of career development opportunities. As one white
male reporter put it, "The *Post* is a brutal, tough, often unforgiving
place to work. There's lots of fear about one's standing here—fear
brought to life by the seemingly arbitrary destruction of careers of
some fine journalists among us."[36]

At Gannett, Bonner became a newsroom recruiter, working
from 1986 to 1989 as part of a team "assigned to recruit and refer
journalists of all ethnic backgrounds and genders for the company's ninety newspapers," she said.[37] She later served as director of journalism education programs for the Freedom Forum,
an outgrowth of the Gannett Foundation, which worked for
First Amendment rights and more diversity in newsrooms. After
receiving a doctorate in journalism and mass communications
from the University of North Carolina in 1999, Bonner taught
at the University of Southern California and the University of
Maryland.

LaBarbara Bowman, one of the original Metro Seven, did not
stay with the *Post* either. She moved to Gannett and became managing editor of its newspaper in Utica, New York, before being
named diversity director of the American Society of Newspaper
Editors in Reston, Virginia, in 1999. She held the post for ten
years, coordinating efforts of the organization to increase racial
and ethnic hiring in U.S. daily newspaper operations.[38]

Gannett, the nation's largest media corporation in the 1980s,
started its daily newspaper, *USA Today,* in 1982. It reached a circulation figure of more than one million seven months later. Headquartered in Northern Virginia, the new publication aimed itself
at a national audience via satellite printing technology and made

no attempt, like the *Post,* to serve as both a national and a local newspaper. Under Al Neuharth, the founder of *USA Today* and chairman of Gannett, the company had an expressed policy of hiring and promoting women and minorities.

By 1989 Gannett's women publishers represented one-fourth, or twenty-one of the eighty-four women newspaper publishers in the United States, a fact that Neuharth, who had watched his widowed mother struggle with pay discrimination for years in South Dakota, reported with pride.[39] Neuharth set affirmative action goals for Gannett executives tied to their annual bonuses. "Even the most chauvinistic of our male managers got the message when it hit their pocketbooks," he contended.[40]

In 1983 Neuharth made headlines by hiring Cathie Black, the publisher of *New York* magazine and a super advertising saleswoman with no experience in newspapers, as president of *USA Today* at a time when the newspaper was hemorrhaging money.[41] She stayed for eight years with Neuharth, who called her a "good-looking blonde" and wrote that her "total annual take approaches a million dollars."[42] Named publisher of *USA Today* in 1984, the charismatic Black put the newspaper on the track to success. She left to become head of the American Newspaper Publishers Association (ANPA), soon renamed the Newspaper Association of America, and in 1995 the president of the magazine division of the Hearst Corporation, amassing a personal fortune while showing what a woman could do.[43]

Black joked that "Gannett was one of the few companies where, at management meetings, there was a line outside the ladies' room."[44] She praised Neuharth's interest in diversity as "smart business sense."[45] Years later, in 2010, Black was chosen by New York's Mayor Michael R. Bloomberg to be the new head of the city's troubled public school system, although she had no experience in education, fueling speculation she might have political ambitions. She left the position five months later.

Gannett and the *Washington Post,* whose executives feuded publicly, did not always see eye-to-eye on diversity matters. An annual study of ten major U.S. newspapers from around the country—begun in 1989 by the Women, Men and Media group, set up by Betty Friedan and Nancy Woodhull, a Gannett executive—showed that *USA Today* had the highest average of women's bylines on the front page, 41 percent.[46] The feature-oriented *USA Today* assigned far more stories to women than the *New York Times,* which had only 5 percent front-page female bylines, leading Max Frankel, the *Times'* executive editor, to comment sarcastically, "If you are covering local teas, you've got more women [on the front page] than if you're the *Wall Street Journal.*"[47]

Although the *Post* came out better in the survey than the *Times,* ranking ahead of *USA Today* in the number of women featured in front-page photographs (42 percent in 1990 compared to 41 percent for *USA Today* the previous year), Bradlee agreed with Frankel. "I am damned if I can see what conclusions should be drawn from your findings," Bradlee wrote the sponsoring group, adding, "The wisdom of the ages appears to cry out for silence."[48]

Neuharth did not practice reticence. He claimed that he "maneuvered" Katharine Graham into a position to become the first woman chairman and president of the ANPA, but that she did not push hard enough to ensure that other women would follow her. "Her example of leadership should have been enough [but] it wasn't," Neuharth said.[49]

To many mainstream journalists, *USA Today,* with its mixture of colorful news and graphics in a smooth, slick package sold in machines that looked like television sets, resembled fast food rather than weighty fare. It acquired the nickname of McPaper, first bestowed by the *Post*.[50] Quoting this term of derision as shorthand for his aim of informing and entertaining the public, Neuharth boosted confidence in his staff, including Woodhull, who previously had been managing editor of the Gannett newspaper at Rochester, New York. "He knew we were hanging the world of journalism and laughed at the critics," she said.[51]

At *USA Today* Woodhull had more extensive responsibilities than a typical managing editor because of the novel nature of a newspaper geared to a television generation.[52] As one of the top planning editors, she helped design the publication and subsequently took charge of story selection for page one. Having dropped out of Trenton State College after only one year to pursue a career in journalism, Woodhull was determined to succeed as managing editor, even though "she felt that some people did not trust her in that position," according to the official history of *USA Today*.[53]

The demands of launching the new newspaper led to long hours and a pressure-cooker office atmosphere that did not fit well with family life. Woodhull had an infant daughter whom she rarely saw because she left home early in the morning and did not return until 11:00 P.M. or later. Finally she arranged to have the child brought to the *USA Today* building at 6:00 P.M. every evening so she could spent forty-five minutes with her in a restaurant.[54] She was afraid to tell Ron Martin, the executive editor, what she was doing, so she instructed an assistant to run down and get her if Martin wanted to see her while she was with her daughter.[55]

At the age of thirty-seven Woodhull developed cancer and had to leave her job temporarily. She returned in 1983 and three years later was named president of Gannett News Service, the company's national wire service for the eighty-three newspapers it owned at that time.[56] She stood out as Gannett's highest-ranking woman news executive when she left the company in 1990 to become editor in chief of Southern Progress, a Time Warner magazine division.[57] At the time of her death from lung cancer in 1997, a tribute in the *American Journalism Review* paid homage to her mentoring of other women, citing her efforts to "Do something to help another woman every day."[58] This was not an easy matter in the hurly-burly of the *USA Today* newsroom.

Another woman, Nancy Monaghan, who also had been a star at the Gannett newspaper in Rochester, New York, found it hard to deal with the demands of being the dayside news editor of *USA Today*. Every morning before she came to work, she threw up. "Nerves," she explained.[59] Constant office turmoil and second-guessing from superiors wore some staff members down. One reporter crashed under the pressure, breaking down in tears in front of her supervisor, who sent her home to rest. She returned the next day and then disappeared, spending four hours riding the subway because she felt physically unable to stay in the *USA Today* building.[60] The newspaper kept her on but in a less taxing job.

Meanwhile, the competitive atmosphere at the *Washington Post* continued to spawn office discord. As a black woman columnist, Gilliam discovered that her perspective did not always meet with approval. "I got a lot of hate mail," she said, along with a "negative reaction from white colleagues."[61] Some *Post* staffers "thought I wrote about race too much," she explained, and gave her the silent treatment when she entered the newsroom.[62] In writing her column she said she tried to be scrupulously fair, citing her coverage of Washington's controversial African American mayor in the 1980s, Marion Barry. She criticized the *Post* when it based stories about the mayor's drug use and womanizing on rumors, but changed her views when evidence of his misconduct came to light. "I was the first one to call for him to resign," she pointed out.[63]

Gilliam sought to avoid the trap of homogenization that led some African American journalists to be absorbed into the mainstream.[64] She wanted her column to reflect the different experiences of a separate group. Although she often touched on controversial issues, only once did Bradlee question what she wrote. Based on reaction to a Ku Klux Klan rally, she justified violence on one occasion. Looking backward, Gilliam said she should not have taken that position. "As I have learned more about white culture, I've learned you don't ever condone any damage to personal property," she told an interviewer.[65]

Her themes, which often addressed politics, education, racial diversity, and youth, dealt with what it meant to be African American in a white society. Writing about Patricia R. Harris, a railroad waiter's daughter who became the first woman to hold two cabinet posts, Gilliam asked why Harris's commitment to the cause of African American equality had been questioned by some of her peers on the grounds that she was "acting white."[66] Gilliam wrote that Harris believed "blacks could achieve anything they wanted if they didn't buy society's low opinion of them, and, in turn, attempt to hold each other back based on that opinion."[67] Gilliam concluded that "until more black people begin to define themselves, black children will be faced with two subtly conflicting messages from the world: one will say, 'Strive for excellence,' and the other says, 'But only whites are excellent.' "[68]

To Gilliam, who served as president of the National Association of Black Journalists from 1993 to 1995, "The waves of history influenced what I did. I have been part of the diversity movement in media."[69] A former fellow at the Freedom Forum Center at Columbia University and the John F. Kennedy School of Government at Harvard University, she became director of the Young Journalists Development Program after her column ended. This effort was funded by the *Post* to prepare minority high school and college students to go into journalism. Following retirement in 2003, she moved to George Washington University as project director for Prime Movers Media, a similar program to interest disadvantaged young people in media careers.

As Bradlee recognized in his comments on Gilliam's column, the *Post* lacked substantial knowledge of the African American community in Washington, a city that was 70 percent black in the late twentieth century. Top editors failed to recognize the fabrication of a feature story, JIMMY'S WORLD, that purportedly described an eight-year-old black addict in Southeast Washington given heroin by his mother's boyfriend. The writer, Janet Cooke, had been hired on the strength of a résumé that said she had graduated magna cum laude from Vassar College, held a master's degree, and had studied languages at the Sorbonne. She falsified these accomplishments, just as she made up the story about "Jimmy," but the *Post,* seeking promising minorities, had not bothered to check her credentials.[70]

Cooke's falsehoods came to light, to the mortification of the *Post,* when she won the Pulitzer Prize for feature writing in 1981. The newspaper returned the prize and apologized, but was castigated by the public, particularly after Roger Wilkins, a well-known African American journalist, wrote that many blacks in Washington, including Mayor Barry, who ordered police to look for "Jimmy," had expressed doubts about Cooke's story.[71] Graham, then president of the ANPA, denied the incident resulted from "pressures on papers to recruit and promote minorities."[72]

Within the *Post* newsroom itself, Vivian Aplin-Brownlee, an experienced African American journalist who edited the *Post*'s

District Weekly section, stood out among those who had not believed Cooke's "Jimmy" story.[73] When Aplin-Brownlee assigned Cooke to investigate the use of heroin in the city, she returned with notes for what became her prize-winning tale. Questioning its veracity, Aplin-Brownlee told Cooke to discuss it with Milton Coleman, the District editor, and expressed doubts to higher-level editors that Cooke was capable of the reporting she claimed to have done.[74] They paid little attention. Out of town when the story appeared on page one of the Sunday paper on September 28, 1980, Aplin-Brownlee turned to her husband when she saw the story and said, "I don't believe a word of this."[75] After Cooke's Pulitzer Prize was announced, Aplin-Brownlee told Coleman, "I hope that she has committed the perfect crime."[76]

A graduate of Ohio University, Aplin-Brownlee had been the first African American woman reporter at the *Cleveland Plain Dealer*. In 1978 she moved to the *San Diego Union* as an assistant editor. A year later Gilliam recruited her for the *Post,* where she helped train inexperienced reporters like Cooke on the District Weekly staff. When Cooke's story was exposed, Aplin-Brownlee said, "I never believed it. . . . In her eagerness to make a name she [Cooke] would write farther than the truth would allow. When challenged on facts on other stories, Janet would reverse herself, but without dismay or consternation with herself."[77] Refusing to comment further on the Cooke incident, Aplin-Brownlee later moved to the *Post* national staff. She left the newspaper in 1985 to become a full-time mother and homemaker.[78]

After resigning from the *Post,* Cooke attempted to exonerate herself in part by blaming the atmosphere at the *Post*. Appearing on the *Today* show, Cooke said, "Certainly there is an undercurrent [in journalism] of this kind of competitiveness and of the need to be first, flashiest, be sensational. And I think there is more of it in a place like the *Post*."[79]

In her autobiographical look at the *Post,* another African American journalist, Jill Nelson, who was hired in 1986 as the first woman and the first African American to work on the *Post* magazine, endeavored to explain Cooke's actions. Nelson wrote that Cooke "had some severe ethical, moral and psychological problems that caused her to mistake fiction for journalism, and self-hating journalism at that."[80] But, she continued, as an African American woman at the newspaper, Cooke "knew she would be outshone, discarded, and forgotten unless she did something—quick—to earn the notice and approval of the powers that be. What better than following the honored tradition of writing an expose of pathological Negroes?"[81]

At the *Post,* Nelson, a graduate of Columbia University, described herself as caught between a paternalistic white ownership and a desire to identify with African Americans who protested for three months against the debut of the newspaper's million-dollar revamped magazine.[82] The first issue created an uproar by featuring a cover story on a black rapper and a column warning storekeepers to lock their doors to keep out black males who might rob them. Led by Cathy Hughes, owner of a radio station and talk show host, some forty-seven organizations formed the Washington Post Magazine Recall Committee and organized demonstrations in front of the *Post* building to throw copies of the magazine on its steps.

Part of a black women's caucus organized after her arrival at the *Post,* Nelson became the first black woman chair of the Baltimore-Washington Newspaper Guild unit at the newspaper. In 1987 a dozen black women signed a letter to management complaining of disparities in salaries. It used as evidence a Guild report that showed black female reporters earned an average weekly salary of $791.33, white females $859.37, black males $920.46, and white males $988.68.[83] Of the seventeen black women journalists at the *Post,* only two, Gilliam and Nelson, made more than $50,000 annually, the amount Donald Graham had stated publicly was the average for a *Post* reporter.[84] In 1988 the unit filed a complaint with the D.C. Office of Human Rights charging the *Post* with discrimination.

Among those signing the letter along with Gilliam and Nelson was Gwen Ifill, then one of the lowest-paid African American reporters. She worked for the *Post* from 1984 to 1991, when she left for the *New York Times* and subsequently went into broadcasting. Since 1999 she has been the moderator of the PBS program *Washington Week in Review* and senior correspondent for PBS's *NewsHour.*

As a student at Simmons College, Ifill, the daughter of a Methodist minister of Barbadian descent who had immigrated to the United States from Panama, interned for the *Boston Herald-American.* A coworker there left her a note that read, "nigger go home."[85] She put the ugly incident behind her in a career that has been praised for objectivity in political reporting. At the *Post,* Ifill covered what she called "sandpaper politics," the power shift from white to black political leadership in Prince George's County, a Maryland suburb where the African American population soared while the white population declined.[86]

While African American women journalists at the *Post* were fighting pay discrimination and Gilliam's column appeared in its Metro section, *USA Today* featured an outspoken black woman columnist, Barbara Reynolds, on its op-ed page as a member of its editorial board. From 1981 until 1996, when she was abruptly dismissed, Reynolds played what she called "a historic role in

American journalism, after being hired by John Seigenthaler, *USA Today*'s first editorial page editor."[87] Reynolds, one of the first African American women to be awarded a Nieman fellowship at Harvard University, previously had worked for the *Chicago Tribune*'s Washington bureau, where she said she was "excoriated daily" as the only African American and woman on a staff of "twelve white men all of whom treated me with disdain for even thinking I should sit in the same office with them."[88] In contrast, at *USA Today* she initially ranked high in the newspaper's firmament, flying on Neuharth's private plane to interview celebrities and going to the White House to interview presidents.

Her downward trajectory began in 1994, when, as she explained it, Seigenthaler was replaced by a "white woman, who I had heard did not believe in God and who intimated that I must rid myself of so much God-talk and Third World radicalism in my writing."[89] By this time *USA Today* had geared itself to upscale demographics, she explained in her autobiography: "Journalism INC, the age of the big corporation had swallowed up the promises of inclusion and diversity. The nineties and beyond would be devoted to money, mergers and mediocrity."[90]

When Reynolds raised issues of corporate greed or unjust war in her column, she was "pressured more and more not to offend advertisers or corporations."[91] Having become a Christian minister, she insisted, "I could not and would not write and think like privileged white males, which most of my colleagues were."[92] According to Reynolds, "after Seigenthaler left, I was warned to shut up, to be silent, to just fall in line and collect my pay check. But I couldn't. When I wrote about the need for poor children to have health insurance . . . I was told to stop 'whining.'"[93]

In 1996 Reynolds was handed severance papers, told her job had been abolished, and escorted out of the building. "No more was I a founding editor, who had worked day and night, travelling thousands of miles to help start the paper," she said, but "being treated like a criminal, busted, kicked to the curb all for having an opinion unlike those of my white comrades."[94] She subsequently concentrated on a ministry called Harriet's Children to reach women struggling with addictions.

During the years that Reynolds expressed minority opinions at *USA Today,* Jill Nelson left the *Post.* Convinced that she would never fit in there, Nelson quit in 1990 after her feature story on black community reaction to the conviction of Marion Barry on drug charges was buried in the Style section. Resuming her career as a freelance writer, she published *Volunteer Slavery,* the story of her unhappy experiences at the newspaper. In her book she referred to "caucasian women" at the *Post* "who perceived themselves as abused, wronged, and worst of all, trapped," painting a picture of a group of women journalists whose careers had not flourished.[95] Regardless of the accuracy of her description, the Guild figures on salaries showed that the women as a group were paid less than men reporters as a group.

Karlyn Barker, a reporter and editor at the *Post* for more than thirty years, witnessed opportunities for women at the newspaper increase significantly over the decades, but more so for white women than for minorities, whom Barker thought were more likely to leave the *Post.*[96] Barker, who obtained her bachelor's degree at the University of California, Berkeley, and her master's degree at Columbia University, had worked for UPI before being hired by the *Post* in 1971, when there were only seven women on the Metro staff out of about sixty journalists.

"My Metro boss went three years without hiring any women as regular reporters (as opposed to interns) and then made passes at many of those he eventually hired. . . . [He] paid way too much

attention to whom I was dating on the paper and once propositioned me over lunch," she continued.[97] After she declined his advances, he eventually sent her to cover the legislature in Annapolis,
saying, "I was getting the job because he knew he could trust me
not to fool around."[98] He apparently had in mind a couple of married men previously assigned there who had squabbled over the
affections of a woman lobbyist.

A year before Barker arrived at the *Post,* an energetic young
news aide observed the office scene and saw it as a reflection of
both gender and class issues. "When I was in Washington, there
was a lot of shall we say socializing among the older journalists
and the younger members of the staff," Susan Fleming Morgans
commented.[99] "We wouldn't have recognized sexual harassment
if it hit us in the face. But that was back in the days when people
had two or three drinks with lunch."[100]

As an aspiring young journalist, she found that most women
reporters "had some sort of connection to get their jobs—god-
daughter of an ambassador or something like that," she said. "Even
the men were well connected—mostly Ivy League or the son of
the owner of a chain of newspapers or something like that."[101]
Mentors played critical roles, she continued, "and if I had had one
I would probably be working in Washington or New York City
today."[102] Instead she pursued a career teaching and editing in the
Pittsburgh area.

Even when women started to be hired in more numbers in
the 1970s, *Post* editors did not perceive them to be as competent
as men on important breaking stories, remembered Barker—one
of the first women who filed a discrimination complaint against
the newspaper—decades later. "When [presidential candidate]
George Wallace was shot in 1972, I watched as editors first went
to the men on the Metro staff to jump on this story. I watched

an editor look right past me and grab a guy who hadn't been out of the office in so long he had cobwebs on his chair."[103] Having recently been told by Bradlee that men got high-profile assignments because they were more aggressive than women, she and another woman reporter, Claudia Levy, "tested this out by grabbing our notebooks and standing near the assignment editor. But, as I said, he looked right past me to find a male reporter," Barker continued.[104]

Levy, who started on the *Post* in the 1960s, recalled a half century later the different treatment of men and women reporters. "One of my favorite early memories is the time in 1966 the night world editor sent a stylish New York-bred reporter home to change her clothes because she was wearing a PANTS SUIT ... None of us [women] were allowed to leave the building when the riots [after the assassination of Dr. Martin Luther King Jr.] broke out in 1968," she said.[105]

During her years on the *Post,* Barker said she saw unfairness abate "because women have repeatedly proved themselves AND because there are now too many of us on staffs to permit this kind of discrimination."[106] In Barker's view "the sex/race discrimination suits opened up more doors for women and minorities."[107] She remained on the Metro staff until 1993, when she left for three years to work for newspapers in California, returning in 1996 when the *Post*'s first woman Metro editor, Jo-Ann Armao, asked her to help with presidential inaugural coverage. Barker took a buyout a decade later. At the time she still saw "a glass ceiling for women and minorities at the very top of the food chain."[108]

Martha Hamilton, who remained at the *Post* for nearly four decades, including a period of writing guild newsletters outlining pay discrimination, observed enormous changes over the years. In 2008 she explained, "When I came to work in 1972, virtually no one had a picture of children or spouse on desks. Now it is common, and management no longer lauds people who skip [being present for the] delivery of their child to stay at work as management once did. Also there is much less blatant sexism than there once was in terms of guys in the newsroom commenting on women's physical attributes."[109]

But, appearance still remained more important for women than men into the twenty-first century, Hamilton continued. "No woman in the newsroom would dare be as sloppy as some of the men. I also know of one overweight journalist of the first class being rejected out of hand as a possible financial reporter because 'she doesn't look like a financial reporter.' Janet Cooke would have never gotten away with her deceit if she hadn't been so good-looking."[110] She said the *Post* story on how Cooke was forced to admit her guilt ended with a phrase "something like 'In the end, she was still beautiful.'"[111]

A financial news reporter for much of her *Post* career, Hamilton, who is white, donated a kidney to her colleague, Warren Brown, who is African American, in 2001, in a lifesaving operation featured in the newspaper. "Did Martha give you her kidney because you are black?" asked Courtland Milloy, an African American columnist.[112] Hamilton and Brown, both of whom grew up in the segregated South, answered no. "The newsroom was our community, and we were next-door neighbors who looked out for each other," they wrote.[113] "Affirmative action had changed the nature of the workplace."[114] But it did not necessarily lead to an easier working environment. As a 1975 article in the *Washington Monthly* put it, the *Post* Metro staff "is crammed with people who would be stars on most other papers and who are desperate to show their talents."[115]

Even in the early 1970s, however, a few women held jobs on the *Post*'s prestigious national staff. One, Marilyn Berger, performed a bit player role in the *Post*'s coverage of the Watergate scandal that led to the resignation of President Nixon. Berger, a Columbia graduate, arrived at the newspaper in 1970 as a diplomatic correspondent after serving as a United Nations correspondent for *Newsday.* She remained for six years before moving to NBC. Berger told Bob Woodward and Carl Bernstein that Ken Clawson, a former *Post* reporter working at the Nixon White House, had written the bogus "Canuck letter" accusing Sen. Edmund S. Muskie of Maine, a leading Democratic presidential hopeful, of insulting Americans of French Canadian descent.[116] Woodward and Bernstein reported this in October 1972 as one instance of political sabotage connected to bugging the Democratic National Committee offices in the Watergate complex.

In 1973 Susanna McBee returned to the *Post* as a reporter on the national staff and was promoted to assistant national editor. But in 1978, when she asked to cover the Middle East, the foreign editor told her, "No woman could go to Saudi Arabia and get a story because the Saudis wouldn't deal with one."[117] She resigned the next year after President Carter appointed her assistant secretary for public affairs in what was then the Department of Health, Education, and Welfare. Of her *Post* tenure, she said, "It was never easy but I figured that was the way the world was."[118]

Mary Lou Beatty, another woman holding a significant position at the *Post,* followed the convolutions of Nixon's search for a vice presidential candidate in 1968. She recognized that Nixon was serious about choosing Maryland governor Spiro Agnew, even though David Broder thought it so unlikely he buried the idea in his story. Beatty, political editor at the time, rescued the news by pulling it up into the lead.[119] In 1974 she followed Elsie Carper into the ranks of the assistant managing editors, making her the second woman to reach this position at the *Post.*[120]

Beatty joined the Post in 1963 after working for the *Chicago Tribune* and remained there twenty years, directing stories on politics, civil rights, the space program, the Pentagon Papers, and Watergate. She launched the Weekend section in 1977, a popular tabloid listing of events around Washington. According to Hank Burchard, a feature writer, she "specialized in rehabilitation of wounded writers and turning secretaries into reporters."[121]

Leaving the *Post* in 1983, Beatty cofounded a monthly magazine, *Washington Woman,* which folded four years later. She then became publications director of the National Endowment for the Humanities. At the time of Beatty's death in 2007, Ron Sarro—a former *Star* journalist who like Beatty had served as president of the WPC—called her a "leader of people who wanted to make a change in the way women were treated in the profession. And she succeeded."[122]

By the 1980s more and more women had attained responsible positions in Washington journalism. Ann McFeatters, for example, was a White House correspondent and national politics reporter for the Scripps Howard News Service from 1986 until 1999, when she was named bureau chief for the *Pittsburgh Post-Gazette* and the *Toledo Blade.* As a teenage girl, she had gone to her local newspaper editor in Springfield, Ohio, to ask for advice on a career in journalism. "But, you're a girl!" he replied.[123] Not willing to be deterred from her goal, she majored in journalism at Marquette University, graduating in 1966 and finding a job on the *Evansville* (Ind.) *Press.*

As a White House correspondent, McFeatters said she no longer had to fight the rampant battles of discrimination that had affected the women who came before her.[124] Before taking this prize assignment, she had proven herself as an environmental and consumer reporter for the Scripps Howard Washington bureau, which she joined in 1970. "I suppose you could say it was a woman's beat, but I didn't look at it that way," she said.[125] "I could get on page one with no hassle," reporting on the activities of Ralph Nader and other consumer advocates who were pushing for governmental action.[126] "I remember strapping my little baby into the back seat of a rental car and taking off across Pennsylvania looking for acid rain."[127]

What was difficult, she said, was the lack of role models for combining her career with marriage and motherhood. Married to Dale McFeatters, a Scripps Howard editorial writer and columnist, she is the mother of three children. "I continued to work all the time," she said. "There were some tough times, trying to find good baby-sitters and good day-care. My youngest was three years old when I was traveling [with the president]. I went to Russia five times and China five times."[128] Looking back, McFeatters said there were "very few" other women correspondents who had families when she covered the White House. "It was harder than I admitted to myself at the time. You have to have a lot of energy and be pretty well-organized and have good spouses."[129]

In 1980 McFeatters was elected president of the WPC, brought into the group by Wauhillau La Hay, a witty woman proud of her Cherokee Indian background. After a career in New York radio, La Hay had been recruited by Scripps Howard during the Nixon administration to cover the First Lady. "It was a good club and had wonderful parties," McFeatters said. "I still miss it," she added, noting the strong women who played major roles in the club: La Hay, Bonnie Angelo of *Time* magazine, and Elsie Carper of the *Washington Post*.[130]

As women became more integrated into the reportorial scene, McFeatters was chosen to join the Gridiron Club and to be a member of the board of the White House Correspondents' Association. She joined the NPC and became chair of the NPC Foundation. Launched in 1986, her weekly syndicated column, "White House Watch," has appeared in four hundred newspapers for more than two decades. "Covering government in Washington, D.C., is just like covering it in any small town," McFeatters contended. "The most powerful men in American government put their pants on one leg at a time, and the most powerful women have cluttered purses."[131]

Starting in 1978, Judy Luce Mann emerged as the *Washington Post*'s feminist columnist, continuing to speak up for women's equality until her retirement in 2001.[132] At the time of her death four years later, Leonard Downie Jr., the *Post* executive editor, commented, "Her column was widely read, especially by women like herself who believed strongly in expanding the rights of women."[133] Her corps of devoted readers kept the *Post* from canceling her column in the 1990s on grounds that it predictably followed a feminist line. Supporters called and wrote letters to urge the column's continuance. Their pressure resulted in the column remaining a feature of the newspaper, but being moved from the Metro section to the Style section, first adjacent to the comic strips and later to the bottom of a nearby page.[134]

The period of the column coincided with what some considered a backlash against women as efforts mounted to stop passage of the Equal Rights Amendment. Mann's column became a platform for women to advocate for it. During the election of 1980, Mann caught the frustration of Republican women who backed the ERA by quoting one who said, "If he [Reagan] chooses to send a signal that the party is going to reverse a historic trend, that will be truly upsetting. . . . If he wants to keep it [the ERA plank] in, it would be in his interest to send a back channel signal soon before the visibility of the issue is raised."[135]

Unhappily for ERA supporters, Reagan did not signal in their direction. According to Mann, who wrote at a time when the New Right was coalescing, her topics were "frequently unpopular and very often at odds with mainstream orthodoxy."[136] She staunchly supported women's rights, world population control, and child welfare as affirmative action and abortion rights came under heavy attack. In 1984 she was among women columnists who floated the idea of nominating a woman for vice president on the Democratic ticket, which resulted in Geraldine Ferraro running with Walter Mondale in his unsuccessful presidential bid.[137] Her treatment of Ferraro contrasted with that given by the news media to an earlier effort by a woman to campaign for a spot on the Democratic ticket. After Rep. Shirley Chisholm of New York announced her candidacy in 1972, a *Post* feature writer, Myra MacPherson, wrote that Chisholm had been "kissed off as a member of the lunatic fringe . . . politicians narrowly viewed her only as a woman's or black candidate."[138]

The increased presence of women journalists in Washington enhanced the political career of at least one woman, Harriet Woods, a Democrat who narrowly lost a well-publicized, although unsuccessful, race for the U.S. Senate from Missouri in 1982. As Woods recalled the campaign two decades later, "It was hard to gain credibility running against a well-entrenched incumbent like Jack [John] Danforth—particularly [to be taken seriously] in D.C. I wasn't on the map. Male reporters dominated political coverage and I didn't look important."

In Woods's view she gained attention because "it just so happened there was a group of aspiring women journalists also seeking major opportunities. One was Elisabeth Bumiller at *The Washington Post*. She talked her editor into assigning her a feature on my race at a time when no one else was covering it." After Bumiller's story "filled a full page of the 'Style' section, with a huge picture, I instantaneously was on the map in D.C. It made a huge difference," Woods said.[139] She saw the story as stemming from the desire of Bumiller, a recent Columbia University journalism graduate, to get a good assignment at the *Post*.[140]

Bumiller, who had worked at the *Miami Herald* before entering Columbia, was hired at the *Post* to assist Sally Quinn in covering the Washington social scene. Going beyond parties, Bumiller introduced profiles of political figures such as Woods.[141] "It was a win-win," Woods said. "She [Bumiller] was able to do it because of her gender awareness that there was a story there, and the editor's stereotypical assumption that a woman reporter was especially suitable to write about a woman candidate."[142]

According to Woods, "The same combination worked for the new women reporters at NPR (Cokie [Roberts], Linda [Wertheimer], Nina [Totenberg], etc.), who were trying to get more air time."[143] As Woods analyzed her 1982 campaign, she said that the NPR women "were established figures, but I suspect it was a big help to them to have major women candidates emerging who drew coverage—again with the assumption that this was an appropriate assignment for women reporters."[144] She said she recalled having "coffee or lunch in DC with the NPR women after my loss.... We shared war stories of working with male power figures.... Without any suggestion of favoritism in personal coverage."[145] To Woods the camaraderie between her and the women reporters resembled the interaction between Eleanor Roosevelt and the women who covered her press conferences.[146]

Political experts attributed Woods's narrow defeat in part to the fact that she was outspent in the campaign and forced to pull her television ads for a week late in the campaign. Publicity over her loss led to the creation of the political action committee called

Emily's List to back liberal women candidates in 1985.[147] A year earlier Woods won election as lieutenant governor of Missouri, drawing on her name recognition from the Senate race. The first woman elected to statewide office in Missouri, Woods remained in that position until 1989, losing a second bid for U.S. senator from Missouri in another tight race in 1986.

After leaving office, Woods, who had worked as a television producer in the St. Louis area before her political career, served as president of the National Women's Political Caucus from 1991 until 1995. "As a candidate who has been covered by both male and female reporters, I can say firmly that I want GOOD, ACCU-RATE coverage—gender is secondary. I could cite some horrific coverage by women—but I won't," Woods said.[148] Nevertheless, she said she had observed that "there was much more coverage by women reporters [than by men reporters] at press conferences regarding reports on political women.... Interest or opportunity or assignment editor assumptions?"[149]

Woods emphasized that the issues that women most often advocate as legislators "touch women journalists as people: family and medical leave, child care, pay equity, health coverage, breast cancer research. And women politicians are heartened by women's success as journalists and editors.... It's equally important to have women's life experiences included among journalists as ... among legislators."[150]

At the *Washington Post* Mann frequently wrote on the topics that Woods named. Mann's background helped propel her to liberal feminism. Born in Washington, as a child she lived in Paris where her father worked for the Marshall plan. Back in the United States she dropped out of Barnard College to organize protests against the Vietnam War and rent strikes to benefit low-income tenants in New York. In 1964 she defied U.S. law by traveling to

Cuba.[151] Prior to joining the *Post* staff in 1972, she worked for the *Washington Daily News* for four years.

Married three times, Mann was the mother of three children, whom she often referred to in her column with humorous anecdotes. In a collection of columns published in 1990, she said that when she began her career, "the newspapers I worked for presumed that women were cut from the same cloth newspapermen were, and that they put their careers first [ahead of their children]. I never did, and I never had any questions about which gave me more reward and more fulfillment."[152]

"I look at news coverage of women, and I think I've wandered into the fun house at the circus," Mann contended at a 1990 journalism conference. "Women are distorted by the media. We are too tall in our aspirations, too short in our accomplishments, too thin in our talents, too heavy in our personal burdens. And a good deal of the time we simply don't show up in the [media] mirror at all."[153]

When Al Neuharth, following his retirement as chairman of the Gannett Company, wrote a column criticizing commercial airlines for replacing young "sky girls" with aging females and "flighty young men" as flight attendants, Mann accused him of being a "male chauvinist pig."[154] She enumerated his progressive policy at Gannett to court women readers and to promote women to high-ranking positions, but wrote off these efforts as "a cynical ploy to grab circulation, not a genuine personal commitment to enhance the status of women."[155] Neuharth replied in *USA Today* that Mann's "chauvinistic boss, Ben Bradlee, [had] sicked her to 'get' me," but Mann retorted that "I never discussed the column I wrote with Ben or anybody else."[156]

Mann also took after a *Post* columnist, Richard Cohen, for writing in the newspaper's Sunday magazine that feminism had prompted men to "pretend to listen [to women] all the time, lest they be 'accused of not being sensitive.'"[157] To Mann, Cohen's column insulted women and illustrated the kind of male bias that caused women to stop reading newspapers. "From 1982 to 1987 the number of women who read a newspaper four days out of five declined by 26 percent, according to the Newspaper Advertising Bureau," Mann wrote.[158] "Women have money now and they need information. What has happened is that their need for newspapers has declined, and insulting them is not the way to bring them back."[159]

In her last column on December 28, 2001, Mann expressed regret that "there are so few liberal columnists left in the media and so few women writing serious commentary. I have always felt that the media mirror society and that a society in which women are invisible in the media is one in which they are invisible, period."[160] The end of her column made it harder for feminist groups to serve as sources for reporters, according to Martha Burk, former chair of the National Council of Women's Organizations.

"When Judy Mann was writing for the *Post,* she would often talk to us about our agenda and often enough write about our issues," Burk said in 2003.[161] "Our groups intervened on Judy's behalf to keep her from getting fired at least once and I think a couple of times. We really have NO ONE to go to in the way of columnists [now]. . . . Some of us talk to Helen Thomas in social settings, and she is very good about questioning [officials] when she can," Burk added.[162]

While a growing conservative mood in Washington may have limited options for feminist commentators as the twentieth century ended, some women continued to have extremely successful careers. A *Post* staff writer for twenty-five years, Judith Martin, left the newspaper in 1983 to devote full time to her popular feature, "Miss Manners," a tongue-in-cheek etiquette column, syndicated three times a week in more than two hundred newspapers worldwide in 2011.[163] It covers not only matters of behavior but also romance, changing patterns of marriage and relationships, and philosophical and moral dilemmas in a wryly humorous way. A graduate of Wellesley College, Martin covered the White House and diplomatic missions for the women's section of the *Post* in the 1960s and was one of the original staff members assigned to the Style section.

George Will, one of the nation's best-known conservative political columnists, once said Martin actually offered political commentary, particularly in her Sunday column, written in essay form unlike the question-and-answer format of her other work.[164] Martin did not disagree. "In a larger sense of restructuring society, there could hardly be a more political idea than changing our concept of the workplace," she said.[165]

In one of the dozen nonfiction books she has written, *Common Courtesy,* she called for redesigning the workplace to allow both men and women to have time for professional and personal lives. She told an interviewer that writing a column was easier than bucking social norms in the early 1960s and going to work as a married woman with two young children.[166] "What has happened in our time is that the woman has taken over the male pattern, and nobody makes up the slack," she said.[167]

In her autobiography Graham called attention to Martin's work as a reporter for the women's section before she became "Miss Manners." She described an embarrassing telephone conversation with H. R. Haldeman, one of Nixon's top aides, after Martin was banned from covering Tricia Nixon's White House wedding to Edward Cox in 1971 for breaking rules governing the reporting of Julie Nixon's wedding. Concerned about some of the "stiletto" coverage in Style and "how sharp Judith's pen could be," Graham wrote, she found it hard to defend Martin: "I wasn't sure I'd want her to cover my own daughter's wedding. She had, for instance, already compared Tricia to a vanilla ice-cream cone."[168] Reporters from other newspapers, however, all gave Martin their notes on the Nixon-Cox wedding so the *Post* ended up "with the finest pool of material available to any reporter in town," Graham concluded.[169]

While women at the *Post* were endeavoring to break gender barriers, women at the *Washington Times* experienced a different kind of office climate. That daily newspaper was founded in 1982, less than a year after the demise of the *Star.* Funded by the Unification Church, the *Times* provided a conservative voice in the capital, although it trailed the *Post* badly in circulation, advertising, and prestige. Women employees, some of whom previously had worked for the *Star,* enjoyed lively camaraderie with their male colleagues, but they did not think they were paid as much as men doing similar work.[170]

One former staff member recalled that most women did not seem to know how to negotiate for top salaries, whereas most men did.[171] Since there was no union at the newspaper, uniform starting salaries did not exist. Some of the top journalistic jobs were held by men and women who were members of the Unification Church.

In offering a conservative woman's voice, Mary Lou Forbes, who became the commentary editor of the *Times* after the *Star* folded, featured the syndicated columns of Mona Charen, which began in 1987. An honors graduate of Barnard College, Charen earned a law degree at George Washington University. She developed political expertise and close links with the Republican Party as a speechwriter for First Lady Nancy Reagan and Rep.

Jack Kemp during his unsuccessful 1988 bid for the Republican presidential nomination. By 2011 her column ran in about two hundred newspapers, covering various topics such as governmental policy, terrorism, and culture. Writing about her Jewish faith, Charen is seen as offering pro-Israel views.[172]

Charen started her syndicated column after writing a semi-monthly column for the *Republican Study Committee Bulletin,* read by Republican members of Congress.[173] Forbes called Charen "very representative of the new young visionaries who came along during the Reagan years."[174] She also praised her as "an extremely lucid writer, always on top of issues, never afraid to take a strong stand."[175]

Writing from her home in Falls Church, a Northern Virginia suburb of Washington, Charen told an interviewer she wanted to change people's minds: "There is still a view that women aren't as serious as men, are somehow a lesser sex. That is a struggle, and I've been on the ramparts as far as that goes, but I think the feminist movement has been a disaster."[176] Her perception of disintegration of family life and moral values gave her a following among conservative women's groups and pro-life adherents. Married and the mother of three children, when she announced her decision in her column to adopt her first child, she received hundreds of letters of support, but two were hurtful, including one from a reader who wrote, "God knows what he's doing and chose to make you infertile for a reason."[177]

In a typical column in 1992, Charen took on what she named the "liberal agenda" for glorifying the use of condoms. She wrote disapprovingly of a report from the House Select Committee on Children, Youth, and Families in which the Democratic majority recommended more "federal dollars for AIDS education and school-based health clinics (read condom dispensaries)."[178] By contrast she praised the Republican minority report that urged more emphasis in high schools on the importance of abstinence and family values. "Women need to see their perspective on the world presented," Charen said, criticizing feminists who support the sexual revolution and "claim to speak for women, but don't."[179]

Forbes also praised another syndicated woman columnist whose articles appeared in the *Times,* Georgie Anne Geyer, whose background as a foreign correspondent for the *Chicago Daily News* had led to her making her own headlines. In the 1960s, when most women journalists still were relegated to writing society notes, Geyer, a graduate of Northwestern University, covered revolutions in Latin America and roamed the world, witnessing change in the Soviet Union, Middle East, and Far East.[180] As an attractive young woman who met with world leaders, she coped with gossip— usually of the sort that accused her of sleeping with sources—but she learned to laugh it off.[181] In 1973 she was the first Western reporter to interview Saddam Hussein, then vice president of Iraq. She also interviewed Yasser Arafat, Anwar Sadat, King Hussein of Jordan, Muammar al-Qaddafi, and Ayatollah Khomeini.[182]

In 1974 Geyer felt the strain of ceaseless travel and decided to write a column, carried by more than 120 newspapers, from an apartment base in Washington. In 1991 she published a biography of Fidel Castro, based in part on personal interaction with him.[183] Although sometimes described as a conservative, Geyer decried that label. "I'm not ideological and I'm not partisan," she said. "I don't identify with one party or with one type of leader."[184] Forbes called Geyer "extremely knowledgeable about the Middle East and South and Central America," and said she had "achieved a knowledge that few columnists—male or female—have."[185]

Geyer also commented on current domestic politics in her column. In the 1980s she criticized the media for overzealous reporting in its efforts to "get" presidential aspirant Gary Hart in 1987 by tracking his interludes with a girlfriend. In her opinion, by 1989 the press had become prosecutor, judge, and executioner of political candidates by emphasizing so-called character issues.[186]

At the *Post,* Helen Dewar established herself as an outstanding political reporter for four decades, proving that a woman of exceptional ability could win respect from colleagues and news sources alike. A graduate of Stanford University, Dewar joined the *Post* in 1961, covering Northern Virginia suburbs before being assigned to Virginia State government in 1965. Promoted to the national staff a decade later, she tracked Jimmy Carter's presidential campaign in 1976. Three years later she moved to the U.S. Senate, where she stayed until 2005. Through a combination of ceaseless work, scrupulous fairness, and determination to get all sides of a story, Dewar became a *Post* legend. At the time of her death in 2006, David Broder called her "one of the best reporters I ever knew."[187]

A self-effacing individual who devoted herself to her work, Dewar perfected what became known as the "Dewar walk" during the 1990s when congressional leaders tried to bar reporters from waiting for senators outside the doors of their chambers.[188] Aware that she could not be chased away as long as she kept moving, "Dewar would shuffle and amble around the corridors, ready to pounce when senators answered a call to a vote," according to her obituary.[189]

As a woman who personally had worked extremely hard to succeed in a man's occupation, Dewar did not see herself as part of a procession of women who had fought for the right to be journalists. Clearly, Dewar, who won the 1984 Everett McKinley Dirksen Award for distinguished reporting of Congress from the NPC Foundation, did not want to be identified with a historical figure, Anne Royall, the first woman to cover Congress, who symbolized society's ridicule of pioneering women journalists. Dewar boycotted a 1990 ceremony recognizing Royall after trying to block the event by attempting to get the Senate Historical Office to say that Royall had not been the first newspaperwoman at the Capitol.[190]

Dewar, however, was conscious of gender barriers in her own career. She made no secret of the fact that she had started at the *Post* in a temporary job, filling paste pots in the women's department, before working her way up the career ladder. She told a colleague there was no reason a woman could not get ahead at the newspaper—all she had to do was to "be twice as good as a man and work twice as hard."[191]

Unlike Dewar, UPI's Helen Thomas readily spoke at the ceremony honoring Royall and made it an occasion to comment on women's political status. "Women in journalism of our vintage have risen above outrageous prejudice," Thomas emphasized.[192] She said women had advanced "from the blatant—'we don't hire women' pronouncements of editors in an earlier day—to the more subtle forms of discrimination today."[193] Reviewing years of past discrimination against women journalists in Washington, Thomas noted, "Today women are high profile" in professions, but she added that there are "no women top policy makers in the White House where it is a man's world [and only] twenty-nine women out of five hundred and thirty-five members of Congress."[194] She ended, "Yes, we've come a long way but we have miles to go before we sleep."[195]

Interviewed in the White House press room a few months later, Thomas elaborated on her contention that women in the United States still faced gender bias. "As for discrimination, I think that none of us have overcome sex discrimination," she said.[196] "I think it is still blatant in this country and I think that we should never rest until we have equality, true equality."[197]

Looking back, she said, "I felt that I should walk right in and open the door for others, even though sometimes I've been faulted for that," a reference to her becoming the first woman member of the Gridiron Club. "I don't mind being a token if I can just walk in through that door and then open it wider for others." Thomas held the same view toward being one of the first women members of the NPC. Even though "many women reporters who had fought the good fight for equality and for getting into the [National] press club said no, no soap, no dice, that they were not interested anymore after having been shunned," she said, "I didn't think that was the right attitude, frankly."[198]

Thomas equated prejudice against women in general with the lack of women in high political places. "Anybody who thinks that women have reached the top in this country [is wrong]. Every day I walk into the oval office or the cabinet room and the issues of war and peace are being discussed [I see] there is not one woman there," she continued.[199] Linking the general status of women in society, including journalism, to their position in the American political system, she said, "I think in the next century we will have a woman as President."[200]

"Probably we will have [a] black [African American] first, though, I imagine, because they [African Americans] seem to have made bigger strides in politics," she added, offering a prediction that came true in 2008 when Barack Obama was elected president of the United States.[201] In Thomas's view women have to overcome more barriers than men to succeed because "men talk to men and men help men."[202] As she saw it in 1990, women still had to struggle for equality.[203]

Besides Thomas herself, only a few other women were perceived as leaders of Washington journalism during the last decade of the twentieth century. In *Washingtonian* magazine in 1989, Barbara Matusow, drawing on interviews with Washington opinion makers, identified the capital's top fifty journalists. She noted that the number of women had increased since 1983 when the leading fifty last had been picked, but women had hardly broken through the male ranks. In 1989, seven women made the list compared to the four who were named five years previously. They were Meg Greenfield, Mary Hagar, Andrea Mitchell, Cokie Roberts, Lesley Stahl, Helen Thomas, and Judy Woodruff.[204]

The newcomers included Hagar, editor of the *Washington Post*'s Style section, and three broadcast reporters—Mitchell of NBC News, Roberts of ABC News and NPR, and Woodruff of PBS indicating that television was trumping print in giving recognition to women journalists. Hagar was identified as one of the seven *Post* editors included because "there is no way to over-estimate the influence the paper has over the life of the capital."[205] The list had only two minority journalists, neither female: William Raspberry of the *Washington Post* and Bernard Shaw of CNN.

Calling attention to the primacy of television, Matusow wrote, "Television is the great big honey pot, dripping promises of lecture fees, book contracts, and invitations to small, off-the-record briefings at the White House."[206] She continued, "Politicians and journalists alike tend to equate visibility with influence, so we have reporters lobbying to get on the TV talk shows."[207]

Washington reporting no longer consisted simply of news stories dispatched from Capitol Hill and the White House by a group of moderately paid journalists. Matusow lamented that Capitol Hill coverage had shrunk while television networks overemphasized the White House. "Perhaps because it's no longer such a desirable beat, many women have made names for themselves covering the Hill," she commented, citing Roberts, Dewar, Sara

Fritz of the *Los Angeles Times,* and Janet Hook of *Congressional Quarterly.*[208]

In 1992 women made up almost half of the White House press corps, aspiring to cover the president as well as the First Lady. For example, Maureen Santana covered the White House from 1978 until the end of 1992, first for the Associated Press, then for the *New York Daily News.* As a recent graduate of the University of Wisconsin, Santana considered herself fortunate during the Reagan years to get the "unofficial AP spot for women at the White House," reporting on Nancy Reagan.[209]

After Santana moved to the *New York Daily News* in 1987, she advanced professionally, covering the president as well as his wife. Obviously, she pointed out, the president has much more "obligation to be in the regular view of the press," making him far more newsworthy.[210] Jodi Edna, who was assigned to the White House in 1993 by the Knight Ridder newspaper chain, put it this way: "I didn't want to be known as the 'woman's beat' first lady reporter, I wanted to be known as the White House reporter who covered the president."[211]

Indicative of women's increasing stature in Washington reporting, during Bill Clinton's 1992 presidential campaign, Robin Toner, the first woman to be named the national political correspondent of the *New York Times,* led her newspaper's coverage of the election.[212] She subsequently became chief of correspondents on the *Times'* national desk in New York before returning to the Washington bureau as a senior writer.[213] Prior to joining the *Times* in 1985, Toner, an honors graduate of Syracuse University, worked for the *Atlanta Journal-Constitution.*[214] She died of cancer in 2008 at the age of fifty-four.

By 1993 the *Washingtonian* increased the number of women in its top fifty list of journalists to thirteen. Newcomers included

Gloria Borger, *U.S. News,* considered an authority on Congress; Eleanor Clift, *Newsweek,* praised for original insights on politics; Ann Devroy, who covered the White House for the *Washington Post;* Maureen Dowd, *New York Times;* Gwen Ifill, then also of the *New York Times* and the first woman of color to make the list; Diane Rehm, WAMU-FM; Susan Spencer, CBS; and Totenberg and Wertheimer, both of NPR.[215] Thomas had been dropped along with Lesley Stahl and Mary Hador. Most of the women who worked on print publications also appeared on television news shows. IT HELPS TO HAVE A TV DEAL AND AN ATTITUDE, the article's subhead said.[216]

Five years later, however, there were fewer women on the list—only eleven—and three different names: Jill Abramson, *Wall Street Journal;* Linda Greenhouse, *New York Times;* and Ann McDaniel, *Newsweek.*[217] Ifill now was with NBC; Borger, Clift, Mitchell, Spencer, and Totenberg had been dropped. As Matusow put it, "Washington is a fickle place."[218] Most of the powerful journalists remained white males—although a younger, more skeptical and conservative group than their predecessors.

In 1997 the *New York Times* recruited Abramson from the *Wall Street Journal* for its Washington bureau. Described as a "short, droll woman who draws out her words as she speaks," she was known as a "ferocious political reporter."[219] Her best friend at the newspaper was Maureen Dowd, the waspish op-ed columnist who won a Pulitzer Prize for Commentary in 1999, particularly focusing on the impeachment of Bill Clinton for his affair with Monica Lewinsky.

A native Washingtonian and daughter of a police inspector, Dowd, a graduate of Catholic University, joined the *Times*' Washington bureau in 1983 after an interlude at *Time* magazine following the demise of the *Star.* She advanced to being an op-ed columnist in 1995. According to her, when she started as a White

House correspondent, "There was a lot of criticism from guys saying, 'She focuses too much on the person but not enough on policy.' I never understood that argument at all. . . . All the great traumatizing events of American history—Watergate, Vietnam, the Iran/contra stuff—have always been about the president's personal demons and gremlins."[220]

Dowd said she thought "that criticism was just silly—as if it was a *girlish* thing to be focused on the person."[221] Writing columns compared to irreverent political cartoons, Dowd, pictured in feature stories as a glamorous redhead who is appealing to men, frequently referred to gender-related topics.

Before the 2000 presidential election, Dowd described Al Gore, the Democratic candidate, as "so feminized and diversified and ecologically correct that he's practically lactating," and called the Democratic Party the "mommy party."[222] Describing gendered implications as factors in Washington politics and political coverage in a lecture at Harvard University, she pointed to presidents who merged personal drives with political policy. "One [Lyndon B. Johnson] aide told [Arthur M.] Schlesinger," she said, "that Vietnam was all about LBJ proving his manhood and [Henry] Kissinger described a scene in 1968, in the Cabinet room, when Johnson harangued [Defense Secretary] Robert McNamara, growling about the North Vietnamese, 'how can I hit them in the nuts?'"[223] To her the Iraq war "was about W. [President George W. Bush] proving his manhood."[224]

In 2001 Abramson, a Harvard graduate who grew up in New York City, was named the chief of the Washington bureau of the *New York Times*. She became the first woman to hold that rarified position. In addition to her and Dowd, the *Washingtonian* list of the top fifty that year included only six other women.[225] The magazine singled out Roberts for offering "reason and moderation on television," Jane Mayer for describing the "nexus between New York and Washington power players" in the *New Yorker,* and Katherine Boo of the *Washington Post* for winning a Pulitzer Prize after exposing shoddy treatment of the mentally ill.

Jackie Judd of ABC was cited for having taken "more heat during the Monica Lewinsky affair (which she was one of the first journalists to reveal) than any honest reporter should have to."[226] The remaining two: Jonetta Rose Barras, a reporter for the Washington *Afro-American* and the *Washington Times* before moving to the *City Paper,* a free distribution weekly, cited for outstanding political coverage of the capital; and veteran Mary McGrory of the *Post,* called a reflection of "the old traditional liberalism of a generation gone."[227]

The small number of women recognized as outstanding, even though a growing number of Washington correspondents were female, reflected the continuation of conflict between family life and careers. Penny Bender Fuchs, for example, left the Gannett Washington bureau in 1999 after a "tumultuous year, politically and personally," covering the Clinton-Gore administration.[228] The previous year, just after the Lewinsky scandal broke, she returned from taking maternity leave for the birth of her second child, Jonathan, who was unwell, so "I missed work frequently to take him to the doctor," she said.[229]

Even without medical appointments, a typical day generated stress. She recalled, "I dropped John off at the babysitter's home and Katie [his sister] off at her preschool and arrived at work by 8:30 A.M. I worked feverishly to get as much accomplished before I had to pick them both up at 5 P.M."[230] Once at home, she often worked from there, although two or three nights a week she waited for her husband, Michael, a lawyer, to come home at 7:00 P.M. so that she could turn around and go back to the office until 10:00

or 11:00 P.M., or even midnight. "I was working so incredibly hard and it seemed to make little difference to my editors who said I was 'less committed' than I had been a few years earlier. It also was a terrible strain on my marriage," she continued.[231] She quit after covering the Clinton impeachment vote—"because what reasonable, self-respecting reporter walks away from that?"—to pursue graduate work at the University of Maryland where she joined the journalism faculty.[232]

Fuchs, who graduated with a journalism degree from Virginia Commonwealth University in 1984, "thought of myself as part of the generation of women who could do it all."[233] She worked her way up to being a Washington correspondent after proving her abilities on small newspapers in Virginia, not finding it difficult to keep up with male colleagues until she had children. "The men I worked with scratched their heads over this; they interpreted my inability to balance the job with the kids as me making a choice, my children over my career ... that should not have been the case."[234]

Abramson also struggled for gender equality. In mid-2001 she told Gerald Boyd, the *Times'* managing editor, that she thought both he and Howell Raines, the paper's executive editor, were "especially disrespectful to the women managers in the newsroom."[235] When Raines designated Pat Tyler, an old fishing buddy, as the next bureau chief, Abramson found herself in an untenable position. "I went from [being] the first woman ever to be Washington bureau chief of the *Times* to going to book parties in Washington and having people ask me, 'How *are* you?' Like I had cancer," she said.[236] She considered leaving the *Times* and moving to the *Post,* although Boyd counseled Abramson to "fight Pat Tyler for your job."[237]

After Arthur Sulzberger Jr., the *Times'* publisher, asked Abramson to stay at the paper, she told Raines that she intended to remain as bureau chief. An angry Raines told her to make sure Tyler was a star.[238] Following the forced resignations of both Raines and Boyd in the wake of a scandal caused by the fabricated reports of Jayson Blair, a young African American reporter, the *Times* appointed Abramson as a comanaging editor in 2003. She was the first woman named to this position, a symbol of the fight to the top waged by determined Washington women journalists. In 2011 she attained the distinction of being the first woman to be named executive editor of the newspaper.

During the first years of the twenty-first century it appeared easier, or at least more possible than in the past, for women to move ahead in journalism after years of discrimination, but ironically journalism itself was in jeopardy. Newspaper circulations and advertising were falling off as new technologies threatened the future of journalism as it had traditionally been defined. Women had worked hard to achieve a pinnacle that seemed to be collapsing.

───────◇───────

EIGHT

WOMEN JOURNALISTS CONFRONT
TODAY'S MEDIA CHALLENGES

Virtually every media sector—newspapers, network television, local television, cable television, national magazines—is losing readers or viewers. Moreover, most of these venues are investing fewer resources in covering the news. . . . Journalistically, this is a new world, much of which ignores the best of the old-media values.
—*Judy Woodruff, 2007*

The start of the twenty-first century brought sweeping changes to journalism in Washington as well as to the rest of the country. As journalism confronted massive technological upheavals brought by the Internet, newspaper circulation dwindled and news presentation moved to digital formats and social media. With journalists seeking to find places within a new media landscape, a generational gap emerged between younger women, who had not experienced overt discrimination, and older women who remembered it well. Issues of working conditions that made it difficult to combine journalistic careers with family life remained unsolved. The Internet spawned bloggers, some of whose opinionated views and use of sex countered the credibility of mainstream journalists. The twenty-four-hour news cycle of cable television created talk shows geared far more toward entertainment and reinforcement of personal ideology than public enlightenment.

While women journalists achieved visible positions in the capital, relatively few women and even fewer minorities were perceived at the top of their profession. Among the most respected, Gwen Ifill continued as moderator of PBS's *Washington Week in Review* news program and served as senior correspondent for PBS's *NewsHour*. By 2010 she had covered six presidential campaigns and moderated two debates between vice presidential candidates, one in 2004 and the other in 2008. Yet, she was not ranked among Washington's "50 best and most influential journalists" in 2005.[1] Four years later, in 2009, when she was honored with being asked to deliver four commencement addresses in one year, she reappeared on the list.[2]

By that time the nature of Washington journalism had undergone dramatic change, and many new names showed up in the rankings as once-powerful news organizations withered away.[3] Each year of the new century brought retrenchment of the old news establishment and more passing of its influence to a generation enthralled by blogs, websites, and social media. While women played a role in this shift, their roles were far from dominant.

The 2005 list of influential journalists, for example, had even fewer women than the one four years previously. "Anecdotally at least, after a number of years of increasing gender balance, it seems there's been a subtle shift back toward male reporters at the top echelons of Washington reporting," *Washingtonian* magazine reported.[4] Only seven women were named—two mentioned previously from the *New York Times,* Dowd and Greenhouse; two other repeats, Borger and Roberts; and two newcomers from newspapers, Jill Lawrence of *USA Today* and Dana Priest of the *Washington Post,* described as a "top military and intelligence watcher."[5] The remaining figure, Judith Miller of the *New York Times,* was cited as influential but not admired because of controversies surrounding her reporting and jail sentence for refusing to reveal a source.[6] Ironically, Miller gained attention for flaws in her journalistic output, not for integrity or competence.

Miller attracted notoriety for reporting that Iraq allegedly had stockpiled weapons of mass destruction (WMDs). Her disclosures, later proven to be false, helped justify the Bush administration's invasion of Iraq in 2003. She also became a cause célèbre in 2005 when she spent eighty-five days in the Alexandria (Va.) Detention Center, just across the Potomac River from Washington, on civil contempt charges after refusing to reveal a source to a federal prosecutor.

Writing about Miller's walk "through a gantlet of media" into and out of the courtroom where she was sentenced, Robin Givhan, a Pulitzer Prize–winning fashion columnist for the *Post,* reported that the fifty-seven-year-old Miller "looked like she was dashing into the courthouse on her way to an interview."[7] She compared Miller "with her sensible pageboy and its trim bangs" to an "English lecturer at Barnard [College]" and said her black quilted jacket spoke of New York's Upper East Side.[8]

A steady parade of prominent government and media figures, including former Republican presidential candidate Bob Dole and NBC news anchor Tom Brokaw, trekked to the Alexandria jail to visit Miller, saying they wanted to support her right to protect confidential sources.[9] She was allowed to see them on weeknights or during weekends at the maximum security facility where she had to wear a jumpsuit with the word *prisoner* on the back and sleep in a seventy-square-foot cell.[10] Still, according to the *Wash-*

ingtonian, instead of ending her stay as a martyr to principle, Miller "managed to emerge more a pariah than ever."[11]

Her contempt citation came as a result of a subpoena to appear before a Washington grand jury investigating a 2003 leak to journalists that Valerie Plame, the wife of former ambassador Joseph Wilson, a critic of the Iraq war, was an undercover CIA officer. After serving her sentence, Miller said she gained permission from her source to reveal his identity. He was I. Lewis "Scooter" Libby, the chief of staff for Vice President Dick Cheney. The investigation of the leak led to a criminal conviction against Libby, whose thirty-month prison sentence was commuted by President George W. Bush. Miller testified three times for the prosecution at Libby's trial in 2007, first saying that she could not remember her conversations with him.

Miller herself did not write about Plame's identity, but other journalists did.[12] Several testified before the grand jury, saying their source had waived confidentiality, but Miller initially refused to accept such a waiver from Libby, claiming it was not voluntary. She agreed to testify only after receiving a letter and telephone call from him. These circumstances made some journalists speculate on why she had gone to jail at all and wonder if she did so to salvage her professional reputation.[13]

After leaving jail, Miller left her twenty-eight-year-long career with the *New York Times,* which included a Pulitzer Prize, following two weeks of negotiations over severance pay. Detractors said she had been fired. Major journalism organizations praised Miller for protecting her sources, and the Society of Professional Journalists (SPJ) gave her its First Amendment Award, but some journalists, particularly those writing on the web, took a different tack.

In the *Huffington Post,* Arianna Huffington guessed that Miller might be planning to profit from her experiences by writing a book about them. Huffington said, "What would Miller's angle be? I helped the bad guys sell a bogus war that led to tens of thousands of deaths, then went to jail to protect my neocon [neoconservative] pals?"[14] In a series of sensational articles for the *New York Times,* Miller had claimed that Iraq had WMDs, both preceding and following the U.S. invasion there.[15] The reports later were exposed as based on wrong and misleading information.[16] The *Times,* however, contended that Miller was not the only journalist taken in by government intelligence sources and others who claimed Iraq possessed a terrifying arsenal.[17] One *Times* colleague, David Barstow, called it unfair to turn Miller into "the embodiment of all these failures."[18]

On the other hand, one of Miller's strongest critics turned out to be the *Times'* premier woman columnist, Maureen Dowd. Declaring the *Times* would be "in danger" if Miller returned to the newsroom, Dowd called Miller not "credible," contending she had written "bogus" stories about nonexistent Iraqi weapons and alleging she should have been kept on a "tight editorial leash."[19] After tabloids and blogs screamed "Catfight," Dowd commented, "I had written about the WMD scam of the administration. . . . To keep trust with my readers, I needed to address her role in this thing. I knew as a woman writing about another woman I work with, there would be a catfight element, even though . . . it's business, not personal."[20]

In her reporting on WMDs, Miller relied heavily on information from Ahmed Chalabi, head of the Iraqi National Congress, who proved to be untruthful. Salon.com contended, "Lying exile grifter Ahmad Chalabi fed her the worst of the nonsense designed to push America into toppling Saddam Hussein (and giving Iraq to him), and she pushed that nonsense into the newspaper of record."[21] In 2004, after the U.S. government severed ties with

Chalabi, the *Times* admitted that its coverage had depended too heavily on him and other exiles who wanted regime change in the run-up to the war on Iraq.

Critics said Miller's reports encompassed the views of military-minded neoconservatives in the Bush administration, some of whom had personal relationships with Miller. She defended herself by saying she did the best reporting she could do under difficult circumstances. "Was I wrong?" she asked. "Sure, because my sources were wrong."[22]

The daughter of a hotel and nightclub owner, Miller had moved with her family from New York to Las Vegas, where she became interested in the use of the atomic bomb and other weapons. A graduate of Barnard College who obtained a master's degree in public affairs from Princeton University, she joined the *Times* in 1977 after working as a correspondent for *Progressive* magazine and NPR. Known as a tireless reporter who ran roughshod over her colleagues, Miller held major responsibilities for years, first in the paper's Washington bureau, where she covered Congress and foreign affairs, especially those related to the Middle East, and later as the first woman chief of the *Times'* bureau in Cairo.

In 1986 she was named Paris correspondent, but returned to the Washington bureau as news editor and deputy bureau chief the following year. Designated the newspaper's special correspondent for the Persian Gulf in 1990, Miller was embedded with a military unit in Iraq charged with hunting for WMDs.[23] She won a Pulitzer Prize in 2002 for "explanatory journalism" as part of a small team that produced a series for the *Times* the previous year on Osama bin Laden and al-Qaeda.[24]

Salon.com accused her of being a "tool of power," serving as "the voice of the Defense Department, embedded at the *Times*."[25] Her competitiveness led her astray, according to *New York* magazine: "The Judy Miller problem *is* complicated. The very qualities that endeared Miller to her editors at the *New York Times*—her ambition, her aggressiveness, her cultivation of sources by any means necessary, her hunger to be first—were the same ones that allowed her to get the WMD story so wrong."[26]

It noted that when she started in the Washington bureau, almost all of the reporters were men who had risen through the newspaper's ranks, but Miller, hired when the newspaper was fighting its class action gender discrimination suit, "stood out immediately for her sharp elbows."[27] Miller did not deny that she offended some colleagues. "I don't think one can survive in places like Washington or the *Times* without being pushy," she said.[28]

New York magazine pointed out that Miller's blighted career illustrated one of the fundamental problems of journalism—reliance on sources, as she herself admitted. The magazine said the occupation "inevitably relies on people . . . like Miller with her outsize journalistic temperament of ambition, obsession, and competitive fervor," becoming close to "people like Chalabi with his smooth, affable exterior retailing false information for his own motives."[29] The Miller episode also exposed tensions at the *Times,* where editors apparently were unwilling to question her reporting because she seemed to be a favorite of those in charge. While she still was writing page one stories in 2003, *Editor and Publisher* alleged that she was protected because she "delivered 'exclusives,' even if in a prosecutorial, hyperventilated voice," that executives were loath to admit were wrong.[30]

As Miller became the story herself, some saw evidence of gender bias in her media treatment. In a long feature on Miller, the *Washington Post* asked, "Would an aggressive, high-decibel male reporter be embroiled in all the controversy in which Miller finds herself?"[31] In support of Miller, Patricia Cohen, the *Times* theater critic, said, "A man is tough and hard-driving and a woman is a bitch."[32] Others said the *Times* management had trouble handling her volatile personality.

Like Marguerite Higgins's a half century before, Miller's personal relationships as a young woman reporter had become legendary. During her initial tenure in the *Times*' Washington bureau, she lived with a congressman, Rep. Les Aspin (D-Wisconsin), who died in 1995.[33] Another intimate friend, Richard Burt, became an assistant secretary of state in 1982. Miller contended that neither Congress nor the State Department was her beat during these relationships. Questioned about her former romances, she became outraged and claimed discrimination. "What male reporter would be asked about whom he went out with twenty-five years ago?" she exclaimed to a *Post* reporter.[34] She has been married to Jason Epstein, cofounder of the *New York Review of Books,* since 1993.

During her years on the *Times,* Miller frequently appeared on leading television news programs to discuss terrorism, biological warfare, WMDs, and related topics. After leaving the *Times,* she first worked for Fox News, where she appeared on its Fox News Watch program. In 2010 she contracted to write for *Newsmax,* a conservative publication. She has written four books, two of them best sellers, dealing with the Holocaust, Saddam Hussein, Islam, and bioterrorism. Perhaps because of her coauthored book on biological weapons in 2001, Miller was the only major U.S. media reporter to receive an anthrax hoax letter mailed to her *New York Times* office that year.[35]

When Miller left the *Times,* Jay Rosen, a professor at New York University, and other media commentators declared she had done more to damage the reputation of that newspaper than Jayson Blair. Unlike Miller, an experienced journalist with a long record of page-one stories, Blair was a troubled young reporter caught making up news articles in 2003.[36] Miller's rise and fall may have symbolized the tensions facing the mainstream press, even the *Times,* as it sought to maintain readers and lead the news agenda.

As senior correspondent on the PBS *NewsHour,* Judy Woodruff pointed out the anxieties besetting all newspapers in an address at the University of Notre Dame in 2007. She quoted Arthur Sulzberger Jr., publisher of the *Times,* who told an interviewer: "I don't know whether we'll be printing the *New York Times* in five years, and you know what? I don't care," in contemplating a shift to the web.[37] To Woodruff the Scooter Libby trial "revealed a seamy underside of Washington journalism, cozy relationships, and promiscuous promises of anonymity that seemed to put the interests of sources and accessibility ahead of that of readers and viewers."[38]

Another veteran Washington woman journalist became embroiled in controversy that was assumed to close her career during the first decade of the twenty-first century. Helen Thomas kept on winning awards and was professionally active as a columnist for Hearst Newspapers until she was forced to resign in 2010 at the age of eighty-nine after making a remark viewed as callous and hurtful to the citizens of Israel. Yet, she refused to give up journalism. In 2011 the ninety-year-old Thomas reentered the field with a column in a Northern Virginia weekly newspaper.

The publisher and editor, Nicholas Benton, who said he carried Thomas's column when she wrote for Hearst, defended Thomas against charges of being bigoted and antisemitic.[39] He said she misspoke and was misunderstood in July 2010 when she was approached by a rabbi with a video camera during a Jewish Heritage event at the White House and asked if she had any thoughts about Israel. As an American of Arab background, Thomas had long questioned Israeli policy toward Palestinians. She replied: "Tell them [the Israelis] to get the hell out of Palestine."[40] She added that they should "go home" to Poland and Germany.[41]

Since Israel had been founded as a Jewish homeland after Jews in Poland and Germany were murdered in the Holocaust, her remarks received widespread condemnation. Thomas initially apologized, but subsequently said she did not regret her comments and told a Dearborn, Michigan, audience that "Congress, the White House and Hollywood, Wall Street are owned by Zionists," a statement criticized as untrue and hostile to Jews.[42] While Benton acknowledged Thomas's comments were inappropriate, he said the meaning of her July remarks was that "Jewish people can live wherever they want."[43]

The outcry over Thomas's July comments led her alma mater, Wayne State University, to drop an award named after her, and the SPJ to retire a lifetime achievement award that honored her. Her name was removed from the front-row seat in the White House briefing room, where she had sat for decades, although during President George W. Bush's administration, when she was a strong opponent of the Iraq War, she had been moved to the back row. Thomas had been the only reporter to have her own seat in the briefing room where seats are assigned to news organizations, not individuals. As the senior White House correspondent for years, traditionally she had asked the first question during White House press conferences. When relegated to the back, she told observers, "They didn't like me . . . I ask too many questions."[44]

After Thomas called Bush the "worst president in American history" in 2003, for which she later apologized, he did not call on her for three years. When he finally did, in 2006, she brought up the Iraq war and snapped, "Every reason given, publicly at least, has turned out not to be true. . . . Why did you really want to go to war?"[45] Continuing her interrogation, she said, "From the moment you stepped into the White House.... What was your real reason? You have said it wasn't oil ... quest for oil, it hasn't been Israel, or anything else. What was it?"[46] Bush answered by referring to his War on Terror, as well as Saddam Hussein's failure to admit inspectors and to disclose information. Some commentators criticized Thomas for the tone of her questioning.

Thomas's exchange with Bush illustrated one example of growing discord between the White House and its press corps, as well as the public. According to Martha Joynt Kumar, a political scientist who specialized in the relationship between the president and the press, "Reporters do grow sick of being at the White House. They want to be where they can determine more of what they do and how they do it. At the White House, it's decided for them."[47] At the same time the public seemed increasingly unwilling to see the press corps as performing a watchdog function. White House reporters, about half of whom were women in the early twenty-first century, regularly received abusive email messages and read blogs that contended the national media no longer remained relevant.

"This is the punching-bag beat of American journalism," said David E. Sanger, who covered the White House during the George W. Bush administration for the *New York Times*.[48] "And the White House itself has been skillful at diverting tough questions by changing the subject to its battles with the media."[49]

In 2009, at President Obama's first news conference, Thomas was seated again in the front row. Nevertheless, she soon criticized the Obama administration for lack of openness, contending that not even Nixon had tried to control the press to such an extent. Obama himself characterized her remarks on Israel as "offensive," remarking that it was a "shame" for her outstanding career to end so sadly.[50] Similarly, Sam Donaldson, a retired ABC White House correspondent, while not condoning her remarks on Israel, said they should not negate her achievements as a pioneer Washington woman journalist—a fifty-seven-year career with UPI, covering every president from Eisenhower to Obama, and scoring successive "firsts" for women.[51]

In a memoir Thomas said that when she started covering the White House she "didn't think it was possible to do the kind of work I loved to do and still be a wife."[52] Besides, she added, she and the other "ladies of the press" were busy "breaking down the gender-specific walls, either fighting for 'hard news' assignments or trying to kick in the door at the National Press Club."[53] She postponed her marriage to a journalistic rival, Douglas Cornell, who covered the White House for the AP, until Cornell's retirement from the wire service in 1971. After her wedding, she received notes from women friends, "saying I had renewed their hopes— that my getting married was a most encouraging sign for them."[54]

Combining marriage and a family with a journalistic career remained a significant twenty-first century issue for Washington women journalists. Some women managed to combine high-profile careers with a family, while others did not. "First and fore-most, I'm a mother," Woodruff, who has three children, told an interviewer.[55] The condition of her oldest son, Jeffrey, suffering from spina bifida, was made worse by surgery that left him profoundly disabled at the age of sixteen, spurring Woodruff and her husband, Al Hunt, who became executive editor of the Bloomberg News operation in Washington in 2005, to advocate publicly for disabled children. Yet Woodruff, who appears regularly on the PBS *NewsHour,* said that it was difficult for her to find time to attend meetings of the board of the March of Dimes, an organization that raises money for spina bifida. "I essentially have to give up my program that day [when the board meets], and that's really hard," she commented.[56]

Finding that a new century did not bring changes in working routines to accommodate family life, some senior women correspondents gave up the pressures of daily journalism. After winning awards, Marlene Cimons left the Washington bureau of the *Los Angeles Times* in 2001 to spend more time with the two children she had adopted as a single parent. "My editors hated the fact that I chose my children first," she said.[57] "They hated the fact that I could no longer travel."[58]

In 2003 Jodi Enda left the Knight Ridder bureau, for which she had covered the White House, convinced her news organization "that had billed itself as family friendly was not—women with children were treated unfairly as compared to men with children."[59] Enda, who put off having a baby until she was forty-three, said that when she returned from maternity leave, the editors "promised me I wouldn't have to travel," but she was back only three days before being asked to do so.[60] She resigned, struck by the makeup of the traveling White House press and campaign reporting corps—"either unmarried women or women with an older child or married men with children of any age."[61]

Cassandra Clayton was a correspondent for NBC News in New York before moving to the Washington bureau as a part-time contract employee. She created news packages for the *Nightly News Weekend with Brian Williams* for six years, from 1994 to 2000. She also traveled with President Clinton and assisted with coverage of the White House and Congress before leaving the network. "I moved to the District of Columbia from New York City because I thought it would be a better place to raise my then four-year-old daughter," she said.[62] "Tim Russert, the NBC bureau chief, had long entreated me to come work in DC, and offered me a work opportunity that would allow me to . . . take my daughter to school and pick her up almost every day."[63]

In spite of this flexibility, "becoming a mother changed my career, and what I wanted out of a career," she said.[64] "I felt NBC was very supportive, but I made decisions that led me away from the business."[65] She now teaches broadcast journalism at the University of Maryland.

As an experienced observer of television, Clayton, an African American, credited the twenty-four-hour cable news cycle, the explosion of blogs, and other new media with providing increased opportunities for women and minorities. Yet, she said, "it's still very tough to have a high-profile beat, like the White House or Congress and raise children."[66] Calling attention to Norah O'Donnell, Washington bureau chief for MSNBC, Clayton said O'Donnell is raising three-year-old twins and a two-year-old, but she "confesses to getting help from her husband, a nanny, an au pair, and two sets of grandparents. She's very fortunate to have that kind of help."[67]

While women correspondents unquestionably have proved their capability on television, some observers said they still face different standards than men. John Dickerson characterized Campbell Brown of NBC as facing the "same gender categorizing" that his mother, Nancy Dickerson, television's first woman star, did forty years earlier.[68] According to him, when Brown "so ably covered the devastation of Hurricane Katrina in New Orleans in 2005, she was praised as much for still looking sympathetic, soft and feminine as she was for the quality of her reporting."[69] Clayton pointed out that men as well as women must have "a little work" done to improve their appearances on television—"Botox, fillers, and hair pieces abound"—but that women must "use more make-up and hairspray than the men."[70]

As cable television and Internet news fragmented the audience, network news with its frequent Washington reports fell in national prestige. Two years before Couric took over as CBS's *Evening News* anchor in 2006, Tom Rosenstiel, director of the Project for Excellence in Journalism, raised the prospect of "the end of 'network news.'"[71] Pointing out that the average age of viewers of evening network newscasts was close to sixty, Rosenstiel said that network executives no longer cared about the "prestige and influence of their news divisions."[72] The Pew Research Center for the People and the Press reported in 2004 that only 28 percent of Americans regularly watched the nightly network news compared to 60 percent in 1993.[73]

Since morning shows, such as those that Katie Couric and Diane Sawyer had starred in before taking over nightly news, seemed to offer a more promising route for ascension to anchor posts than Washington political beats, the significance of the capital as a news venue diminished somewhat. Younger people turned away from the mainstream political media, preferring to get news via the Internet or entertainment-oriented programs like Comedy Central's *The Daily Show*.[74] Cable television, rather than giving verified reports of actual occurrences, relied on extemporaneous talk from hosts, reporters, and news sources. According to Rosenstiel, "In this new TV journalism, in a sense the news is secondary to the staged debate about the news."[75]

After less than two years in the CBS post, Couric's imminent departure was predicted by dozens of news outlets because she had failed to improve the sagging ratings of the *Evening News*.[76] She determinedly rode out the rumors and fulfilled her five-year contract. Her interview with Republican vice presidential candidate Sarah Palin in September 2008, seen as exposing Palin's lack of a coherent message, raised Couric's ratings and stature at the time.

The presence of Couric and Sawyer at the apex of network news appeared to counter a preponderance of white males who headed the Washington bureaus of U.S. daily newspapers. A 2004 study by UNITY: Journalists of Color, Inc., and the University of Maryland found that fewer than 10.5 percent of the reporters, correspondents, columnists, and bureau chiefs in the Washington daily newspaper press corps were journalists of color—60 out of 574.[77] This figure fell far below 30.9 percent, which represented the non-white U.S. population as a whole, according to the 2000 Census.

The study reported representation particularly low at the top positions in Washington bureaus. Of the thirty-six daily newspapers and groups at the capital, only three had nonwhite heads: the *Chicago Tribune,* Gannett News Service, and the *Detroit News.*[78] Of these, two were women—Vickie Walton-James of the *Tribune* and Alison Bethel of the *Detroit News.* While the study did not track the number of women journalists in the bureaus, according to Chris Callahan of the University of Maryland, only five other bureau chiefs were women.[79]

According to the study, few of the journalists of color believed that the capital press corps did a good job in covering race-related news, with only 13 percent classifying the coverage as "good" and none considering it "excellent" or even "very good."[80] Nearly one-third of the respondents thought that coverage had declined in the past few years.[81] Perhaps surprisingly, only about one-third planned to stay in journalism, although their pay appeared reasonably good—more than one-fourth reported earning more than $100,000 annually from their newspaper jobs, while 51 percent reported making between $75,000 and $100,000.[82]

Some of the dissatisfaction may have been due to the fact that nearly half said they personally had little or no influence over coverage of race-related stories coming out of their own bureaus. The study did not look into whether they felt a sense of empowerment in general, but one might infer that a sizeable number did not. More than 90 percent believed the Washington press corps was at least somewhat out of touch with its audiences in the rest of the nation.[83]

Somewhat similarly, a national study of 273 top editors in 2002 found that almost one out of two of the women editors planned to change newsrooms or leave the news business compared to only one in three of the male editors.[84] The study identified two distinct subsets of women, the career conflicted and the career confident. Almost half fell into the first category, citing sexism and perceived lack of opportunity as obstacles in their paths.[85]

On the brighter side, some Washington women journalists engaged in stellar careers, bridging various kinds of media and having a family at the same time. The energetic Michelle Singletary, a syndicated personal finance columnist for the *Post,* offered plain-spoken advice to readers across the country with her "Color of Money" column that appeared in more than one hundred newspapers. She also wrote three books telling readers how to live well on what they have, appeared on numerous network radio and television programs to help individuals with financial issues, contributed to national magazines, provided a column for a PBS website, hosted a live online chat on the *Post*'s website, and prepared a widely read electronic newsletter distributed by the *Post.*[86]

An African American, Singletary, married and the mother of three children, found time to lead a ministry offering financial advice to members of her Baptist church in Prince George's County, Maryland, and delivered biblically based personal finance presentations at other churches. A graduate of the University of Maryland, she obtained a master's degree in business management from Johns Hopkins University. After starting with the *Post* in 1992, she clearly saw the importance of maneuvering across media platforms in view of the decline of traditional journalism.[87]

By 2006 U.S. newspaper circulation had plunged drastically, dropping by 2.8 percent during a six-month period that ended on September 30, compared with the same period a year earlier, which constituted the steepest decline in any six-month period in at least fifteen years.[88] The losses came as Knight Ridder newspapers were sold and the Tribune Company, publisher of the *Chicago Tribune, Los Angeles Times,* and nine other newspapers, faced a troubled future involving a sale and bankruptcy. As audiences migrated to the online world, studies showed that 60 to 70 percent of the people seeking news from websites of newspapers were male, a higher proportion than the readers of traditional newspapers.[89] According to the Pew Internet and American Life Project and the Pew Research Center for the People and the Press, "The number of men reading online news was 8 to 13 percent higher than women."[90]

As newspaper circulations shrank, the number of Washington reporters also decreased. In 2000, when President George W. Bush took office, Cox Newspapers stationed about thirty journalists in Washington to cover the new administration.[91] Eight years later, as President Barack Obama readied his legislative agenda, Cox Newspapers, which publishes the *Atlanta Journal-Constitution,* the *Austin American-Statesman,* and fifteen other newspapers, closed its Washington bureau for good.[92] At the same time, Advance Publications, which owns twenty-six daily newspapers, including the *Star-Ledger* (Newark, N.J.), the *Cleveland Plain Dealer,* the *Oregonian* (Portland, Ore.), and the *Times-Picayune* (New Orleans, La.), shut down its bureau, which employed about twenty journalists.[93] The bureau also housed the Newhouse News Service, a supplemental wire service.

The closures symbolized decisions by a host of newspapers to concentrate on local news and reduce expenses elsewhere.

Linda Fibich, Newhouse bureau chief, told the AP, "The decision to close followed the direction of our clients, the editors of our papers. They felt they could not afford to pay for a central Washington bureau at a time when they were steering all available resources to local coverage back at home."[94]

Nationally the years 2008 and 2009 were brutal ones for journalists. Jobs disappeared for some 5,900 daily print journalists in 2008 and for another 5,200 the following year, while some 1,600 lost jobs in local television news and networks also cut back.[95] No precise statistics were kept on cutbacks in the mainstream Washington press corps. Yet by the start of the Obama presidency in 2009, observers noted substantial changes.

According to Joe Keenan, superintendent of the Senate Press Gallery, representatives of general circulation newspapers left the capital to be replaced by employees of small, narrowly focused publications, especially those related to finance. "It seems like for every newspaper that leaves, a niche publication comes in," he said.[96] If bureaus did not vanish altogether, they declined markedly in size—the Tribune Company, for instance, merged the bureaus of all its newspapers, pruning the number of employees from seventy to about half that total.[97]

As bureaus dwindled in size, Deborah Howell, a formidable force in journalism at a time when women rarely advanced as far as she did, left her position as head of the Newhouse News Service in 2005. Named bureau chief in 1990, Howell, a well-respected professional who inspired other women to follow her example, expanded coverage on such subjects as race, gender, sexuality, technology, and religion, instead of concentrating on governmental matters.[98] "She developed beats and story ideas that people were not doing in Washington," Fibich said.[99]

Howell, whose father was a Texas newspaperman and broadcaster, was a 1962 graduate of the University of Texas who suffered from asthma throughout her life. Refusing to work on women's pages, she sought reporting jobs like male graduates but was repeatedly turned down because of her gender. Finally, on the strength of her father's name, she was offered an eighty-dollar-a-week job at a broadcasting station in Corpus Christi. "I was thrilled," she recalled, even though she had to put in sixty hours a week and work six days a week.[100] She soon moved to the *Corpus Christi Caller-Times* as a copy editor before relocating in Minnesota, both to follow a boyfriend and to enhance her journalistic skills on a major regional newspaper.

At the age of thirty-four, Howell became city editor of the *Minneapolis Star,* where she proved herself as tough and aggressive as the men under her.[101] "If the guy reporters accepted you, you know, you went down to the bar with them and you drank, you became one of the boys," she said in an oral history interview.[102] She became furious when she learned her pay was less than that of the men under her: "I blew up. I went in and pasted myself all over the managing editor's office, then went and did the same thing to the editor, and I said they'd better do something about it, because in about twenty-four hours I was going to call my lawyer."[103] Actually, she added, she would not have carried out her threat—"I never did that kind of thing."[104]

Switching to the *St. Paul Pioneer Press,* she rose to executive editor, overseeing feature stories that led the paper to win its first two Pulitzer Prizes, in 1986 and 1988. Known as both a fierce competitor and a kindly mentor, the small and slender Howell, said to "curse like a longshoreman," gloried in two nicknames given her in the Twin Cities: Mother Mary Deborah and the Dragon Lady.[105] After the death of her first husband, Nicholas D. Coleman, Democratic majority leader of the Minnesota Senate, she married

C. Peter Magrath, who served as president of three universities. During her fifteen years at Newhouse, she led her staff in winning a Pulitzer Prize. After leaving the bureau, Howell acted as ombudsman of the *Washington Post* from 2005 to 2008, where she pushed for higher ethical standards.

The same year Howell joined the *Post,* it lost one of its most promising women staff members, Marjorie Williams, a columnist known for her trenchant profiles of the politically elite. She died of cancer at the age of forty-seven. Williams, who dropped out of Harvard University to work in book publishing in New York, decided to try Washington journalism in 1986. She soon drew admirers to her Style profiles and op-ed columns that deflated pompous politicians with insightful yet homey comparisons. She also wrote for *Vanity Fair.*

A *Post* editorial at the time of Williams's death quoted one column in which she wrote: "Official Washington is implacably, impartially hostile to family life. You can tinker with this truth only at the margins, and to pretend otherwise is just to write one more chapter in the big book of lies titled 'Having It All.' "[106] Married to Tim Noah, an online columnist for Slate.com, and the mother of two young children, Williams did not gloss over the trials of working mothers as she leveled her elegant, withering prose at the foibles of official Washington.

In one column she zeroed in on rhapsodizing about men who behaved the way women had been expected to for years without being praised: "In years of writing about political figures, I have heard the friends and associates of a really striking number of men offer, as proof of the great men's warmth and cuddliness, that when their children call during work hours, they actually take the calls," Williams commented.[107] In a profile on Clark Clifford, considered the quintessential Washington insider before his career ended in scandal, Williams asked "the intriguing question of how Washington came to repose so much confidence in a corporate lawyer-lobbyist, making him the personification, the very definition, of integrity. The answer to that mystery lies in . . . how eager Washington always is to think of its fixers as statesmen."[108] According to Bob Thompson, one of her *Post* editors, "She had an extraordinary concern for getting it right, not just in the details, but in the context."[109]

The themes of getting it right and being truthful with readers occupied Howell as ombudsman. Howell publicly chastised her colleagues for journalistic flaws at the same time she won their admiration. A strong believer in honest and fair journalism, she raised ethical flags about famous *Post* journalists accepting large speaking fees from groups that might want to influence news coverage.[110] Her stance led the paper to make key changes, including more attention to timely corrections and accountability to readers.[111]

Howell died in 2010 when she was struck by an oncoming car when she tried to take a picture on vacation in New Zealand. At the time, Karen Tumulty, a *Time* magazine reporter, wrote, "She was a source of inspiration, having made her way up in this business at a time when the newsroom was hostile territory for women who didn't want to spend their careers writing wedding announcements."[112] Tumulty added, "Because of her, it was a lot easier for those of us who followed."[113]

One of Howell's biggest controversies occurred in 2006 when she wrote a column supporting the work of *Post* reporter Susan Schmidt, who had exposed the tactics of Jack Abramoff, a lobbyist eventually convicted of mail fraud and conspiracy. Howell erroneously wrote that he had given money to both Republicans and Democrats, when in fact he had contributed only to the Republicans, although he directed others to donate funds to both parties.[114]

Howell corrected the statement, but outraged readers who accused her of favoring the Republican Party by attempting to portray Abramoff as linked to Democrats as well as the GOP. Readers sent emails so abusive and obscene that part of the *Post*'s website was shut down.[115] In her column she wrote that "a few curse words (which I use frequently) are not going to hurt my feelings."[116] But, she continued, "This unbounded, unreasoning rage is not going to help this newspaper, this country or democracy."[117]

During her last month as ombudsman, Howell criticized the *Post* for allowing men to dominate the news. She said that a study of two weeks of *Post* content showed that men were the subjects of many more stories than women, were quoted far more often, and appeared in more photos than women. She referred to a study by a group of women in the *Post* newsroom that urged top male editors to pay more attention to news that attracted women, including reports on women's sports.[118] While the newsroom was split, with about 60 percent men and 40 percent women in professional jobs, and there were many mid-level women editors, only two women were near the top, she said. "And Page 1 decisions ultimately are made only by men."[119]

The previous May, Howell tore into the *Post*'s op-ed page, calling it "too male and too white," as well as lacking in "youthful opinions."[120] She noted that since the first of the year the newspaper had printed 654 op-ed pieces—575 by men, but only 79 by women and about the same number by minorities.[121] She also pointed out that of nineteen weekly or biweekly columnists, seventeen were men.[122] The only two women were Ruth Marcus, a *Post* editorial writer, and Anne Applebaum, a former *Post* editorial writer.

Earlier in the year Howell had taken on a column in the Outlook section by a woman writer who wondered whether "we
women" aren't the "weaker sex after all" if not the "stupid sex."[123]
Charlotte Allen, the author, went on to quote studies that showed
women have more car accidents than men, lack masculine spatial
awareness, and "have smaller brains."[124] Howell called it "insulting" and questioned the judgment of the Outlook assignment
editor, Zofia Smardz, who thought the article "funny," and the
male editor who approved publication on the grounds that it was
"different."[125] The article generated outpourings of rage from
women readers.

At the same time Howell lamented the *Post*'s orientation to
males, both women and men were losing their jobs on its staff.
More than 100 journalists took early retirement packages in
2008 that were designed to replace senior reporters with cheaper
help—or not to replace them at all. Following a peak of 900 employees, the 2008 buyout was the third in five years, shrinking the
newsroom to 680 employees—offset by some 20 new hires.[126]
Circulation had fallen from 813,000 daily in 2000 to 673,000 daily
in 2008, although the *Post* on the web drew 9.4 million unique
visitors a month, 85 percent of them outside the newspaper's circulation area. Unfortunately, those readers did not provide the
revenue that the print subscribers did.[127]

Some journalists who left cited increased tensions and the pressures of a twenty-four-hour news cycle as factors in their decision
to depart. In 2007 Leslie Walker, the *Post* technology editor and
former head of its web division, resigned to write fiction, determined that she "wasn't going to drop dead in the newsroom."[128]
Walker said she wanted to experience life outside the newsroom
and work "in a setting that was less driven by hourly, or even mi-
nutely deadlines."[129]

The challenge of revamping the *Post* fell to its new publisher, Katharine Weymouth, forty-one, the granddaughter of Katharine Graham. In a message to the staff Weymouth said, "The ways in which we break news and tell stories will continue to evolve and change as technology and readers' habits evolve and change. The challenge is at once daunting and thrilling; reinventing the news-paper—in some senses, the news itself—for a new century."[130] Yet, Weymouth herself, a lawyer who had been the *Post*'s vice president of advertising before becoming publisher in 2008, had to deal with the old scourge of sexism. She told a Women's History Month audience at the National Archives in 2009 that she had agreed to wear "hot pants" to please an advertiser who wanted to play golf with her.[131]

Among those who left the *Post* in the 2008 buyouts was Susan Schmidt, the Pulitzer Prize winner who had been instrumental in exposing the lobbying corruption of Jack Abramoff. She cited frustration in getting her work printed and a dwindling of re-sources for investigations. With the departure of senior people, the newspaper had less ability to correct reportorial mistakes, ac-cording to Schmidt.[132] She told the *American Journalism Review* that the *Post* had not even tried to set the record straight after incor-rectly intimating that a federal regulator had cashed out to work for bankers who had wrecked the economy. In the past, she said, experienced editors and reporters would have caught the error, but they were no longer there: "That's the kind of institutional memory that's missing."[133]

Schmidt moved to the *Wall Street Journal* where she met Glenn Simpson, another investigative journalist interested in uncovering "dirty money."[134] After less than a year at that paper she left, along with Simpson. Both feared their efforts were not getting any-where. The two teamed up to do private investigations, launching a firm described as "investigative journalism for rent," aimed at assisting people who have had no success in getting government or media to right wrongs.[135]

As Washington journalism struggled to find its way in the new world of technology, the outlook for watchdog reporting dimmed in many news organizations. Bureau cutbacks led to diminished coverage of administrative agencies, and investigative reporters, except for a few notable exceptions, got the ax. At the new *Tribune* bureau, for instance, only one reporter was assigned to investigative work. This represented a drastic reduction from the days when Deborah Nelson, who won a Pulitzer Prize for uncovering improprieties in the federal Indian Housing Program, headed an eight-member investigative unit for the *Los Angeles Times*.[136]

Before moving to the *Times* in 2001, Nelson ran a metropolitan investigative team for the *Post*. Foreseeing the future, Nelson, who holds a law degree and is a past president of Investigative Reporters and Editors, resigned from the *Times* in 2006 to teach journalism and write books. "Everybody was so hung up on looking backward and holding on to what we had," she said. "And I thought, 'We're not going to be able to hold on to what we've had.'"[137]

Even though she won some seventy-five awards during three decades as a local and network television reporter, Roberta Baskin, director of the investigative team at WJLA-TV, Washington's ABC affiliate, found herself out of a job in 2009.[138] On the day she was in New York receiving a prestigious duPont-Columbia Award for exposing a chain of pediatric dental clinics called Small Smiles that abused Medicaid children, she received a call from her news director.[139] He told her that she was among twenty-six being let go, and said, "The bean counters upstairs say they can no longer afford investigative reporting."[140]

Baskin began her television career in 1978 in Chicago, exposing high levels of cancer-causing nitrosamines in beer. Her investigation sent shock waves through the brewing industry and resulted in brewers changing their malting processes.[141] Perhaps her best-known investigation, conducted for the CBS newsmagazine *48 Hours,* detailed Nike's exploitation of workers in Vietnam. Her protests against newscasters wearing Nike emblems led to her demotion to the network's morning program.[142] Her disclosures of the company's sweatshop practices also led to boycotts, picketing, and debates about Nike as a global citizen.[143] After moving on to ABC and from there to a year as Washington correspondent for *NOW with Bill Moyers* on PBS, she returned to WJLA, where she had worked some twenty-five years before.

In 2010 Baskin took a job as senior communications adviser in the office of the inspector general of the Department of Health and Human Services. "When the ax fell, it was predictable and not personal," Baskin said.[144] "I've been watching newsrooms implode for years as budgets hemorrhaged and people turned to online sources for their information. . . . When I think about my career, I reflect on what is being lost. . . . Investigative reporting matters, and it can't be replaced on the cheap."[145] When the *Washingtonian* named its fifty top journalists in 2009, it pointed out that the "creative destruction brought about by the rise of the web had accelerated."[146] It stressed "impact" reporters, those whose work moved the news cycles, identifying *Politico* as one of the few "successful new journalism models around being the first with every small tidbit of news" and causing the *Post* leadership "indigestion."[147]

More women than ever before—fourteen—showed up in the fifty selections, although the grand total of women was only one more than in 1993. In addition to Ifill and the acerbic Maureen

Dowd, the *Washingtonian* picked eleven others, roughly divided between representatives of print and traditional broadcasting: Helene Cooper of the *New York Times,* Jane Mayer of the *New Yorker,* Lara Logan of CBS, Andrea Mitchell of NBC, Michele Norris and Nina Totenberg of NPR, Dana Priest of the *Post,* Lynn Sweet of the *Chicago Sun-Times,* and Karen Tumulty of *Time.*[148] One represented cable—Candy Crowley of CNN—and two worked for publications appealing primarily to a web-based audience, Jeanne Cummings of *Politico* and Amy Walter of *Hotline,* which offered a daily political briefing aimed mainly at congressional staffers and political operatives.[149] Some familiar names appeared from other years—Dowd, Mitchell, Totenberg, and Priest—but the array of newcomers personified the increasing fragmentation of the media.

As a group the women seemed well situated in the Washington political-media landscape. About half of the women were married, generally to others in the same milieu, and several had children. The *Washingtonian* pointed out that Mitchell, "the peacock channel's go-to reporter for just about any major Washington story—also known socially as Mrs. Alan Greenspan—is incredibly well connected with her husband being the former chairman of the Federal Reserve."[150] Norris, the mother of three, also fit into the "power couple" rubric. Her husband, Broderick Johnson, a lawyer and lobbyist, acted as President Clinton's chief lobbyist for legislative affairs and was the senior congressional affairs adviser for the presidential bid of Democratic Sen. John Kerry in 2004. As a result NPR took Norris off 2004 campaign coverage.[151]

Two women listed were married to other journalists: Mayer, who has one child, to William B. Hamilton, a *Post* editor, and Tumulty, the mother of two, to Paul Richter, who covered the State Department for the *Los Angeles Times.* Priest, a two-time Pulitzer Prize winner and mother of two, is the wife of William

Goodfellow, executive director of the privately funded Center for International Policy in Washington, a liberal think tank that advocates for human rights.

Most of the women singled out by the *Washingtonian* had worked at other well-established news organizations before joining the ones at which they were employed in 2009. This showed that they, like their male colleagues, tended to move around within the perimeters of mainstream media, although an increasing number blogged and utilized the web. As might have been expected following the presidential election of 2008, which featured the hotly contested race between Hillary Clinton and Barack Obama for the Democratic presidential nomination, a sizeable number of the women on the 2009 *Washingtonian* list specialized in political reporting. In addition to Ifill, the magazine singled out two other African Americans, Cooper and Norris, giving more recognition to minority women journalists than previously.

The presence of notable women journalists on the campaign trail did not necessarily lead to improved coverage of women, according to critics. As Women's eNews' "Cheers and Jeers" put it, "After Fox News referred to Sen. Barack Obama's wife, Michelle Obama, as 'Obama's baby man' in news captions," observers continued to debate "the role of sexist coverage in the presidential campaign following months of controversy over the way Sen. Hillary Clinton was characterized for her gender."[152] In a video post on the CBS website, Katie Couric said, "Like her [Clinton] or not, one of the great lessons of that campaign is the continued— and accepted—role of sexism in American life, particularly in the media."[153]

Possibly another lesson was that women did not cover politics much differently than men—an observation made by Judy Woodruff during the preceding decade. Noting that more than one-third of the reporters covering Sen. Bob Dole, the Republican presidential candidate in 1996, were women, Woodruff wrote, "Women today no longer hear the familiar refrain that greeted me in 1969 when, as a secretary, I asked for a reporting opportunity: 'We already have a woman reporter,' the news director replied."[154] Although the increased numbers are "easy to measure," she continued, "the effect is less so."[155]

Woodruff quoted Susan Page of *USA Today* and CNN's Candy Crowley, both of whom contended sex was irrelevant because both genders employed the same journalistic standards. She tempered their remarks, however, by referring to Gwen Ifill and others who said women journalists provided a different perspective than men on selected issues—Ifill, for example, thought women more likely to cover welfare reform.[156] Woodruff concluded that women political reporters did not appear to have a women's agenda.

Certainly Maureen Dowd dived into Hillary Clinton, characterizing her as masculine and domineering. In Clark Hoyt's "Public Editor" column, the *New York Times* itself conceded that Dowd "went over the top this election season."[157] Hoyt assessed Dowd's columns on Clinton as "loaded with language painting her as a fifty-foot woman with a suffocating embrace, a conniving film noir dame and a victim dependent on her husband."[158] Dowd defended herself by claiming she was being asked "to treat Hillary differently than I've treated the male candidates all these years, with kid gloves."[159] Hoyt granted that as a columnist Dowd had much leeway to express her opinion, but replied there had never been a male commentator as sardonic as she and that he did not think anyone else would have used Dowd's language.[160]

Kim Gandy, president of the National Organization for Women, complained that television coverage of Clinton ridiculed "her voice, her laugh, her clapping, her clothing, even her ankles—not to mention calling her a bitch and a she-devil, and comparing her to a crazed murderer, a hated ex-wife or a scolding mother."[161] In NOW's "Media Hall of Shame" for the 2008 election, Dowd was named twice, but NBC and MSNBC were branded the "chief offenders."[162] Robin Givhan, the *Post* fashion columnist, was chastised for bringing "attention to Hillary's cleavage."[163] *US Weekly* was accused of misogyny for a cover showing the face of Sarah Palin, the Republican vice presidential nominee, and equating her with "Babies, Lies & Scandal."[164]

Lack of any overriding agenda other than professional success marked the variegated careers of the women selected for the 2009 *Washingtonian* list. The fourteen notables displayed flexibility and use of new media as well as old. Print-oriented women demonstrated proficiency in writing blogs and giving interviews on network or cable television as well as reporting for traditional media. As a group the women, like their male counterparts, surmounted barriers between different forms of the news.

For instance, Sweet, bureau chief for the *Chicago Sun-Times,* wrote a column and blog for her newspaper and was a regular guest on MSNBC programs. She also contributed to two Internet newspapers, the *Huffington Post* and *Politics Daily;* wrote for the *Hill,* a publication aimed at Congress; and appeared on CNN, Fox, NBC, and CBS broadcasts talking about politics.[165] A member of the *Sun-Times* Washington staff since 1993, Sweet, who received a master's degree in journalism from Northwestern University, focused on the Obama presidential campaign and traveled to Africa with the then-senator Obama in 2006. The *Washingtonian* called her a "one-woman multimedia newsroom who often seems to out-produce whole teams of correspondents."[166] Her membership in the Gridiron Club testified that she stood in the inner circle of Washington journalists.

Cummings, *Politico*'s assistant managing editor, like Cooper as a former *Wall Street Journal* reporter, won attention for scooping other journalists during the 2008 campaign with news that the Republican National Committee had bought an expensive wardrobe for Sarah Palin's vice presidential bid.[167] Experienced in covering politics at every level, Cummings was cited as "perhaps Washington's best expert on the business of making policy."[168] She was a regular panelist on broadcast news programs, including *Washington Week with Gwen Ifill* on PBS and *The Diane Rehm Show* on NPR.

A national political correspondent for *Time* for more than a decade, Tumulty, who received a master's degree in business administration from Harvard University in 1981, previously worked for the *Los Angeles Times.* The *Washingtonian* noted, "Increasingly you can find her all over the web."[169] During the 2008 presidential race, Sen. John McCain, the Republican candidate, accused her of "hysterical liberal bias" after she claimed a McCain television ad showed the candidate "playing the race card" against Obama.[170] When McCain objected to her characterization of his ad, Tumulty responded, "I grew up in Texas. I know what this stuff looks like."[171] In 2010 Tumulty left *Time* to become a national political correspondent for the *Post.*

According to the *Washingtonian,* "Few people in TV journalism are as respected, balanced, or hard-working as 'Candy' [Crowley], who seems to know most campaign developments before the campaigns do."[172] Crowley, CNN's chief political correspondent who joined the cable network in 1987 after working in NBC's Washington bureau, had amassed an eye-popping array of major broadcasting awards. From a start as a newsroom assistant at a local radio station in Washington, the graduate of Randolph-Macon Woman's College moved to the

AP as a White House correspondent during the Reagan years and then into television.[173]

She drew particular attention, however, for her slimmer, healthier appearance, not her credentials, in 2010 when CNN named her anchor of its Sunday morning *State of the Union* political talk show that analyzes important issues. As James Rainey wrote in the *Los Angeles Times,* "A career of sophisticated political observation, graceful writing and determined fairness earns you this: speculation about your metabolism and guesses about your turns under the surgeon's knife."[174] Initially reluctant to discuss her "new incarnation," Rainey reported, Crowley finally agreed to explain that she had been "dieting, swimming and working out, sometimes with a trainer," as well as engaging in Transcendental Meditation.[175] "I'm lighter now in a lot of ways," she said.[176]

Bloggers speculated that had the sixty-one-year-old Crowley not lost weight (she would not say how much), she would not have been picked for the anchor slot.[177] "Would I have gotten the job without having lost the weight? I don't know," Crowley told TVNewser's Gail Shister.[178] "I readily admit I'm not the most obvious pick, from a purely cosmetic point of view. I'm not going to argue that when you turn on the TV, you basically [do not] get young, blonde, thin women," although she added, "This is changing."[179]

Maybe, but speculation arose on the web regarding the ability of Lara Logan, CBS's chief foreign affairs correspondent, to use her good looks to enhance her career. Logan made the 2009 list for "balancing globetrotting with motherhood," having given birth to a son in January 2009.[180] A native of South Africa, Logan joined CBS News in 2002 and received numerous awards for reporting from war zones in Afghanistan, Iraq, and the Middle East.[181]

Before joining CBS, Logan gained more than a decade of international broadcast news experience working for British television and as a freelance correspondent covering global hot spots. Despite her journalistic credentials, pictures on the web showing her modeling swimsuits during her student days in England provoked comment that physical appearance figured prominently in her career success.[182] In addition, her personal relationships led to a front-page story in the *New York Post,* which called her a "sexy CBS siren" when she was expecting a baby before her divorce from her first husband became final.[183]

At the time, Joseph Burkett, a federal defense contractor who was the father of her child, was involved in a messy divorce from his wife, who accused Logan of stealing her husband. Logan and Burkett married in 2009. When CBS brought Logan back to Washington before she gave birth, Howard Kurtz, the media critic of the *Post,* called her situation "an all-too-familiar tale of someone consumed by a career and needing a partner who understands the peculiar pressures involved."[184] He might have changed the "someone" to "woman," since one could hardly imagine a man being referred to as a "sexy siren." In February 2011 Logan was sexually assaulted while covering uprisings in Cairo, giving rise to controversy over her right as a woman journalist to report on war in the Muslim world.

Two other women on the *Washingtonian* list—Cooper, the White House correspondent for the *New York Times,* and Mayer of the *New Yorker*—both stood out as authors as well as journalists. Cooper was born in Liberia into a privileged family that descended from American freed slaves who colonized the African country. A journalism graduate of the University of North Carolina, she wrote a critically acclaimed account of her girlhood in Liberia before her family was forced to flee the country during a coup in 1980.[185] She moved to the *Times* in 2004 as assistant editorial page editor following twelve years at the *Wall Street Journal,* where she reported on international economic trends before becoming assistant Washington bureau chief. Prior to taking the *Times'* White House assignment, she was the paper's diplomatic correspondent.[186]

A writer for the *New Yorker* since 1995, Mayer, a graduate of Yale University, previously worked for the *Wall Street Journal* for twelve years. During that time she became the newspaper's first woman White House correspondent, served as a war correspondent in the Middle East, and covered the last days of communism in the former Soviet Union. She also wrote three books, including the 2008 best seller *The Dark Side,* which disclosed the use of torture by the CIA to interrogate detainees during the War on Terror. She made numerous television appearances in connection with her award-winning book.

Norris, a graduate of the University of Minnesota, was named Journalist of the Year in 2009 by the National Association of Black Journalists, which recognized her for two decades of journalistic achievement as well as her coverage of the 2008 presidential campaign. Norris, the first African American woman weekday host of NPR's newsmagazine *All Things Considered,* public radio's longest-running national program, assumed that role in 2002 after nearly a decade as a correspondent for ABC News.[187] Previously she reported for the *Post, Chicago Tribune,* and *Los Angeles Times.* In 2010 she published *The Grace of Silence,* a book that began as an elaboration of an NPR series on race relations but ended as an autobiography.

Perhaps, of all the women listed, the most impressive and controversial résumé belonged to Priest, an investigative reporter who concentrated on national security issues for the *Post.* As the *Washingtonian* put it, "Priest's byline often means that someone will soon be facing a congressional-oversight hearing."[188] Along with a colleague, Anne Hull, Priest reported on degrading living conditions for wounded Iraq War soldiers and veterans at Walter Reed Army Medical Center. As a result of Priest and Hull's exposé of unsanitary outpatient housing, the *Post* won the Pulitzer Prize for Public Service in 2008. Public outcry ended in the resignation of the secretary of the army and a shake-up in overseeing health care for injured military personnel.[189]

Two years earlier Priest won a Pulitzer Prize in Beat Reporting for an article on so-called black sites, secret prisons overseas that the CIA used for interrogation of suspected terrorists. The disclosure led to a worldwide debate on whether these sites existed. President George W. Bush later confirmed that the CIA did operate secret prisons.[190] Conservatives denounced Priest's article, and some members of Congress called for an inquiry into whether she or her sources had broken laws pertaining to classified intelligence.

Priest denied that she had done so, saying in a television interview, "We tried to figure out a way to get as [much] information to the public as we could without damaging national security."[191] In 2010 the *Post* published TOP SECRET AMERICA, an ambitious project on the nation's security buildup since the attacks on September 11, 2001. Priest collaborated with William Arkin on this report, which took almost two years to complete.[192]

A graduate of the University of California at Santa Cruz, Priest, a veteran of two decades at the *Post,* was assigned to the Pentagon for seven years before spending three years on a national intelligence beat. She covered the invasion of Panama (1989), reported from Iraq (1990) and Kosovo (1999), and traveled with army special forces in Asia, Africa, and South America.[193] Priest, who also contributed to CBS news, won numerous national awards for reporting on foreign affairs. Her book, *The Mission: Waging War and Keeping Peace with America's Military* (2003), was a finalist for a Pulitzer Prize in General Nonfiction.

In a sense Priest and Hull's reporting on Walter Reed conditions displayed the primacy of print over online reporting. In a review of investigative reporting, the *American Journalism Review* noted that Mark Benjamin had publicized the squalid arrangements for outpatients at the medical center for two years on Salon.com before the story hit the *Post*. In a *Nieman Reports* article, Benjamin wrote, "It was as though until headlines blared from newsstands in the nation's capital, the trees in this forest weren't really falling."[194]

To gain attention as a Washington political commentator on the web, at least one woman resorted to sex and sensationalism. In 2004, Ana Marie Cox, a University of Chicago graduate and former editor at Suck.com, became the founding editor of the political blog *Wonkette,* published by Gawker Media that presented politics irreverently. Writing at home in her pajamas, Cox combined profanity with witty, ironic political coverage that included naughty references to anal sex and alcohol. *Wonkette* publicized the story of "Washingtonienne," a woman staffer on Capitol Hill who took money from a Bush administration official and others in exchange for sex.[195]

Two years later, Cox announced her transition to *Wonkette Emerita* and subsequently was named the Washington editor of Time.com, writing for both *Time* magazine and its website. The next year Cox apologized on the website for appearing on Don Imus's radio show, where he made racist and sexist comments until finally forced off the air. "I did the show almost solely to earn my media-elite merit badge," she wrote. "It's depressingly easy to find female journalists who will tolerate or ignore bigotry if it means getting into the boys' club someday (If only I were the only one.) . . . He [Imus] and his cronies seemed to enjoy having the occasional guest they could leer at."[196] In 2010 Cox became the Washington correspondent for *GQ* magazine.

Whether women are likely to dominate Washington reporting in the years ahead remains an open question. The idea of news itself as a distinctive aspect of journalism eroded in an era in which the line between news content, entertainment, and public advocacy became thinner and thinner. Some media organizations left news behind, leading women journalists to switch from one medium to another within the communications field.

Consider the career of Pamela J. Gentry, who over a span of three decades went from broadcasting to cable television to the web with time out to work in public affairs for the federal government. Experienced as a general assignment reporter for a newspaper and broadcasting stations in Tennessee and Kentucky, Gentry arrived in Washington in 1984. Starting as a producer and assignment editor for Channel 9, the CBS affiliate, she developed news programming for three daily newscasts before leaving that job to become a director of media relations for the Department of Health and Human Services, and subsequently associate administrator for external affairs. In 1999 she switched to C-SPAN as a producer of political programs and host of *The Washington Journal,* a public affairs program.

Three years later Gentry joined Black Entertainment Television, opening a Washington bureau for a CBS/BET Nightly News program, which covered Capitol Hill and the White House. In 2005, as BET's senior political analyst, she created *Pamela on Politics,* the first political blog on BET.com. When BET shut down its news operation in 2008, she kept on with the blog. She also appeared on political talk shows for national and international broadcasting outlets, including Fox News, CNN, BBC, Sky News,

NPR, XM Radio, and PBS, and was a guest blogger for the *Huff-ington Post*.

As Gentry's experience shows, the current media scene requires adaptability by journalists. "You can't be tied to decisions made by the corporate types," Gentry said, in commenting on BET's decision to drop news.[197] "BET has been criticized for not having it. People didn't support it. It was not given a good marketing and promotion budget."[198]

An African American who has won awards from the National Association of Black Journalists and other groups, Gentry expressed particular concern about the career paths of minorities. "People who do the hiring are still more comfortable with people who look like them," she said. "The numbers [of minorities in management] don't look much different than in the 1980s. Minorities are on the air but they don't have hiring authority. No one is grooming the next generation in management."[199]

Changes in print and broadcasting have made it more difficult for journalists to make a living, she continued. Since cuts have come in budgets for news, "young women and experienced women are working harder for a lot less," she said. "There is so much citizen journalism out there; they [media organizations] don't have to pay professionals. The audiences don't know the difference."[200] If she were advising aspiring young women, she would tell them to go into journalism only "if it is your passion and you would do it for free."[201] These days, they may have to.

Ironically, after years of fighting for opportunities, women have ascended during a communications revolution that threatens the continuation of established models in print and broadcasting. Now women are being called on to rescue traditional media from financial disaster. Journalism, as it has been known, no longer seems commercially viable, although long-established news media, referred to as legacy media, continues to draw readers and viewers and wants to stay in business.

In 2009 the *Post* named its first woman managing editor, Elizabeth Spayd, who had been running the *Post*'s online operation after years of experience on the newspaper itself. Not given the title individually, Spayd was paired with a male outsider, Raju Narisetti, brought to the *Post* after launching a national business newspaper in his native India. Narisetti previously had worked with the *Post*'s executive editor, Marcus Brauchli, at the *Wall Street Journal,* where Brauchli had been the top editor until pressured to leave by owner Rupert Murdoch in 2008. Never before had the *Post* had two managing editors.

Spayd, who started work at the *Post* in 1988, said that it felt "pretty cool" to break the newspaper's gender barrier and that she hoped to increase the newspaper's appeal to women readers.[202] Charged to merge the company's print and online newsrooms, Spayd was to oversee the main news operation while Narisetti took charge of the feature sections. Both called attention to the sharp decline in newspaper revenue and staffing. "The industry is in such trouble that there is a will-power to try a lot of things that maybe five years ago we wouldn't have considered trying," Narisetti, the first minority to be named a *Post* managing editor, said.[203]

At present women journalists like Andrea Roane of WUSA-TV (Channel 9), the CBS Washington affiliate, remain fixtures on the capital scene. Roane, an African American, started with the station in 1981 as a news anchor and has remained in that role for three decades, with the time slots in which she has broadcast varying over the years. During her on-air career, she has interviewed first ladies, generals, entertainers, and other notable figures—including Archbishop Desmond Tutu—and covered numerous Republican and Democratic conventions.[204]

Well known for her efforts to publicize breast cancer awareness, she was named one of *Washingtonian* magazine's "Washingtonians of the Year" in 2006 for her campaign to encourage early detection of the disease. Washington's Sibley Memorial Hospital Foundation has honored her with its Community Service Award for advocating breast cancer awareness. Roane initiated an innovative program that encouraged viewers to team up on the ninth of each month to follow the National Cancer Institute's three-step breast examination program.[205]

Still, the days of local news broadcasts such as the one that Roane coanchored from 4:25 A.M. to 7:00 A.M. in 2011 may not survive the technological onslaught of increased demand for mobile data services. Broadcasters, already smarting from declining viewership, are fighting a plan by the Federal Communications Commission to encourage voluntary auction of airwaves now set aside for television to allow more expansion of wireless networks.[206] While such a move would take time to work out, broadcasters fear it would set a precedent for future government mandates to force them to give up channels used for news and popular programs.

Those concerned about sufficient infrastructure for mobile devices like iPhones and Xoom tablets see it differently.[207] "The reality is that fewer people are watching over-the-air television, and we're fighting for our future of innovation," said Gary Shapiro, president of the Consumer Electronics Association.[208]

At the *Post* publisher Weymouth pulled back from an idea that critics called influence peddling in an effort to stem recurring losses. Possibly keeping in mind that her grandmother, Katharine Graham, had been famous for dinner parties that attracted the capital's elite, in 2009 Weymouth and Brauchli proposed a series of eleven salons at Weymouth's home. Unlike Graham's private parties, these would have been highly commercial events. Sponsors would have paid at the rate of $25,000 a night or $250,000 for the entire series. The gatherings would have brought together Washington's most powerful individuals—government officials, lobbyists, and *Post* staff members—for what was promised as "news-driven and off-the-record conversation."[209]

When *Politico* posted a story about the proposed dinners, a furious outcry over the plan caused it to be dropped amid expressions of embarrassment and apology from Weymouth and Brauchli. Ironically, a health care lobbyist had gone to *Politico* with the story because he considered it a conflict of interest for the *Post* to charge for access to reporters and editors following health care issues. As *Politico* expressed it, "The offer—which essentially turns a news organization into a facilitator for private lobbyist-official encounters—is a new sign of the lengths to which news organizations will go to find revenue at a time when most newspapers are struggling for survival."[210] It added, "And it's a turn of the times that a lobbyist is scolding the *Washington Post* for its ethical lapses."[211]

The *New York Times* put it more succinctly: "Theoretically, you can't buy *Washington Post* reporters, but you can rent them."[212] Jack Shafer of *Slate,* an online magazine, complained, "What really stinks about the now-aborted salon-for-dollars scheme is that Katharine Weymouth appears to have contemplated the sale of something that wasn't hers to sell—the *Post*'s credibility."[213] The *Post*'s ombudsman, Andrew Alexander, termed the salon proposal "pretty close to a public relations disaster."[214]

To Dave Kindred, a sportswriter granted access to the *Post* to write a history of its financial woes, Weymouth's proposed salons mattered less ethically than her disapproval of a story expected to run in the *Post* magazine in 2009.[215] According to Shafer, Weymouth expressed hostility to a proposed article on a young woman who had lost her arms and legs, thinking the story depressing and not attractive to advertisers.[216] Shafer quoted Weymouth as saying, "I would never interfere in an editorial decision," but he discounted her denial: "Can you believe for a moment that Katharine Weymouth's ideas *don't* drive what the *Post* prints ... or that [they] *shouldn't* ... Weymouth is the one in charge!"[217] A graduate of Harvard University and Stanford University Law School, Weymouth, a divorced mother of three, is considered the heir to Donald E. Graham, chairman and chief executive of the Washington Post Company.

In 2011 Warren Buffett, the billionaire financier who controls Berkshire Hathaway, which is the largest shareholder in the *Post,* announced that he would step down from the board of the Washington Post Company. Buffett said he would not sell his stock, but he foresaw "the newspaper business will be tougher and tougher and tougher, and it is already plenty tough."[218] While the newspaper lost money in recent years, the Post Company itself thieved on profits from its Kaplan education division, which operates for-profit tutoring and educational institutions and accounted for about two-thirds of the company's total revenue. In 2010, however, the federal government raised questions about marketing and student loan practices of Kaplan and other for-profit schools and threatened to regulate them more tightly.[219]

Against this background the *Post*'s ombudsman, Andrew Alexander, wrote a farewell column on January 23, 2011, asking, "Can *The Post* restore its luster?"[220] After praising Priest and Arkin's TOP SECRET AMERICA, Alexander hit his dominant theme: that the *Post*'s journalistic quality has declined as the newspaper became "riddled with typos, grammatical mistakes and intolerable 'small' factual errors"; local news coverage has "withered"; the "excessive use of anonymous sources has expanded into blogs"; and "the list goes on."[221] Alexander blamed this on "upheaval, disruption and neces-

sary cost-cutting" aimed at "trying to preserve a dying print prod-
uct while building a new digital one."[222] Although the *Post* and its
journalism will survive, he wrote, "the question is: At what level
of quality? That depends largely on those in the newsroom."[223]

As old models of journalism give way to new, the voices of
Washington women journalists were heard, trying to stimulate
the field that they once had been barred from entering. Would
women like Priest and Weymouth be equal to the task? Certainly,
they intended to try, even as print was giving way to multimedia.
In 2009 Priest said she could not imagine not being an investigative reporter. Weymouth said she was planning to "improve" on
the salon/conference idea, presumably to keep the *Post* in the
center of communication among Washington's power elite.[224] As
Geneva Overholser, a former ombudsman for the *Post* and now
director of the Annenberg School of Journalism at the University
of Southern California, expressed it, if one era was closing, another
was opening and "therein lay the peril and the promise."[225]

EPILOGUE

In summary, Washington journalism has owed more than it has recognized to the women who have sought to enter its ranks in spite of overwhelming discrimination that marked most of the decades in which they attempted to establish careers. As the governing center of the nation—and in the view of some—the most significant force on the international scene, Washington has been attuned chiefly to politics. Its most important journalists to date have been those with the best political contacts. Until recently most women and minorities in journalism faced extraordinary challenges in establishing reportorial relationships with political leaders, most of whom were white males accustomed to dealing with those most like themselves. The same challenges confronted women and minorities in news organizations headed with white male superiors. The fact that women and minorities succeeded to the extent they did stands as a tribute to their intelligence and perseverance in response to changing political and social conditions, which they themselves helped to bring about.

While seeking to be accepted as objective professionals competing on an even field with men, for more than a century women journalists fought against gender subordination. True, their individual opinions varied widely on the extent of their commitment to feminist issues. Sometimes they promoted political causes such as suffrage and an active role for First Ladies as illustrated by their championing of Eleanor Roosevelt. Sometimes they attempted to showcase through women's and society pages construction of a social culture with a significant political dimension. Sometimes they fought to gain access to professional organizations. Sometimes they used their own good looks and personalities, along with keen intelligence, to move into broadcasting. Sometimes they took advantage of legal redress to seek employment and promotion opportunities under the federal Civil Rights Act. One woman, Katharine Graham, displayed her innate strength by inheriting a good newspaper and leaving it a much stronger one while she turned her company into a media empire. But most of all women as a group simply insisted on their rights to work as journalists like men in the center of national power. Their story needs to be told as part of the American experience.

Whatever the future holds in new media for Washington journalism, women can be expected to play a vital part at a time when a technological revolution has enormously expanded opportunities for individuals to make their voices heard. Old structures for news may have changed, but the determination of women, now estimated to make up at least half of the Washington press corps, to move ahead remains, even though solutions to issues of family versus career still need to be worked out. Women may have arrived in a field at a time when it is losing its well-defined perimeters, but based on their history they have the ingenuity and forward thinking to create new ones. Although they may not agree on political goals, they are worthy successors to their foremother, Anne Royall, who was determined to earn her living as a journalist in the nation's capital.

ABBREVIATIONS

BFP, MD, LOC	Bess Furman Papers, Manuscript Division, Library of Congress
CRWJA, WPCF, NPCA	Cora Rigby Washington Journalism Archives, Washington Press Club Foundation, and National Press Club Archives
EBHP, MD, LOC	Edith B. Helm Papers, Manuscript Division, Library of Congress
ERPCAP, FDRL	Eleanor Roosevelt Press Conference Association Papers, Franklin D. Roosevelt Library
FDRP, FDRL	Franklin D. Roosevelt Papers, Franklin D. Roosevelt Library
LHP, FDRL	Lorena Hickok Papers, Franklin D. Roosevelt Library
MCP, MD, LOC	May Craig Papers, Manuscript Division, Library of Congress
MHP, UW	Mary Hornaday Papers, University of Wyoming
MSP, UW	Martha Strayer Papers, University of Wyoming
RBP, MD, LOC	Ruby A. Black Papers, Manuscript Division, Library of Congress
STEP, FDRL	Stephen T. Early Papers, Franklin D. Roosevelt Library

NOTES

PREFACE

1. "Barbara Cochran '68," *Columbia Journalism School* (Winter 2010): 10.
2. Ibid.
3. Donald A. Ritchie, email message to author, June 18, 2007.
4. Quoted in Howard Kurtz, "Sex and the Single Stiletto," *Washington Post,* November 5, 2005.
5. Herbert J. Gans, *Deciding What's News: A Study of CBS Evening News, NBC Nightly News, Newsweek and Time* (New York: Vintage, 1980), 43.

CHAPTER ONE

1. See Alice S. Maxwell and Marion B. Dunlevy, *Virago! The Story of Anne Newport Royall (1796–1854)* (Jefferson, N.C.: McFarland, 1985), 179–96. The authors considered the trial a political persecution.
2. *Intelligencer* (Harrisburg, Pa.), August 4, 1829, quoted in Bessie Rowland James, *Anne Royall's U.S.A.* (New Brunswick, N.J.: Rutgers University Press, 1972), 262.
3. George Stuyvesant Jackson, *Uncommon Scold* (Boston: Bruce Humphries, 1937), 11–12.
4. Anne Royall, *The Black Book II* (Washington, D.C.: privately printed, 1828–29), 110.
5. See Maurine Beasley, "Anne Royall: Huntress with a Quill," *Quill* 78 (May 1990): 32–35.
6. Helen Dewar, in-person interview by author, who nominated Royall for the plaque, May 15, 1990.
7. Helen Thomas, remarks prepared for Anne Royall Historic Site marking, Washington, D.C., May 22, 1990.

8. Jane G. Swisshelm, *Half a Century* (1880; repr., Boston: IndyPublish, 2006), 97.

9. "Mrs. Swisshelm's Letter," *New York Tribune,* April 15, 1850.

10. Ibid., April 19, 1850.

11. Ibid., April 22, 1850.

12. Swisshelm, *Half a Century,* 100.

13. Ibid., 98–99.

14. Irving H. Bartlett, *Daniel Webster* (New York: Norton, 1978), 286.

15. Barbara Welter, "The Cult of True Womanhood: 1820–1860," *American Quarterly* 18 (Summer 1966): 151.

16. Ibid.

17. Swisshelm, *Half a Century,* 192; see also *New York Tribune,* May 22, 1863.

18. Swisshelm, *Half a Century,* 97.

19. Judy Yaeger Jones and Jane E. Vallier, eds., *Sweet Bells Jangled: Laura Redden Searing, A Deaf Poet Restored* (Washington, D.C.: Gallaudet University Press, 2003), 6.

20. Beth Haller, "Laura Redden Searing, 1840–1923, Journalist, Writer, Poet," in *Encyclopedia of American Disability History,* ed. Susan Burch (New York: Facts on File, 2009), entry #707.

21. Lois Bryan Adams, *Letter from Washington: 1863–1865,* ed. Evelyn Leasher (Detroit: Wayne State University Press, 1999), 10.

22. Ibid., 37.

23. Arthur J. Larsen, ed., *Crusader and Feminist: Letters of Jane Grey Swisshelm 1858–1865* (St. Paul: Minnesota Historical Society, 1934), 308–9.

24. Adams, *Letter from Washington,* 24.

25. Ibid.

26. Ibid., 344.

27. Sylvia D. Hoffert, *Jane Grey Swisshelm: An Unconventional Life, 1815–1884* (Chapel Hill: University of North Carolina Press, 2004), 128–29.

28. Barbara Welter, "Sara Jane Clarke Lippincott," in *Notable American Women 1607–1950: A Biographical Dictionary,* ed. Edward T. James, Janet Wilson James, and Paul S. Boyer, vol. 2 (Cambridge, Mass.: Belknap Press, 1971), 408.

29. Ibid.

30. Nan Robertson, *The Girls in the Balcony: Women, Men, and the "New York Times"* (New York: Random House, 1992), 43–44.

31. Sara Clarke Lippincott [Grace Greenwood, pseud.], "Washington Notes," *New York Times,* February 1, 1873.

32. Ibid.

33. Mary Clemmer Ames, "A Woman's Letter from Washington," *Independent,* March 7, 1878.

34. Ibid.

35. Sara Jane Clarke [Grace Greenwood, pseud.], *Greenwood Leaves,* 1st ed. (Boston: Ticknor, Reed and Fields, 1850), 311.

36. Sara Clarke Lippincott [Grace Greenwood, pseud.], "Washington Notes," *New York Times,* April 13, 1873.

37. Our Special Correspondent [Sara Clarke Lippincott], dispatch to *New York Times,* July 3, 1877.

38. Ames, "Woman's Letter from Washington," May 24, 1866.

39. Donald A. Ritchie, *Press Gallery: Congress and the Washington Correspondents* (Cambridge, Mass.: Harvard University Press, 1991), 61–62.

40. Ames, "Woman's Letter from Washington," March 24, 1870.

41. Ibid.

42. Ibid., October 10, 1872.

43. Ibid., December 27, 1866.

44. Ibid., March 24, 1870.

45. Mary Abigail Dodge [Gail Hamilton, pseud.], *Gail Hamilton's Life in Letters,* ed. Augusta H. Dodge, vol. 1 (Boston: Lee and Shepard, 1901), 203.

46. Mary Abigail Dodge, [Gail Hamilton, pseud.] *Gail Hamilton's Life in Letters,* ed. Augusta H. Dodge, vol. 2 (Boston: Lee and Shepard, 1901), 698.

47. Mary Abigail Dodge [Gail Hamilton, pseud.], "The Display of Washington Society," *Galaxy* 21 (June 1876): 768.

48. *Hamilton's Life in Letters,* vol. 2, 645.

49. Mary Clemmer Ames, *Life and Scenes in the National Capital* (Hartford, Conn.: Worthington, 1874), 253.

50. Quoted in Emily A. Green, *First Lady: The Life of Lucy Webb Hayes* (Kent, Ohio: Kent State University Press, 1984), 138.

51. Ibid.

52. Emily Edson Briggs [Olivia, pseud.], *Philadelphia Press,* March 16, 1868.

53. Ibid., January 19, 1870.

54. Ibid., February 2, 1871.

55. Quoted in Ritchie, *Press Gallery,* 156.

56. Ibid.

57. Emily Edson Briggs, *The Olivia Letters* (New York: Neale, 1906), 412–13.

58. Ritchie, *Press Gallery,* 145.

59. F. B. Marbut, *News from the Capital: The Story of Washington Reporting* (Carbondale: Southern Illinois University Press, 1971), 154.

60. Ibid., 154–55.

61. Ritchie, *Press Gallery,* 145.

62. Ibid., 145–46.

63. Austine Snead to Rutherford B. Hayes, January 10, 1887, Austine and Fayette Snead letters and clippings file, Rutherford B. Hayes Library, Fremont, Ohio.

CHAPTER TWO

This chapter's epigraph is from Frances Parkinson Keyes Papers, box 1, Special Collections, Tulane University Library.

1. Frances Parkinson Keyes, *Letters from a Senator's Wife* (New York: D. Appleton, 1924), 98.

2. Ibid.

3. See Agnes Hooper Gottlieb, *Women Journalists and the Municipal Housekeeping Movement 1868–1914* (Lewiston, N.Y.: Edwin Mellen, 2001), 5–18.

4. Karen J. Blair, "General Federation of Women's Clubs," in *The Reader's Companion to U.S. Women's History,* ed. Wilma Mankiller et al. (Boston: Houghton Mifflin, 1998), 242.

5. Maurine H. Beasley, "The Emergence of Modern Media: 1900–1945," in *The Media in America,* ed. W. David Sloan, 5th ed. (Northport, Ala.: Vision Press, 2002), 284.

6. *Reliable Sources: 100 Years at the National Press Club* (Nashville: Turner, 2008), 39.

7. John P. Cosgrove, ed., *Shrdlu: An Affectionate Chronicle* (Washington, D.C.: National Press Club, 1958), 19.

8. Ritchie, *Press Gallery,* 161.

9. Gottlieb, *Municipal Housekeeping Movement,* 37–41.

10. Mrs. J. C. Croly [Jennie June, pseud.], *The History of the Woman's Club Movement in America* (New York: Henry C. Allen, 1898), 340–41. See also "The Woman's National Press Association," *New Cycle* (organ of the General Federation of Women's Clubs) (October 1895): 296–97.

11. Ritchie, *Press Gallery,* 161.

12. Ishbel Ross, *Ladies of the Press* (New York: Harper and Brothers, 1936), 331–32.

13. Donald A. Ritchie, *Reporting from Washington: The History of the Washington Press Corps* (New York: Oxford University Press, 2005), 161.

14. Ritchie, *Press Gallery,* 162.

15. M. S. Burke, "Women and the Reporters' Gallery," *Journalist* 11 (May 24, 1890): 13, quoted in Ritchie, *Press Gallery,* 161.

16. Elizabeth S. Tilton, *The League of American Pen Women in the District of Columbia* (Washington, D.C.: District of Columbia branch, League of American Pen Women, 1942), 1, 4–6.

17. Keyes, *Letters from a Senator's Wife,* 66.

18. Ibid.

19. Ibid., 44.

20. Frances Parkinson Keyes, "Letters from a Senator's Wife," *Good Housekeeping* 76 (May 1921): 52.

21. Quoted in *Reliable Sources,* 41.

22. Ibid., 43.

23. Ibid., 43–44.

24. Ibid., 45.

25. Ibid., 46.

26. Ross, *Ladies of the Press,* 122.

27. Ellen Carol DuBois, "Suffrage Movement," in Mankiller et al., *Women's History,* 580.

28. Amelia Roberts Fry, "Alice Paul," in *Notable American Women:*

A Bibliographical Dictionary, ed. Susan Ware and Stacy Braukman, vol. 5 (Cambridge, Mass.: Belknap Press, 2004), 501.

29. *Congressional Directory,* 66th Cong., 2d sess. (Washington, D.C.: Government Printing Office, 1920), 443–45.

30. Delbert Clark, *Washington Dateline: The Press Covers the Capital* (New York: Frederick Stokes, 1941), 205.

31. *Reliable Sources,* 81.

32. Lonnelle Aikman, "An End and a Beginning," chapter 1 from proposed book on Women's National Press Club (unpublished manuscript, 1968), TS, 8–10, 16, Cora Rigby Washington Journalism Archives, Washington Press Club Foundation, and National Press Club Archives (hereafter cited as CRWJA, WPCF, NPCA).

33. Open letter from E. M. King, Cora Rigby, Caroline [*sic*] Vance Bell, Eleanor Taylor Marsh, and Florence Brewer Boeckel, September 23, 1919, TS, CRWJA, WPCF, NPCA.

34. Ibid.

35. *Reliable Sources,* 81.

36. Carolyn Vance Bell, "Founding," 1968, TS, 4, 7, CRWJA, WPCF, NPCA.

37. Ibid.

38. Christine Sadler, "The Poe Sisters," n.d., TS, 3, CRWJA, WPCF, NPCA.

39. Ross, *Ladies of the Press,* 507.

40. Membership qualifications as listed in the WNPC's 1924 directory, CRWJA, WPCF, NPCA.

41. Ibid.

42. Minute Books for 1921–1924 and 1928–1930, box 2, Records of District of Columbia Federation of Women's Clubs, Washington Historical Society, Washington, D.C.

43. Winifred Mallon, "The Whole Truth, as Far as It Goes About Ourselves," July 1937, TS, 1, CRWJA, WPCF, NPCA.

44. Ross, *Ladies of the Press,* 334.

45. Ibid., 333–34.

46. Ibid., 333.

47. Frances Parkinson Keyes, *Capital Kaleidoscope: The Story of a Washington Hostess* (New York: Harper, 1937), 281.

48. Ibid., 282.

49. Ibid., 281.

50. Quoted in Ritchie, *Reporting from Washington,* 162.

51. Notes from Lily Lykes Shepard for proposed WNCP history, CRWJA, WPCF, NPCA.

52. Ibid.

53. Mallon, "Whole Truth," 4, CRWJA, WPCF, NPCA; and Aikman, "An End and a Beginning," 33, CRWJA, WPCF, NPCA.

54. For a full discussion of the women's agenda after suffrage, see Jan Doolittle Wilson, *The Women's Joint Congressional Committee and the Politics of Maternalism, 1920–30* (Urbana: University of Illinois Press, 2007).

55. Keyes, "Letters from a Senator's Wife."

56. Keyes, *Letters from a Senator's Wife,* 74.

57. Ibid.

58. Quoted in Ritchie, *Reporting from Washington,* 161.

59. Ibid.

60. *Reliable Sources,* 82.

61. Quoted in Beatrice Fairfax [Marie Manning, pseud.], *Ladies Then and Now* (New York: Dutton, 1944), 204.

62. Corinne Frazier Gillette, ed., "Pardon Our Petticoats" (unpublished manuscript, 1961), 36, CRWJA, WPCF, NPCA.

63. Ross, *Ladies of the Press,* 312.

64. Bell, "Founding," 3, CRWJA, WPCF, NPCA.

65. Carl Sferrazza Anthony, *Florence Harding* (New York: Morrow, 1998), 392.

66. Ross, *Ladies of the Press,* 312.

67. Anthony, *Florence Harding,* 392.

68. Aikman, chapter 1, 33, CRWJA, WPCF, NPCA.

69. Ibid.

70. Gillette, "Pardon Our Petticoats," 3, CRWJA, WPCF, NPCA.

71. Manning, *Reliable Sources,* 135.

72. *Toaster,* February 9, 1931, 1. In the author's possession.

73. Ibid., 2.

74. Ibid.

75. Ibid., 1.

76. "Color Is Factor in Social Swing," *Toaster,* February 9, 1931, 4.

77. Ibid., 2.

78. Ibid.

79. Keyes, *Capital Kaleidoscope,* 318.

80. Ishbel Ross, *Grace Coolidge and Her Era* (New York: Dodd, Mead, 1962), 85.

81. Gladys Moon Jones, "WPC Now in Its 27th Year Looks Backward and Forward," WNPC folder, box 63, Bess Furman Papers, Manuscript Division, Library of Congress (hereafter cited as BFP, MD, LOC).

82. Ibid.

83. Ross, *Ladies of the Press,* 445.

84. Ibid.

85. Keyes, *Capital Kaleidoscope,* 286.

86. Ibid.

87. Ibid., 285.

88. See "Sallie Pickett Dies: Rites to Be Held Today," *Washington Post,* July 26, 1939; and "Mrs. Sallie V. Pickett Funeral Services at National City Church," *Evening Star,* July 26, 1939.

89. Ross, *Ladies of the Press,* 446.

90. "Ruth Jones, Long Noted as Capital Society Editor, Dies," *Washington Times-Herald,* September 18, 1940.

91. Ibid.

92. Ross, *Ladies of the Press,* 446.

93. Keyes, *Capital Kaleidoscope,* 286–87.

94. Ibid., 287.

95. David Denker, "Eleanor Medill Patterson," in James, James, and Boyer, *Notable American Women,* 27.

96. Gillette, "Pardon Our Petticoats," 32, CRWJA, WPCF, NPCA.

97. Membership directory, American News Women's Club, 1997–1998, American News Women's Club Archives, Special Collections, University of Maryland Libraries.

98. Ibid.

99. Ibid.

100. Ritchie, *Reporting from Washington,* 160.

101. Ross, *Ladies of the Press,* 342–43.

102. See Winifred Mallon scrapbooks, 1903–1920, box 51, BFP, MD, LOC.

103. Ritchie, *Reporting from Washington,* 162; and Ross, *Ladies of the Press,* 342.

104. Ibid., 162; and ibid., 344.

105. Ross, *Ladies of the Press,* 345.

106. Ibid., 344.

107. Maurine Beasley, *Eleanor Roosevelt and the Media: A Public Quest for Self-Fulfillment* (Urbana: University of Illinois Press, 1987), 155; and see also Ross, *Ladies of the Press,* 345.

108. Quoted in Ritchie, *Reporting from Washington,* 162.

109. Bess A. Furman, *Washington By-Line: The Personal Story of a Newspaperwoman* (New York: Knopf, 1949), 26.

110. Ibid.

111. Ibid., 36.

112. Ibid.

113. Ibid.

114. Susan Ware, "Bess Furman," in *Notable American Women: A Bibliographical Dictionary,* ed. Barbara Sicherman and Carol Hurd Green, vol. 4, *The Modern Period* (Cambridge, Mass.: Belknap Press, 1980), 257.

115. Furman, *Washington By-Line,* 44.

116. Ross, *Ladies of the Press,* 7.

117. Ibid.

118. Ibid., 342.

119. Ibid.

120. Ware, "Bess Furman," in Sicherman and Green, *Notable American Women,* 257.

121. Furman, *Washington By-Line,* 40.

122. Ibid., 55.

123. Ibid.

124. Ibid.

125. Ross, *Ladies of the Press,* 354.

126. Ibid., 352–54.

127. Ritchie, *Reporting from Washington,* 163.

CHAPTER THREE

This chapter's epigraph is from a statement by Eleanor Roosevelt on holding press conferences, March 6, 1933, box 76, BFP, MD, LOC.

1. Eleanor Roosevelt, *This I Remember* (New York: Harper, 1937), 102.

2. Ibid.

3. Quoted in Beasley, *Eleanor Roosevelt and the Media,* 43.

4. Ross, *Ladies of the Press,* 204.

5. See "Front-Page Girl," in Ross, *Ladies of the Press,* 1–13.

6. See figures cited in Kathleen Endres, "Women in Journalism" (unpublished paper, University of Maryland, 1973), chart 1.

7. Ross, *Ladies of the Press,* 208.

8. India Edwards, telephone interview by author, April 27, 1983.

9. Ibid.

10. Ibid.

11. Lorena A. Hickok, *Reluctant First Lady* (New York: Dodd, Mead, 1962), 96.

12. Lorena A. Hickok, "Nation's 'First Lady' Outlines Plans as She Begins White House Residence," *LaCrosse* (Wis.) *Tribune,* March 5, 1933, Ruby A. Black Papers, Manuscript Division, Library of Congress (hereafter cited as RBP, MD, LOC).

13. Hickok, *Reluctant First Lady,* 151; and Furman, *Washington By-Line,* 150–51.

14. The letters, which raise the possibility of a lesbian relationship between Roosevelt and Hickok, were opened to the public in 1978 at the Franklin D. Roosevelt library in Hyde Park, New York, and first published in part in Doris Faber, *The Life of Lorena Hickok: E. R.'s Friend* (New York: Morrow, 1980).

15. Ibid., 102.

16. Entry from Bess Furman diary, January 25, 1933, TS, box 51, BFP, MD, LOC.

17. Furman, *Washington By-Line,* 138–39.

18. Hickok, *Reluctant First Lady,* 63.

19. "New Mistress of White House Plans Conferences with Press," *Christian Science Monitor,* March 4, 1933, box 1, Mary Hornaday Papers, University of Wyoming (hereafter cited as MHP, UW).

20. Ibid.

21. Ruby A. Black to Nelson A. Crawford, May 26, 1929, and Crawford to Black, June 8, 1929, RBP, MD, LOC.

22. Black to Eleanor Roosevelt, January 12, 1933, RBP, MD, LOC.

23. Ibid.

24. Roosevelt to Black, January 24, 1933, RBP, MD, LOC.

25. Black to Roosevelt, January 30, 1933, RBP, MD, LOC.

26. Ibid.

27. Ruth E. Jones to Stephen T. Early, February 24, 1932, president's personal file, Franklin D. Roosevelt Papers, Franklin D. Roosevelt Library (hereafter cited as FDRP, FDRL).

28. Appendix A, "Newspaper Representatives," in *The White House Press Conferences of Eleanor Roosevelt,* ed. Maurine H. Beasley (New York: Garland, 1983), 337.

29. Quoted in Paul F. Healy, "Cissy's Feuds," *Washingtonian,* April 1966, 52.

30. Quoted in Ralph G. Martin, *Cissy* (New York: Simon and Schuster, 1979), 323–24.

31. Paul F. Healy, "Cissy," *Washingtonian,* March 1966, 22, 36.

32. Paul F. Healy, *Cissy* (New York: Doubleday, 1966), 321.

33. Martin, *Cissy,* 359.

34. Ibid.

35. Mildred Gilman Wohlforth to author, March 23, 1983, quoted in Beasley, *Eleanor Roosevelt and the Media,* 75.

36. Martin, *Cissy,* 386–87.

37. Mary Matthews, "Bread Firm's Survey Picks Times-Herald," October 13, 1939, clipping file, "Newspapers, *Times-Herald,* 1939–1949," Washingtonian Division, Martin Luther King Public Library, Washington, D.C.

38. Roosevelt, *This I Remember,* 102.

39. Mary Hornaday, interview by author, May 21, 1979, quoted in Beasley, *Eleanor Roosevelt and the Media,* 43.

40. Roosevelt, *This I Remember,* 102.

41. Quoted in Ritchie, *Reporting from Washington,* 164.

42. Dorothy Roe Lewis, "A First Lady as an Inside Source," *New York Times,* March 13, 1981, A31.

43. Ibid.

44. Dorothy Ducas Herzog, interview by author, September 11, 1982, quoted in Beasley, *Eleanor Roosevelt and the Media,* 42.

45. Ibid.

46. Furman notes on Roosevelt's press conference, March 6, 1933, TS, box 77, BFP, MD, LOC.

47. "All Alike in Crisis," *New York Times,* March 7, 1933, Mallon scrapbooks, box 154, BFP, MD, LOC.

48. Notes from Furman's letter to her family, March 1933, TS, box 51, BFP, MD, LOC.

49. Beasley, *Eleanor Roosevelt and the Media,* 47.

50. Furman, *Washington By-Line,* 153.

51. Mary Hornaday (unpublished manuscript on Eleanor Roosevelt's press conferences, May 21, 1979), quoted in Beasley, *Eleanor Roosevelt and the Media,* 48.

52. Ross, *Ladies of the Press,* 316.

53. Quoted in Beasley, *Eleanor Roosevelt and the Media,* 105.

54. Ross, *Ladies of the Press,* 309.

55. Entry from Furman diary, March 15, 1933, box 51, BFP, MD, LOC.

56. Ruby A. Black, "Covering Mrs. Roosevelt," *Matrix* 18 (April 1933): 1.

57. Hope Ridings Miller, interview by author, May 3, 1979, quoted in Beasley, *Eleanor Roosevelt and the Media,* 194.

58. Rosamond Cole, interview by author, April 20, 1979, quoted in Beasley, *Eleanor Roosevelt and the Media,* 49.

59. Ibid.

60. Entry from Furman diary, April 20, 1933, box 1, BFP, MD, LOC.

61. Roosevelt to Furman, April 15, 1933, box 32, BFP, MD, LOC.

62. Black, "Covering Mrs. Roosevelt," 1.

63. Lewis, "Inside Source," A31.

64. Hickok to Malvina Thompson, July 23, 1949, box 17, LHP, FDRL.

65. Ibid.

66. Ibid.; see also Roosevelt, *This I Remember,* 78.

67. Hickok to Thompson, July 12, 1949, box 17, LHP, FDRL.

68. Roosevelt, *This I Remember,* 78.

69. Keyes, *Capital Kaleidoscope,* 298; see also Edwards, interview.

70. Ross, *Ladies of the Press,* 539–41.

71. Ibid., 543–44.

72. Edwards, interview.

73. Martin, *Cissy*, 383.

74. Edwards, interview.

75. Martha Strayer to Eleanor Roosevelt, March 30, 1933, topical file, press conferences, 1933–1935, Eleanor Roosevelt Papers (hereafter cited as ERPCAP, FDRL); and "Beer to Be Served at White House," *New York Times*, April 4, 1933, box T-121, Roosevelt scrapbooks, FDRP, FDRL.

76. Martha Strayer ("Eleanor Roosevelt," unpublished manuscript on Eleanor Roosevelt's press conferences), box 2, TS, 11 (hereafter cited as MSP, UW).

77. "Women's Forest Work Camps May Be Set Up," *New York Times*, May 24, 1933, box 154, Winifred Mallon scrapbooks, BFP, MD, LOC.

78. Furman, *Washington By-Line*, 173–74.

79. "Mrs. Roosevelt Hits Low Pay for Women Enrolled as Skilled Relief Workers," *New York Times*, December 5, 1933, box 154, Mallon scrapbooks, BFP, MD, LOC.

80. Eleanor Roosevelt statement to the press, January 29, 1934, box 76, BFP, MD, LOC; and Ruby A. Black, "'New Deal' for News Women in Capital," *Editor and Publisher*, February 10, 1934, 11.

81. Roosevelt, *This I Remember*, 104.

82. Black to Roosevelt, November 2, 1933, RBP, MD, LOC.

83. *Time*, February 19, 1934, quoted in Faber, *Life of Lorena Hickok*, 158–59.

84. Ruby A. Black, United Press dispatch from Washington, March 3, 1935, RBP, MD, LOC.

85. See "Personal Finances," in *The Eleanor Roosevelt Encyclopedia*, ed. Maurine H. Beasley, Holly C. Shulman, and Henry R. Beasley (Westport, Conn.: Greenwood Press, 2001), 180–84.

86. See Eugene A. Kelly, "Distorting the News," *American Mercury* (March 1935): 308–13.

87. Dorothy Dunbar Bromley, "The Future of Eleanor Roosevelt," *Harper's* 180 (January 1940): 134.

88. Liz Watts, "Covering Eleanor Roosevelt," *Journalism History* 36 (Spring 2010): 46.

89. Ann Cottrell Free, "Ruby Aurora Black," in Beasley, Shulman, and Beasley, *Eleanor Roosevelt Encyclopedia,* 64.

90. Roosevelt to Hickok, April 3, 1933, box l, LHP, FDRL.

91. Ross, *Ladies of the Press,* 317.

92. Ibid., 353.

93. Ibid.

94. Ibid.; see also Ritchie, *Reporting from Washington,* 164.

95. Entries from Furman diary, March 25 1935; May 27, 1935; and February 10, 1936, box 1, BFP, MD, LOC.

96. Quoted in Watts, "Covering Eleanor Roosevelt," 50.

97. Eleanor Roosevelt to Lorena Hickok, January 15, 1934, box 1, LHP, FDRL.

98. Kathleen McLaughlin, "Mrs. Roosevelt Goes Her Way," *New York Times Magazine,* July 5, 1936, 7.

99. Furman, *Washington By-Line,* 177.

100. Ibid.

101. Ducas Herzog, interview, quoted in Beasley, *Eleanor Roosevelt and the Media,* 66.

102. Hornaday, interview, quoted in Beasley, *Eleanor Roosevelt and the Media,* 109.

103. Frances M. Lide, interview by author, November 1, 1984, quoted in Beasley, *Eleanor Roosevelt and the Media,* 102.

104. Strayer, notes on Eleanor Roosevelt's press conference, May 15, 1936, TS, box 2, MSP, UW.

105. Ibid.

106. Beasley, *Eleanor Roosevelt and the Media,* 103.

107. Roosevelt, *This I Remember,* 164.

108. Ibid., 327.

109. Furman, *Washington By-Line,* 153.

110. Watts, "Covering Eleanor Roosevelt," 52.

111. Ibid., 48.

112. Kathleen McLaughlin to Maurine Beasley, July 7, 1979, quoted in Beasley, *Eleanor Roosevelt and the Media,* 66.

113. Ibid., 262.

114. Furman, notes on Mrs. Roosevelt's press conference, May 4, 1939, TS, box 78, BFP, MD, LOC.

115. Alice Albright Hoge, *Cissy Patterson* (New York: Random House, 1966), 141.

116. Ibid.

117. Ducas Herzog, interview, and Hornaday, interview, May 21, 1979, quoted in Beasley, *Eleanor Roosevelt and the Media,* 97.

118. Stephen Early to Eleanor Roosevelt, June 23, 1937, box 15, Stephen T. Early Papers, Franklin D. Roosevelt Library (hereafter cited as STEP, FDRL).

119. Ibid.

120. Emma Bugbee, "'Mrs. Roosevelt' of Press Skit Stages White House Sit-Down," *New York Herald Tribune,* March 2, 1937, scrapbook, MHP, UW.

121. Entry from Furman diary, February 15, 1938, box 1, BFP, MD, LOC; and Black to Roosevelt, February 16, 1938, RBP, MD, LOC.

122. Drew Pearson and Robert S. Allen, "Washington Merry-Go-Round," May 14, 1938, unidentified newspaper, box 27, May Craig Papers, Manuscript Division, Library of Congress (hereafter cited as MCP, MD, LOC).

123. Ibid.

124. Beth Campbell Short, interview by author, November 1, 1984, quoted in Beasley, *Eleanor Roosevelt and the Media,* 113.

125. See Winifred Mallon, "Map Party Backing for Doris Stevens," *New York Times,* February 17, 1939, 3; and see also Albert L. Warner, "Roosevelt Ousts Doris Stevens and Stirs a Women's Tempest," unidentified newspaper, February 16, 1939, Mallon scrapbooks, box 156, BFP, MD, LOC.

126. Furman, notes on Mrs. Roosevelt's press conference, February 17, 1939, TS, box 78, BFP, MD, LOC.

127. Ibid.

128. Ibid.

129. Ibid.

130. List of newspaperwomen and governmental representatives eligible to attend Mrs. Roosevelt's press conferences, June 18, 1941, box 6, Eleanor Roosevelt Press Conference Association Papers, Franklin D. Roosevelt Library (hereafter cited as ERPCAP, FDRL).

131. Early to Roosevelt, February 10, 1941, STEP, FDRL.

132. Ibid.; and see also Betty H. Winfield, "Mrs. Roosevelt's Press Conference Association: The First Lady Shines a Light," *Journalism History* 8 (Summer 1981): 63.

133. Early to Malvina Thompson, November 17, 1941, STEP, FDRL.

134. List of those eligible to attend Mrs. Roosevelt's press conferences, June 18, 1941, box 6, ERPCAP, FDRL.

135. Ibid.

136. Ibid.

CHAPTER FOUR

This chapter's epigraph is quoted from Kay Mills, *A Place in the News: From the Women's Pages to the Front Page* (New York: Dodd, Mead, 1988), 53.

1. Abbie A. Amrine, "This Is Our Day," *Matrix* 27 (October 1941): 15.

2. Ibid.

3. "Employers' Symposium," *Matrix* 26 (October 1940): 7–8.

4. Marion Marzolf, *Up from the Footnote* (New York: Hastings House, 1977), 69.

5. Ritchie, *Reporting from Washington,* 162.

6. "Mrs. Craig 'Hell Fire' on Women's Equality," *Editor and Publisher,* June 17, 1944. See also Jennifer L. Tebbe, "Elizabeth May Craig," in Sicherman and Green, *Notable American Women,* 171–73.

7. Helen M. Staunton, "Mary Hornaday Protests Bars to Newswomen," *Editor and Publisher,* July 15, 1944.

8. John O'Donnell and Doris Fleeson, "Capitol Stuff," *Washington Times-Herald,* May 19, 1941.

9. Ibid.

10. Minutes, organizing meeting, Mrs. Roosevelt's Press Conference Association, December 22, 1942, box 6, ERPCAP, FDRL.

11. Mohr transcription of Strayer shorthand notes, February 9, 1942, in Beasley, *Press Conferences of Eleanor Roosevelt,* 264–73.

12. Quoted in Beasley, *Eleanor Roosevelt and the Media,* 147.

13. See Appendix C, in Beasley, *Press Conferences of Eleanor Roosevelt,* 344.

14. Minutes of temporary standing committee of Mrs. Roosevelt's Press Conference Association, January 31, 1942, ERPCAP, FDRL.

15. Minutes of Mrs. Roosevelt's Press Conference Association meeting, December 19, 1942, box 6, ERPCAP, FDRL.

16. Ibid.

17. Ritchie, *Reporting from Washington,* 168.

18. Mary Hornaday to Eleanor Roosevelt, November 28, 1942, and minutes of meeting with Eleanor Roosevelt, December 7, 1942, box 6, ERPCAP, FDRL.

19. Minutes of meeting with Roosevelt, December 7, 1942, box 6, ERPCAP, FDRL.

20. Quoted in Beasley, *Eleanor Roosevelt and the Media,* 155.

21. Ann Cottrell, "Mrs. Roosevelt Assails Stories About Waacs," *New York Herald Tribune,* June 8, 1943.

22. Quoted in Ritchie, *Reporting from Washington,* 168.

23. See Ann Cottrell Free, "Eleanor Roosevelt and the Female White House Press Corps," *Modern Maturity* (October–November 1984): 98–99.

24. Quoted in Ritchie, *Reporting from Washington,* 168.

25. Bert Andrews to Eleanor Roosevelt, September 25, 1943, ERPCAP, FDRL.

26. James T. Howard, "Males Squirm at First Lady's Parley," *PM* September 28, 1943, RBP, MD, LOC.

27. Ibid.

28. Helen Essary, "Dear Washington," *Washington Times-Herald,* September 28, 1943, RBP, MD, LOC.

29. Supplemental report on results of meeting of Mrs. Roosevelt's Press Conference Association, February 13, 1943, box 5, ERPCAP, FDRL.

30. Ibid.

31. Ruth Montgomery, *Hail to the Chief* (New York: Coward, McCann, 1970), 16–17.

32. Ibid.

33. Marzolf, *Up from the Footnote,* 69.

34. Lilya Wagner, *Women Correspondents of World War II* (Westport, Conn.: Greenwood Press, 1989), 2.

35. Ross, *Ladies of the Press,* 550–51.

36. Julia Edwards, *Women of the World: The Great Foreign Correspondents* (New York: Ivy, 1988), 142–43.

37. Ibid., 144.

38. Ritchie, *Reporting from Washington,* 166.

39. Mary McGrory, "Doris Fleeson," in Sicherman and Green, *Notable American Women,* 240.

40. Ibid.

41. Mills, *Place in the News,* 50.

42. Stanley Frank and Paul Sann, "Paper Dolls," *Saturday Evening Post,* May 20, 1944, 95.

43. Quoted in Ritchie, *Reporting from Washington,* 167.

44. Marzolf, *Up from the Footnote,* 69.

45. Quoted in Mills, *Place in the News,* 51.

46. Ibid.

47. Helen Thomas was the first recipient of the prize established in her name by the White House Correspondents' Association, the Helen Thomas Lifetime Achievement Award. See her memoir, Helen Thomas, *Front Row at the White House* (New York: Scribner, 1999).

48. Jane Eads Bancroft, oral history interview, June 4, 1988, Washington Press Club Foundation, http://npc.press.org, sess. 3, 38.

49. Virginia Van der Veer Hamilton, *Looking for Clark Gable and Other 20th-Century Pursuits* (Tuscaloosa: University of Alabama Press, 1996), 94–95.

50. Ibid., 102.

51. Ritchie, *Reporting from Washington,* 167.

52. Mills, *Place in the News,* 51.

53. James Reston, *Deadline* (New York: Random House, 1991), 241.

54. Tom Kelly, *The Imperial Post: The Meyers, the Grahams, and the Paper That Rules Washington* (New York: Morrow, 1983), 93.

55. Quoted ibid.

56. Katharine Graham, *Personal History* (New York: Vintage, 1998), 148.

57. Ibid., 149.

58. Chalmers M. Roberts, *The Washington Post: The First 100 Years* (Boston: Houghton Mifflin, 1977), 217.

59. Quoted ibid., 248.

60. Agnes Meyer, "Rio Grande Problem: Migrant Mexican and Anglo Labor," *Washington Post,* April 23, 1946.

61. Kelly, *Imperial Post,* 92.

62. Graham, *Personal History,* 148.

63. Roberts, *Washington Post,* 242.

64. Ibid.

65. Quoted ibid.

66. Ibid.

67. Ibid.

68 Martin, *Cissy,* 434.

69. Healy, *Cissy,* 239.

70. Martin, *Cissy,* 441.

71. Healy, *Cissy,* 355.

72. Ibid.

73. Inga Arvad, "Did You Happen to See Katherine Smith?" *Washington Times-Herald,* April 17, 1942.

74. Ibid.

75. See "Another Day at the Office," *Washington City Paper,* May 21, 2004, 27; and see also Carol Hymowitz and Michaele Weissman, *A History of Women in America* (New York: Bantam, 1978), 312.

76. Healy, "Cissy," 36.

77. Ibid.

78. Ibid.

79. David Denker, "Eleanor Medill Patterson," in James, James, and Boyer, *Notable American Women,* 28.

80. Hoge, *Cissy Patterson,* 206–7.

81. Martin, *Cissy,* 449.

82. Ibid., 472.

83. Quoted in ibid., 474.

84. Betty Boyd Caroli, "Jacqueline (Lee Bouvier) Kennedy (Onassis)," in Lewis L. Gould, *American First Ladies: Their Lives and Their Legacy* (New York: Garland, 1996), 478.

85. Ibid.

86. Quoted in Martin, *Cissy,* 331.

87. Quoted ibid.

88. Quoted in Healy, *Cissy,* 387–88.

89. Quoted in Mills, *Place in the News,* 114.

90. Kimberly Wilmot Voss, "Redefining Women's News: A Case Study of Three Women's Page Editors and Their Framing of the Women's Movement" (Ph.D. dissertation, University of Maryland, 2004), 113.

91. Ibid.

92. Dorothy Jurney, oral history interview, "Women in Journalism," 1990, Washington Press Club Foundation, http://npc.press.org, sess. 4, 126.

93. Ibid.

94. Quoted in Mills, *Place in the News,* 114.

95. Marzolf, *Up from the Footnote,* 112.

96. Ibid., 71.

97. Quoted ibid.

98. Adam Bernstein, "D.C. Journalists Netted Pulitzer for Schools Coverage," June 30, 2009, http://www.washingtonpost.com/wp-dyn/content/article/2009/06/29.

99. Liz Carpenter, *Ruffles and Flourishes* (College Station: Texas A&M Press, 1993), 20.

100. Ibid.

101. Edwards, *Women of the World,* 177.

102. Carpenter, *Ruffles and Flourishes,* 20.

103. Ibid., 22.

104. Ibid.

105. Ritchie, *Reporting from Washington,* 167.

106. Sarah McClendon, *My Eight Presidents* (New York: Wyden, 1978), 21.

107. Ibid.

108. Sarah McClendon, oral history interview, June 27, 1989, Washington Press Club Foundation, http://npc.press.org, sess. 3, 47–48.

109. Ibid.

110. McClendon, *My Eight Presidents,* 23.

111. Ibid., 135.

112. "Washington Merry-Go-Round," *Washington Post,* April 8, 1945, RBP, MD, LOC.

113. Ibid.

114. See notes from Black Papers, quoted in Beasley, *Press Conferences of Eleanor Roosevelt,* 335–36.

115. Ibid., 336.

116. *New York Times* news copy marked "First Lady," April 12, 1945, box 51, BFP, MD, LOC.

117. Quoted in Kati Marton, *Hidden Power* (New York: Pantheon, 2001), 96.

118. See Margaret Truman, *Bess W. Truman* (New York: Macmillan, 1986), 276.

119. Ibid.

120. Quoted in Ritchie, *Reporting from Washington,* 168.

121. Summary of questions answered by Mrs. Truman, n.d., box 32, Edith B. Helm Papers, Manuscript Division, Library of Congress (hereafter cited as EBHP, MD, LOC).

122. Memo on press meeting, December 6, 1945, box 32, EBHP, MD, LOC.

123. Attendance roll for press briefings, 1952–1953, box 32, EBHP, MD, LOC.

124. Maurine H. Beasley, *First Ladies and the Press: The Unfinished Partnership of the Media Age* (Evanston, Ill.: Northwestern University Press, 2005), 68.

125. Judy Luce Mann, *Mann for All Seasons* (New York: MasterMedia, 1990), 6.

126. Marzolf, *Up from the Footnote,* 74.

127. Ibid.

128. Linda Lumsden, "Recipe for a Fifties' Feminist: Ruth Cowan Reports the Woman's Angle in Cold War Washington" (paper given at the American Journalism Historians Association Convention, San Antonio, October 6, 2005), 8.

129. Malvina Lindsay, "The Gentler Sex," *Washington Post,* February 28, 1946, quoted in Judith Paterson, *Be Somebody: A Biography of Marguerite Rawalt* (Austin: Eakin Press, 1986), 87.

130. "Reporter for the Star Wins Pulitzer Prize for Series," *Washington Star,* May 3, 1960, A3.

131. Marzolf, *Up from the Footnote,* 81.

132. "Crime Fighters Honor Mss Ottenberg of Star," *Washington Star,* May 30, 1958.

133. Miriam Ottenberg, *The Federal Investigators* (Englewood Cliffs, N.J.: Prentice Hall, 1962), vii.

134. "Reporter for the Star Wins."

135. Nancy Beckham Ferris, interview by author, July 5, 2010.

136. Adam Bernstein, "D.C. Journalists Netted Pulitzer."

137. Ibid.

138. Donald Lambro, "Pulitzer-Winning Journalist Mary Lou Forbes Dies at 83," *Washington Times,* June 29, 2009, A10.

139. Ibid.

140. Ibid.

141. Quoted in "Miriam Ottenberg," *Washington Post,* November 11, 1982, A26.

142. Miriam Ottenberg, *The Pursuit of Hope* (New York: Rawson, Wade, 1978), 5.

143. Ibid.

144. Rodger Streitmatter, "Alice Allison Dunnigan," in Ware, *Notable American Women,* 184.

145. See Rodger Streitmatter, *Raising Her Voice* (Lexington: University Press of Kentucky, 1994), 107–17.

146. Alice Allison Dunnigan, *A Black Woman's Experience from School-house to White House* (Philadelphia: Dorrence, 1974), 220.

147. Streitmatter, "Alice Allison Dunnigan," in Ware, *Notable American Women,* 184.

148. Alice Dunnigan, oral history interview by Marcia Greenlee, April 8, 1977, Oral history-31, Schlesinger Library, Radcliffe College, 25–26.

149. Quoted in Ritchie, *Reporting from Washington,* 159; and see also Marzolf, *Up from the Footnote,* 79.

150. Robertson, *Girls in the Balcony,* 102–3.

151. Quoted in Mills, *Place in the News,* 141.

152. Ibid.

153. McGrory, "Doris Fleeson," in Sicherman and Green, *Notable American Women,* 239.

154. Ibid., 240.

155. Quoted in Carolyn Sayler, *Doris Fleeson: Incomparably the First Political Journalist of Her Time* (Santa Fe: Sunstone Press, 2010), 208–9.

156. Doris Fleeson to Henry L. Mencken, August 19, 1945, and August 27, 1945, quoted in ibid., 165.

157. Ibid., 166.

158. Mencken to Fleeson, October 9, 1945, quoted in ibid., 166.

159. Marzolf, *Up from the Footnote,* 57.

160. Fred Hobson, quoted in Sayler, *Doris Fleeson,* 132.

161. Ibid.

162. Doris Fleeson, "McCarthyism in Full Bloom," June 10, 1954, quoted in ibid., 227.

163. Marzolf, "Marguerite Higgins," in Sicherman and Green, *Notable American Women,* 340.

164. Edwards, *Women of the World,* 188.

165. See Marguerite Higgins, *War in Korea: The Report of a Woman Combat Correspondent* (Garden City, N.Y.: Doubleday, 1951); *News Is a Singular Thing* (Garden City, N.Y.: Doubleday, 1955); *Red Plush and Black Bread* (Garden City, N.Y.: Doubleday, 1955); and *Our Vietnam Nightmare* (New York: Harper and Row, 1965).

166. Quoted in Marzolf, "Marguerite Higgins," in Sicherman and Green, *Notable American Women,* 341.

167. Quoted in Mills, *Place in the News,* 326–27.

168. See Peter Noel Murray, "Marguerite Higgins: An Examination of Legacy and Gender Bias" (Ph.D. dissertation, University of Maryland, 2003), 277–95.

169. Ibid., 179–80.

170. Ibid., 181.

171. Ibid.

172. Quoted in Ritchie, *Reporting from Washington,* 170.

173. Quoted in Murray, "Marguerite Higgins," 182.

174. Marzolf, "Marguerite Higgins," in Sicherman and Green, *Notable American Women,* 341.

175. Ritchie, *Reporting from Washington,* 173.

176. Ibid., 174.

177. Maurine Beasley, "The Women's National Press Club: Case Study of Professional Aspirations," *Journalism History* 15 (Winter 1988): 119.

178. *Reliable Sources,* 87.

179. Eileen Summers, "Women Say 'No Thanks' to Bid for Admission to Male Press Club," *Washington Post,* February 23, 1955, C1.

180. "Why Not Women?" *Newsweek,* February 28, 1955, 81.

181. Quoted in Robertson, *Girls in the Balcony,* 101.

182. Ibid.

183. Ibid.

184. Ibid.

185. *Reliable Sources,* 89.

186. Ritchie, *Reporting from Washington,* 175.

187. *Reliable Sources,* 67–68.

188. Ibid., 88.

189. Quoted in "Hagerty Suggests a Summit," *Washington Post,* October 30, 1959, C1.

190. Quoted in Ritchie, *Reporting from Washington,* 175.

191. Ibid.

192. Patricia Sullivan, "Journalist an Effective Voice for Women," *Washington Post,* December 7, 2008, C7.

CHAPTER FIVE

1. Mei-ling Yang, "Women's Pages of the *Washington Post* and Gender Ideology in the Late 1940s and the 1950s" (master's thesis, University of Maryland, 1992), 60.

2. "Flight from Fluff," *Time,* March 20, 1971, 52–53.

3. Mei-ling Yang, "Women's Pages or People's Pages: The Production of News for Women in the *Washington Post* in the 1950s," *Journalism and Mass Communication Quarterly* 73 (Summer 1996): 368.

4. Yang, "Women's Pages of the *Washington Post,*" 129.

5. Yang, "Women's Pages or People's Pages," 366.

6. Quoted in Yang, "Women's Pages or People's Pages," 367.

7. Ibid., 368.

8. Yang, "Women's Pages of the *Washington Post,*" 55.

9. Ibid., 80, 84.

10. Chalmers M. Roberts, *In the Shadow of Power: The Story of the "Washington Post"* (Cabin John, Md.: Seven Locks Press, 1989), 392.

11. Ibid., 345.

12. Ritchie, *Reporting from Washington,* 169; and Betty Beale, *Power at Play: A Memoir of Parties, Politicians and the Presidents in My Bedroom* (Washington, D.C.: Regnery Gateway, 1993), 3.

13. Beale, *Power at Play,* 3.

14. Adam Bernstein, "Washington Star Society Columnist Betty Beale, 94," *Washington Post,* June 8, 2006, B6.

15. Ibid.

16. Beale, *Power at Play,* 31.

17. Bernstein, "Washington Star Society Columnist."

18. Beale, *Power at Play,* 162.

19. Ibid., 47–48.

20. Ibid., 48.

21. Roberts, *In the Shadow of Power,* 345.

22. Maxine Cheshire with John Greenya, *Maxine Cheshire, Reporter* (Boston: Houghton Mifflin, 1978), 28.

23. Ibid.

24. Ibid., 37–38.

25. Streitmatter, *Raising Her Voice,* 121.

26. Dorothy Gilliam, "Ethel L. Payne," in Ware, *Notable American Women,* 503.

27. Ibid.

28. Ibid.

29. Ethel L. Payne, oral history interview by Kathleen Currie, September 8, 1987, Washington Press Club Foundation, National Press Club Archives, 48.

30. Ibid.

31. Streitmatter, *Raising Her Voice,* 123.

32. Ibid., 124.

33. Ibid.

34. Quoted in ibid., 123.

35. Gilliam, "Ethel L. Payne," in Ware, *Notable American Women,* 502.

36. Mills, *Place in the News,* 179.

37. "Dorothy B. Gilliam: Lincoln University Dream Recipient," Lincoln University, Mo., http://www.Lumoalumni-washdc.org/Dream Recipients/Dorothy Butler Gilliam.htm., accessed August 15, 2010.

38. Quoted in Mills, *Place in the News,* 179.

39. Ibid., 180.

40. Dorothy Butler Gilliam, oral history interview by Donita Moorhus, "Women in Journalism," March 17, 1993, Washington Press Club Foundation, http://www.wpcf.org/oralhistory/gill.html.

41. Ibid., 77–78.

42. Ibid., 72.

43. Ibid., 181.

44. Ibid.

45. Susanna McBee, interview by author, October 18, 2010.

46. Ibid.

47. Quoted in Roberts, *In the Shadow of Power,* 171.

48. Winzola McLendon and Scottie Fitzgerald Smith, *Don't Quote Me: Washington Newswomen and the Power Society* (New York: Dutton, 1970), 198.

49. Helen Thomas, *Dateline White House* (New York: Macmillan, 1975), 11–12.

50. Ibid., 12.

51. Quoted in C. David Heymann, *A Woman Named Jackie* (New York: Carol Communications, 1989), 223.

52. McLendon and Smith, *Don't Quote Me,* 71–72.

53. Ibid.

54. Heymann, *Woman Named Jackie,* 275.

55. Quoted in ibid.

56. Thomas, *Dateline White House,* 7.

57. Heymann, *Woman Named Jackie,* 272.

58. Bonnie Angelo, interview by author, March 2, 2005.

59. Ibid.

60. Ibid.

61. Ibid.

62. Thomas, *Dateline,* 79.

63. Lewis L. Gould, *Lady Bird Johnson and the Environment* (Lawrence: University Press of Kansas, 1988), 61.

64. Betty Beale, "A Plea for U.S. Beauty," *Washington Evening Star,* September 8, 1965, B1, and Beale, "First Lady Discusses Beauty," September 8, 1965, B5.

65. American News Women's Club Archives, box 1, unprocessed collection, University of Maryland Libraries, College Park, Md.

66. Ibid.

67. Ibid., box 18.

68. Ibid., membership directories, box 1.

69. Ibid., box 13.

70. Ibid., business meeting file, 1969–1970, box 5.

71. William H. Chafe, *The American Woman* (New York: Oxford University Press, 1972), 218.

72. Patricia Bradley, *Mass Media and the Shaping of American Feminism: 1963–1975* (Jackson: University Press of Mississippi, 2003), 24.

73. Charles W. Whalen Jr., "Unlikely Hero," *Washington Post,* January 2, 1984, A21.

74. Quoted in McLendon and Smith, *Don't Quote Me,* 122.

75. Roberts, *In the Shadow of Power,* 400–401.

76. Graham, *Personal History,* 450.

77. Ibid., 465.

78. Ritchie, *Reporting from Washington,* 260.

79. Quoted in Roberts, *In the Shadow of Power,* 437.

80. Ibid., 479.

81. Ibid., 498.

82. Ibid.

83. McLendon and Smith, *Don't Quote Me,* 234.

84. Ibid.

85. Ibid., 162.

86. Ibid., 164.

87. Ibid., 401.

88. Kelly, *Imperial Post,* 157–58.

89. Ibid., 158.

90. Roberts, *In the Shadow of Power,* 401.

91. Quoted in Ritchie, *Reporting from Washington,* 172.

92. Kelly, *Imperial Post,* 160.

93. Quoted in Ritchie, *Reporting from Washington,* 172.

94. Quoted in Kelly, *Imperial Post,* 161.

95. McLendon and Smith, *Don't Quote Me,* 164.

96. Ibid., 167.

97. Kelly, *Imperial Post,* 226.

98. Thomas, *Dateline,* 160.

99. Ibid., 200.

100. Quoted in Kelly, *Imperial Post,* 197.

101. Quoted in McLendon and Smith, *Don't Quote Me,* 177.

102. Ibid.

103. Ritchie, *Reporting from Washington,* 171.

104. Ibid.

105. Ibid., 172.

106. Peggy A. Simpson, "Covering the Women's Movement" (Summer 1979), reprinted in *Nieman Reports* 53–54 (Winter 1999 and Spring 2000), and Vera Glaser Papers, National Press Club Archives, 2.

107. Quoted in Bradley, *Mass Media,* 208.

108. Ibid.

109. Mills, *Place in the News,* 124.

110. Ibid.

111. Nicholas Von Hoffman, "Women's Pages: An Irreverent View," *Columbia Journalism Review* 10 (1971): 52–54.

112. David S. Broder, *Behind the Front Page: A Candid Look at How News Is Made* (New York: Simon and Schuster, 1987), 127–28.

113. Mills, *Place in the News,* 130.

114. Ibid.

115. Ibid.

116. Rosalynn Carter, *First Lady from Plains* (Boston: Houghton Mifflin, 1984), 173.

117. Marlene Cimons, interview by author, March 5, 2004.

118. Ibid.

119. Ibid.

120. Ibid.

121. Ibid.

122. Ritchie, *Reporting from Washington,* 170.

123. McLendon and Smith, *Don't Quote Me,* 23.

124. Marianne Means, "After 50 Years, a Fond Farewell—Till Next Time," *Seattle Post-Intelligencer,* October 5, 2008, B9.

125. McLendon and Smith, *Don't Quote Me,* 26.

126. Means, "After 50 Years."

127. McLendon and Smith, *Don't Quote Me,* 28–29.

128. Ibid.

129. Means, "After 50 Years."

130. Ibid.

131. Ibid.

132. Quoted in Ritchie, *Reporting from Washington,* 170.

133. Quoted in McLendon and Smith, *Don't Quote Me,* 27.

134. Ibid.

135. Ibid., 29.

136. Marzolf, *Up From the Footnote,* 80.

137. John Hohenberg, *The Pulitzer Prize Story II 1959–1980* (New York: Columbia University Press, 1980), 228–29.

138. Ibid., 228.

139. Quoted in McLendon and Smith, *Don't Quote Me,* 35–36.

140. Ibid., 36.

141. Quoted in Ritchie, *Reporting from Washington,* 170.

142. McLendon and Smith, *Don't Quote Me,* 19–20.

143. Ibid., 20.

144. Ibid., 21.

145. See Myrna Blyth, "The Witches of Washington," *Cosmopolitan,* March 1972, 162, 164–67.

146. Ibid., 167.

147. Ibid., 162.

148. Beale, *Power at Play,* 189.

149. Ibid., 162.

150. Ibid.

151. Ibid.

152. Ibid., 166.

153. Timothy Crouse, *The Boys on the Bus: Riding with the Campaign Press Corps* (New York: Random House, 1972), 209–10.

154. Ibid.

155. Sam Donaldson, "Introduction," in Sarah McClendon, *Mr. President, Mr. President: My Fifty Years of Covering the White House* (Los Angeles: General, 1996), 5.

156. Blyth, "Witches of Washington," 167.

157. Ibid.

158. Simpson, "Covering the Women's Movement," 3.

159. Ibid.

160. Ibid.

161. Crouse, *Boys on the Bus,* 210.

162. Ibid.

163. Simpson, "Covering the Women's Movement," 3.

164. Ibid., 2–3.

165. Ibid., 3.

166. Mills, *Place in the News,* 58–59.

167. Eileen Shanahan, oral history interview by Mary Marshall Clark, "Women in Journalism," Washington Press Club Foundation, Columbia University, May 21, 1994, http://npc/press.org/wpforal, 239.

168. Ibid.

169. Ibid.

170. Ibid.

171. Robertson, *Girls in the Balcony,* 10.

172. Ibid., 113.

173. Ibid.

174. Bill Kovach, interview by author, March 7, 2005.

175. Ibid.

176. Ibid.

177. Ibid.

178. Ibid.

179. Robertson, *Girls in the Balcony,* 13.

180. Quoted in Irvin Molotsky, "Marjorie Hunter, 78, a Pioneering Washington Correspondent for the Times," April 4, 2011, http://www.nytimes.com/2001/04/11/us/marjorie-hunter-78-a-pioneering-washington-correspondent-for-the-times.html.

181. Quoted in Peggy Simpson, "The Shock of Recognition," *Quill* 78 (February 1990): 34.

182. Marion Marzolf, "The History of Women Journalists" (paper, Distinguished Lecture Series on Women in the Mass Media, University of Maryland College Park, February 24, 1977), 19.

183. Mills, *Place in the News,* 149.

184. Ibid., 91.

185. Quoted in ibid., 153.

186. Ibid., 131.

187. Frances L. Lewine, oral history interview by Anne S. Kasper, November 12, 1991, Washington Press Club Foundation, National Press Club Archives, 66.

188. Ibid.

189. Ibid.

190. Quoted in Ritchie, *Reporting from Washington,* 171.

191. Ibid.

192. Graham, *Personal History,* 425.

193. Ibid.

194. Ibid., 422.

195. Ibid.

196. Ibid., 411.

197. Quoted in ibid., 424.

198. Ibid.

199. Ibid., 426.

200. Nancy Beckham Ferris, interview by author, July 5, 2010.

201. Ibid.

202. Ibid.

203. Joe Holley, "Betty Miles James: One of First Women at Star," *Washington Post,* April 2, 2008, B7.

204. Ibid.

205. Ferris, interview.

206. Ibid.

207. Ibid.

208. Ibid.

209. Roberts, *In the Shadow of Power,* 426.

210. Ibid., 427.

211. Ibid., 428.

212. "From EEOC Findings of Sex Discrimination at *The Washington Post,*" reprinted in Maurine H. Beasley and Sheila Gibbons, *Taking Their Place: A Documentary History of Women and Journalism,* 2nd ed. (State College, Pa.: Strata Publishing, 2003), 189.

213. Ibid.

214. Ibid., 189–90.

215. Roberts, *In the Shadow of Power,* 429.

216. Graham, *Personal History,* 426.

217. Ritchie, *Reporting from Washington,* 178.

218. Ibid., 179.

219. Ibid., 180.

220 Quoted in Mills, *Place in the News,* 107.

221. Graham, *Personal History,* 429.

222. Mills, *Place in the News,* 107.

223. Marlene Cimons, responses to questionnaire on Washington women journalists and interview by author, February 10, 2004.

224. Ibid.

225. Mills, *Place in the News,* 181.

226. Jody Beck, responses to a questionnaire on Washington women journalists by author, May 14, 2004.

227. Ibid.

228. Ibid.

CHAPTER SIX

1. Ruth Crane Schaefer, oral history interview by Pat Mower, November 18, 1975, American Women in Radio and Television, Library of American Broadcasting.

2. Ibid.

3. Ibid.

4. Michele Hilmes, *Only Connect: A Cultural History of Broadcasting in the United States* (Belmont, Calif.: Wadsworth/Thomson Learning, 2002), 98.

5. Ibid., 48.

6. Rick Ball and NBC News, *Meet the Press: Fifty Years of History in the Making* (New York: McGraw-Hill, 1998), 3.

7. Ibid., 4.

8. Ibid., 19.

9. Ibid., 13.

10. David H. Hosley and Gayle K. Yamada, *Hard News: Women in Broadcast Journalism* (Westport, Conn.: Greenwood Press, 1987), 75.

11. Mary E. Beadle, "Martha Rountree," in Ware, *Notable American Women,* 560.

12. Tebbe, "Elizabeth May Adams Craig," in Sicherman and Green, *Notable American Women,* 170.

13. McClendon, *My Eight Presidents,* 41.

14. Patty Cavin, oral history interview by Frank Harrison, March 31, 1984, Library of American Broadcasting, University of Maryland, College Park.

15. Ibid.

16. Ibid.

17. Ibid.

18. Ibid.

19. Ibid.

20. John Dickerson, *On Her Trail: My Mother, Nancy Dickerson: TV News' First Woman Star* (New York: Simon and Schuster, 2007), 110.

21. Marzolf, *Up from the Footnote,* 165.

22. Nancy Bernhard, "Pauline Frederick," in Ware, *Notable American Woman,* 223.

23. Quoted in Marzolf, *Up from the Footnote,* 159.

24. Ibid.

25. Marlene Sanders and Marcia Rock, *Waiting for Prime Time: The Women of Television News* (Urbana: University of Illinois Press, 1988), 10.

26. Quoted in Hosley and Yamada, *Hard News,* 64.

27. Ibid., 66.

28. Dickerson, *On Her Trail,* 110.

29. Quoted in Hosley and Yamada, *Hard News,* 82.

30. Ibid.

31. Ibid.

32. Ibid., 83.

33. Donna L. Halper, "Nancy Dickerson," in Ware, *Notable American Women,* 174.

34. Dickerson, *On Her Trail,* 48.

35. Ibid., 10.

36. Ibid.

37. Nancy Dickerson, *Among Those Present: A Reporter's View of 25 Years in Washington* (New York: Ballantine, 1976), 70.

38. Dickerson, *On Her Trail,* 110.

39. Quoted in Hosley and Yamada, *Hard News,* 83.

40. Dickerson, *Among Those Present,* 159.

41. Dickerson, *On Her Trail,* 239.

42. Dickerson, *Among Those Present,* 172.

43. Ibid., 208.

44. Dickerson, *On Her Trail,* 205.

45. Dickerson, *Among Those Present,* 207–8.

46. Hosley and Yamada, *Hard News,* 57.

47. Bart Barnes, "Fay G. Wells Dies at 94; Sought Out Adventure," *Washington Post,* December 6, 2002, B7.

48. Hosley and Yamada, *Hard News,* 106.

49. Ibid.

50. Quoted in Dickerson, *On Her Trail,* 252.

51. Louise Crosby Spieler, "Catherine Mackin: Trailblazer for Women in Broadcast Journalism" (master's thesis, 1990, University of Maryland, College Park), 3.

52. Ibid., 59.

53. Sanders and Rock, *Waiting for Prime Time,* 80.

54. Barbara Matusow, *The Evening Stars* (Boston: Houghton Mifflin, 1983), 182.

55. Sanders and Rock, *Waiting for Prime Time,* 80.

56. "Ann Compton, ABC News," ABC News, http://abcnews.go.com/Politics/story?id=6433048&page=1, accessed September 21, 2010.

57. Hosley and Yamada, *Hard News,* 108.

58. Ibid., 111.

59. Lesley Stahl, *Reporting Live* (New York: Simon and Schuster, 1999), 13.

60. Roger Mudd, *The Place to Be: Washington, CBS, and the Glory Days of Television News* (New York: Public Affairs, 2008), xiv.

61. Ibid.

62. Quoted in ibid., 248.

63. Hosley and Yamada, *Hard News,* 93.

64. Mudd, *Place to Be,* 276.

65. Ibid.

66. Ibid., 277.

67. Ibid.

68. Ibid.

69. Ibid., 279.

70. Stahl, *Reporting Live,* 11.

71. Ibid., 25.

72. Matusow, *Evening Stars,* 181.

73. Ibid.

74. Hosley and Yamada, *Hard News,* 111.

75. Mudd, *Place to Be,* 339–41; and see also Stahl, *Reporting Live,* 51–53.

76. Matusow, *Evening Stars,* 182.

77. Ibid.

78. Ibid., 167.

79. Ibid., 179.

80. Quoted in ibid.

81. Stahl, *Reporting Live,* 81.

82. Ibid.

83. Ibid.

84. Ibid.

85. For a discussion of the Craft case, see Beasley and Gibbons, *Taking Their Place,* 248.

86. Stahl, *Reporting Live,* 171.

87. Ibid., 171–72.

88. Ibid., 83.

89. Ibid., 103.

90. Ibid., 125.

91. Andrea Mitchell, *Talking Back* (New York: Viking, 2005), 135.

92. Ibid., 136.

93. Ibid.

94. Quoted in Sanders and Rock, *Waiting for Prime Time,* 81–82.

95. Mitchell, *Talking Back,* 136.

96. Ibid., 135.

97. Sanders and Rock, *Waiting for Prime Time,* 80.

98. Crouse, *Boys on the Bus,* 15–16.

99. Susan G. Kahlenberg, "Constance (Connie) Yu-Hwa Chung," in *Women in Communication: A Biographical Sourcebook,* ed. Nancy Signorielli (Westport, Conn.: Greenwood Press, 1996), 70.

100. Connie Chung, oral history interview by Donita M. Moorhus, "Women in Journalism," March 30, 1994, Washington Press Club Foundation, 99.

101. Hosley and Yamada, *Hard News,* 140.

102. Quoted in ibid., 141.

103. Quoted in Sanders and Rock, *Waiting for Prime Time,* 96.

104. Ibid., 97.

105. "Katie Couric," NNDB, http://www.nndb.com/people/487/000025412, accessed November 2, 2010.

106. Ibid.

107. Ibid.

108. "Katie Couric," Wikipedia, http://en.wikipedia.org/wiki/Katie_Couric, accessed November 1, 2010.

109. Amber J. Tresca, "Colorectal Cancer and the Katie Couric Effect," About.com, http://ibscrohns.about.com/cs/colorecalcancer/a/ktiecouric.htm, accessed November 2, 2010.

110. Ibid., 93.

111. Ibid., 59.

112. Ibid., 60.

113. Betsy Ashton, email message to author, September 7, 2010.

114. Ibid.

115. Ibid.

116. Ibid.

117. Ibid.

118. Ibid.

119. Ibid.

120. Ibid.

121. Connie Lawn, *You Wake Me Each Morning* (San Jose, Calif.: Writers Club Press, 2000), 81.

122. Ibid.

123. Ibid., 107.

124. Ibid., 107–8.

125. Ibid., 122.

126. Ibid., 129.

127. Ibid.

128. Ibid., 130.

129. Ibid.

130. Ibid., 147.

131. Matusow, *Evening Stars,* 181.

132. Stahl, *Reporting Live,* 47.

133. Ibid.

134. Sanders and Rock, *Waiting for Prime Time,* 152.

135. Ibid.

136. Hosley and Yamada, *Hard News,* 92.

137. Barbara Ruben, "Anchor Celebrates 36 Years on TV," *Senior Beacon,* February 2008, 1.

138. Ibid., 41.

139. Ibid.

140. "Maureen Bunyan," Zonta Club of Washington, D.C., http://www.zontawashingtondc.org/Gala_2006/MaureenBunyanBioInsert.pdf, accessed September 17, 2010.

141. Quoted in Betsy Covington Smith, *Breakthrough: Women in Television* (New York: Walker, 1981), 12.

142. Ibid., 15.

143. Ibid.

144. Ibid., 17.

145. Ibid., 9.

146. Ibid.

147. Ibid., 14.

148. Scott Shindell, "Visionary Renee Poussaint '66," Sarah Lawrence College, http://www.slc.edu/magazine/mtm/glimpse_pouissant.php, accessed October 27, 2010.

149. Lee Thornton, interview by author, March 11, 2004.

150. Ibid.

151. Ibid.

152. Quoted in Marzolf, *Up From the Footnote,* 194.

153. Ibid.

154. Lee Thornton, responses to a questionnaire by author, September 30, 2003.

155. Ibid.

156. Ibid.

157. Ibid.

158. Ibid.

159. Payne, interview, reprinted in Beasley and Gibbons, *Taking Their Place,* 233.

160. Ibid., 234.

161. Gilliam, "Ethel Payne," in Ware, *Notable American Women,* 503.

162. Streitmatter, *Raising Her Voice,* 127.

163. Quoted in Gilliam, "Ethel Payne," in Ware, *Notable American Women,* 503.

164. Cokie Roberts, *We Are Our Mothers' Daughters* (New York: Morrow, 1998), 122.

165. Ibid.

166. Thornton, responses to questionnaire.

167. Dickerson, *On Her Trail,* 317.

168. Claudia Dreifus, "Cokie Roberts, Nina Totenberg and Linda Wertheimer," *New York Times Magazine,* January 2, 1994, http://www.nytimes.com/1994/01/02/cokie-roberts-nina-tote, 3.

169. Ibid., 1.

170. Ibid.

171. Ibid.

172. Ibid., 5.

173. Ibid.

174. Sanders and Rock, *Waiting for Prime Time,* 199.

175. Ibid.

176. J. Max Robins, "Cokie Faux Pas Upsets Arledge," *Variety,* February 13, 1994, http://www.variety.com/article/VR118288.html?categoryid=14&cs=1.

177. "Cokie Roberts," Wikipedia, http://en.wikipedia.org/wiki/Cokie_Roberts, accessed October 30, 2010.

178. Burt Solomon, *The Washington Century: Three Families and the Shaping of the Nation's Capital* (New York: Morrow, 2004), 371.

179. Ibid.

180. Quoted in ibid., 371.

181. Ibid., 372.

182. Bill Buzenberg, foreword to *Listening to America: Twenty-Five Years in the Life of a Nation, as Heard on National Public Radio,* ed. Linda Wertheimer (Boston: Houghton, Mifflin, 1995), xi.

183. "Linda Wertheimer," NPR, http://www.npr.org/templates/story/story.php?storyId=1931801, accessed November 6, 2010.

184. Wertheimer, introduction to *Listening to America,* xx.

185. Ibid.

186. Hosley and Yamada, *Hard News,* 117.

187. Susan Stamberg, "Mama Stamberg's Cranberry Relish Recipe," NPR, http://www.npr.org/templates/story/story.php?storyId=4176014, accessed November 4, 2010.

188. Ibid., 38–39.

189. Ibid., 192.

190. Dreifus, "Cokie Roberts," 3.

191. Ibid.

192. Wertheimer, *Listening to America,* 114.

193. Ibid.

194. Ibid., 282.

195. Ibid., 110.

196. "Wertheimer," NPR.

197. Dreifus, "Cokie Roberts," 3.

198. Ibid.

199. "Nina Totenberg," Wikipedia, http://en.wikipedia.org/wiki/Nina_Totenberg, accessed November 1, 2010.

200. Ibid.

201. Ibid.

202. Trudy Lieberman, "Plagiarize, Plagiarize, Plagiarize . . .," *Columbia Journalism Review* (July–August 1995).

203. "Totenberg," Wikipedia.

204. Ibid.

205. John Wilner, "Nina Totenberg: 'You Can't Do Good Investigative Work Without Making Some People Mad,'" Current, December 16, 1991, http://www.current.org/people/peop123t.html.

206. "Nina Totenberg," Academic.ru, http://en.academic.ru/dic.nsf/enwiki/1041231, accessed November 7, 2010.

207. "Nina Totenberg," Current.

208. Ibid.

209. Ibid.

210. "Nina Totenberg," Academic.ru.

211. "Juan Williams Talks Back on 'O'Reilly Factor,'" CBS News, October 23, 2010, http://www.cbsnews.com/stories/2010/10/22/national/main6983495.shtml.

212. "Nina Totenberg," Wikipedia.

213. Diane Rehm, *Finding My Voice* (New York: Knopf, 1999), 44–47.

214. Ibid., 93, 96.

215. Ibid., 116.

216. Ibid., 117.

217. Ibid., 180.

218. Ibid., 172.

219. Ibid., 150.

220. Ibid., 240.

221. "Diane Rehm," The Diane Rehm Show, http://thedianerehm show.org/diane, accessed November 12, 2010.

222. Ibid.

223. Quoted in Hosley and Yamada, *Hard News,* 119; and see also Alanna Nash, *Golden Girl* (New York: Signet, 1988), 57.

224. Nash, *Golden Girl,* 57–60.

225. Hosley and Yamada, *Hard News,* 120.

226. Ibid., 121.

227. Ibid.

228. Nash, *Golden Girl,* 227.

229. Ibid., 286.

230. See Jessica Savitch, *Anchorwoman* (New York: G. P. Putnam's Sons, 1982). The book received relatively poor reviews.

231. Hosley and Yamada, *Hard News,* 120.

232. Nash, *Golden Girl,* ix.

CHAPTER SEVEN

This chapter's epigraph is Judy Luce Mann, quoted in Maria Braden, *Women Politicians and the Media* (Lexington: University of Kentucky Press, 1996), 180.

1. Braden, *Women Politicians and the Media,* 181.

2. Ibid.

3. Quoted in David S. Broder, *Behind the Front Page* (New York: Simon and Schuster, 1987), 142.

4. Michael Kilian and Arnold Sawislak, *Who Runs Washington?* (New York: St. Martin's, 1982), 170–78.

5. Ibid., 174.

6. Ibid., 175.

7. Ibid., 177.

8. Jim Bellows, *The Last Editor* (Kansas City, Mo.: Andrews McMeel, 2002), 220.

9. Ibid.

10. Ibid.

11. Broder, *Behind the Front Page,* 141.

12. Ibid., 142.

13. Ibid.

14. Ibid., 193.

15. Ibid., 195, 199.

16. Quoted ibid., 197.

17. Ibid., 205.

18. Reprinted ibid., 193.

19. Ibid., 194.

20. Ibid.

21. Joe Holley, "Nancy Maynard, 61: Newspaper Owner Pressed for Diversity," *Washington Post,* September 22, 2008, B6.

22. Ibid.

23. Dorothy Gilliam, interview by author, November 10, 2010.

24. Ibid.

25. Ibid.

26. Ibid.

27. Ibid.

28. See "Dorothy Gilliam," in Maria Braden, *She Said What? Interviews with Women Newspaper Columnists* (Lexington: University of Kentucky Press, 1993), 110–22.

29. Ibid., 114.

30. Quoted ibid., 110–22.

31. Alice Bonner, response to questionnaire on Washington women journalists by author, October 31, 2003.

32. Ibid.; and see also letter to Leonard [Downy] signed by twelve women, January 2, 1987, private collection.

33. Bonner, response to questionnaire.

34. Ibid.

35. "Minority Report Jolts the Post," *Washington Journalism Review,* December 1985, 8.

36. Ibid.

37. Bonner, response to questionnaire.

38. "ASNE Losing Diversity Director," Maynard Institute, http://mije.org/richardprince/asne-losing-diversity-director, accessed December 6, 2010.

39. Al Neuharth, *Confessions of an S.O.B.* (New York: Doubleday, 1989), 245.

40. Ibid., 243.

41. Cathie Black, *Basic Black: The Essential Guide for Getting Ahead at Work (and in Life)* (New York: Crown Business, 2007), 108–9.

42. Neuharth, *Confessions of an S.O.B.,* 250, 252.

43. David M. Halbfinger, Michael Barbaro, and Fernanda Santos, "A Trailblazer with Her Eye on the Bottom Line," *New York Times,* November 19, 2010, A1, 21.

44. Black, *Basic Black,* 253.

45. Ibid.

46. "Where Are Women in the Media? A Summary of Two New Studies" (press kit, Women, Men and Media Conference, Washington, D.C., April 10, 1989).

47. Quoted in Eleanor Randolph, "The Newspaper Editors, at a Loss for Words," *Washington Post,* April 4, 1990, B1, 4.

48. "About and by Women" (report, Human Resources Committee, American Society of Newspaper Editors, Reston, Va., 1990), 7.

49. Neuharth, *Confessions of an S.O.B.,* 246.

50. Ibid., 157.

51. Quoted in ibid., 246.

52. Beth Haller, "Nancy Woodhull," in Ware, *Notable American Women,* 700.

53. Peter Prichard, *The Making of McPaper: The Inside Story of USA Today* (Kansas City, Mo.: Andrews, McMeel and Parker, 1987), 12.

54. Ibid.

55. Ibid.

56. Ibid., 239.

57. Haller, "Nancy Woodhull," in Ware, *Notable American Women,* 701.

58. Quoted in ibid.

59. Ibid.

60. Ibid., 186–87.

61. Gilliam, interview.

62. Ibid.

63. Ibid.

64. Braden, *She Said What?* 115.

65. Quoted in ibid.

66. Dorothy Gilliam, "You Define Yourself," *Washington Post,* 29, 1985, reprinted in ibid., 117–18.

67. Ibid., 118.

68. Ibid.

69. Gilliam, interview.

70. Roberts, *In the Shadow of Power,* 485.

71. Ibid.

72. Quoted in ibid., 486.

73. Patricia Sullivan, "Aplin-Brownlee, 61: Former Post Editor Had Smelled Scandal," *Washington Post,* October 26, 2007, B7.

74. Ibid.

75. Ibid.

76. Ibid.

77. Ibid.

78. Ibid.

79. Quoted in Roberts, *In the Shadow of Power,* 485.

80. Jill Nelson, *Volunteer Slavery: My Authentic Negro Experience* (Chicago: Noble Press, 1993), 87.

81. Ibid., 87–88.

82. See ibid., 69–76.

83. Letter to Leonard [Downie].

84. Ibid.

85. "Gwen Ifill," Wikipedia, http://en.wikipedia.org/wikiGwen-Ifill, accessed November 28, 2010.

86. Gwen Ifill, *The Breakthrough: Politics and Race in the Age of Obama* (New York: Doubleday, 2009), 5.

87. Rev. Dr. Barbara A. Reynolds, *Out of Hell and Living Well* (Xulon Press, 2004), 106.

88. Ibid., 91.

89. Ibid., 115.

90. Ibid., 116.

91. Ibid., 117.

92. Ibid.

93. Ibid.

94. Ibid., 118.

95. Nelson, *Volunteer Slavery,* 140.

96. Karlyn Barker, responses to questionnaire on Washington women journalists by author, October 2007.

97. Ibid.

98. Ibid.

99. Susan Fleming Morgans, email responses to a survey on Washington women journalists by author, February 2, 2008. Morgans worked as a news aide at the *Washington Post* in 1969 and 1970.

100. Ibid.

101. Ibid.

102. Ibid.

103. Barker responses to questionnaire.

104. Ibid.

105. Alan E. Phelps to Martha Hamilton, November 11, 2003, private collection.

106. Barker responses to questionnaire.

107. Ibid.

108. Ibid.

109. Martha Hamilton, responses to questionnaire on Washington women journalists by author, January 7, 2008.

110. Ibid.

111. Ibid.

112. Martha McNeil Hamilton and Warren Brown, *Black and White and Red All Over* (New York: Public Affairs, 2002), xvii.

113. Ibid., xix.

114. Ibid.

115. Quoted in Roberts, *"Washington Post,"* 424.

116. Carl Bernstein and Bob Woodward, "FBI Finds Nixon Aides Sabotaged Democrats," *Washington Post,* October 10, 1972, http://www.washingtonpost.com/wp-dyn/content/article/2002/06/03/; and see also Broder, *Behind the Front Page,* 46.

117. McBee, interview.

118. Ibid.

119. Broder, *Behind the Front Page,* 95.

120. Patricia Sullivan, "Mary Lou Beatty; Editor at NEH, Post," *Washington Post,* February 9, 2007, B6.

121. Quoted in ibid.

122. Ibid.

123. "Defining a Beat," *Money,* April 17, 1977, 47.

124. Ann McFeatters, oral history interview by author, National Press Club, August 3, 2007.

125. Ibid.

126. Ibid.

127. Ibid.

128. Ibid.

129. Ibid.

130. Ibid.

131. Ann McFeatters, "Politics in Washington," *St. Augustine* (Fla.) *Record,* October 6, 2004.

132. Patricia Sullivan, "*Post* Columnist Judy Mann Dies," *Washington Post,* July 9, 2005, http://www.washingtonpost.com/wp-dyn/content/article/2005/07/08.

133. Ibid.

134. Ibid.

135. Quoted in Tanya Melich, *The Republican War Against Women* (New York: Bantam, 1996), 116–17.

136. Sullivan, "Judy Mann Dies."

137. Braden, *Women Politicians and the Media,* 106.

138. Quoted in ibid., 188.

139. Harriet Woods, email message to author, October 13, 2003.

140. Ibid.

141. "Alumni Profile: Elisabeth Bumiller '79," *One Hundred Sixteenth and Broadway* (Summer 2006): 7.

142. Woods, email.

143. Ibid.

144. Ibid.

145. Ibid.

146. Ibid.

147. "Harriett Woods," Wikipedia, http://en.wikipedia.org/wiki/Harriett_Woods, accessed December 23, 2010; and see also Patricia Sullivan, "Harriet Woods: Inspired Creation of Emily's List," *Washington Post,* February 10, 2007.

148. Woods, email.

149. Ibid.

150. Ibid.

151. Sullivan, "Judy Mann Dies."

152. Mann, *Mann for All Seasons,* 255–56.

153. Braden, *Women Politicians and the Media,* 94.

154. "Neuharth's USA of Yesterday," *Washington Post,* August 2, 1989, reprinted in Mann, *Mann for All Seasons,* 50.

155. Ibid., 51.

156. Quoted in ibid., 49.

157. Judy Luce Mann, "The Great Pretender," *Washington Post,* August 18, 1989, reprinted in Mann, *Mann for All Seasons,* 52.

158. Ibid., 53.

159. Ibid.

160. Sullivan, "Judy Mann Dies."

161. Martha Burke, email message to author, October 21, 2003.

162. Ibid.

163. "Miss Manners," Universal Uclick, http://www.universaluclick.com/text_features/missmanners, accessed December 18, 2010.

164. Braden, *She Said What?* 128.

165. Quoted in ibid.

166. Ibid., 129.

167. Quoted in ibid., 128.

168. Graham, *Personal History,* 444.

169. Ibid.

170. Chris Harvey, discussion with author, December 3, 2010.

171. Ibid.

172. "Mona Charen," Wikipedia, http://en.wikipedia.org/wiki/Mona_Charen, accessed December 18, 2010.

173. Braden, *She Said What?* 138.

174. Ibid., 139.

175. Ibid.

176. Quoted in ibid., 141.

177. Ibid., 142.

178. Mona Charen, "Worshipping the Condom God," April 16, 1992, reprinted in ibid., 144.

179. Ibid., 140.

180. Ibid., 62.

181. Ibid., 65.

182. "Georgie Anne Geyer," Wikipedia, http://en.wikipedia.org/wiki/Georgie_Anne_Geyer, accessed December 19, 2010.

183. See Georgie Anne Geyer, *Guerilla Prince: The Untold Story of Fidel Castro* (Boston: Little, Brown, 1991).

184. Quoted in Braden, *She Said What?* 64.

185. Ibid., 63.

186. Braden, *Women Politicians and the Media,* 163.

187. Patricia Sullivan, "Helen Dewar, 70: Distinguished Post Senate Reporter," *Washington Post,* November 5, 2006, C09.

188. Ibid.

189. Ibid.

190. Personal recollection of author, chair of the Society of Professional Journalists Committee in charge of the ceremony honoring Royall in the Senate Hart Office building, May 22, 1990.

191. Personal recollection of author, who worked with Dewar at the *Post* in the 1960s.

192. Remarks by Helen Thomas at ceremony on May 22, 1990, to precede placement of plaque in Senate Press Gallery.

193. Ibid.

194. Ibid.

195. Ibid.

196. Helen Thomas, interview by author, December 20, 1990.

197. Ibid.

198. Ibid.

199. Ibid.

200. Ibid.

201. Ibid.

202. Ibid.

203. Ibid.

204. Barbara Matusow, "Washington's Journalism Establishment," *Washingtonian,* February 1989, 97.

205. Ibid., 96.

206. Ibid.

207. Ibid., 98.

208. Ibid., 268.

209. Maureen Santini, interview by author, April 27, 2004.

210. Ibid.

211. Jodi Enda, interview by author, June 21, 2004.

212. Braden, *Women Politicians and the Media,* 180.

213. Ibid.

214. Ibid.

215. "Washington's Media Elite," *Washingtonian,* May 1993, 39.

216. Ibid.

217. "Here's the Media Elite," *Washingtonian,* August 1997, 63.

218. Barbara Matusow, "Powers of the Press," *Washingtonian,* August 1997, http://we.lexis-nexis.com/universe/printdoc, 2.

219. Seth Mnookin, *Hard News: The Scandals at "The New York Times" and Their Meaning for American Media* (New York: Random House, 2004), 66.

220. Ariel Levy, "The Redhead and the Gray Lady," *New York,* October 31, 2005. http://nymag.com/nymetro/news/people/features/14946.

221. Ibid.

222. "Maureen Dowd: Biography from Answers.com," Answers.com, http://www.answers.com/topic/maureen-dowd, accessed December 20, 2010.

223. "Theodore H. White Lecture with Maureen Dowd" (lecture, Shorenstein Center, Harvard University, Cambridge, Mass., 2007), 24.

224. Ibid.

225. Kim Isaac Eisler, "The Journalism 50 Establishment," *Washingtonian,* March 2001, http://web.lexis-nexis.com/universe/printdoc, 1–11.

226. Ibid., 6, 8, 9.

227. Ibid., 10.

228. Penny Bender Fuchs, email message to author, December 31, 2010.

229. Ibid.

230. Ibid.

231. Ibid.

232. Ibid.

233. Ibid.

234. Ibid.

235. Quoted in Mnookin, *Hard News,* 69.

236. Ibid., 77.

237. Ibid., 79.

238. Ibid.

CHAPTER EIGHT

This chapter's epigraph is from Judy Woodruff, "Are Journalists Obsolete?" (Red Smith Lecture in Journalism, University of Notre Dame, September 2007).

1. Garrett Graff, "50 Best and Most Influential Journalists," *Washingtonian,* December 2005; http://web.lexis-nexis.com/universe/printdoc.

2. Garrett M. Graff, "50 Top Journalists 2009," *Washingtonian,* June 1, 2009, http://www.washingtonian.com/print/articles/6/174/12512.html.

3. Ibid.

4. Graff, "Most Influential Journalists," 4.

5. Ibid., 4, 5, 7, 8–9.

6. Ibid., 7.

7. Robin Givhan, "No False Moves in These Sentencing Walks," *Washington Post,* July 8, 2005, C1, 2.

8. Ibid., C2.

9. Carol D. Leonig, "Jailed Reporter Is Distanced From News, Not Elite Visitors," *Washington Post,* September 17, 2005, 1.

10. Lorne Manly, "Jail Where Reporter Is Held: Maximum, Modern Security," *New York Times,* July 8, 2005, A18.

11. Graff, "Most Influential Journalists," 8.

12. Howard Kurtz, "The Judith Miller Story: Not Ready Yet," *Washington Post,* October 13, 2005, C1, 8.

13. Ibid.

14. Arianna Huffington, "Making Faux Martyrdom Pay: Judy Miller Lands a Book Deal," *Huffington Post,* October 3, 2005, http://www.huffingtonpost.com/arianna-huffington/making-faux-martyrdom-pay_b_8268.html.

15. "Judith Miller," SourceWatch, http://www.sourcewatch.org/index.php?title=Judith_Miller, accessed January 3, 2011.

16. "Judith Miller (journalist)," Wikipedia, http://en.wikipedia.org/wiki/Judith_Miller, accessed, January 3, 2011.

17. Lorne Manly, "A Difficult Moment, Long Anticipated," *New York Times,* July 7, 2005, A16.

18. Quoted in ibid.

19. Kurtz, "Sex and the Single Stiletto."

20. Ibid.

21. Alex Pareene, "Judith Miller: From the Times to the Nuts," Salon.com., December 30, 2010, http://www.salon.com/2010/12/30/judy_miller_newsmax/singleton/.

22. Manly, "Difficult Moment."

23. "Biography: Judith Miller," Pundicity: Informed Opinion and Review, http://www.judithmiller.com/about/, accessed January 3, 2011.

24. Ibid.

25. Pareene, "Judith Miller."

26. Franklin Foer, "The Source of the Trouble," *New York,* May 21, 2005, http://nymag.com/nymetro/news/media/features/9226/.

27. Ibid.

28. Quoted in Manly, "Difficult Moment."

29. Foer, "Source of the Trouble."

30. William E. Jackson Jr., "Miller's Star Fades (Slightly) at 'NY Times,'" *Editor and Publisher Online,* October 2, 2003, http://www.commondreams.org/scriptfiles/views03/1002-09.htm.

31. Lynne Duke, "The Reporter's Last Take," *Washington Post,* November 10, 2005, C1, 8.

32. Ibid.

33. Ibid.

34. Ibid.

35. See Judith Miller, William Broad, and Stephen Engelberg, *Germs: Biological Weapons and America's Secret War* (New York: Simon and Schuster, 2001).

36. Graff, "Most Influential Journalists," 3.

37. Quoted in Woodruff, "Are Journalists Obsolete?" 8.

38. Ibid.

39. Roxanne Roberts and Amy Argetsinger, "Still Fit to Print," *Washington Post,* January 7, 2011, C2.

40. Keach Hagey, "Anxieties Provoke Quick Media Responses in 2010," Politico.com, January 2, 2011, http://www.politico.com/news/stories/1210/46780.html.

41. Ibid.

42. Ibid.

43. Roberts and Argetsinger, "Still Fit to Print."

44. "Helen Thomas," Wikipedia, http://en.wikipedia.org/wiki/Helen_Thomas, accessed January 2, 2011, 4.

45. Ibid.

46. Ibid.

47. Katharine Q. Seelye, "Another White House Briefing, Another Day of Mutual Mistrust," *New York Times,* February 27, 2006, C1, 6.

48. Ibid., 6.

49. Ibid.

50. "Helen Thomas," Wikipedia, 7.

51. Ibid.

52. Thomas, *Front Row,* 227.

53. Ibid., 227–28.

54. Ibid., 233.

55. Rob Capriccioso, "Judy Woodruff: A Personal Path to Advocacy," SparkAction, September 13, 2004, http://sparkaction.org/node/616.

56. Ibid.

57. Cimons, responses to questionnaire.

58. Ibid.

59. Enda, interview.

60. Ibid.

61. Ibid.

62. Cassandra Clayton, responses to questionnaire on Washington women journalists by author, December 1, 2010.

63. Ibid.

64. Ibid.

65. Ibid.

66. Ibid.

67. Ibid.

68. Dickerson, *On Her Trail*, 111.

69. Ibid.

70. Clayton, responses to questionnaire.

71. Tom Rosenstiel, "The End of 'Network News," *Washington Post,* September 12, 2004, B7.

72. Ibid.

73. Quoted in Philip S. Balboni, "Cable News Future Depends on Quality," *Columbia Journalism Alumni Journal* (Winter 2007): 3.

74. Bryan Keefer, "You Call That News? I Don't," *Washington Post,* September 12, 2004, B2.

75. Rosenstiel, "End of 'Network News.'"

76. Ibid.

77. "Diversity in the Washington Press Corps," joint project of UNITY: Journalists of Color Inc. and Philip Merrill College of Journalism, 2004, 2.

78. Ibid.

79. Ibid.

80. "Washington Press Corps," 3.

81. Ibid.

82. Ibid.

83. Ibid.

84. "The Great Divide: Female Leadership in U.S. Newsrooms," study conducted for American Press Institute and Pew Center for Civic Journalism, September 2002, 3.

85. Ibid.

86. "About Michelle," Michelle Singletary, http://www.michelle singletary.com/about/default.html, accessed March 20, 2011.

87. Ibid.

88. Katharine Q. Seelye, "Newspaper Circulation Falls Sharply," *New York Times,* October 31, 2006, 1.

89. Laila Weir, "News Sites, Where the Men Are," *Wired News,* August 4, 2004, http://www.wired.com/news/business/0,1367,64439,00.html.

90. Ibid.

91. Richard Perz-Pena, "Big News in Washington, but Far Fewer Cover It," *New York Times,* December 18, 2008, A1.

92. Ibid.

93. Ibid.

94. Associated Press, "Newhouse News Service to Close," July 29, 2008.

95. Figures supplied by the American Society of News Editors and Radio Television Digital News Association as reported in Mary Walton, "Investigative Shortfall," *American Journalism Review* (Fall 2010): 20.

96. Quoted in Perez-Pena, "Big News in Washington," A24.

97. Ibid.

98. Matt Schudel, "Former Post Ombudsman Helped Break Glass Ceiling," *Washington Post,* January 3, 2010, http://www.washingtonpost.com/wp-dyn/content/article/2010/01/01.

99. Ibid.

100. Deborah Howell, oral history interview by Donia Moorhus, "Women in Journalism," April 22, 1993, 20, Washington Press Club Foundation, http://www.wpcf.org/oralhistory/how.html.

101. Richard Perez-Pena, "Deborah Howell, One of the First Women to Lead a Big U.S. Paper, Dies at 68," *New York Times,* January 3, 2010, http://www.nytimes.com/2010/01/04/business/04howell.html.

102. Quoted in ibid.

103. Ibid.

104. Ibid.

105. Ibid.

106. "Marjorie Williams," *Washington Post,* January 17, 2005, A16.

107. Quoted in David Von Drehle, "Post Columnist Marjorie Williams Dies," *Washington Post,* January 17, 2005, B5.

108. Quoted in ibid.

109. Ibid.

110. Schudel, "Former Post Ombudsman."

111. Ibid.

112. Quoted in ibid.

113. Ibid.

114. Ibid.

115. Ibid.

116. Quoted in ibid.

117. Ibid.

118. Deborah Howell, "Getting Women into the News," *Washington Post,* December 14, 2008, B6.

119. Ibid.

120. Deborah Howell, "An Op-Ed Need for Diverse Voices," *Washington Post,* May 25, 2008, B6.

121. Ibid.

122. Ibid.

123. Deborah Howell, "The Outrage over an Outlook Piece," *Washington Post,* March 9, 2008, B6.

124. Ibid.

125. Ibid.

126. Howard Kurtz, "Post Buyouts Come with an Emotional Cost," *Washington Post,* May 26, 2008, C1, 8.

127. Ibid.

128. Leslie Walker, interview by author, July 1, 2008.

129. Walker, email message to author, March 21, 2011.

130. Quoted in Kurtz, "Post Buyouts."

131. "Women in Leadership: Journalism," March 15, 2010, YouTube video, http://www.youtube.com/watch?v=nqCJdX9_610.

132. Walton, "Investigative Shortfall," 26.

133. Ibid.

134. Ibid., 30.

135. Ibid., 31.

136. Ibid., 21.

137. Quoted in ibid., 26.

138. Ibid., 24.

139. Roberta Baskin, "Investigative Reporting/A Reporter's Notebook," *Kosmos* (Fall–Winter 2010).

140. Ibid.

141. Ibid.

142. Walton, "Investigative Shortfall," 24.

143. Baskin, "Investigative Reporting."

144. Ibid.

145. Ibid.

146. See Garrett M. Graff, "50 Top Journalists 2009," *Washingtonian,* 1.

147. Ibid.

148. Ibid., 2–5.

149. Ibid.

150. Ibid., 4.

151. See T. A. Frank, "Look Who's Hitched! The Secret Lives of Washington's Power Couples," *Washington Monthly,* May 2007, http://www.washingtonmonthly.com/features/2007/0705.frank.html.

152. Reported in "NOW President Gandy: Will Media Gauntlet Challenge Future Female Candidates?" *Media Report to Women* (Summer 2008): 2.

153. Quoted in ibid.

154. Judy Woodruff, "Covering Politics—Is There a Female Difference?" *Media Studies Journal* (Spring 1997): 157.

155. Ibid.

156. Ibid., 157, 158.

157. Clark Hoyt, "Pantsuits and the Presidency," *New York Times,* Sunday Opinion, June 22, 2008, 10.

158. Ibid.

159. Ibid.

160. Ibid.

161. "NOW President Gandy," 1.

162. NOW, "2008 Election Edition," National Organization of Women's Web page: NOW's Media Hall of Shame, http://www.now.org/issues/media/hall_of_shame/, accessed December 30, 2011.

163. Ibid.

164. Ibid.

165. "Lynn Sweet Biography," *Chicago Sun-Times* Website, http://

www.suntimes.com/news/sweet/2353260-452/story.html, accessed December 30, 2011.

166. Graff, "50 Top Journalists 2009," 5.

167. "Jeanne Cummings," Politico.com, http://www.politico.com/reporters/JeanneCummings.html, accessed January 14, 2011.

168. Graff, "50 Top Journalists 2009," 3.

169. Ibid., 5.

170. "Karen Tumulty," Wikipedia, http://en.wikipedia.org/wiki/Karen_Tumulty, accessed January 15, 2011.

171. Ibid.

172. Graff, "50 Top Journalists 2009," 2.

173. "Candy Crowley," CNN, http://www.cnn.com/CNN/anchors_reporters/crowley.candy.html, accessed January 15, 2011.

174. James Rainey, "She's Lighter 'In a Lot of Ways,'" *Los Angeles Times,* November 18, 2009, http://articles.latmes.com/2009/nov/18/entertainment/et-onthemedia18.

175. Ibid.

176. Ibid.

177. Danny Shea, "Candy Crowley: Would I Have Gotten 'State of the Union' If I Didn't Lose Weight?" *Huffington Post,* April 7, 2010, http://www.huffingtonpost.com/2010/02/05/candy-crowley-would-i-hav_n_451121.html.

178. Quoted in ibid.

179. Ibid.

180. Graff, "50 Top Journalists 2009," 4.

181. "Lara Logan," CBS News, http://www.cbsnews.com/stories/2002/12/02/broadcasts/main531421.shtml, accessed January 15, 2011.

182. "Lara Logan Swimsuit Photos," Mahalo, http://www.mahalo.com/lara-logan-swimsuit-photos, accessed January 15, 2011.

183. Howard Kurtz, "Back from War, into Tabloid Territory," *Washington Post,* July 8, 2008, http://www.washingtonpost.com/wp-dyn/content/article/2008/07/07/AR2008070702662.html.

184. Ibid.

185. See Helene Cooper, *The House at Sugar Beach: In Search of a Lost African Childhood* (New York: Simon and Schuster, 2008).

186. "Helene Cooper," Wikipedia, http://en.wikipedia.org/wiki/Helene_Cooper, accessed January 17, 2011.

187. "Michele Norris," NPR, http://www.npr.org/people2100974/michele-norris, accessed January 17, 2011.

188. Graff, "50 Top Journalists 2009," 4.

189. "Dana Priest," Wikipedia, http://www.en.wikipedia/org/wiki/Dana_Priest, accessed January 18, 2011.

190. Ibid.

191. Quoted in ibid.

192. Ibid.

193. "Dana L. Priest," *Washington Post,* http://projects.washingtonpost.com/staff/articles/dana+priest/, accessed January 18, 2011.

194. Mark Benjamin, "Reporting a Scandal When No One Bothers to Listen," *Nieman Reports* (Summer 2008), http://www.nieman.harvard.edu/reports/article/100032/Reporting-a-Scandal-When-No-One-Bothers-to-Listen.aspx.

195. "Ana Marie Cox," Wikipedia, http://en.wikipedia.org/wiki/Ana_Marie_Cox, accessed January 18, 2011.

196. "An Imus Guest Says No More," *Time,* April 12, 2007, http://www.time.com/time/magazine/article/0,9171,1609766,00.html.

197. Pamela J. Gentry, interview by author, May 26, 2010.

198. Ibid.

199. Ibid.

200. Ibid.

201. Ibid.

202. Howard Kurtz, "*Washington Post* Names Two Managing Editors," *Washington Post,* January 14, 2009, A2.

203. Ibid.

204. "Andrea Roane," WUSA9.com., http://www.wusa9.com/company/bios/story.aspx?catid=133&storyid=37259, accessed December 30, 2011.

205. Ibid.

206. Cecilia Kang, "Broadcasters Resist Plan to Cede Airwaves," *Washington Post,* January 20, 2011, A12.

207. Ibid.

208. Quoted ibid.

209. David Kindred, *Morning Miracle: Inside the Washington Post* (New York: Doubleday, 2010), 228.

210. Quoted ibid., 227–28.

211. Ibid., 228.

212. Ibid.

213. Ibid.

214. "Katharine Weymouth News," *New York Times*, July 6, 2009, http://topics.nytimes.com/topics/reference/timestopics/people/w/katharine_weymouth/index.html.

215. Kindred, *Morning Miracle,* 231.

216. Jack Shafer, "Katharine Weymouth Steps in It Again," *Slate,* September 15, 2009, http://www.slate.com/id/2228413.

217. Ibid.

218. Steven Mufson, "Buffett Will Leave Post Co.'s Board," *Washington Post,* January 21, 2011, A13.

219. Ibid.

220. Andrew Alexander, "Can the Post Restore Its Luster?" *Washington Post,* January 23, 2011, A17.

221. Ibid.

222. Ibid.

223. Ibid.

224. Kindred, *Morning Miracle,* 254.

225. Geneva Overholser, "The Imperiled Media," in *The Edge of Change,* ed. June O. Nicholson et al. (Urbana: University of Illinois Press, 2009), 176.

BIBLIOGRAPHY

BOOKS, BOOK CHAPTERS, AND ENCYCLOPEDIA ARTICLES

Adams, Lois Bryan. *Letter from Washington: 1863–1865.* Edited by Evelyn Leasher. Detroit: Wayne State University Press, 1999.

Ames, Mary Clemmer. *Life and Scenes in the National Capital.* Hartford, Conn.: Worthington, 1874.

Anthony, Carl Sferrazza. *Florence Harding.* New York: Morrow, 1998.

Ball, Rick, and NBC News. *Meet the Press: Fifty Years of History in the Making.* New York: McGraw-Hill, 1998.

Bartlett, Irving H. *Daniel Webster.* New York: Norton, 1978.

Beale, Betty. *Power at Play: A Memoir of Parties, Politicians and the Presidents in My Bedroom.* Washington, D.C.: Regnery Gateway, 1993.

Beasley, Maurine H. *Eleanor Roosevelt and the Media: A Public Quest for Self-Fulfillment.* Urbana: University of Illinois Press, 1978.

———. "The Emergence of Modern Media: 1900–1945." In *The Media in America,* edited by W. David Sloan, 283–303. 5th ed. Northport, Ala.: Vision Press, 2002.

———. *First Ladies and the Press: The Unfinished Partnership of the Media Age.* Evanston, Ill.: Northwestern University Press, 2005.

———, ed. *The White House Press Conferences of Eleanor Roosevelt.* New York: Garland, 1983.

Beasley, Maurine H., and Sheila Gibbons. *Taking Their Place: A Documentary History of Women and Journalism.* 2nd ed. State College, Pa.: Strata Publishing, 2003.

Beasley, Maurine H., Holly C. Shulman, and Henry R. Beasley. *The Eleanor Roosevelt Encyclopedia.* Westport, Conn.: Greenwood Press, 2001.

Bellows, Jim. *The Last Editor.* Kansas City, Mo.: Andrews McMeel, 2002.

Bernhard, Nancy. "Pauline Frederick." In Ware, *Notable American Women,* 223–24.

Black, Cathie. *Basic Black: The Essential Guide for Getting Ahead at Work (and in Life).* New York: Crown Business, 2007.

Blair, Karen J. "General Federation of Women's Clubs." In Mankiller, Mink, Navarro, Smith, and Steinem, *Reader's Companion,* 242.

Braden, Maria. *Women Politicians and the Media.* Lexington: University of Kentucky Press, 1996.

Bradley, Patricia. *Mass Media and the Shaping of American Feminism: 1963–1973.* Jackson: University Press of Mississippi, 2003.

Briggs, Emily Edson. *The Olivia Letters.* New York: Neale, 1906.

Broder, David S. *Behind the Front Page: A Candid Look at How News Is Made.* New York: Simon and Schuster, 1987.

Caroli, Betty Boyd. "Jacqueline (Lee Bouvier) Kennedy (Onassis)." In *American First Ladies: Their Lives and Their Legacy,* edited by Lewis L. Gould, 476–95. New York: Garland, 1996.

Carpenter, Liz. *Ruffles and Flourishes.* College Station: Texas A&M Press, 1993.

Chafe, William H. *The American Woman.* New York: Oxford University Press, 1972.

Cheshire, Maxine, with John Greenya. *Maxine Cheshire, Reporter.* Boston: Houghton Mifflin, 1978.

Clark, Delbert. *Washington Dateline: The Press Covers the Capital.* New York: Frederick Stokes, 1941.

Congressional Directory. 66th Cong., 2d sess. Washington, D.C.: Government Printing Office, 1920.

Cooper, Helene. *The House at Sugar Beach: In Search of a Lost African Childhood.* New York: Simon and Schuster, 2008.

Cosgrove, John P., ed. *Shrdlu: An Affectionate Chronicle.* Washington, D.C.: National Press Club, 1958.

Croly, J. C., Mrs. [Jennie June, pseud.]. *The History of the Woman's Club Movement in America.* New York: Henry C. Allen, 1898.

Denker, David. "Eleanor Medill Patterson." In James, James, and Boyer, *Notable American Women,* 26–28.

Dickerson, John. *On Her Trail: My Mother, Nancy Dickerson: TV News' First Woman Star.* New York: Simon and Schuster, 2007.

Dickerson, Nancy. *Among Those Present: A Reporter's View of 25 Years in Washington.* New York: Ballantine, 1976.

Dodge, Mary Abigail [Gail Hamilton, pseud.]. *Gail Hamilton's Life in Letters,* edited by Augusta H. Dodge, vol. 1, 203. Boston: Lee and Shepard, 1901.

Dowd, Maureen. *Are Men Necessary? When Sexes Collide.* New York: Putnam, 2005.

DuBois, Ellen Carol. "Suffrage Movement." In Mankiller, Mink, Navarro, Smith, and Steinem, *Reader's Companion,* 580.

Dunnigan, Alice Allison. *A Black Woman's Experience from Schoolhouse to White House.* Philadelphia: Dorrence, 1974.

Edwards, Julie. *Women of the World: The Great Foreign Correspondents.* New York: Ivy, 1988.

Faber, Doris. *The Life of Lorena Hickok: E. R.'s Friend.* New York: Morrow, 1980.

Fry, Amelia Robert. "Alice Paul." In Ware, *Notable American Women,* 500–502.

Furman, Bess A. *Washington By-Line: The Personal Story of a Newspaperwoman.* New York: Knopf, 1949.

Gans, Herbert J. *Deciding What's News: A Study of CBS Evening News, NBC Nightly News, Newsweek and Time.* New York: Vintage, 1980.

Geyer, Georgia Anne. *Guerilla Prince: The Untold Story of Fidel Castro.* Boston: Little, Brown, 1991.

Gilliam, Dorothy. "Ethel L. Payne." In Ware, *Notable American Women,* 502–4.

Gottlieb, Agnes Hooper. *Women Journalists and the Municipal Housekeeping Movement 1864–1914.* Lewiston, N.Y.: Edwin Mellen, 2001.

Gould, Lewis L. *Lady Bird Johnson and the Environment.* Lawrence: University Press of Kansas, 1988.

Graham, Katharine. *Personal History.* New York: Vintage, 1998.

Green, Emily A. *First Lady: The Life of Lucy Webb Hayes.* Kent, Ohio: Kent State University Press, 1984.

Haller, Beth. "Laura Redden Searing, 1840–1923, Journalist, Writer, Poet." In *Encyclopedia of American Disability History,* edited by Susan Burch. New York: Facts on File, 2009. Entry #707.

———. "Nancy Woodhull." In Ware, *Notable American Women,* 701.

Halper, Donna L. "Nancy Dickerson." In Ware, *Notable American Women,* 175–77.

———. *Invisible Stars.* Armonk, N.Y.: M. E. Sharpe, 2001.

Hamilton, Martha McNeil, and Warren Brown. *black and white and red all over.* New York: Public Affairs, 2002.

Hamilton, Virginia Van Der Veer. *Looking for Clark Gable and Other 20th-Century Pursuits.* Tuscaloosa: University of Alabama Press, 1996.

Healy, Paul F. *Cissy.* New York: Doubleday, 1966.

Heymann, C. David. *A Woman Named Jackie.* New York: Carol Communications, 1989.

Hickok, Lorena A. *Reluctant First Lady.* New York: Dodd, Mead, 1962.

Higgins, Marguerite. *News Is a Singular Thing.* Garden City, N.Y.: Doubleday, 1955.

———. *Our Vietnam Nightmare.* New York: Harper and Row, 1965.

———. *Red Plush and Black Bread.* Garden City, N.Y.: Doubleday, 1955.

———. *War in Korea: The Report of a Woman Combat Correspondent.* Garden City, N.Y.: Doubleday, 1951.

Hilmes, Michele. *Only Connect: A Cultural History of Broadcasting in the United States.* Belmont, Calif.: Wadsworth/Thomson Learning, 2002.

Hoffert, Sylvia D. *Jane Grey Swisshelm: An Unconventional Life, 1815–1884.* Chapel Hill: University of North Carolina Press, 2004.

Hoge, Alice Albright. *Cissy Patterson.* New York: Random House, 1966.

Hosley, David H., and Gayle K. Yamada. *Hard News: Women in Broadcast Journalism.* Westport, Conn.: Greenwood Press, 1987.

Hymowitz, Carol, and Michaele Weissman. *A History of Women in America.* New York: Bantam, 1978.

Ifill, Gwen. *The Breakthrough: Politics and Race in the Age of Obama.* New York: Doubleday, 2009.

Jackson, George Stuyvesant. *Uncommon Scold.* Boston: Bruce Humphries, 1937.

James, Bessie Rowland, *Anne Royall's U.S.A.* New Brunswick, N.J.: Rutgers University Press, 1972.

James, Edward T., Janet Wilson James, and Paul S. Boyer, eds. *Notable American Women 1607–1950: A Biographical Dictionary.* Vol. 2. Cambridge, Mass.: Belknap Press, 1971.

Jones, Judy Yaeger, and Jane E. Vallier, eds. *Sweet Bells Jangled: Laura Redden*

Searing, A Deaf Poet Restored. Washington, D.C.: Gallaudet University Press, 2003.

Kahlenberg, Susan G. "Constance (Connie) Yu-Hwa Chung." In *Women in Communication: A Biographical Sourcebook,* edited by Nancy Signorielli, 66–78. Westport, Conn.: Greenwood Press, 1996.

Kearney, James M. *Anna Eleanor Roosevelt: The Evolution of a Reformer.* Boston: Houghton Mifflin, 1968.

Kelly, Tom. *The Imperial Post: The Meyers, the Grahams, and the Paper That Rules Washington.* New York: Morrow, 1983.

Keyes, Frances Parkinson. *Capital Kaleidoscope: The Story of a Washington Hostess.* New York: Harper, 1937.

———. *Letters from a Senator's Wife.* New York: D. Appleton, 1924.

Kilian, Michael, and Arnold Sawislak. *Who Runs Washington?* New York: St. Martin's, 1982.

Kindred, David. *Morning Miracle: Inside the Washington Post.* New York: Doubleday, 2010.

Larsen, Arthur J., ed. *Crusader and Feminist: Letters of Jane Grey Swisshelm 1858–1865.* St. Paul: Minnesota Historical Society, 1934.

Lawn, Connie. *You Wake Me Each Morning.* San Jose, Calif.: Writers Club Press, 2000.

Lippincott, Sara Clarke [Grace Greenwood, pseud.]. *Greenwood Leaves.* 1st ed. Boston: Ticknor, Reed and Fields, 1850.

Mankiller, Wilma, Gwendolyn Mink, Marysa Navarro, Barbara Smith, and Gloria Steinem, eds. *The Reader's Companion to U.S. Women's History.* Boston: Houghton Mifflin, 1998.

Mann, Judy Luce. *Mann for All Seasons.* New York: MasterMedia, 1990.

Manning, Marie [Beatrice Fairfax, pseud.]. *Ladies Then and Now.* New York: Dutton, 1944.

Marbut, F. B. *News from the Capital: The Story of Washington Reporting.* Carbondale: Southern Illinois University Press, 1971.

Martin, Ralph G. *Cissy.* New York: Simon and Schuster, 1979.

Marton, Kati. *Hidden Power.* New York: Pantheon, 2001.

Marzolf, Marion. "Marguerite Higgins." In Sicherman and Green, *Notable American Women,* 340–41.

———. *Up from the Footnote.* New York: Hastings House, 1977.

Matusow, Barbara. *The Evening Stars.* Boston: Houghton Mifflin, 1983.

Maxwell, Alice S., and Marion B. Dunlevy. *Virago! The Story of Anne Newport Royall (1796–1854)*. Jefferson, N.C.: McFarland, 1985.

McClendon, Sarah. *My Eight Presidents*. New York: Wyden, 1978.

McLendon, Winzola, and Scottie Fitzgerald Smith. *Don't Quote Me: Washington Newswomen and the Power Society*. New York: Dutton, 1970.

McGrory, Mary. "Doris Fleeson." In Sicherman and Green, *Notable American Women*, 239–41.

Melich, Tanya. *The Republican War Against Women*. New York: Bantam, 1996.

Meltzer, Kimberly. *TV News Anchors and Journalistic Tradition*. New York: Peter Lang, 2010.

Miller, Judith, William Broad, and Stephen Engelberg. *Germs, Biological Weapons and America's Secret War*. New York: Simon and Schuster, 2001.

Mills, Kay. *A Place in the News: From the Women's Pages to the Front Page*. New York: Dodd, Mead, 1988.

Mitchell, Andrea. *Talking Back*. New York: Viking, 2005.

Mnookin, Seth. *Hard News: The Scandals at "The New York Times" and Their Meaning for American Media*. New York: Random House, 2004.

Montgomery, Ruth. *Hail to the Chief*. New York: Coward, McCann, 1970.

Mudd, Roger. *The Place to Be: Washington, CBS, and the Glory Days of Television News*. New York: Public Affairs, 2008.

Nash, Alanna. *Golden Girl*. New York: Signet, 1988.

Nelson, Jull. *Volunteer Slavery: My Authentic Negro Experience*. Chicago: Noble Press, 1993.

Neuharth, Al. *Confessions of an S.O.B.* New York: Doubleday, 1989.

Norris, Pippa, ed. *Women, Media, and Politics*. New York: Oxford University Press, 1997.

Ottenberg, Miriam. *The Federal Investigators*. Englewood Cliffs, N.J.: Prentice Hall, 1962.

———. *The Pursuit of Hope*. New York: Rawson, Wade, 1978.

Overholser, Geneva. "The Imperiled Media." In *The Edge of Change*, edited by June O. Nicholson, Pamela J. Creedon, Wanda S. Lloyd, and Pamela J. Johnson. Urbana: University of Illinois Press, 2009.

Paterson, Judith. *Be Somebody: A Biography of Marguerite Rawalt.* Austin: Eakin Press, 1986.

Prichard, Peter. *The Making of McPaper: The Inside Story of USA Today.* Kansas City, Mo.: Andrews, McMeel and Parker, 1987.

Rehm, Diane. *Finding My Voice.* New York: Knopf, 1999.

Reliable Sources: 100 Years at the National Press Club. Nashville: Turner, 2008.

Reston, James. *Deadline.* New York: Morrow, 1983.

Reynolds, Barbara A. *Out of Hell and Living Well.* Xulon Press, 2004.

Ritchie, Donald A. *Press Gallery: Congress and the Washington Correspondents.* Cambridge, Mass.: Harvard University Press, 1991.

———. *Reporting from Washington: The History of the Washington Press Corps.* New York: Oxford University Press, 2005.

Roberts, Chalmers M. *In the Shadow of Power: The Story of the "Washington Post."* Cabin John, Md.: Seven Locks Press, 1989.

———. *"The Washington Post": The First 100 Years.* Boston: Houghton Mifflin, 1977.

Roberts, Cokie. *We Are Our Mothers' Daughters.* New York: Morrow, 1998.

Robertson, Nan. *The Girls in the Balcony: Women, Men and the "New York Times."* New York: Random House, 1992.

Roosevelt, Eleanor. *This I Remember.* New York: Harper, 1937.

Ross, Ishbel. *Grace Coolidge and Her Era.* New York: Dodd, Mead, 1962.

———. *Ladies of the Press.* New York: Harper and Brothers, 1936.

Royall, Anne. *The Black Book II.* Washington, D.C.: privately printed, 1828–29.

Sanders, Marlene, and Marcia Rock. *Waiting for Prime Time: The Women of Television News.* Urbana: University of Illinois Press, 1988.

Savitch, Jessica. *Anchorwoman.* New York: Putnam's, 1982.

Sayler, Carolyn. *Doris Fleeson: Incomparably the First Political Journalist of Her Time.* Santa Fe: Sunstone Press, 2010.

Sicherman, Barbara, and Carol Hurd Green, eds. *Notable American Women: A Bibliographical Dictionary.* Vol. 4, *The Modern Period.* Cambridge, Mass.: Belknap Press, 1980.

Smith, Betsy Covington. *Breakthrough: Women in Television.* New York: Walker, 1981.

Solomon, Burt. *The Washington Century: Three Families and the Shaping of the Nation's Capital.* New York: Morrow, 2004.

Stahl, Lesley. *Reporting Live.* New York: Simon and Schuster, 1999.

Streitmatter, Rodger. "Alice Allison Dunnigan." In Ware, *Notable American Women,* 183–84.

———. *Raising Her Voice.* Lexington: University Press of Kentucky, 1994.

Swisshelm, Jane G. *Half a Century.* Chicago: McClurg, Jensen, 1880. Reprinted. Boston: IndyPublish, 2006. Page references are to the 2006 edition.

Tebbe, Jennifer L. "Elizabeth May Craig." In Sicherman and Green, *Notable American Women,* 171–73.

Thomas, Helen. *Dateline White House.* New York: Macmillan, 1975.

———. *Front Row at the White House.* New York: Scribner, 1999.

Tilton, Elizabeth S. *The League of American Pen Women in the District of Columbia.* Washington, D.C.: District of Columbia branch, League of American Pen Women, 1942.

Truman, Margaret. *Bess W. Truman.* New York: Macmillan, 1986.

Wagner, Lilya. *Women Correspondents of World War II.* Westport, Conn.: Greenwood Press, 1989.

Ware, Susan. "Bess Furman." In Sicherman and Green, *Notable American Women,* 256–57.

Ware, Susan, and Stacy Braukman, eds. *Notable American Women: A Bibliographical Dictionary.* Vol. 5, *Completing the Twentieth Century.* Cambridge, Mass. Belknap Press, 2004.

Welter, Barbara. "Sara Jane Clarke Lippincott." In James, James, and Boyer, *Notable American Women,* 407–9.

Wertheimer, Linda, ed. *Listening to America: Twenty-Five Years in the Life of a Nation, as Heard on National Public Radio.* Boston: Houghton Mifflin, 1995.

Wilson, Jan Doolittle. *The Women's Joint Congressional Committee and the Politics of Maternalism, 1920–1930.* Urbana: University of Illinois Press, 2007.

NEWSPAPER AND PERIODICAL ARTICLES

Alexander, Andrew. "Can The Post Restore Its Luster?" *Washington Post,* January 23, 2011.

"Alumni Profile: Elisabeth Bumiller '79." *One Hundred Sixteenth and Broadway* (Summer 2006): 7.

Ames, Mary Clemmer. "A Woman's Letter from Washington." *Independent,* December 27, 1866; March 24, 1870; October 10, 1872; and March 7, 1878.

Amrine, Abbie A. "This Is Our Day." *Matrix* 27 (October 1941): 15.

"Another Day at the Office." *Washington City Paper,* May 21, 2004.

Arvad, Inga. "Did You Happen to See Katherine Smith?" *Washington Times-Herald,* April 17, 1942.

Associated Press. "Newhouse News Service to Close." July 29, 2008.

Balboni, Philip S. "Cable News Future Depends on Quality." *Columbia Journalism Alumni Journal* (Winter 2007).

"Barbara Cochran '68." *Columbia Journalism School* (Winter 2010): 10.

Barnes, Bart. "Fay G. Wells Dies at 94; Sought Out Adventure." *Washington Post,* December 6, 2002.

Baskin, Roberta. "Investigative Reporting/A Reporter's Notebook." *Kosmos* (Fall–Winter 2010).

Beale, Betty. "First Lady Discusses Beauty." *Washington Star,* September 8, 1965, B5.

———. "A Plea for U.S. Beauty." *Washington Star,* September 8, 1965.

Beasley, Maurine. "Anne Royall: Huntress with a Quill." *Quill* 78 (May 1990): 32–35.

———. "The Women's National Press Club: Case Study of Professional Aspirations." *Journalism History* 15 (Winter 1988): 112–21.

Bernstein, Adam. "D.C. Journalist Netted Pulitzer for Schools Coverage." *Washington Post,* June 30, 2009.

———. "Washington Star Society Columnist Betty Beale, 94." *Washington Post,* June 8, 2006.

Bernstein, Carl, and Bob Woodward. "FBI Finds Nixon Aides Sabotaged Democrats." *Washington Post,* October 10, 1972.

Black, Ruby A. "Covering Mrs. Roosevelt." *Matrix* 18 (April 1933): 1.

———. "'New Deal' for News Women in Capital." *Editor and Publisher,* February 10, 1934, 11.

Briggs, Emily Edson [Olivia, pseud.]. *Philadelphia Press,* March 16, 1868; January 19, 1870; and February 2, 1871.

Bromley, Dorothy Dunbar. "The Future of Eleanor Roosevelt." *Harper's* 180 (January 1940): 129–39.

Cottrell, Ann. "Mrs. Roosevelt Assails Stories About Waacs." *New York Herald Tribune,* June 8, 1943.

"Crime Fighters Honor Miss Ottenberg of Star." *Washington Star,* May 30, 1958.

"Defining a Beat." *Money,* April 17, 1977, 47.

Dodge, Mary Abigail [Gail Hamilton, pseud.]. "The Display of Washington Society." *Galaxy* 21 (June 1876): 768.

Dreifus, Claudia. "Cokie Roberts, Nina Totenberg and Linda Wertheimer." *New York Times Magazine,* January 2, 1994, http://www.nytimes./com/1994/01/02/cokie-roberts-nina-tote, 1–4.

Duke, Lynne. "The Reporter's Last Take." *Washington Post,* November 10, 2005.

Eisler, Kim Isaac. "The Journalism 50 Establishment." *Washingtonian* (March 2001), http://web.lexis-nexis.com/universe-printdoc.

"Employers' Symposium." *Matrix* 26 (October 1940): 7–8.

"Flight from Fluff." *Time,* March 20, 1971, 52–53.

Frank, Stanley, and Paul Sann. "Paper Dolls." *Saturday Evening Post,* May 20, 1944, 20, 93–96.

Frank, T. A. "Look Who's Hitched! The Secret Lives of Washington's Power Couples." *Washington Monthly,* 2007, http://www.washingtonmonthly.com/feataures/2007/0705.frank.html.

Free, Ann Cottrell. "Eleanor Roosevelt and the Female White House Press Corps." *Modern Maturity* (October–November 1984): 98–99.

Givhan, Robin. "No False Moves in These Sentencing Walks." *Washington Post,* July 8, 2005.

Graff, Garrett. "50 Best and Most Influential Journalists." *Washingtonian,* December 2005, http://web.lexis-nexis.com/universe/printdoc.

———. "50 Top Journalists 2009," *Washingtonian,* June 1, 2009, http://www.washingtonian.com/print/articles/6/174/12512.html.

"Hagerty Suggests a Summit." *Washington Post,* October 30, 1959.

Halbfinger, David M., Michael Barbaro, and Fernanda Santos. "A Trailblazer with Her Eye on the Bottom Line." *New York Times,* November 19, 2010.

Healy, Paul F. "Cissy." *Washingtonian,* March 1966, 22–36.

————. "Cissy's Feuds." *Washingtonian,* April 1966, 23–51.

"Here's the Media Elite." *Washingtonian,* August 1997, 63.

Holley, Joe. "Nancy Maynard, 61: Newspaper Owner Pressed for Diversity." *Washington Post,* September 22, 2008.

Howell, Deborah. "Getting Women into the News." *Washington Post,* December 14, 2008.

————. "Op-Ed Need for Diverse Voices." *Washington Post,* May 25, 2008.

————. "Outrage Over an Outlook Piece." *Washington Post,* March 9, 2008.

Hoyt, Clark. "Pantsuits and the Presidency." *New York Times,* Sunday Opinion, June 22, 2008.

Jackson, William E., Jr. "Miller's Star Fades (Slightly) at 'NY Times.'" *Editor and Publisher Online,* October 2, 2003, http://www.commondreams.org/cgi-bin/print.cgi?file=/views03/1002-09.htm.

Kang, Cecilia. "Broadcasters Resist Plan to Cede Airwaves." *Washington Post,* January 20, 2011.

"Katharine Weymouth News." *New York Times,* July 6, 2009.

Keefer, Bryan. "You Call That News? I Don't." *Washington Post,* September 12, 2004.

Kelly, Eugene A. "Distorting the News." *American Mercury,* March 1935, 307–18.

Keyes, Frances Parkinson. "Letters from a Senator's Wife." *Good Housekeeping* 76 (May 1921): 52, 74.

Kurtz, Howard. "Back from War into Tabloid Territory." *Washington Post,* July 8, 2008.

————. "The Judith Miller Story: Not Ready Yet." *Washington Post,* October 13, 2005.

————. "Post Buyouts Come with an Emotional Cost." *Washington Post,* May 26, 2008.

————. "Sex and the Single Stiletto." *Washington Post,* November 5, 2005.

————. "*Washington Post* Names Two Managing Editors." *Washington Post,* January 14, 2009.

Lambro, Donald. "Pulitzer-Winning Journalist Mary Lou Forbes Dies at 83." *Washington Times,* June 29, 2009.

Leonig, Carol D. "Jailed Reporter Is Distanced from News, Not Elite Visitors." *Washington Post,* September 17, 2005.

Levy, Ariel. "The Redhead and the Gray Lady." *New York,* October 31, 2005, http://nymag.com/nymetro/news/people/features/14946.

Lewis, Dorothy Roe. "A First Lady as an Inside Source." *New York Times,* March 13, 1981.

Lieberman, Trudy. "Plagiarize, Plagiarize, Plagiarize . . ." *Columbia Journalism Review* (July–August 1995), http://archives,cjr.org/year/95/4/plagiarize.asp.

Lippincott, Sara Clarke [Grace Greenwood, pseud.]. "Washington Notes." *New York Times,* February 1, 1873; April 13, 1873; and July 3, 1877.

Mallon, Winifred. "Map Party Backing for Doris Stevens." *New York Times,* February 17, 1939.

Manly, Lorne. "A Difficult Moment, Long Anticipated." *New York Times,* July 7, 2005.

———. "Jail Where Reporter Is Held: Maximum, Modern Security." *New York Times,* July 8, 2005.

"Marjorie Williams." *Washington Post,* January 17, 2005.

Matusow, Barbara. "Powers of the Press." *Washingtonian,* August 1997, http://we.lexis-nexis.com/universe/printdoc.

———. "Washington's Journalism Establishment." *Washingtonian,* February 1989, 95–101, 265–70.

McFeatters, Ann. "Politics in Washington." *St. Augustine (Fla.) Record,* October 6, 2004.

McLaughlin, Kathleen. "Mrs. Roosevelt Goes Her Way." *New York Times Magazine,* July 5, 1936, 7, 15.

Meyer, Agnes. "Rio Grande Problem: Migrant Mexican and Anglo Labor." *Washington Post,* April 23, 1946.

"Minority Report Jolts the Post." *Washington Journalism Review,* December 1985, 8.

"Miriam Ottenberg." *Washington Post,* November 22, 1982.

"Mrs. Sallie V. Pickett Funeral Services at National City Church." *Evening Star,* July 26, 1939.

Mufson, Steven. "Buffett Will Leave Post Co.'s Board." *Washington Post,* January 21, 2011.

"NOW President Gandy: Will Media Gauntlet Challenge Future Female Candidates?" *Media Report to Women* (Summer 2008).

O'Donnell, John, and Doris Fleeson. "Capitol Stuff." *Washington Times-Herald,* May 19, 1941.

Perz-Pena, Richard. "Big News in Washington, for Far Fewer Cover It." *New York Times,* October 31, 2006.

———. "Deborah Howell, One of the First Women to Lead a Big U.S. Paper, Dies at 68." *New York Times,* January 3, 2010.

Randolph, Eleanor. "The Newspaper Editors, at a Loss for Words." *Washington Post,* April 4, 1990.

"Reporter for *The Star* Wins Pulitzer Prize for Series." *Washington Star,* May 3, 1960.

Roberts, Roxanne, and Amy Argetsinger. "Still Fit to Print." *Washington Post,* January 7, 2011.

Rosenstiel, Tom. "The End of 'Network News.'" *Washington Post,* September 12, 2004.

Ruben, Barbara. "Anchor Celebrates 36 Years on TV." *Senior Beacon,* February 2008, 1.

"Ruth Jones, Long Noted as Capital Society Editor, Dies." *Washington Times-Herald,* September 18, 1940.

"Sallie Pickett Dies: Rites to Be Held Today." *Washington Post,* July 26, 1939.

"Sarah Booth Conroy, 81, Post Reporter and Editor, 'Chronicler' of Life in D.C." *Washington Post,* January 14, 2009.

Schudel, Matt. "Former Post Ombudsman Helped Break Glass Ceiling." *Washington Post,* January 3, 2010, http://www.washingtonpost.com/wp-dyn/content/article/2010/01.

Seelye, Katharine Q. "Another White House Briefing, Another Day of Mutual Mistrust." *New York Times,* February 27, 2006.

———. "Newspaper Circulation Falls Sharply." *New York Times,* October 31, 2006.

Simpson, Peggy A. "Covering the Women's Movement." Summer 1979. Reprinted in *Nieman Reports* 53–54 (Winter 1999, Spring 2000), http://www.nieman.harvard.edu/reports/article/102010/1979-Covering-the-Womens-Movement.aspx.

Sullivan, Patricia. "Aplin-Brownlee, 61: Former *Post* Editor Had Smelled Scandal." *Washington Post,* October 26, 2007.

———. "Harriet Woods: Inspired Creation of Emily's List." *Washington Post,* February 10, 2007.

———. "Helen Dewar, 70: Distinguished *Post* Senate Reporter." *Washington Post,* November 5, 2006.

———. "Mary Lou Beatty; Editor at NEH, *Post.*" *Washington Post,* February 9, 2007.

———. "*Post* Columnist Judy Mann Dies." *Washington Post,* July 9, 2005.

Summers, Eileen. "Women Say 'No Thanks' to Bid for Admission to Male Press Club." *Washington Post,* February 23, 1955.

Swisshelm, Jane. "Mrs. Swisshelm's Letter." *New York Tribune,* April 15, April 19, and April 22, 1850.

Utting, Mary E. "Through the Years, Women Find Niche in Newspapers." *Women in Communication Inc. National Newsletter,* October 1979, 5.

Von Drehle, David. "Post Columnist Marjorie Williams Dies." *Washington Post,* January 17, 2005.

Von Hoffman, Nicholas. "Women's Pages: An Irreverent View." *Columbia Journalism Review* 10 (1971): 52–54.

Walton, Mary. "Investigative Shortfall." *American Journalism Review* (Fall 2010).

"Washington's Media Elite." *Washingtonian,* May 1993, 39.

Watts, Liz. "Covering Eleanor Roosevelt." *Journalism History* 36 (Spring 2010): 45–54.

Weir, Laila. "News Sites, Where the Men Are." *Wired News,* August 4, 2004, http://www.wired.cm/news/business/0,1367,64439.00.html.

Welter, Barbara. "The Cult of True Womanhood: 1820–1860." *American Quarterly* 18 (Summer 1966): 151–74.

Whalen, Charles W., Jr. "Unlikely Hero." *Washington Post,* January 2, 1984.

"Why Not Women?" *Newsweek,* February 28, 1955.

Winfield, Betty H. "Mrs. Roosevelt's Press Conference Association: The First Lady Shines a Light." *Journalism History* 8 (Summer 1981): 54–55, 63–67.

"The Woman's National Press Association." *New Cycle* (October 1985): 296–97.

Woodruff, Judy. "Covering Politics—Is There a Female Difference?" *Media Studies Journal* (Spring 1997): 155–58.

Yang, Mei-ling. "Women's Pages or People's Pages: The Production of News for Women in the Washington Post in the 1950s." *Journalism and Mass Communication Quarterly* 73 (Summer 1996): 368.

INTERVIEWS BY AUTHOR

Ashton, Betsy. Email. September 7, 2010.

Barker, Karlyn. Personal interview and responses to questionnaire. October 2007.

Beck, Jody. Responses to questionnaire. May 14, 2004.

Bonner, Alice. Responses to questionnaire. October 31, 2003.

Burke, Martha. Email. October 21, 2003.

Callahan, Chris. Email. August 17, 2004.

Cimons, Marlene. Personal interview and responses to questionnaire. February 10, 2004.

Dewar, Helen. Personal conversation. May 15, 1990.

Edwards, India. Telephone interview. April 27, 1983.

Enda, Jodi. Personal interview. June 21, 2004.

Ferris, Nancy Beckham. Personal interview. July 5, 2010.

Fuchs, Penny Bender. Email. December 31, 2010.

Gentry, Pamela J. Personal interview. May 26, 2010.

Gilliam, Dorothy. Personal interview. November 20, 2010.

Harvey, Chris. Personal conversation. December 3, 2010.

McBee, Susanna. Personal interview. October 18, 2010.

McFeatters, Ann. Oral history interview. August 3, 2007, National Press Club.

Morgans, Susan Fleming. Email responses to questionnaire. February 2, 2008.

Ritchie, Donald A. Email. June 18, 2007.

Santini, Maureen. Email. April 20, 2004.

———. In-person interview. April 27, 2004.

Thomas, Helen. Personal interview. December 20, 1990.

Thornton, Lee. Personal interview. March 22, 2004.

————. Responses to questionnaire. September 30, 2003.

Woods, Harriet. Email. October 13, 2003.

SPEECHES, REPORTS, UNPUBLISHED MATERIALS, AND ORAL HISTORIES

"About and by Women." Report of the Human Resources Committee, American Society of Newspaper Editors, Reston, Va., 1990.

Cavin, Patty. Oral history interview by Frank Harrison, 1984. Library of American Broadcasting, University of Maryland, College Park.

Chung, Connie. Oral history interview by Donita M. Moorhus, "Women in Journalism," March 30, 1994. Washington Press Club Foundation. Columbia University.

"Diversity in the Washington Press Corps." Joint report by UNITY: Journalists of Color Inc., and Philip Merrill College of Journalism, 2004.

Dunnigan, Alice. Oral history interview by Marcia Greenlee, April 8, 1977. Oral history-31, Schlesinger Library, Radcliffe College, 25–26.

Endres, Kathleen L. "Women in Journalism." Unpublished paper, University of Maryland, 1973.

Gilliam, Dorothy Butler. Oral history interview by Donita Moorhus, "Women in Journalism," March 17, 1993. Washington Press Club Foundation, http://beta.wpcf.org/oralhistory/gill.html.

"The Great Divide: Female Leadership in U.S. Newsrooms." Study conducted for the American Press Institute and the Pew Center for Civic Journalism, September 2002.

Hamilton, Martha. Private collection.

Howell, Deborah. Oral history interview by Donia Moorhus, "Women in Journalism," April 22, 1993. Washington Press Club Foundation, http://beta.wpcf.org/oralhistory/how.html.

Jurney, Dorothy. Oral history interview by Anne S. Kasper, "Women in Journalism," 1990. Washington Press Club Foundation, http://beta.wpcf.org/oralhistory/jurn.html.

Lumsden, Linda. "Recipe for a Fifties' Feminist: Ruth Cowan Reports the Woman's Angle in Cold War Washington." Paper given at the American Journalism Historians Association convention, San Antonio, October 6, 2005.

McClendon, Sarah. Oral history interview by Margot Knight, "Women in Journalism," June 27, 1989. Washington Press Club Foundation, http://beta.wpcf.org/oralhistory/sarah.html.

Murray, Peter Noel. "Marguerite Higgins: An Examination of Legacy and Gender Bias." Ph.D. dissertation, University of Maryland, 2003.

Payne, Ethel L. Oral history interview by Kathleen Currie, "Women in Journalism," September 8, 1987. Washington Press Club Foundation, http://beta.wpcf.org/oralhistory/payn.html.

Schaefer, Ruth Crane. Oral history interview by Pat Mower, November 18, 1975. American Women in Radio and Television, Library of American Broadcasting, University of Maryland, College Park.

Shanahan, Eileen. Oral history interview by Mary Marshall Clark, May 21, 1994, "Women in Journalism." Washington Press Club Foundation, Columbia University, http://beta.wpcf.org/oralhistory/shan.html.

Spieler, Louise Crosby. "Catherine Mackin: Trailblazer for Women in Broadcast Journalism." M.A. thesis, University of Maryland, College Park, 1990.

"Theodore H. White Lecture with Maureen Dowd." Lecture, Shorenstein Center, Harvard University, Cambridge, Mass., 2007.

Thomas, Helen. Remarks prepared for Anne Royall Historic Site marking, Washington, D.C., May 22, 1990.

Voss, Kimberly Wilmot. "Redefining Women's News: A Case Study of Three Women's Page Editors and Their Framing of the Women's Movement." Ph.D. dissertation, University of Maryland, 2004.

Woodruff, Judy. "Are Journalists Obsolete?" Red Smith Lecture, University of Notre Dame, September 2007.

Yang, Mei-ling. "Women's Pages of the *Washington Post* and Gender Ideology in the Late 1940s and the 1950s." Master's thesis, University of Maryland, 1992.

ARCHIVAL MATERIALS

American News Women's Club Archives. Special Collections, University of Maryland Libraries.

Austine and Fayette Snead. Letters and clipping file. Rutherford B. Hayes Library.

Bess Furman Papers. Manuscript Division, Library of Congress.

Cora Rigby Washington Journalism Archives, Washington Press Club Foundation, and National Press Club Archives. National Press Club.

District of Columbia Federation of Women's Clubs Records. Washington Historical Society.

Edith B. Helm Papers. Manuscript Division, Library of Congress.

Eleanor Roosevelt Papers. Franklin D. Roosevelt Library.

Frances Parkinson Keyes Papers. Special Collections, Tulane University Library.

Lorena A. Hickok Papers. Franklin D. Roosevelt Library.

Martha Strayer Papers. University of Wyoming.

Mary Hornaday Papers. University of Wyoming.

May Craig Papers. Manuscript Division, Library of Congress.

Mrs. Roosevelt's Press Conference Association Papers, Franklin D. Roosevelt Library.

"Newspapers, *Times-Herald,* 1939–1949." Washingtonian Division, Martin Luther King Public Library.

President's Personal File. Franklin D. Roosevelt Papers, Franklin D. Roosevelt Library.

Roosevelt scrapbooks. Franklin D. Roosevelt Library.

Ruby A. Black Papers. Manuscript Division, Library of Congress.

Stephen T. Early Papers. Franklin D. Roosevelt Library.

Vera Glaser Papers. National Press Club Archives.

WEB REFERENCES

"Ana Marie Cox." Wikipedia, http://en.wikipedia.org/wiki/Ana-Marie-Cox, accessed January 18, 2011.

"Andrea Roane." WUSA9.com, http://www.wusa9.com/company/bios/ story.aspx?catid=133&storyid=37259, accessed January 19, 2011.

"Ann Compton, ABC News." ABC News, http://abcnews.go.com/ Politics/story?id=6433048&page=1, accessed September 21, 2010.

"ASNE Losing Diversity Director." Maynard Institute, http://mije.org/ richardprince/asne-losing-diversity-director, accessed December 6, 2010.

Benjamin, Mark. "Reporting a Scandal When No One Bothers to Listen," *Nieman Reports* (Summer 2008), http://www.nieman.harvard.edu/ reports/article/100032/Reporting-a-Scandal-When-No-One -Bothers-to-Listen.aspx.

"Biography: Judith Miller." Pundicity: Informed Opinion and Review, http://www.judithmiller.com/about, accessed January 3, 2011.

"Candy Crowley." CNN, http://www.cnn.com/CNN/anchors_reporters/crowley.candy.html, accessed January 15, 2011.

Capriccioso, Rob. "Judy Woodruff: A Personal Path to Advocacy," SparkAction, September 13, 2004, http://sparkaction.org/node/616.

"Dana Priest." Wikipedia, http://www.en.wikipedia/org/wiki/Dana_ Priest, accessed January 18, 2011.

"Dana L. Priest." *Washington Post,* http://projects.washingtonpost.com/ staff/articles/dana+priest, accessed January 18, 2011.

"Diane Rehm." The Diane Rehm Show, http://thedianerehmshow.org/ diane, accessed November 12, 2010.

Foer, Franklin. "The Source of the Trouble," *New York,* May 21, 2005, http://nymag.com/nymetro/news/media/features/9226.

"Georgie Anne Geyer." Wikipedia, http://en.wikipedia.org/wiki/Georgie_Anne_Geyer, accessed December 19, 2010.

"Gwen Ifill." Wikipedia, http://en.wikipedia.org/wikiGwen-Ifill, accessed November 28, 2010.

Hagey, Keach. "Anxieties Provoke Quick Media Responses in 2010," Politico.com, January 2, 2011, http://www.politico.com/news/ stories.

"Harriett Woods." Wikipedia, http://en.wikipedia.org/wiki/Harriett_ Woods, accessed December 23, 2010.

"Helen Thomas." Wikipedia, http://en.wikipedia.org/wiki/Helen_ Thomas, accessed January 2, 2011.

"Helene Cooper." Wikipedia, http://en.wikipedia.org/wiki/Helene_Cooper, accessed January 17, 2011.

Huffington, Arianna. "Making Faux Martyrdom Pay: Judy Miller Lands a Book Deal," *Huffington Post,* October 3, 2005, http://www.huffingtonpost.com/arianna-huffington/making-faux-martyrdom-pay_b_8268.html.

"An Imus Guest Says No More." *Time,* April 12, 2007, http://www.time.com/time/magazine/article/0,9171,1609766,00.html.

"Jeanne Cummings." Politico.com, http://www.politico.com/reporters/JeanneCummings.html, accessed January 14, 2011.

"Juan Williams Talks Back on 'O'Reilly Factor.'" CBS News, October 23, 2010, http://www.cbsnews.com/stories/2010/10/22/national/main6983495.shtml.

"Judith Miller." SourceWatch, http://www.sourcewatch.org/index.php?title=Judith_Miller, accessed January 3, 2011.

"Judith Miller (journalist)." Wikipedia, http://en.wikipedia.org/wiki/Judith_Miller, accessed January 3, 2011.

"Karen Tumulty." Wikipedia, http://en.wikipedia.org/wiki/Karen_Tumulty, accessed January 15, 2011.

"Katharine Weymouth News." *New York Times,* July 6, 2009, http://topics.nytimes.com/topics/reference/timestopics/people/w/katharine_weymouth/index.html.

"Katie Couric." NNDB, http://www.nndb.com/people/487/000025412, accessed November 2, 2010.

———. Wikipedia, http://en.wikipedia.org/wiki/Katie_Couric, accessed November 1, 2010.

"Lara Logan." CBS News, http://www.cbsnews.com/stories/2002/12/02/broadcasts/main531421.shtml, accessed January 15, 2011.

Lara Logan Swimsuit Photos. Mahalo, http://www.mahalo.com/lara-logan-swimsuit-photos, accessed January 15, 2011.

"Linda Wertheimer." NPR, http://www.npr.org/templates/story/story.php?storyId=1931801, accessed November 6, 2010.

"Lynn Sweet Biography." *Chicago Sun-Times* Website, http://www.suntimes.com/news/sweet/2353260-452/story.html, accessed December 30, 2011.

"Marjorie Hunter, 78, a Pioneering Washington Correspondent for the

Times." Obituary by Irvin Molotsky, April 4, 2011, http://www
.nytimes.com/2001/04/11/us/marjorie-hunter-78-a-pioneering
-washington-correspondent-for-the-times.html

"Maureen Bunyan." Zonta Club of Washington, D.C., http://www.zonta
washingtondc.org/Gala_20006/MaureeBunyanBioInsert.pdf, accessed September 17, 2010.

"Maureen Dowd: Biography from Answers.com." Answers.com, http://
www.answers.com/topic/maureen-dowd, accessed December 20,
2010.

"Michele Norris." NPR, http://www.npr.org/people2100974/michele
-norris, accessed January 17, 2011.

"Miss Manners." Universal Uclick, http://wwunitedfeatures.com/?title
=Bio:MissManners, accessed December 18, 2010.

"Mona Charen." Wikipedia, http://en.wikipedia.org/wiki/Mona_Charen,
accessed December 18, 2010.

"Nina Totenberg." Wikipedia, http://en.wikipedia.org/wiki/Nina
-Totenberg, accessed November 1, 2010.

————. Academic.ru, http://en.academic.ru/dic/nsf/enwiki/1041231,
accessed November 7, 2010.

NOW. "2008 Election Edition," National Organization of Women's Web
page: NOW's Media Hall of Shame, http://www.now.org/issues/
media/hall_of_shame/, accessed December 30, 2011.

Pareene, Alex. "Judith Miller: From the Times to the Nuts," Salon.com,
December 30, 2010, http://www.salon.com/2010/12/30/judy
_miller_newsmax/singleton/.

Rainey, James. "She's Lighter 'In a Lot of Ways,'" *Los Angeles Times,* November 18, 2009, http://articles.latmes.com/2009.nov.18/enter-
tainment/et-onthemedia18.

Robins, J. Max. "Cokie Faux Pas Upsets Arledge," *Variety,* February 13, 1994, http://www.variety.com/article/VR118288.html
?categoryid=14&cs=1.

Shafer, Jack. "Katharine Weymouth Steps in It Again," Slate.com, September 15, 2009, http://www.slate.com/id/2228413.

Shea, Danny. "Candy Crowley: Would I Have Gotten 'State of the Union'
If I Didn't Lose Weight?" *Huffington Post,* April 7, 2010, http://

www.huffingtonpost.com/2010/02/05/candy-crowley-would-i-hav_n_451121.html.

Shindell, Scott. "Visionary Renee Poussaint '66," Sarah Lawrence College, http://www.slc.edu/magazine/mtm/glimpse_pouissant.php, accessed October 27, 2010.

Stamberg, Susan. "Mama Stamberg's Cranberry Relish Recipe," NPR, http://www.npr.org/templates/story/story/php?storyID+4176014, accessed November 4, 2010.

Tresca, Amber. "Katie Couric," About.com, http://ibscrohns.about.com/cs/colorecalcancer/a/ktiecouric.htm, accessed November 2, 2010.

"Women in Leadership: Journalism." March 15, 2010, YouTube video, http://www.youtube.com/watch?v=nqCJdX9_610.

INDEX

Maurine H. Beasley is a professor emerita of journalism at the University of Maryland, College Park. She is the author of *First Ladies and the Press: The Unfinished Partnership of the Media Age* (Northwestern, 2005) and *Eleanor Roosevelt and the Media: A Public Quest for Self-Fulfillment,* as well as the coeditor of *Taking Their Place: A Documentary History of Women and Journalism* and *The Eleanor Roosevelt Encyclopedia.*

Sandy Johnson has worked as a journalist in Washington, D.C., for twenty-eight years, including a decade as the Associated Press Washington bureau chief.